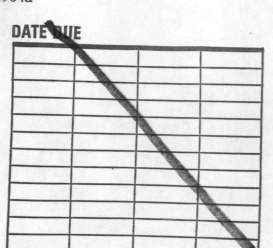

The Molly Maguires

The Molly Maguires

WAYNE G. BROEHL, JR.

✣ ✣ ✣ ✣ ✣ ✣ ✣ ✣ ✣

HARVARD UNIVERSITY PRESS

CAMBRIDGE, MASSACHUSETTS

Distributed in Great Britain by
Oxford University Press, London

Publication of this work has been aided by
a grant from the Ford Foundation

♣

Library of Congress Catalog Card Number
64–21239

Printed in the United States of America

Book design by David Ford

Preface

*T*HIS IS a new book on a famous old story—the Molly Maguire incidents. The locale of the climax is the anthracite fields of eastern Pennsylvania, the time the decade of the 1870's. The main characters are Franklin B. Gowen, the flamboyant president of a major railroad and coal combination; Allan Pinkerton, chief of the detective agency carrying his name; James McParlan, Pinkerton's key operative in the case; and a group of Irish miners who played major roles in the drama. (Over a hundred participants are listed and briefly identified in the appendix.)

Since early in the Civil War there had been persistent rumors that a shadowy Irish secret society—the "Molly Maguires"— was responsible for a continuing series of murders of mine bosses. Through the same period, the miners were attempting to form a labor union in spite of a laissez-faire environment and the operators' rampant economic individualism. Bitter social tensions brought about by differing national backgrounds and religious beliefs complicated both problems. Most of the mine bosses and owners were English or Welsh, and were Protestant; the miners were predominantly Irish and Roman Catholic. Inevitably, the Catholic hierarchy, from parish priest to bishop, became enmeshed in the situation.

Gowen, the dominant business personality of the area, had personal and corporate stakes in most of these tensions. After he first attempted to conciliate the existing union—and failed—he apparently decided to break the struggling labor organization by painting it with the brush of "Molly Maguireism."

Using the violence connected with the murders as his rationale, Gowen hired Allan Pinkerton to infiltrate the alleged secret society. The detective president then sent McParlan into the fields disguised as a criminal running from the law. The young operative spent a harrowing two and a half years in the fields, where he joined the society and became increasingly privy to its plans. Finally, on the point of being discovered, McParlan escaped from the fields with enough information to bring a large group of the Irish to trial. These widely publicized court cases brought many guilty verdicts, and twenty of the Irish were hanged, ten in one day.

The story has elements of the wildest of detective lore, and has become a classic for writers of both fiction and fact. Unfortunately for those wishing to stick to the facts, a sizable part of the firsthand documentation for the case has been unavailable. Most of the missing links are now released, and are used for the first time in this book. The complete Reading Railroad files have been made available— they include many of McParlan's daily reports and expense statements that fill significant gaps in the story. The Allan Pinkerton letterbooks have likewise been released, and provide new insights into the detective agency's involvement in the story. Even a few of Gowen's letters have been found, although the lack of his private correspondence remains the most serious blind spot in the case.

And fresh information from Ireland allows a more authoritative view of the affair than has been possible before. A crucial link was lacking in most of the previous studies—the heritage of secret society beliefs and tactics brought over from Ireland by the Irish miners. Many of the seemingly random attitudes and devices in the Pennsylvania story actually had deep roots in Irish history. For this reason, I spent a year in Ireland pursuing the threads of the Irish land question and the secret society that so often resulted. Again a wealth of firsthand documentation became available, documentation that has not been treated authoritatively up to now, even by the Irish themselves. The Pennsylvania story is clearer because of this addition.

The "Molly Maguire" story is at the same time labor history, business history, and social history. It relates deeply to the general histories of both Ireland and the United States. Its enigmas cannot be answered by economic analysis alone; the cultural dimensions— ethnic, religious, nationalistic—are decisively influential.

The Alfred P. Sloan Foundation underwrote the research for the Pennsylvania story, and the Scholarship Exchange Board of the Republic of Ireland sponsored the research on Irish secret societies. I especially thank the holders of four key manuscript collections for their cooperation, free of restrictions: Pinkerton's National Detective Agency; the Reading Railroad; Mrs. George Keiser of Pottsville, Pennsylvania; and Major John Shirley of Carrickmacross, Ireland.

Dartmouth College   WAYNE G. BROEHL, JR.
Hanover, New Hampshire
April 3, 1964

Contents

Illustrations

Part One ✦ *Ireland Sends a Legacy*

Chapter 1 • *Night Riders and Informers*

*E*NGLISH RULE of Ireland was achieved by force, maintained by force. Counter-efforts by the Irish to wrest control from the English were also built upon force. From both sides, through almost all periods of English-Irish relationships, this force was of such brutality as to shame any thinking descendant of either. Military victories were all too often followed by massacres of women, children, and other noncombatants. The heights of barbarity, during the Cromwellian period, saw whole towns of civilians murdered by Cromwell's armies in retaliation for equally appalling murders of the English in the Irish rising of 1641. Even the eighteenth and nineteenth centuries were filled with harrowing tales of agrarian and political murders by the Irish, followed by harshly retaliative police action by the English, typically culminating in a hanging.

It is important to understand this enmity before we assess the American Molly Maguire story. During the first half of the nineteenth century the Irish came in large numbers to the Pennsylvania coal fields. This period in Irish history was the seedtime that formed the attitudes and outlook of the Pennsylvania Irish. Some of the miners involved in the Molly incidents emigrated from Ireland during (or just before or after) the 1846–1852 famine.[1] For the rest, born in America of Irish immigrant parents, cultural ties with the immediate past in Ireland were still powerful. There is little doubt that Irish history had a direct bearing on the evolution of the Molly Maguire incidents.

The secret society itself was a revered, though clandestine, Irish institution. One society in Ireland was actually called the "Molly Maguires." On both sides of the Atlantic the antagonists of the Irish were the same—the English. In Ireland they were landlords and agents; in Pennsylvania they were mine owners and mine bosses. And the unwilling but deep involvement of the Roman Catholic Church was as decisive in Ireland as it was in Pennsylvania. A true understanding of the Pennsylvania incidents depends on an underlying understanding of the Irish secret society.

✤ ✤ ✤ ✤ ✤

What brought such bitterness between two peoples? The answers lie imbedded in a subtle combination of political, religious, economic, and personal issues.

Politics often dominates Irish thinking. The ancient Gaels established concepts of rule that gave the Irish a sense of the importance of political institutions. When these institutions were swept away first by the Vikings and then by the English, a deep bitterness was born. The Irish were not by heritage receptive to political domination no matter how benevolent (and it typically was not). The English experimented with a variety of devices to rule Ireland, ranging from semiautonomous Irish Parliaments to strong-willed resident Lord Lieutenants with weak representation for the Irish in the English Parliament. The half-century 1800–1850 turned politically in the latter direction. The 1798 rebellion had been crushed, the home-rule Irish Parliament was dissolved, and legislative Union with England was pushed through. The Irish people were indignant, and most of this period was marked by vigorous agitation for repeal under the leadership of "The Liberator," Daniel O'Connell.

Political domination begat control of other institutions, and here one of Ireland's profound problems emerged. England had been predominantly a Protestant nation from the time of Elizabeth I. Ireland, since the days of St. Patrick, had been almost exclusively a Roman Catholic nation. Perhaps nowhere within the dominions of the English Crown did the split between Henry VIII and Rome have more serious consequences. Whereas English domination of Ireland prior to Henry was essentially political and economic, a religious dimension was now added, with fateful consequences. During the reign of Elizabeth, Irish history ran into a mold that held it hardened for three hundred years. The Queen, seeing in Ireland a potential haven for Spanish Catholics threatening England, used great cruelty in extinguishing Irish Catholic landowning classes. The Cromwellian period was again particularly illustrative of anti-Catholic bias. Even in less vindictive periods, England's policy toward the Roman Catholic was that of hostility. The English colonists in Ireland, as distinguished from the old Anglo-Irish nobility, identified Protestantism with their own racial ascendancy, to maintain which they regarded as a solemn duty to God and to England. The Irish, in turn, identified Roman Catholicism with a passionate hatred of the English.[2] Though the situation eased during the early part of the reign of George III, the 1798 rebellion dispelled any hopes that the religious issue would die.

As compelling as were politics and religion, the economic problem was even more traumatic. In 1767 there were just over 3,400,000 people in Ireland. By the 1841 census this had jumped to 8,175,124.[3] The reasons for this population explosion are still elusive, but there is ample evidence that the Irish during this period married early, desired to conceive almost as many children as it was possible for the mother to bear, and indulged this desire prolifically.[4] Rapid overcrowding resulted, with families crowded onto smaller and smaller plots of land. This succeeded only in persuading the peasants that their outlook was further poverty and hopelessness, so "why not get married and enjoy that bit of life" before the all-too-frequent early grave. There is little evidence that a declining death rate helped to swell the increase. The almost total dependence on the potato as a staple for subsistence made for both ease of feeding this large a population (potato crops required minimum effort) and for a terrifyingly dangerous situation if the potato crop failed.

The Irish farmer was typically a tenant farmer, renting from landlords who had seized the properties in the great seventeenth-century confiscations. By the nineteenth century many of these holdings had been consolidated into great estates. The landlord was most often English or of English origin, and quite frequently an absentee, living in splendor in England from the rental income of his Irish estate. Between the landlord and the tenant was often interposed an agent —a man noted, and rightly in most cases, for grinding the last penny of rent from his estate. Eviction for nonpayment of rent (often for less understandable reasons) was common. The landlord-tenant economic relationship was tenuous in good times, outright chaos in poorer periods. In the words of one historian, Ireland was "heading for the human disaster which came with greater force and horror than its people could possibly anticipate."[5]

One more problem intruded. This was the personal attitude of the English to the Irish. Quite simply, most Englishmen all through this period had little or no respect for the Irish, treated them as a class lower than themselves, and created an incalculable personal animosity by their high-handed actions. Far back in the early years of English lordship in Ireland—in 1310—Parliament had passed an act that "no mere Irishman shall be received into a religious order among the English in the land of peace."[6] The phrase "land of peace" meant the shires in England; the Irish lands of the great feudal lords were "march lands" and that part of Ireland still held by the native Irish was a "land of war." No more inflammatory phrase could have been devised than the soon-famous "mere Irish" (*merus hibernicus*). The original purpose of the act was to prevent Gaels living by Irish law and under their own chiefs from enjoying any civil rights under English law. But after 1366 the English held that all the "mere Irish" living under Brehon law were "of Irish and servile condition."[7] A neat distinction was made between the Irish (the "King's Irish enemies") and the Anglo-Irish (the "King's Irish rebels"). The former had no rights under English law; the latter never lost the protection of common law and the Magna Carta. Even when the Anglo-Irish lord was altruistic and benevolent, his treatment of tenants tended all too often to be paternalistic and patronizing.

But the fault lay not alone with the English. The Irish exhibited traits which were extremely irritating, calculated to bring about many of the retaliatory acts that occurred. From the start of their relationship, the English had viewed the Irish as combative, argumentative, and unruly. Another trait attributed to the Irish by many Englishmen was improvidence. The peasant was said to be lazy and ignorant, unwilling to work hard and incapable of turning any improvement in conditions to long-term advantage. There was surface truth to this. The dependence on the potato as the main crop, the subdivision that lowered the farm size to miniature proportions, and the constant threat of eviction led almost inevitably to a feeling of frustration and resignation that bred such improvidence. When the fruits of the tenant's labor went not to him but to his landlord, motivation for betterment was almost totally absent.

But surface truth often hides complications. Difficulties here in determining true causal relationships are very real. It seems wise, then, to take a closer look at one particular facet of Irish history—

the landlord-tenant relationship and two of its devastating aberrations, agrarian crime and the secret society.

After 1780, under the Irish Parliament, many earlier repressive trade restrictions were removed; and the Act of Union in 1800 threw open the marts of England on an even more favorable basis. During the eighteenth century there had been a marked move toward using Irish land for grazing, often leading to tenant ejectments and clearances to provide the space. But the system of bounties and encouragement under the Corn Laws (from 1784) had turned a good part of Irish agriculture toward wheat growing.[8] Ever-increasing demands (particularly during the Napoleonic Wars) soon bred overemphasis —and overproduction. Glut in the grain markets forced prices down precipitously, and landlords saw their high profits melt away. The end of the war in 1815 quickly brought economic chaos.

The solution, thought the landlord, appeared to lie in shifts to livestock. This required pasturage. And building a pasture meant eliminating both grain growing and grain growers. Hence, clearances. In 1816 an Ejectment Act was passed—of such stringency that the already easy process of tenant ejectment was greatly facilitated (the process became less expensive, the time needed far shorter).[9] Other acts followed, all designed to augment the landlord's powers of ejectment.

Though the short-lived wartime prosperity had filtered down in only modest proportions to the tenant, there had been prospects for eventual betterment of his conditions. But the sharp downturn following Waterloo took away both the modest gain itself and killed the hope for any future improvement. Within a generation the Irish tenant farmer was living close to subsistence; by 1845—on the eve of the famine—he was a ripe target for disaster.

What brought this desolate condition about? A look at the Irish cottier's way of life in this period will give some clues.

By 1841, when the census counted just over 8,100,000 people, there were about 820,000 individual holdings supporting something over one million families.[10] Of these holdings, only seven per cent were over thirty acres; forty-five per cent were from one to five acres.[11] If we took a particularly rosy view we might class men with more than thirty acres as reasonably independent "farmers," although one historian commented that the only difference from those holding lesser amounts was that "he has probably an additional compartment, hardly divided, for a sleeping place or a dairy."[12] But the tenant holding a plot of an acre or two was, clearly, an agricultural laborer who was forced to supplement his earnings by cultivating a small plot of land.

Patently, the income from such a plot was too small to support a family, as witnesses before the "Devon" Parliamentary Commission in 1843 testified. One commented, "I think he is a very poor man who cannot have a cow—and he cannot rear a cow upon four or five acres." Another noted, "I have seen a farmer, if you may call him a farmer, support himself and family upon one acre of land . . . he sows one-half of the acre with wheat and the other with potatoes, and feeds two pigs." The commissioners concluded that "in *ordinary land* . . . about eight acres, well improved and well managed, would be a minimum average."[13]

Further, the use of the word "holding" is also stretching the truth, for most of these cottiers on small "holdings" were at best operating under a yearly lease, and more frequently were subject to ejectment with only the briefest notice. Both law and practice did vary, though, depending on the region. Tenure in Ulster was generally more secure than in the rest of the country. But these were only relative differences. In absolute terms, the Irish tenant farmer had only a tenuous hold on his few acres; the specter of eviction always followed him about.

Several practices aggravated the problem. The Irish tenant typically subdivided among his children as they married. The exploding population, when combined with the desire to provide all male adults (and often the females, too) with land, soon multiplied the numbers of holdings and decreased the sizes. As one contemporary observer put it, "every patch produces a new family, every member of a family a new patch, and so on. Hence, a country covered with beggars—a complete pauper warren."[14] And one of the Devon Commission witnesses commented that "they have gone on subdividing so far that instead of its being called a 'cow's grass' it is gone down to a 'cow's foot' which is one-fourth of a cow's grass—nay, they have gone so low as a 'cow's toe' which is one-eighth of a cow's grass."[15]

The evils of subdivision were enormously accentuated in many places (especially in Mayo and Donegal) by an ancient Irish practice called "rundale." Instead of receiving his pitifully small holding in one plot, the peasant obtained it in various pieces representing the various grades of land available. Each patch was too small to cultivate successfully, and too small to fence in economically. As a result, the tenant found himself exposed to forays by his neighbor's cattle, leading to continual bickering as to responsibility and often to full-scale family feuds. The Devon Commission findings turned up some amazing examples, as shown by the testimony of a Donegal proprietor that "one man had his land in forty-two different places, and gave it up in despair declaring that it would take a very keen man to find it," and that "one field of half an acre of oats, near the police barracks, was held by twenty-two persons."[16]

In some cases there would be a middleman, himself a farmer, between the landlord and the cottier. The cottier subleased from this middleman, and seldom had any contact with the landlord. In other cases the cottier leased directly from the landlord. But, again, between the cottier and the landlord was a closer adversary, the landlord's agent. When the landlord was an absentee, there was opportunity for exploitation by this agent if he so desired. And many did. The level of the rents was often abused—set at a rate above the actual value of the property for farming. The tenacious desire of the tenant to hold on to the land, coupled with the practice of putting available land up for bidding, succeeded in drawing up rents beyond what even the tenant himself knew he could pay, his hope being that the landlord or agent would tire of pressing him for the rent or, if not, that the secret society would back him in an emergency. It was difficult to generalize about rents, though, for a figure might be exorbitant in one district and reasonable in another. Rents were sticky, and tended to remain immobile in periods of general economic downturn. One analyst has estimated the average annual income of a tenant during the period just before the Great Famine as varying from £6 10s to £8 0s; at the same period his annual rental might be from £6 0s to £10 0s, depending on the quality of land.[17]

The tenants at the bottom of the ladder did not even have full rights to the land that they held so precariously, for another Irish practice—"conacre"—was very common at this time. Under this system, a holder of a piece of land (who was typically a tenant himself) would sublet a small section of this to a subtenant for the growing season of a particular crop. The lessor provided the manuring, the lessee the seed and the work. If the lessor was also the lessee's employer, he would generally take the rent in labor, usually pre-empting the busy season and leaving the lessee little time to do his own cultivation. For this reason potatoes were generally the conacre crop. Abuses of conacre were widespread, especially when the system of payment-in-labor was used. The County Clare tenants who called conacre "mock ground" were probably close to the truth.

If there was a deficit in the rent due, it was made up in a variety of ways. Sometimes the family pig was the wedge against eviction. More frequently, one or more members of the family were sent to adjoining counties in Ireland or to England to pick up whatever possible during the harvest season——"spalpeening," as it was dubbed. Begging was resorted to as a last hope and was widespread during all this period.

One of the most biting provisions facing the tenant was "distraining," the right of the landlord who was owed rent to appropriate the tenant's growing crops, keep title to them until ripe, and then to sell them, charging the tenant with the accumulation of expense involved. Tenants were particularly agitated by distraining of livestock—which were driven away and impounded in a town pound. The family cow was closer to being a member of the family than most household pets today. It represented both a productive source of family subsistence, and a hedge against future catastrophe, in effect a living "savings bank." The pounds, as one analyst put it, were "evilly constructed,"[18] and even if the animals were not physically harmed, the mental torture for the entire tenant family was profound.

If the accumulation of all this did not explain the tenant's frequent indolence and lack of initiative, one further practice did. This was the prevailing custom concerning improvements. Generally the landlord rented only the naked land. It was then the tenant's responsibility to provide the necessary dwellings and farm buildings, fencing, manuring, and the other necessities of successful agriculture. But any such improvements became, by the law of most counties, the property of the landlord. The Devon Commissioners called the abuses here the most serious of all land problems.[19] What possible motivation was there to improve beyond the barest necessities of subsistence if the landlord could confiscate by evicting the tenant and taking over all his improvements? The English economist John Stuart Mill scathingly denounced the system:

In such a condition, what can a tenant gain by any amount of industry or prudence, and what lose by any recklessness? If the landlord at any time exerted his full legal rights, the cottier would not be able even to live. If by extra exertion he doubled the produce of his bit of land, or if he prudently abstained from producing mouths to eat it up, his only gain would be to have more left to pay to his landlord; while, if he had twenty children, they would still be fed first, and the landlord could only take what was left. Almost alone among mankind, the Irish cottier is in this condition, that he can scarcely be either better or worse off by any act of his own. If he was industrious or prudent, nobody but his landlord would gain; if he is lazy or intemperate, it is at his landlord's expense. A situation more devoid of motives to either labor or self-command, imagination itself cannot conceive. The inducements of free human beings are taken away, and those of a slave not substituted.[20]

Mill's statement introduces a point that is often ignored by writers on Irish land questions. The system had some very pernicious facets for the landlord, too. Though the weight of sympathy tends to tip heavily in the direction of the tenant, the landlord was caught within forces that made him, too, less a master of his destiny than he was generally considered to be.

True, the pre-Waterloo days had been halcyon ones for him—prosperity allowed high rents and high income from property. Whereas the holder of land in England had substantial charges against his income (land tax, poor rates, and tithes), his Irish counterpart had none of these before the 1830's. As a result, his gross rental income became his net income. The thesis has been advanced that this bred the inclination to do nothing in the way of land improvement. Though a case could be made that improvements in the condition of the tenantry would have made the estates more stable, the fact remains that there was a pervasive unwillingness by landlords to put any money back into their estates.

But the postwar depression hit the Irish landlord badly—nonpayment of rent increased and his position worsened. With new legislation in the 1830's, he was faced with poor-law charges and tithe payments. The profligate lives led by many landlords had already left them in debt. Now the combination of circumstances brought many of them face to face with financial ruin. The heavily encumbered estate, slowly falling to bankruptcy, was all too common in the decades after 1815 (and especially after the famine years, when a special "Encumbered Estates Court" was necessary to clear the way to new ownership). Nonpayment of rent continued to increase, the specter of ruin panicked many landlords, and many of the tenant-damaging excesses of the landlords during this period were carried through with private misgivings. Eviction, in particular, was thought to be necessary as a device to clear the land for more productive worth, and the laissez-faire economic philosophy of this period, while not countenancing distress, nevertheless held it to be a necessary corollary of progress. The nineteenth-century landlord, looking out through the glasses of English conservatism, was appalled by the rapidly increasing hordes of tenants unemployed because of lack of work (seemingly unwilling to work even when work was available) and in all cases unable to pay rent. The Devon Commission put the landlord's side well:

If the gross produce derived from a limited holding amount to £8, and that it be occupied by a family of five persons . . . where there is little or no assistance for them in the way of profitable or casual labour, we find a most difficult and embarrassing situation, both as regards the land proprietor and the tenant; and yet this is by no means an exaggerated or uncommon case . . .

The most moderate calculation of a year's maintenance for such a family would amount to £24 . . . thus the gross produce would amount to only one-third of the sum requisite to support the family, without allowing for either rent, seed or taxes . . .

The landlord then looks for his rent. His just claim is not the point which the debtor or the public considers when he seeks for its liquidation. The broad fact of a rich man pressing a wretchedly poor man for a payment of money is the point that arrests attention . . .

Goods are distrained, or legal proceedings instituted, and the landlord at once acquires the character of an oppressive rack-renter. Inattentive management permits the subdivision of farms to increase: the £8 worth of gross produce must now provide for two or three families. This needy class of tenants increases in number and destitution, and the landlord's character for oppression increases in a like proportion . . .

The evil grows to such an extent that threatens the annihilation of the landlord's income; a clearance of the tenants, or consolidation of farms is resorted to, and forms the climax of tyrannical landlordism . . . Nor would his granting these holdings to such tenants free of rent materially mend these cases . . .[21]

Thus, both landlord and tenant thought themselves caught up within forces they could little understand and less control. Both did what they did because of knowing little else to do. And the result was chaotic.

George O'Brien, one of the most perceptive Irish economic historians, has maintained that there were three possible remedies for this desperate situation: increase the amount of produce per acre, or, increase the amount of land under cultivation, or, lastly, secure a more equitable division of the produce of the soil between landlord and tenant.[22]

There might have been definite possibilities in the first two of these suggestions, but little resulted from either during the early nineteenth century. The third meant trouble for all concerned, particularly because of the way the tenant enforced his side of the argument. For he frequently turned to one of the most pervasive and infamous of Irish land reform devices, the secret society.

Peaceful persuasion by the peasant to alleviate his personal distress was difficult, if not impossible. He was uneducated, unorganized for peaceful pressure, and unable to hold his own in debate or other parliamentary avenues. If he resorted to the courts for redress of his grievances he was likely to find a landlord or his agent sitting as magistrate, an all-Protestant jury assessing his claims. The scales of justice were tipped heavily toward the landowner.

And, unfortunately, the tenants' strongest political representative during the first half of the nineteenth century, the famous and revered Daniel O'Connell, was more interested in political reform, Catholic emancipation, and abolition of Union than in specific land reforms. That O'Connell's dreams, if realized, would later bring better conditions was not obvious to the peasant. His ills were "now"; they were direct; and they were being suffered day by day under conditions brought about by a specific person. The situation begged for more direct action. And this the peasant supplied through agrarian disturbance.

Taking direct action by force to combat a presumed evil was an ancient tradition in Ireland. Faction fights between Irish families or between the forces of two townlands, the settlement of a personal quarrel by a fight—these are as old as Ireland itself. And the further refinement of banding together in a secret society (loosely knit in most cases) goes far back in Irish history.[23] For the Molly Maguire story our interest will center on the nineteenth-century varieties. But their predecessors laid important groundwork; a brief look at them is in order.

✤   ✤   ✤   ✤   ✤

The "Whiteboys" were the first to gain national notoriety. Their name came from their practice of wearing a white shirt over their clothes while on a night raid. In the early 1760's Irish agriculture began shifting from tillage to pasturage. This often brought the "enclosure of commons"—the fencing in by landlords of pasture lands that were being used by the peasants on a "squatters' rights" basis. The peasants had used this land (and their fathers before them) as a matter both of right and economic necessity, for the peasantry's cows often meant the difference between survival and starvation. As enclosures increased, the peasants banded together under cover of darkness and threw down the fences (thus the alternate name, "Levellers"). And their defiance was soon being directed against another peasant grievance, the payment of church tithes.

The tithe was a profound irritant. Its incidence was heavy and its collection often brutally handled by the "tithe proctor." Most galling of all, though, was the fact that the overwhelmingly Roman Catholic peasantry were required by law to pay the tithes to the Established Church, the Protestant Episcopal Church. (The substantial number of Presbyterian dissenters in the North therefore were equally hit.)

The Whiteboy movement thus struck at deep-rooted grievances—and spread rapidly over many counties. It was temporarily driven underground by the Whiteboy Act of 1765, but new grievances brought new attacks in Kildare, Kilkenny, and Queen's Counties in 1775, and incidents continued sporadically until 1785, when Whiteboyism again burst through central and southern Ireland. Every season of distress brought further disturbances, and the system prepared the way for a host of nineteenth-century adaptations. Beatings of tithe proctors, landlords, and any others who irritated its "members" were common. Incendiary fires were a revered device. Threatening letters and placards found wide use. And even more refined brands of torture were sometimes resorted to—for example, imprisonment of a naked victim in a hole in the ground, buried up to the chin in briars.

The Whiteboys were at first viewed with diffidence by the authorities, but, as the violence increased, diffidence turned to alarm. English troops were called in; their efficiency was far superior to the local forces, and in brutality they were often the equal of the worst of the Whiteboys. "Eye-for-an-eye" retaliation by the authorities was abetted by the series of "Whiteboy" crime acts of terrible severity passed by the Irish Parliament.[24] Their enforcement was often graphically reported in the provincial newspapers. In Clonmel, in early 1776, two men (one going under the name "Captain Slasher") were tried for complicity in a Whiteboy murder, sentenced to death and "immediately conducted from the dock to the main street, opposite the courthouse, where a wooden gallows being erected, they were immediately hanged . . . without being allowed a clergyman . . . and after hanging for a few moments, they were cut down whilst life still remained, after which they were quartered and beheaded."[25]

The North of Ireland was itself nurturing the embryos of future secret societies. Here the peasant situation contained a different set of premises. The Protestant population represented a much higher proportion than in the South. The peasant position was sometimes bettered by the granting of a modest form of "tenant right" (in respect to both tenant improvements and tenant lease). The practice grew that a tenant could not be evicted without following a specified set of legal steps, and if evicted was allowed to sell his "tenant rights" to the next renter. Too much should not be made of this difference, as it still left the tenant with only rudimentary protection. But Ulster was not quite the same as Kilkenny or Tipperary, where Whiteboyism was so often rampant.

The first Ulster movement, in 1763, was the Hearts of Oak, or "Oak boys," whose bands of men wearing oak branches in their hats ranged the northern counties aggressively protesting both tithes and the application of the "road acts" of several of the counties, which generally required that all highways should be repaired by the householders themselves. This concept might have engendered little heat had it not been that many of the roads were for use of the landlord as estate byways. The county officials acted quickly, though, repealing the more stringent aspects of the Road Act and bringing about a reduction in tithes, and the "Oak boys" soon died out.[26]

A more lasting organization was the Hearts of Steel, which first made its appearance in 1770.[27] At that time there was a general depression, brought about by worsening conditions in the linen trade,[28] but the prime force seems to have been a series of wholesale evictions from the estate of the Marquis of Donegal. Most of those evicted were Presbyterians. Violence first was directed at cattle, and an ancient device—"houghing," or the cutting of leg tendons—was widely used. Soon violence was turned on humans. Arrests came, and a general fear of enmeshment led many of the Presbyterians to emigrate to the United States. Unlike the Whiteboys, the Hearts of Steel finally died out completely. But the North did not remain calm for long. For the most famous of all northern societies soon came into the picture—the Orangemen.

Though tensions between the Episcopalians and the Presbyterians continued through this period, the two Protestant groups generally stood together in opposition to the Roman Catholics. Increasing clashes soon led to repressive measures by the government. Protestants could legally carry arms; Catholics could not. The Protestants were thus in a position to swagger and boast, and to disarm Catholics with the full backing of the law. Catholics depended on the blackthorn stick, and thus were inferior as a fighting force. Protestant (especially Presbyterian) "volunteers" often aided government forces and carried out searches for arms without any legal fiat. Their custom of entering peasant cottages by surprise at daybreak soon brought them the name "Peep of Day Boys" (sometimes Break of Day Boys).[29] Against them were arrayed the Catholic group, the Defenders. A series of incidents soon hardened lines and built up a furious desire for revenge. Finally, on September 21, 1795, it came to a head in the infamous Battle of the Diamond, in Armagh County. Whoever was the aggressor (it is generally presumed to have been the Catholic group), a pitched battle was fought, and when it was over upwards of twenty people were dead.[30] That night a large band of the Protestant side congregated and formed the "Orange Society." It had ritual and hierarchy, and a requirement for an oath, the wording of which has since been the subject of much difference of opinion among scholars.

It was widely believed by the ignorant peasant that each side meant to extirpate the other. The Catholic peasant was particularly fearful of the Orange order. The undeclared religious war that resulted found both sides committing acts of terror. Often the Catholics were willing to bid higher for land than Protestants, and thus set in motion fierce anti-Catholic outbursts in mid-Ulster which under the Orange cry "To Hell or Connaught" drove large numbers of the more peaceful Catholics altogether out of the North and into the wilder regions of western Ireland. What a shock to have had the following notice stuck in one's cottage door: "Peter Brady, you have five days your goods to sell, and get to Connaught or hell, for here you may not dwell."[31]

By the end of the eighteenth century secret societies were well embedded in both the South and North. But worse was to come. With the crushing of the United Irishmen in the 1798 rebellion, this terrible device began to loom ever more importantly. The nineteenth century was the heyday of the agrarian secret society.

✣   ✣   ✣   ✣   ✣

Few of the Irish in the Pennsylvania anthracite fields in the 1870's would have personally remembered the 1798 rebellion (barroom boastings to the contrary notwithstanding). But a great many had searing personal memories of the Irish land tensions in the first half of the nineteenth century.

The smashing of the rebellion led to an uneasy peace. England kept large numbers of troops in the country. Successively stronger "convention and coercion" acts and the continued suspension of habeas corpus made melancholy partners. Just under the surface simmered disorder, wanting only the right circumstances to break again into armed combat. There had been a connection with the French in the 1798 insurrection, and though this connection had been abortive, hopes for French aid lingered on for several years, to be fully extinguished only by the fall of Napoleon in 1815. Ties with the French were alleged in police reports.[32] In 1803, for example, French agents were reputed to be passing out "guineas among the disaffected" near Mallow.[33] In 1805 priests were said to be teaching their parishioners to speak French.[34] "Bonaparte" bobbed up as a benefactor and as a favorite signature for the threatening notice:

> Bonaparte is our Friend.
>
> B. Ready[35]

> No Labourer to Work Under Two
> Shillings a Day or Suffer Death.
> Bonaparte[36]

But the latter notice telegraphed how shallowly the average peasant really felt about invasion and political overthrow, and how deeply ran the grievances connected with everyday life—rents, wages, tenancy. Legislative union with England had not changed the landlord–tenant relationship, and soon new versions of earlier agrarian outrages claimed the attention of the authorities. As the outrages cumulated, fresh rumors of the presence of societies were relayed to Dublin Castle by the local authorities. New names had replaced the old, and new leaders affixed their signatures to the notices. In Counties Cavan and Monaghan an organization called the "Black Conclusion" was rumored; in County Londonderry in 1807 it was the "Standardmen."[37] Both names dropped out of the police reports within months of their first mention. But meanwhile the first truly new group of substantial impact in the new century had appeared —the "Threshers."

The first Thresher activity came in 1806, when magistrates in several western counties reported outrages connected with tithe collection. Payment of tithes in kind rather than money was common at that time (few peasants would have had much cash anyway, as large parts of the South and West were essentially barter economies). A tenth of the crop "above the ground" was generally asked; as grudgingly as this was given, the occasional demand for a tenth of the crop "below the ground" (i.e., potatoes) was even more bitterly opposed. The Threshers gained their name from their initial passive resistance to tithes by leaving a tenth of the crop in the field to deteriorate. Frequently these tithe sheaves were burned by night riders, who always seemed able to find the tenth part for the torch. Special vitriol was directed against tithe proctors; a rigged system of auction of the tithe crops added additional grievances. The Earl of Rosslyn in County Mayo described one of these auctions, "which takes place commonly at night and the bidders are encouraged by great quantities of whiskey," and decried the windfall profits that accrued to the proctor.[38]

Threshers in County Sligo soon encouraged like efforts by peasant groups in Leitrim and Longford, and the movement's seepage was threatening Cavan. Up to that point the apparent concentration on tithes had appeared to be no direct threat against the government and little action had been taken; there was a general feeling among the peasants that the Threshers were countenanced—"Oh! Government knows very well we only mean to put down the tythes."[39] But the turn to increased violence and the broader agrarian base of the crimes finally led Dublin Castle to order suppression. In mid-1807 the British Parliament passed a stringent insurrection act[40] which renewed with modifications a Whiteboy Act of 1796. Trial by jury now could be suspended. Persons out of doors between sunset and sunrise were liable to arrest, and if convicted could be transported out of the country for a period of years (a frequent penalty for crimes of less than capital nature).

Ambivalence had generally typified government efforts—the countenancing of crime and outrage as long as it appeared non-insurrectionary, with abrupt change to severe repression when the disturbances took on any semblance of coordinated effort or were directed against the collection of rents. Further, the ability of England to spare manpower and money for controlling disturbances in Ireland varied sharply according to conditions in England. At this time the French involvement left the English armies in Ireland understaffed.

Before the clampdown the Threshers were quite bold, not only operating at night but marching about the country in large mobs by daylight. One of their favorite devices was using the secret oath to swear in peasants, who either by willingness or as the result of a threat were required to pledge allegiance to Thresher objectives. The method was well calculated to strike fear in the heart of the peasant. The band would rendezvous at night at a prearranged spot, arrayed in white sheets. The leader, generally decked out in a distinctive uniform (in one case an old cavalry uniform, a green cockade, a green sword and a green sash[41]), arranged the group in military formation, those on horseback in front, followed by those on foot. Some would be armed, with old fowling pieces or whatever arms were available, others would carry a favorite blackthorn stick. They then marched up to a peasant's cottage in well-disciplined silence. A gentle knock awoke the tenant who was "fairly" asked if he wanted to "become acquainted with Captain Thresher's laws." Terrified, he was then sworn to whatever the "laws" advocated at the moment—to pay tithes only to the Episcopal rector rather than the tithe proctor, or in some cases to pay reduced fees to the Roman Catholic priest. After he was also sworn to secrecy, the mob, silent until now, would typically break into one loud "huzzah" and then silently melt away, leaving the thunderstruck peasant quaking lest they return and "scourge" him.[42]

Most of the tithe defiance was directed at the Established Church. But the Roman Catholic Church came in for its share of antipathy; and the control of priests' fees for weddings, funerals, and other services of the Church were often at issue.[43]

Economics, too, occupied the Threshers. Efforts were made to control the price of potatoes, despite the fact that there was no shortage nor evidence of any substantial profiteering.[44] The trade-union analogy was even closer in the occasional efforts to circumscribe methods of farming—an 1804 notice threatened reprisals "against all that plant potatoes otherwise than by the spade,"[45] signaling the lack of employment for a rapidly increasing population. More frequent were outrages designed to prevent the shipping of potatoes and grain out of the area. Three boats visiting Limerick "had their rigging cut to pieces"[46] and in Galway port a ship's captain had his sails "taken away by a mob."[47] "Captain Thresher's price for potatoes" terrified both merchants and peasants. The officials often took this fear to be apathy; one magistrate commented (on such outrages) that "their number and atrocity is only to be equalled by the apathy with which they have been suffered." He added that "if possible I will shame them into something like activity . . ."[48]

Outlaw elements took advantage of Thresher activity to perpetrate armed robbery and extortion, and thus added to the peasant's fears. A gang terrorized Kilkenny for several years, with the populace unwilling to assist the authorities in any way, until one day the police surprised the leader and killed him. Upon this, the now-courageous people rose up in a posse and captured the remainder of the gang. So great had been the fear of the leader that only his death had brought any resistance.[49] The Irish peasant, like his counterparts all over the world, was universally uneducated and almost universally filled with superstitious fears; many ghost stories were invented by gangs or secret societies to keep strangers away from a favorite meeting place.[50] The choice of a feared name for the mythical leader of their organizations was in large part due to the very respect the name itself would gain among the peasantry. "Captain Rock" was the favorite, but "Captain Rouser," "Captain Thresher" and others were found in this period (with many ingenious adaptations in later decades).

The authorities frequently attempted to use citizens, generally Protestants, as "yeomanry," in both the eighteenth and nineteenth centuries, but the scheme was generally ineffectual. Great bodies of the peasantry were too timid to be helpful and those who did join were too frequently guilty of their own excesses. Beyond this, the English found that the yeomanry were continually defecting to the side they were sworn to fight. One observer of a Thresher foray noted that yeomen participated, as evidenced "from the circumstance of *bright arms* being frequently seen."[51] But the question of arms was a thorny problem for the English. Periodic arms acts contained confiscatory clauses for disarming the peasantry, but were only partially successful, for the peasant had many sources. In addition to the defecting yeoman, the English had recurring problems with their own men illegally selling arms to the peasant.[52] And some of the peasant groups had their own armorers, who, if detected repairing arms, were subject to arrest (the "Caravats," in 1811, were found employing their own specialists).[53]

The Threshers were active for only a few years; trials and hangings in Sligo in 1807 drove most of the dissidents underground and the name soon dropped out of the lexicon of Irish society names. But others soon appeared. In 1808, in Kilkenny and Tipperary, two factions, the "Shanavests" and the "Caravats," fought extensively at fairs; in a particularly brutal encounter in Whitechurch parish troops were required.[54] Soon, others not connected directly with the two groups adopted their names for fighting and outrages of their own, and police reports in 1811 spoke of "the System of Shanavests spreading,"[55] and of "Caravat mania" in the counties of Waterford, Limerick, Westmeath, Roscommon, and Kings.[56] Again, as with the Threshers, there appeared to be little contact among the various groups and little formal structure within any of them. The names lingered on for many years.

About this time another loosely knit organization with a particularly brutal device made its appearance—the "Carders." The name itself appears to have been used first in County Dublin in 1811,[57] but the method was much older. The device, quite simply, was to card individuals, rather than wool. The razor-sharp card was slashed down the back of the victim and only a few strokes were needed to rip large patches of skin away, quickly baring the bones. Sometimes the carding was not confined to the head of the house; one police report noted that "they beat Neale severely and then carded his wife and son on their bare backs after which they placed Neale and son on their knees and swore them to give up their farm in ten days."[58] The Carders soon became notorious all over Ireland, their aims ranging from religious to economic. An illustration of economic motive is found in a report that, in Galway and Mayo Counties in 1812, "the Carders aim at regulating prices of provisions and liquor, preventing persons from taking land over the heads of old tenants and deterring new settlers from coming into the country."[59]

Another form of outrage common through all this period (already mentioned in connection with earlier times) was "houghing." Although most often applied to cattle, it was sometimes used on humans. The cutting of the tendons forced the destroying of the cattle; in the case of the men houghed, they were crippled for life. In 1804 a certain battalion of soldiers was particularly hated; one night in Dublin three men met a lone soldier walking, asked him if he was of this group, and, getting an affirmative reply, pulled him down on his face and cut his Achilles tendon just above the heel of the left leg. The examining surgeon confirmed that the cut "will prevent his ever having the use of the limb."[60]

Chapter 2 • Who Was Molly Maguire?

*T*HE PHENOMENON of "Whiteboyism" had prevailed from the 1760's through 1780's, "Defenderism" was widespread in the North in the last two decades of that century, and the first few years of the new century brought "Threshers," "Carders" and others. Now, between 1810 and 1820, a new name appears—a name coming to stand pre-eminently for the Irish secret society—the "Ribbonmen." The title was first used in the North, and the wide variety of local groups under a wide variety of local names all were called loosely the "Ribbon Conspiracy." Soon the name Ribbon came to be a generic term for peasant agitation, wherever it was (although "Whiteboy" and "Rockite" remained more popular terms in the southernmost counties).

The words "society" and "conspiracy," if applied literally, would stretch the truth. The actual structure was very loose, almost non-existent beyond the particular locality. Local agitation for local reasons would crop up, a name of local renown would be adopted as it was discussed around the shebeens and town squares, and certain local luminaries of reputation (good or bad as the case might be) would become its leaders. Violence would take place, obviously on a planned basis. The movement would likely spread to other localities in the area and soon the violence in the other areas would become "the work of the Ribbonmen." There must have been some contact among the several groups in a great many cases. The notion of importing a stranger from across the mountain or lake to perpetrate the crime in return for a similar act in the stranger's territory was used often enough to suggest that more than just informal word-of-mouth contacts were involved. But the insinuation that there was a giant Ribbon conspiracy being organized all over Ireland and controlled by an unknown but powerful and diabolical "central committee"—a belief held at various times by many of the English administrators—does not appear warranted by the facts. There were Irishmen who hoped, schemed and planned for a universal uprising, and who attempted national political and agrarian organization. But their efforts generally went unrewarded.

The Ribbonmen now provided several new chapters to the mounting list of outrages—and the government new chapters in retaliation and repression. Specific cases will help to illustrate the trend.

In June 1816, the Lord Lieutenant of Ireland, Charles Whitworth, addressed a long memorandum to Viscount Sidmouth (Henry Addington) on "the Nature and Extent of the Disturbances which have Recently Prevailed in Ireland." The tone is that of frustration, frenzy, and exasperation—and the feeling that the situation was getting completely out of hand. Whitworth noted that his making "severe examples" in some convictions in Tipperary and Waterford had seemed not to have produced "any lasting effect or materially checked the bad spirit." On the contrary, the Irish were apparently stepping up their attacks. Worse, potential Crown witnesses were being intimidated, so that it became almost impossible to procure satisfactory evidence. "Sufferers from such atrocities, when visited by a magistrate, would depose only generally to the facts . . . and not denying their knowledge of the offenders, would yet steadily refuse to disclose their names . . . " Whitworth dolefully listed a wide range of crimes, including murders, burnings, beatings, threats. A police barracks in the barony of Kilnamanagh, near Limerick, was attacked by a large body of men, who, after burning the building to the ground, left a notice that they would do the same to any other house used as a barracks. Whitworth noted that, "fortunately for the peace of the country," fourteen persons were captured, found guilty and hanged for this episode.[1]

In another case, Whitworth told of the killing of William Baker, a wealthy farmer in Tipperary, because Baker had aided aggressively in the detection of a party who had burned his house down. But the Lord Lieutenant failed to note (and probably didn't know of) an incident which, whether it happened or not, came to be a lasting anecdote of this period. Baker's presumed murderer was finally found, after vast sums had been offered as rewards for information. And, so the story goes, the police then offered the man freedom if he would inform on the others involved. As embroidered by succeeding generations of folk-story tellers, the murderer was about to succumb to the bribe when his wife tearfully came to him and on her knees begged him to "die rather than betray his comrades." His backbone straightened by this (presumably) unselfish courage of his wife, he closed his mouth and, unabashed, went forth to the gallows.

Even if this particular story is false, the situation itself rings true. During this period the government placed heavy dependence on a system of public rewards and private under-the-table payments for information concerning past crimes or future plottings. Substantial numbers of people availed themselves of these opportunities, undoubtedly for a wide mixture of motives. Some probably wished to have the lawless brought to justice, for idealistic or vindictive reasons. Others, quite baldly, wanted the money. The system was widespread enough to make the "informer" one of the most hated persons in Ireland. The ill feelings concerning informers, particularly as augmented in the 1880's, remain so close to the surface in Ireland today that many aspects of the secret-society question cannot yet be openly discussed there.

Some fascinating and macabre tales of the pillory of the informer have resulted. Fear of being called an informer came not only from the actual physical danger this might bring but also the bitter social recriminations that would come. The hated name would follow the family for generations. In one case in 1829 a man stopped to talk with a constable about a levy warrant for wages due him. As soon as he was finished, three people came up to him and accused him of conveying intelligence to the police. Worse yet, the following Sunday the parish priest denounced him at the service as an informer. The terrified man pleaded with the constable to give him an affidavit that he was innocent. No record remains of what happened to him, but we can assume that at the least his life was made miserable by his fellow parishioners for some time afterward.[2]

The position of a young man in County Monaghan was even more uncomfortable. The Chief Secretary in Dublin received the following letter:

I feel it my duty as one of his majestys loyal subjects to let your Excellency know that since Easter Monday the 10th of April a number of the Pentioners in the place where I reside has become Repealers against the Crown. Therefore I apply for to be known wheather their conduct is wright or Rong and on answer to this I will send you their addresses and proof for what they have done.

(signed) Hugh Flemming

So the Chief Inspector of County Monaghan sent a sub-inspector to interview Flemming. Flemming vehemently denied any knowledge whatsoever of the letter, and the sub-inspector was inclined to believe him, as he was a "simple looking young boy of nineteen." The sub-inspector then checked the postoffice, and the postmaster happened to remember the sender—a young girl of about the same age! It was not further reported whether the young woman was disappointed in love, but whatever the reason, the device was about as revengeful as possible.[3]

Some writers have suggested that not only did the police sergeants have informers in the county lodges and organizations of the Ribbonmen, but that these would be composed of two classes—those who would agree to appear as witnesses, and those whose names would never be divulged under any circumstances. According to these writers, the second group often included the most active people in the organization itself.[4] Checking the authenticity of such notions is close to impossible now, and secondary sources furnish our only clues. But there was probably considerable substance to these accusations.

Police methods during this period were all too often crude and harsh—designed, as implied by the Lord Lieutenant's statements, to put down insurrection by fear. The stories of police brutality were often magnified out of proportion and fed the minds of the people until they were poisoned with hatred. In 1821 a major in the Limerick barracks was assassinated, after which, according to the *Limerick Chronicle*, "there was a joyous shout through the country which re-echoed from place to place; lighted heaps of straw also were at night exhibited on the different hills in triumph of the accomplishment of this horrible deed." The paper went on to quote the current rumor as to why the major was killed: that he had ordered one of the men who had been shot in an affray with the police at Askeaton to be buried in quicklime "before life was extinct." The *Chronicle* pointed out that in fact this was not true, as there was a record of an inquest for the dead peasant. But the paper implied that it *was* true that the major had ordered burials in quicklime of peasants shot or hanged for agrarian crimes as "the best for deterring all other deluded people."[5]

Secret-society vengeance was sometimes directed at the women; later, in the time of the Land League, there were cases in which wives and daughters of victims had their hair shorn. In the main, though, it was the male who suffered the atrocity. Likewise, women did not frequently participate in the avenging. Only very occasionally is there mention of female participants in night riding, although both women and children were prominent in certain daytime riots (and became noted for their rock-throwing ability). On many occasions the wife of a victim attempted to intervene when her husband was being beaten, and there were examples where the wife was shot after throwing herself in front of her husband. And personal intervention by the wife to prevent attack (generally involving the giving of a bribe to the intended assailants without the knowledge of the husband) was sometimes used. But the lack of involvement of the women is a remarkable element of the Irish agrarian and political disturbances of the eighteenth and nineteenth centuries.

But if women themselves were not frequently involved, the same cannot be said of their *clothing*. Disguises had been common from the earliest agrarian agitation. One of the favorite tricks was dressing in women's clothes. W. E. H. Lecky recounts the story of how a private army in the wildest districts of Kerry in the 1660's attacked collectors of hearth money, bailiffs and informers, dressed in women's clothing with faces blackened and armed with stout hazel sticks; they became widely known as "fairesses."[6] Few instances are recorded of Whiteboys disguised as women, but this was a widely used practice of the Peep-of-Day Boys in the North. By the 1820's the "Lady Rocks" were frequent; their robing was complete with bonnet and veil.[7] In the early 1830's a whole new society calling themselves the "Lady Clares" was to mushroom in Clare and adjoining counties; in this case the "official" costume was women's clothing.

During the period 1823–1829 violence was somewhat overshadowed by political activity. Daniel O'Connell formed the Catholic Association of Ireland in 1823, dedicated to win Catholic emancipation through open organization via peaceful means. The ability of O'Connell to catch the imagination of the Irish people and his resourcefulness and ingenuity during this period marked him for what he soon became—the key Irish figure of the first half of the nineteenth century, the "Uncrowned King of Ireland."[8] O'Connell vehemently opposed the use of force and began teaching the Irish people to trust in methods that no army could be called on to suppress. In a speech at Limerick in March 1822, referring to the terrible outrages in Cork and Kerry, he said: "Many a widow, many an orphan, grieves over the consequences of these disturbances.

Murder—oh, it brings the curse of heaven on their heads; the hand of man pursues to punish it; the red right arm of God's avenging justice hangs over the head of the murderer and of the midnight assassin!"[9] In extended testimony before an investigating committee of the House of Commons in 1825, O'Connell again castigated agrarian crime. Contrasting the Ribbonmen in the north with Whiteboyism in the south, he remarked that "the Ribbonmen do not, if I may say so, choose to fritter away their strength in those driftless acts of outrage which the peasantry in the south do." But, O'Connell continued, "we have a great deal more trouble to check Ribbonism than to check Whiteboyism in the south. By we, I mean the Catholic Association, and those who have taken an active part in Catholic politics."[10]

How much impact did O'Connell have on the people? His following was enormous and his influence great. Probably he did succeed in putting additional caution and responsibility into the picture. Certainly the period from 1823 to 1829 was relatively quiet. But Irish leaders appear always to have had trouble in building a sense of personal responsibility in certain groups of the Irish, particularly the uneducated. And soon the incidence of outrages began to rise, for little had been done to alleviate the basic causes. There were no substantial changes in the landlord–tenant relationship, and the tithe was still a very sensitive issue. So from 1829 through the famine of 1846–1852 (and afterward, too) substantial agrarian disorders were the rule. Few years from 1829 to the 1850's could be classed as peaceful. New names spread under the broad umbrella of "Ribbonmen," and the lexicon of Irish secret societies took on its colorful and unique fabric. In addition to "Rockites," far the most common name during this period, there were Whitefeet and Blackfeet, Three-Year Olds and Four-Year Olds, Black Hens and Black Conclusions, Riscarvilles, Moll Doyle's Men and Padreen Gar's Men, Terryalts and Billy Welters, Northerns (called Widgeons), Sons of Irish Freedom, Sons of Erin, and Shamrock Societies. Some were agrarian, some political, others both. Many existed primarily as faction-fighting groups. Few had any substantial structure, few lasted for any time as distinct entities. But all entered the vocabulary of the Irish people and became important additions to the Irish way of life.

❖   ❖   ❖   ❖   ❖

Thomas Foster, an English lawyer and journalist, sent back to the London *Times* a series of articles on his travels in Ireland between August 1845 and January 1846, and these were reprinted in book form. From County Cavan he asked, "What is the 'Molly Maguireism' which has disturbed this county?" He continued, "It is the same as 'Ribandism,' say the magistrates, in their placards offering rewards for the apprehension of 'Molly Maguires' . . . it is then, in fact, but the embodyment of the spirit of discontent; it is an old existing malady with a new name."[11] Foster said Molly Maguireism was concentrated in Cavan, Longford, and Leitrim, and had its headquarters in the parish of Clune in Leitrim. He traced the beginnings of the movement to the famous wholesale eviction by Lord Lorton, a landlord in Ballinamuck, Longford, in 1835, when he razed the whole village in the ensuing disturbance.

In another notable nineteenth-century book, *Realities of Irish Life*, published in 1868, an Irish land agent, W. S. Trench, recounted a series of events on the Shirley Estate in County Monaghan in 1843, where an organization called the Molly Maguires was said to operate.[12] Those events have a special place in our story and must be investigated presently.

In the middle and late 1840's the name was well-known not only in the north central region around County Cavan, but also as far south as Clare[13] and as far north as Donegal and Tyrone. A Tyrone landlord received a threatening letter: "Mr. Todd, don't think that I want Quinn, only Molly Maguire is angry that you would turn out one tenant and give it to another. I have bargained to shoot a few others as well as you, but I think you will be shot in Dublin to save your widow the expense of taking your corpse home . . . Molly Maguire and her children have been watching you."[14]

Was there ever an authentic Molly Maguire? Legends and stories make up in ingenuity and wildness for the lack of agreement on the facts. Once the name had achieved international notoriety in the Pennsylvania coal field incidents, highly conflicting versions were put forth, all couched in most positive tones, but all probably rooted primarily in folklore.

The most famous of the stories was that Molly was a poor widow, evicted from her home after the landlord's agent "severely abused she and her daughter."[15] One report ran as follows:

The bailiffs, supported by the constabulary, appeared near Ballymena, County Antrim, in June, 1839, to eject the Widow Maguire from her little farm. The people from the neighboring parishes assembled, and determined, if possible, to prevent the ejectment. Resistance, however, was of little avail, as the bailiffs and constabulary were in great force. The widow was old, and as the constabulary and bailiffs led the aged woman out of her cabin, her feeble and helpless appearance produced a great impression upon the spectators. Next came her little grandchildren and their mother in tears. The bailiffs cast their bed and bedding, with what little furniture they possessed, into the road and leveled the house to the ground. This eviction made such a sensation . . . that the name quickly became famous.[16]

Alternately, Molly's house was said to have been used as the first meeting place of a new secret society.[17] Another version held that Molly was a huge, fierce Irish woman with a pistol strapped to each thigh, who led gangs of young Irishmen dressed in women's clothing on night raids. A well-known Irish version maintained that the Mollies were the result of a schism within a Ribbon grouping, "the name being given in derision by their rivals, after a crazy old woman in County Fermanagh, who imagined she had great armies and organizations of men under her control."[18]

But, whichever story one likes, the fact remains that the Molly Maguires contributed some of the lasting exploits and legends of nineteenth-century Ireland. There is a famous Molly Maguire song which was probably constructed around the circumstances connected with the murder of a justice of the peace (an Orangeman) in County Cavan in 1845.[19] Here is one of the many versions of the song:

Pat Dolan is my christian name, likewise my surname, too, sir,
An' if ye listen to me awhile I'll sing ye something new, sir,
To sweet Miltown I did go down, against tyrants to conspire,
Where I saw youth and bold recruits well headed by Molly Maguire.
    Chorus: With my rigadum-doo! to hell with the crew
              Wouldn't come to aid the nation;
              When I look back, I count them slack—
              Wouldn't join the combination.
Says Mollie to her darling sons, "those tyrants we must tumble
Such filthy tribe we can't abide—we'll rule them meek and humble.
There is one Bell, an imp from hell, a land agent by station—
Lots must be drew to see which of you will tumble him to damnation!"

Chorus: So let the toast go merrily round,
          Each Irish heart conspire;
          Those tyrant hounds will be crushed down
          By matchless Molly Maguire!

It's lots were drew, and cuts went through—I scorn to tell a lie, sir;
But as for me, ye may plainly see, I own I won the prize, sir.
It's to Crossdoney I did go to meet big Andrew Bell, sir;
It was at his brains I took fair aim—"Come down, ye imp of hell, sir!"

Chorus: With my swaggering bob, wasn't that a good job
          To tumble him out of his phaeton,
          An' Molly's sons with swords and guns
          To keep us from bein' taken.

Then I was on my banishment, wanderin' up and down, sir,
For to catch poor Pat was all their chat, an' they offered five hundred
     poun', sir.
The polis, too, that traitor crew, oft ran my trace breath high, sir;
But when they would see Pat's pistols cocked, they'd sooner pass him
     by, sir!

Chorus: So let the toast go merrily round,
          Each earnest heart conspire;
          Those tyrant hounds will be crushed down
          By matchless Molly Maguire!

One night as I lay in a shed I found a terrible rattle
The ghost of Bell came back from hell to fight me another battle
Then at his brains I took good aim—he vanished off in fire,
And in sulphur flames he thus exclaims, "I'm conquered by Molly
     Maguire."

Chorus: So let the toast go merrily round,
          Each Irish heart conspire;
          Those Brunswick hounds we will crush down
          By matchless Molly Maguire![20]

This song captures—more eloquently and accurately than any police report or newspaper article—the spirit and bravado of organizations like the Molly Maguires. The killing of the "tyrant" was fully rationalized and no moral stigma was attached. "Youth and bold recruits" were the nucleus; they "came to the aid of the nation" by joining the combination. The age-old system of drawing lots, the killing in ambush, the behind-the-scenes protection by "Molly's sons with swords and guns" all ring true. And even the mystical and superstitious reappearance of the murdered man, to be dispatched again by the defiant firing of the gun, recalls the Irish attitude toward those dying by violence.

Though one might be hard pressed to make any neat distinctions among the various Ribbon outrages, a legend has grown in Ireland that the Molly Maguires were a more desperate and bloodthirsty lot than the rest—in effect, a criminal lunatic fringe that used the "better" reasons for murder and outrage as a cloak to perpetrate crimes of a more personally oriented origin. Michael Davitt, the famous leader in the Land League days in the 1880's, held that the Mollies of the 1840's and 1850's were a "rural body" to the Ribbonmen, committing "more outrages of a shocking kind which were unjustly fathered upon the larger society. They anticipated the 'Moonlighters' of a later period in mere senseless lawlessness."[21] John O'Dea, in his sprawling official history of the American version of the Ancient Order of Hibernians, made the same distinction: "The 'Molly Maguires' were a distinct body from the Ribbonmen, and in many places brought discredit upon the National cause through crimes committed in their name by men of much violence and poor judgment."[22]

It is hard to put much credence in this view. By its very nature, *any* secret society laid itself bare for exploitation and settling of personal grudges. If the caliber of the leaders at a particular time and place was low, the ends were also low. Many of the northern secret societies were designed to combat religious intolerance and the Orangemen directly; perhaps the Mollies concentrated more heavily on agrarian ills, and thereby played down the religious side. In any case, though, the end product of murder was a corpse, whether it was for "the national purpose" or for plain robbery.

Nevertheless, it is true that the legends and stories of the Mollies remain in sharp focus even today in the less-settled regions in the northwest of Ireland. This is particularly true in County Donegal. The Irish Folklore Commission, realizing that there are still elderly residents alive who as children heard adults discussing Molly Maguire forays, has captured many of these reminiscences through personal interviews. They are eloquent testimony to the impact of the secret society. One Donegal oldster said of the Mollies:

They had their good and bad points. At the time they were going strong, the country was in a bad state . . . Here in the Glenties mountains where I was born and brought up, the men and women spent most of the year in their bare feet although they could buy a pair of shoes for about half a crown. But in them days the half crown was as hard to get as five pounds now.

They used to hold meetings in secret all over the place in different centres. A meeting would be held this month in this town and next month the meeting might be held in a townland ten miles away, and one or two men from each district would attend . . . they never fixed punishment locally for a local person. They always got strangers to do this, and when there was any dirty job to be done, it was strangers that were brought in to do it . . .

As I said, the good and the bad was in this society. They didn't want anybody to be taking advantage of the poor by overcharging. Even some of the shopkeepers were afraid of them and they daren't charge a penny over the market price . . . For all these reasons at the start a whole lot of people had a certain amount of respect for them.

In the end they became very cruel and they did things like what is going on in Africa today . . . sometimes they wouldn't bother with the cards, but they would take a man into a quarry or an old house and make him take off his clothes and then tie him up and take a rough stone and they would keep rubbing him with that stone until the blood would be streaming out of him.[23]

Most often the stories evolved around the pervasive struggle for the land, as exemplified by this 1961 statement of an old-timer concerning one of his elders, long since dead:

He told me that he was only sixteen years of age when he joined up with them. The first case he was out on was in an elderly woman's house in the townland of Dearrachan, on this side of Fintown. There was some other party that thought she got the place just not according to their liking. So the Mollies came this night and Jack told me that he was there and that the job he got to do was to hold the candle for them . . . "They went in there," he says, "and caught this woman . . . and threw her across the 'bac' and she fell on the floor, and the other party on the other side picked her up and threw her back, and they kept throwing her around like this till they killed the woman. They didn't leave a sound bone in her body."[24]

But Donegal was also fertile ground for faction fighting, often with the Mollies on one side:

It seems the wedding party didn't belong to the Mollies. These were great fighting men and they would boast of themselves and they had a very cross name. Well, this man's daughter got married in Glenties. They went around and they asked picked men to the wedding—men that they knew had nothing to do with the Mollies . . . The Mollies then went out and collected their picked men . . . When the couple were getting married they went and got saws and axes, and there was plenty of thorn hedges about the Big Glen of Glenties . . . They cut down these hedges and they put a thorn ditch across the county road. About twenty yards away from that one they built a second ditch and in twenty yards more they made a third . . .

When the couple were married and I suppose they took a couple of drinks they made for the bride's home up the Big Glen of Glenties. When they reached the first barrier the men commenced to knock it down but the Mollies that were lying in hiding came on them and the battle started. They made their way through the first barrier and the Mollies were getting the better of them and then the girls and women had to help.

They had to fight their way the whole way till they went into the wedding house. Some of them were laid up for a month afterwards . . .[25]

The Molly Maguires, then, were well known in Donegal—feared and respected, remembered vividly. A Donegal emigrant leaving for America during the 1840's or 1850's would not likely forget that name.

✤   ✤   ✤   ✤   ✤

And when he had reached America, he quite likely would have been greeted by a group of fellow Irishmen calling themselves by a new name, albeit with familiar words. This group was destined to be, by the 1870's, the most powerful benevolent and immigrant-aid lodge in the country. Its name was the Ancient Order of Hibernians.

The AOH loomed large in the Pennsylvania Molly Maguire story. To understand how it got there, and where it came from, we need to explore another facet of Irish history, the relation of the Roman Catholic Church to the secret society.

In 1825 the Apostolic Constitution of Pope Leo XII put together the acts and decrees of former pontiffs on the subject of secret societies, ratifying and confirming the earlier prohibitions.[26] In particular, the Church prohibited the binding of a Roman Catholic to an oath-bound organization that made its members agree to obey without question a temporal authority. Quite directly this ban encompassed the activities of oath-bound Irish secret societies. By the threat of excommunication (sometimes carried through), the Church tried to put pressure on its members to stay completely out of secret societies. Although the Church had had little effect in the eighteenth century, it began to have more in the nineteenth. In particular, Bishop James Doyle of Kildare took a strong stand. As early as 1819 he denounced the Ribbon organization,[27] and after the terrible disturbances in 1821 and 1822 wrote a lengthy letter which he ordered to be read from the pulpit of all churches in his diocese.[28] This famous document, if not fully deserving the praise given it by Doyle's biographer ("This letter, for point, clearness, argument and scriptural illustration, was perhaps never equalled."[29]), nevertheless had a profound effect on the country. It was reprinted (some said by pressure from the government) and widely distributed over Ireland.

The oath itself struck most sensitively at the Church. Yet it was integral to the concept of a secret society. There were about as many such oaths as there were members, for a local leader would frequently adapt the oath to his own particular designs; nevertheless, in every case they required some form of unquestioning allegiance to a temporal authority. This was anathema to the Church.

As a result of this stepped-up pressure from the Church, particularly after Leo XII's ban, groups of men evidently closely associated with Ribbonism formed an organization (or organizations) variously titled "St. Patrick's Fraternal Society," "Knights of St. Patrick," "Sons of the Shamrock," "Patriotic Association," "The Shamrock Society," and, later, the "Religious Liberty System."[30] Very soon a form of the same type of organization was active in Liverpool under the name of "The Liverpool Hibernian Benevolent Burial Society."[31] The exact relationship of these groups, each to the others and outward to the many "Ribbon" societies, remains very unclear. But it was some sort of amalgam of these that became the Ancient Order of Hibernians, first in America, then later in a reverse transplant, back in Ireland.

James Bergin, in his history of the Ancient Order of Hibernians, written in 1910 as the presumed official history of the Irish brand of the AOH, devotes a chapter to "St. Patrick's Fraternal Society," and describes the group as follows:

Branches of Ribbonmen sprang up in several counties, under different designations. In England and Scotland divisions were formed under the name "Hibernian Funeral Society," while in several counties in Ireland the name "Molly Maguires" was used . . . In 1825 the Ribbonmen changed the name of their organization into "St. Patrick's Fraternal Society," or otherwise known as "St. Patrick's Boys." The Executive sanctioned this change in the name of the organization, owing to the fact that the Ribbonmen had incurred the censure of the Church, but it is not to be supposed that all the branches gave up their old title.[32]

An American AOH history, published in 1898, had a slightly different interpretation:

In 1825 the name in Ireland was changed from the Ribbonmen to that of St. Patrick's Fraternal Society. It is not to be supposed that all these changes took place in harmony, as there was a large number of members who rebelled against those changes and withdrew from the order and continued under the name of Molly Maguires and Ribbonmen, especially in the County Antrim.[33]

The use of the name of the hallowed patron saint himself was natural enough, and had a long history in secret-society nomenclature. Legends relate that there was a famous organization in Dublin in the 1750's known as the Ancient Order of the Friendly Brothers of St. Patrick, and secondary sources even give us the constitution of this group. One of the self-styled "fundamental laws" in this constitution is most intriguing, for the concept involved occurs over and over in later Irish groups—and in the Molly Maguire story in Pennsylvania: "The order is divided into two classes—one comprehending all the members of the order, styled the Regular Friendly Brothers, the other consisting of such regulars as for their well-tried fidelity and friendship have been initiated into the grand and solemn mysteries of the order, and are styled the approved and perfect Friendly Brothers."[34]

In short, there was an "inner circle," available only to those with "well-tried fidelity." The very nature of a secret society militates in favor of having several classes of members. No secret society could justly claim the designation unless it had "secrets," and not everyone can keep a secret well. Most secret societies have had probationary periods of membership, and the notion of degrees of membership survives widely in today's lodges.

But when the secrets of the secret society are nefarious, the "inner circle" changes its complexion, and takes on overtones of "master criminals" plotting outrage under the cover of a front organization.

There is little doubt that the Bavarian Illuminati and Italian Carbonari had such inner circles, and only these knew of the revolutionary plots and plans. By the very character of the Irish secret societies it would be logical to have an inner circle. Informers and spies were rampant, the penalty for discovery was bitter, the need for secrecy crucial. So the nineteenth-century agrarian societies, though loosely organized, inevitably had some sort of classification of "membership." The northern Ribbon groups must have been influenced to develop a reasonably well-defined local structure, for their counterparts, the Orangemen, were highly structured. And there were insistent rumors that there were inner circles—"Black Lodges"—within the main Orange orders, composed of men who would take on the most violent (and secret) activities, leaving the order itself to parade publicly and to publicly fight the Catholics. One of the more perceptive witnesses at the House of Commons hearings on the Orange Society in 1835 admitted the presence of the Black Lodge, but held that it "arose from desire of the lower orders to have something more exciting or alarming in the initiation of members . . . a species of mummery innocent in itself and originating in the strong desire that vulgar minds in general manifest for awful mysteries and ridiculous pageantry."[35]

Few Ribbon apologists would admit to any such inner circle. But these same people (especially those in the twentieth century) were quick to adduce great national and even international significance to the Ribbon "confederation." John O'Dea in his official American AOH history stated flatly that "the St. Patrick's Fraternal Society, in Ireland, and Hibernian Society and Hibernia Sick and Funeral Society, in England, Scotland, and Wales, exchanged communications and passwords." He wrote that "in all matters affecting the advancement of the race and the faith these societies acted as one body," and that "travelling cards and passwords were recognized all over the three kingdoms and Wales, and if any travelling member was in distress he did not appeal in vain to his fellow members." But O'Dea admitted that there were no national or international officers, and "only a common sympathy and understanding bound the various branches together."[36] This seems more likely; the locus of power was probably centered in the hands of the local parish or "body" master, and the activities concentrated on local problems. Nevertheless, the rumor persisted that there was a national Ribbon conspiracy, and this rumor was widely believed by the English rulers of Ireland during this period.

This pervasive self-delusion about a national conspiracy was well illustrated in the hearings on crime and outrage held by the Roden Committee of the House of Lords in 1839. Much of the testimony dealt with the Ribbon societies, most of it based on hearsay and inflammatory allegations from irresponsible sources. The specter of a huge, monolithic confederation loomed larger and larger. But one witness at these hearings—perhaps the person most knowledgeable on agrarian crimes alive at that time—sharply differed with the prevailing testimony. This man was Thomas Drummond, who held the critical post of Under Secretary to the Lord Lieutenant of Ireland from 1835 to 1839.

Historians generally agree that Drummond's term of office was one of the highlights of English civil administration in Ireland after the Union. Under the policy of Lord Melbourne's British government, Drummond was charged with the ticklish responsibility of discouraging Orange spirit and seeing that rich and poor, Catholic and Protestant, fared equally before the law. He established a new police force, the Royal Irish Constabulary, whose ranks were filled with native Irishmen. It became a model of efficiency and fairness, at least in nineteenth-century terms.

Drummond's appearance before the Roden Committee unleashed a frontal attack on him for his handling of the office of Lord Lieutenant. The chairman, Robert Jocelyn, third Earl of Roden, lived in Northern Ireland and was himself the grand master of the Orange Order. Drummond had been singularly unsympathetic about Orangeism. Much of Drummond's testimony was devoted to defending his choices for stipendiary magistrates and the handling of police investigations. In the course of his testimony, however, the question of Ribbonism was introduced.

Drummond corroborated previous evidence that several associations under such names as Shamrock Society had been reported in County Sligo, that there had been considerable activity in County Dublin by several faction-fighting groups (under the names of Billy Welters and Widgeons), and that similar evidence was reported in several other counties. But, cautioned Drummond, one had to use great care in dignifying the testimony of informers, for "very different conclusions may be come to by different individuals accord-

ing to the degree of credit they are disposed to attach to it." Many
oaths had been reported, he continued, but "the most common one
is, as far as I recollect, unexceptional in terms—it is a printed oath
or pledge." True, he noted, "there are other Oaths of a highly
treasonable and seditious Character, but we have no Authority but
that of Informants to prove that such oaths are in use." Nor, Drummond admitted, "have we in any one instance been able to detect
them in administering those oaths."[37]

Queried about the presence of a universal password system, Drummond substantiated that there were some cases where similar passwords were found in several different districts. Asked the reason for
the similarities, he introduced a factor seldom taken into account at
that time:

The whole is a Scheme, a Business for raising Money . . . with regard
to the Promotors of it, there is less Difficulty in coming to a Conclusion
as to their Objects. They are almost all Publicans—Publicans of a very
low Class and of a very bad Character. All the meetings are held in the
Houses of Publicans to whom regular Quarterly payments are made . . .
they have a further Advantage in their Houses being constantly frequented by them. These Publicans appear to keep up a Sort of Connexion
one with another, and in order to maintain their Influence more securely,
affect a certain Degree of Mystery. They gave out that they act under
some high and nameless Authority, and that Leaders will be forthcoming,
when the Time is ripe, who will ensure the Restoration of the forfeited
Estates, and such other Objects as the lowest and most needy commonly
look to . . . Their Object is, manifestly, to keep up a Delusion among
the ignorant, and to conceal their real Motive, which is nothing more
or less than to raise Money . . . the Promotors are Knaves and the members their Dupes.[38]

Drummond depreciated the ability of the societies to effect anything
more than a purely local disturbance; if they were to turn out for a
more general purpose, "they would fall instantly to pieces like a
Rope of Sand." In short, Drummond concluded, "I think no conclusion can be drawn as to the existence of such secret combination
at all."[39]

The name Ancient Order of Hibernians was not used in Ireland
at this time—this designation first appeared when the organization
was transplanted to America. (In the 1830's, though, the Sons of the
Shamrock often called themselves "Hibernians."[40]) For this Ameri-

can transplantation we must again fall back on secondary sources. Both the Irish and American official histories tell essentially the same story. In 1836 some of the members of St. Patrick's Fraternal Society in New York City began discussing the advantages of affiliating with "the parent body" back in Ireland. "In this discussion," relates one historian, "they were joined by Ribbonmen in Schuylkill County, Pennsylvania."[41] Contact was arranged via sailors on one of the shiplines, and a charter was sent over to "our few Brothers in New York" with authority to set up branches in America. The qualifications for membership were set: All members had to be Roman Catholics and Irish or of Irish descent, and none "shall join in any secret societies contrary to the laws of the Catholic Church." A paragraph was devoted to certain pious declarations concerning brotherly love and charity. The remainder of the document, well over half of the entire piece, was devoted to a curious side-issue:

Also be it Known to you that our wish and prayer is that when you form your Society, in many cities and towns, that you will do all that is in your power to aid and protect your Irish Sisters from all harm and temptation. As the Irish woman is known for her chastity all over the world, and though some of them may differ from you in religion, brothers, bear in mind that our good Lord died for us all; therefore, be it known to you that our wish is that you do all you can for the Irish emigrant girls, no matter who they may be, and God will reward you in your new country, and doing this, you will keep up the high standing of the Irish in America.[42]

What events prompted this interest in the Irish women—even the non-Catholic ones—is unexplained. But it seems an incongruous note in what purports to be the definitive charter authorization. The document, according to Bergin and O'Dea, the official historians who quoted it, was signed by twelve county chairmen in Ireland, plus a representative from Glasgow and one from Liverpool. The counties represented were largely northern.

Within a few years there were a sizable number of lodges in America (under the AOH name after 1838). There also appears to have been some direct link between the Irish and American organizations through an Irish over-body called the Board of Erin. Through this central "headquarters" came quarterly passwords (soon called, widely, "the goods"). How much more came from the Board of

Erin in the way of instructions and prohibitions is unclear. Bergin's book, the Irish version of AOH history, attempts to prove that the AOH was really an Irish-controlled organization, and speaks of "levies paid to the Irish governing body up to the year 1898, so recognizing the indisputable fact that the headquarters of the order was in Ireland and not America."[43] Whether the relationship went beyond the payment of dues from America and the relaying of passwords back from Ireland is indeterminate.

If the Hibernians in America received only the passwords for their money, it was perhaps a fair bargain, for the ingenuity and complexity of these were remarkable. Not only were there signs and toasts for normal occasions, but even "quarreling toasts," which could be used not only to cool tempers among members but also to identify friend from foe at a faction fight.

There are hundreds of versions of these toasts and passwords already in print; we note here one version used in the Pennsylvania coal fields in the 1870's:

Q. What is the best remedy for Irish grievances?
A. An Irish Parliament in College Green.
Q. Will the Irish hold on for their rights?
A. Yes; their rights they will fight for, and in justice must have.
QUARRELING TOAST.—Q. What is the meaning of all this?
A. I am insulted.
SIGN.—Two first fingers of the right hand downwards on the apple of the throat.
Answer.—Two first fingers of the left hand to the side of the nose.
BODY-MASTER'S TOAST.—Q. May the exiles so noble and brave still firm stand!
A. Yes; for tyrants we make tremble and hope our country to save.
PRIVATE MARK.—Dot on last o but one on card.
TOAST.—Q. What do you think of our nation?
A. The land question will cause great vexation.
Q. The tory landlords will oppose the bill.
A. Yes; Bishop McHale will praise their master still.
WINTER NIGHT PASSWORDS.—Q. The winter nights are sharp and clear.
A. Yes; I hope heresy will soon disappear.[44]

❖　❖　❖　❖　❖

Thus certain patterns of the Irish secret societies emerged. Though often politically tinged, they were most deeply influenced by agrarian tensions. Though religious differences added an incendiary issue, the most critical relationship was still that between the landlord and his tenant. The secret society was most often a short-term and local reaction to a direct, personal problem with a specific individual. There were so many of these problems over such a wide area for so long a period that it is quite understandable that the English assumed a national conspiracy.

But the real key was found on individual estates, peopled by individual landlords and their tenants. An analysis of one estate—the Shirley property in County Monaghan—is illuminating. This estate was an important one in Ireland, and the Shirley family's concepts of estate management were interesting, perhaps unique. The Shirleys, by a combination of seemingly minor events, were suddenly projected into a limelight that left them as one of the most famous of Irish landlord families. And, most importantly for our story, the Shirley case was to become—in the great Molly Maguire trials of Pennsylvania—the prime illustration of Irish secret-society tactics.

Chapter 3 * Tenant Troubles

*W*AS THE Irish landlord a "pimpled, beef-eating, ignorant, self-satisfied country squire" who hunted four days a week, blew his pheasants to pieces on two other days, and "slept like a wart-hog" the seventh?[1] Was it his pleasure to "eat and drink more than enough, to beget children, to marry off his daughters to his neighbors' sons, to swear a good deal and think not at all?" Did he really place "implicit confidence in the best tone of country society," shunning a self-made man and courting a noble one? Did he truly care so little about the principles of Irish justice that, having inherited his money and landed estate, he felt it was his "indisputable, inalienable right to spend the one and idle out his days on the other?" Was it "impossible to make him aware that, in spite of his possible good fellowship and coarse good nature, he was a profitless lump of clay, his sporting instincts as vulgar as his conversation, his life radically unsound and worthless for all purposes of social progress?" There were Irish landlords who could match this image line by line. And there were others, undoubtedly the minority, who made sincere though often misguided and ineffective efforts to manage their estates humanely. The less attractive cases have already been well-documented by countless tracts; let us document the other situation with an examination of the Shirley Estate.

The Shirley family traced its descent, according to *Burke's Landed Gentry*, "in a direct male line from Seawallis or Saswalo, who held the Lordship of Ettington (still in possession of his descendants) under Henry de Ferrers at the time of the compilation of Domesday (1086)."[2] The family had held property in Warwickshire, England, since that time, and had held a large estate in Ireland dating from a direct grant by Queen Elizabeth in 1576.[3] The Irish estate was a tract of over 30,000 acres in the Barony of Farney, near Carrickmacross in County Monaghan. This county, along with County Cavan, formed the southern tier of Ireland's northern province, Ulster. A Shirley residence had been maintained at Ettington,

Warwickshire, for centuries; but the Irish property had been visited only occasionally by the family.

In 1810, however, Evelyn John Shirley came to Farney with his new bride and set in motion steps that were to carry the family deeply into Irish life. Appointed High Sheriff for the county in 1824, he decided to build a home on the estate as a residence for part of the year. As the house took shape, it was clear that Shirley intended "Lough Fea" to be a showpiece. Erected entirely of free-stone found on the estate, it was patterned in the manner of a College, with a chapel on the left, principal living rooms in the center and a "Great Hall" on the right.[4] By the time the latter was completed in 1842, the house was a landmark in nineteenth-century Irish country estates.

The Great Hall became the hub of much activity, also a subject for pointed discussion by those unsympathetic to the Shirleys. The proportions were massive—it was seventy-five feet long, thirty-three wide, and thirty-three high. Paneled in wood, with the shields of Shirley and Devereux in alternate panels, and with two huge free-stone chimneys, the hall was a showpiece room for a showpiece house. It was a magnificent location for entertainment now that the family spent a good portion of the year in Ireland. Though Irish country society could not compare with its counterpart in Dublin during the previous century, nevertheless it could be dazzling in its brilliance and pomp. For these occasions, the Great Hall was ideally suited.

A local newspaper once lyrically reported:[5] "The Ball on Friday night last eclipsed any oblation at the shrine of *Terpsichore* ever before offered up to that muse, nor could *Comus* himself have with-held his admiration had he the good fortune to have been translated to it on that happy evening." The appearance in Carrickmacross of an unusual number of vehicles gave evident indication of an immense attendance; Shirley's son, Evelyn Philip, a colonel, had even ordered the band of his regiment to attend. Scarcely had "the sable train of night veiled the horizon" when the doors of the baronial hall were thrown open, "to present a scene worthy of Paradise, when upwards of two hundred of the rank, beauty, talent and distinction of the Kingdom graced its boards."

Dancing commenced, opening with the Shirley quadrille. "The scene was now exquisitely brilliant, variable and enchanting, the

Gallope, Polka, and Waltz and the Quadrilles had each its charms, and the moving multitude of matchless splendor gliding thro' the gentle mazes of the one while at intervals convolving in the angelic circle of sublime commotion in the other produced a 'scene so charming' that the senses were almost lost in admiration."

Time "stole on unmarked" until supper was announced at the witching hour of one, "when the table presented a variety of sweets such as wanton on the busom of the spring, but in winter's cold embrace die!" Fruits of every variety, venison pastries, game pies, *pièce-montées* decorated with bonbons, *gatens napolitinnes*, creams, jellies, custards, ices were served by the Dublin caterers imported for the occasion. In the center of the table was a massive gold and silver epergne, flanked by two pair of antique candelabra "of chaste design and matchless beauty." All the choicest and rarest wines "contributed their exhilarating quota to render perfections still more perfect."

Soon "smiling Hygeia summoned all her willing votaries," and "dancing was resumed with new-born spirit." Nor did the assemblage think of parting "till the intruding moon commenced his rosy progress, and jocund day sat gaily dressed." All in all, the editor concluded, " 'twas a scene upon which the fancy will yet delight to dwell."

It was, however, a moot point whether many of the Shirley tenants could long let their "fancy dwell" on this party. For its date was November 1848, in the third year of the Great Famine.

* * * * *

But the use of the Great Hall and the estate as centers for social life illustrated only one side of Evelyn Shirley's interest in Farney. He also recognized the problems of the estate, and made efforts to alleviate them. His motivations for doing this were undoubtedly mixed. It was to his personal advantage to have the estate prosper— the income was very sizable, in the best years exceeding £20,000. If the tenantry could maintain the rent payments, it would be highly advantageous to the family. But it also seems clear from his actions that Shirley had a sincere interest in the tenants, and in his own way was concerned to see that they had a better life.

Nevertheless, Shirley's outlook was vastly different from that of his tenants, in view of the wide gulf between any member of the English landed gentry and an Irish peasant.[6] Shirley was, in the words of his son, "an ultra-Tory, opposed to every species of radical innovation and change."[7] This conservatism was remarkably illustrated in a series of handbills addressed to his tenantry and distributed before he left for his annual trip back to Ettington. Over the years he left little doubt as to where he stood on a number of issues affecting the estate.

Farming was Shirley's first concern. He asked, "How often are your crops to be seen overrun with unprofitable Weeds whilst many of the young people are idling?" He pleaded for better methods: "Without manure you can do nothing . . . the keeping of your cattle in the house *all the year round* is of first importance . . . you must have Green Crops in succession . . . " But, inveigh though he might, he found his advice often unheeded. Then, in pique, he would loose a blast. He particularly resented the apparent laziness of the tenants. "Now it is my duty to tell you that you do not value your time . . . I saw numbers of the tenantry lounging and idling about, their turf still in the Bog, their Hay still uncut, and the weeds growing plentifully . . . Pro. Ch. XV, verse 19, 'The way of the slothful man is as a hedge of thorns.' "[8]

To combat what Shirley felt was excessive lethargy, he set up a remarkably ingenious system of rewards for performance. Awards were made for the best fencing, manuring, and draining of an individual farm, for "the best and most convenient Pig Stye," and even for the tenant "who has had his children within the last three years best educated and placed out at or taught useful trades." Even the peasant *wife* came in for approbation and a cash award for keeping "the clothing of herself and family in the best state of cleanliness and repair and whose children shall have been remarkable for their tidiness."[9]

But Shirley was not content to confine himself to farming practices. He was particularly disturbed at the excessive use of alcohol on the estate: "I feel called upon to notice (most unwillingly) the scenes of Drunkenness . . . of the quarrels of the nearest and dearest friends, whose blood, like that of the bitterest foes, is often shed—of the wailings of Wives and Children, alike bereft of the support of Husbands and Parents." He added that "if this will not suffice to curb the use of this maddening spirit, surely the knowledge of what it is composed, and the deadly poison therein contained, would perhaps restrain, for safety sake, the rejected draught." Shirley blamed the innumerable markets and fairs for being breeding grounds for tippling, and exhorted the tenants that "should you want any trifling article, do not go yourself with all your family to buy it," for by foregoing the fair "you save *time* as well as the *Money* you would have been tempted to lay out in Whiskey." Do not suppose, he concluded, "that your vices can be hidden from your children."[10]

Overcrowding was one of the most serious problems on the estate, and Shirley bitterly fought the long-standing practices in subdividing. "Take notice," he cautioned, "abstain from leaving to your family in your Wills what is not yours to leave." If some of the smaller holders of land continued to allow cottiers on their property, he warned, he would force these tenants to give up a portion of their land. "I am obliged to have as few under tenants as possible."[11]

But if these cottiers were willing to emigrate, Shirley promised help: "It must be evident to all that holders of two or three acres cannot possible thrive—let me entreat such as are young and active to make preparation to visit our Colonies and I will endeavor to facilitate such arrangements."[12]

But entreaties made no dent on the numbers, and Shirley decided to attack the problem at its very source, the institution of marriage itself:

The necessity of consideration before engaging in marriage is self-evident; and yet how many hasten to become united for life without at all considering the consequence . . . Let those who are about to enter into the married state be asked if they are aware of the duties and burthens it will bring . . . remember that you injure your neighbors by throwing upon them the burthen of supporting those whom you ought yourself to support. You are bringing labourers into the world, and taking employment and food from those who already have not enough . . . Keep animal impulses under the control of reason.[13]

One of the inevitable sources of irritation among Irish tenants was their representation in the English Parliament. Since the Union in 1800 the members of Parliament from Ireland had been made up predominantly of the Anglo-Irish aristocracy, elected to their posts under the same antiquated system that had brought such a public outcry in England.[14] Shirley stood for election to Parliament as representative for Monaghan Borough in 1826 and was unopposed. There were two posts to be filled, though, and the second was contested. Colonel Leslie, a close friend of Shirley, unexpectedly faced opposition from Henry Westenra. Shirley and Leslie traveled around the country, meeting with the tenantry in the streets and bars, soliciting votes for Leslie.[15] But, in spite of their large expenditures, Westenra's views in favor of Catholic emancipation and nationalism appeared to be giving him an edge. Finally, Shirley appealed directly to his tenants: "Prove your attachment to *my* and to *your own* interests by rallying round me and exerting yourselves to oppose the attempts of your enemies, who are endeavouring to ruin you and your cause, by persuading you to give your Votes against the wishes of your Landlord."[16] Even so the election went to Westenra.

Shirley's years representing Monaghan in Parliament were marked by recurrent complaints. Though he seldom spoke in debates, he rarely omitted to vote, and uniformly along a conservative line. As a result, he was often subjected to attack in handbills, distributed throughout Monaghan. They were generally signed "Verax," and frequently bordered on the scurrilous. Shirley was taken to task for his continued support of Tory tax bills, and needled about his high incomes from the Irish estate. These snipings took their toll, and much of Shirley's efforts to bring order and prosperity to the estate were dissipated by his political involvements. His votes in Parliament were consistent with his over-all philosophy, and were honestly and openly stated many times over. But the overpopulated, economically distressed tenantry were not receptive.

The issue that proved to be the most irritating to both Shirley and his tenantry evolved around the issue of education. When Shirley first traveled to Farney he found a tenantry almost completely uneducated. The only schools, if they could be called such, were the "hedge schools," conducted along informal lines and with generally low standards. Only a small proportion of the Farney population could even read and write in a rudimentary way.

Shirley attacked this problem frontally—he established a series of schools over the estate, without cost to the tenants. But this praiseworthy objective was clouded by one sensitive issue—the extent and type of religious training. The tenantry were almost completely Roman Catholic, Shirley was Anglican. Shirley, further, was an active member of the Kildare Street Society in Dublin, who were advocates for reading the Bible, but also proselyters for Protestantism. Shirley shared their views and probably would have liked to see his tenantry converted to Protestantism. In this he would have been no different from most of the other Protestant Anglo-Irish landlords. He was not, however, a militant anti-Catholic, and through all the school difficulties he seems to have been willing to recognize the realities of the situation. His schools were taught by laymen and they were predominantly Catholic laymen. But he set a condition for the teaching that soon drew the ire of the Catholic hierarchy. For he insisted that the Bible be read in the schools by the teachers. Though the Bible read—the Douay Bible—was the authorized Roman Catholic version, the whole plan quickly came under fire from the local parish priests. By the mid-1830's the school population was dwindling and Shirley began stringent exhortations via handbills: "Why do these most useful Institutions droop while other matters thrive around us? . . . Can YOU object because the SACRED WORD OF GOD is daily read, and fear that the knowledge of the Scriptures should instil bad notions into the minds of your Children? Impossible, I will never believe it!!! No, my friends, you are too shrewd thus to conclude . . . Send your Children *without fear of Man*, to my schools, where the Bible (even your own Douay Version) is daily read."[17]

By such provocative wording Shirley led many to believe he was intent on converting the Roman Catholics on his estate to Protestantism. Soon anonymous handbills and letters to the newspapers took up this issue. It was "Vindex" this time that chided Shirley in one of the local newspapers about a servant boy in Lough Fea House: "After all, where are your converts? Oh Yes, there was one—a wretched lad, of the name of Smyth, who from your school conformed, was taken into your cottage as a menial—in proof of his Protestantism and *grace*, ate flesh-meat on Fridays—broke the sixth commandment with your favourite housemaid—forsook his new creed and connexions and returned to the errors of Popery to do penance, and abstain from fleshly lusts . . ."[18] Others blamed Shirley's agent, and one threatened that "things are hastening on your estate [toward] the wild justice of revenge."[19] Shirley abhorred violence, and the implied threat was disturbing. Ugly incidents came—several of the school houses were looted and books burned, the homes of teachers attacked. In 1839 a Roman Catholic priest in the barony proposed to build his own school, and asked Shirley for a piece of property for it. Shirley was adamant at first, refusing both the land and the right to materials to build it. But the passage at this time of the bill providing for a national school system soon gave opportunity for compromise. Shirley granted land for several national schools, with an agreement that "Mr. Shirley's schools still to continue for the use of those tenants who will take advantage of them; but every Roman Catholic tenant is to use his own discretion as to where he will send his children to be educated."[20]

The economic distress deepened in the 1830's and County Monaghan began to show increased tensions. Agents and bailiffs were beaten for seizing crops, new tenants threatened for "taking land over others." By 1835 the crimes looked to be organized efforts. Men who dressed in women's clothing and blackened their faces appeared more frequently, and one of the constables reported that "the system here is to employ strangers from a different county to execute those outrages which in turn they do for them."[21] Though the other large estate in the Barony of Farney, that of the Marquis of Bath, was quite agitated, the Shirley estate maintained a surface calm. But the seeds of trouble went beyond the school issue itself. Shirley's agent during this period was accused of acting in an unduly harsh manner. He was thought to be too unbending on the punctuality of rent payments and niggardly in providing money or materials for tenant improvements. Shirley had allowed "tenant right," the system common in Ulster of allowing a leaving tenant to sell his rights to the farm to the incoming tenant. Though any improvements legally remained Shirley's, the "tenant right" price could be considerably boosted. The accusation that Shirley's agent was picayune was not strictly true, for Shirley was always willing to provide lime for painting and fertilizing, and he encouraged the building of outbuildings. But Shirley and his agent always expected strict accountability and this annoyed the tenants.[22]

More serious accusations were leveled at the agent, though. He was said to have an ingenious spy system operating on the estate that persuaded tenants to become informers concerning other tenants' shortcomings. There were even rumors that the agent "was in the habit of arranging matrimonial alliances, pointing out this girl as a suitable match for that boy, and the boy must marry the girl or give up his farm."[23] Meddling in marriages of tenants was not a common thing—most agents were primarily concerned with collecting rents.

But with Shirley's concern for the overpopulation of the estate and his evident intent to secure a responsible and "improving" tenantry, it may have been that the agent discouraged matches that would bring a known idler to the land. But, even for the best motives, the attempt would have been galling to many.

An abrupt event in early 1843 brought all these latent feelings of hostility to a violent head. The agent died suddenly of a heart attack. That night bonfires were set ablaze on many of the hills in the barony, reminiscent of the earlier bonfire celebrations in Limerick and Tipperary after successful outrages.

Shirley was in Ettington at the time, but acted quickly to fill the vacancy. He called a young Anglo-Irishman, William Steuart Trench, to London for interviews, quickly arrived at an agreement, and proceeded with Trench to Lough Fea to install the new agent in his job. Little did they realize that the events of the next few days would provide one of the best-known incidents in nineteenth-century land agitation.

According to Trench's account, he and Shirley went directly to the agent's office in Carrickmacross. When they stepped outside a few hours later, they found themselves surrounded by a large crowd of tenants, who immediately demanded in loud and threatening tones that their rents be reduced and their grievances met. Shirley was taken aback by the presumptuousness of previously servile tenants, but recovered himself enough to promise that if they came the following Monday, "you shall have an answer to your demands."

"Monday! Monday!" was shouted on all sides. The most frenzied excitement ensued. Hats were thrown in the air, sticks flourished on all sides. After a little while the crowd dispersed, and the news flew like wildfire over the barony that the whole tenantry were to come in on Monday, that they might know the amount of reduction to be granted and to have all their grievances removed.

Shirley now realized the forces he had loosed. The tenants, according to Trench, had clearly misunderstood their landlord—he intended no rent reduction. Shirley quickly had a handbill printed, to be posted all over the estate, informing the tenantry that "the present distress has not been caused . . . by high Rents, and that therefore, although both willing and anxious to relieve the really distressed, yet he does not feel bound to make at present either a temporary or permanent reduction in the Rent." Under these circumstances, Shirley con-

tinued, he "must decline meeting the Tenantry on Monday next and
. . . trusts the Tenantry will on that day remain at home."[24]

The enraged tenants tore down the placards and on that Sunday
gathered in throngs at all the churches to plan a mammoth demonstration the following day.

At the dawn of the next day, April 3, 1843, an immense crowd,
probably over ten thousand men, surrounded the agent's house.
Shirley, who was there, stayed inside, and decided to send Trench
out to state once again the landlord's decision.

"A chair! A chair!" was shouted on all sides. "Put him on a chair
so we can hear him." One was procured, and Trench stood facing
the now-silent crowd. The new agent tried to explain Shirley's stand.

There was a dead silence when he stopped. It was broken by a
stentorian voice, "Then you won't reduce our rents?"

Trench admitted that he would not.

"Down on your knees, boys!" shouted the same voice, and to
Trench's consternation the huge mob got down on their knees before
him.

Trench pleaded with them to get up, but when queried again
about the rent, was forced to reiterate the same refusal.

At this the crowd went wild. Seizing Trench, they began hustling
him down the road toward Shirley's mansion a mile or two from the
town. The tenants apparently were determined to see Shirley himself,
and hadn't realized that he was back at the agent's house.

Pushed and buffeted, his clothes torn off his back, Trench was
finally presented, almost exhausted, at the door of Lough Fea. Again
a chair was produced, and Trench summoned his strength to address
the crowd again. The agent now decided that his life was in real
danger unless he stood up to the crowd. So he roundly berated the
assembled group for treating a stranger so poorly. The surprised
tenants fell silent, and Trench used the pause to enter the house.
Shirley's architect, who was visiting, finally got the crowd to
disperse.

Trench's exciting account of the day later later beame a key
chapter in his book *Realities of Irish Life*,[25] which went through six
printings and titillated thousands of English readers who wanted to
vicariously sample Irish "realities." His account of the facts may
have been dressed to suit his own reputation, but was probably close
to the actual events. There were other versions, though. According to

one writer, "The events point to the affair having been arranged by agents provocateur, everything happened at the time, place and in the manner that suited the narrator [Trench]. He never appears to have been in any real danger himself, although his bailiffs may have been; his residence was fortified, bullet proof, loop holed shutters, etc."[26]

This implication seems farfetched. True, the previous agent had maintained an espionage system, and agents could presumably have been planted to carry through the assault. But Shirley's moral integrity—never questioned at any time—would seem to have militated against such a device. The mob scene was undoubtedly spontaneous, well illustrative of the essentially local and intermittent nature of most Irish tenant outrages at that time.

The remarkable fact about the incident, though, is that it became remarkable. It was a minor happening; no one was harmed in any way. Far worse things were occurring all over Ireland but were dying away after brief notices in the local papers. Not so here. The "Shirley case" became a *cause célèbre* in nineteenth-century Ireland.

Shirley was aghast at such an evident outpouring of resentment and ill-will among his tenantry. All his efforts at amelioration of his tenants' difficulties seemed brushed aside. He decided to meet the issue head-on, and immediately wrote the Lord Lieutenant at Dublin Castle for "a Troop of Dragoons," adding for good measure that "it is desirable that a Company of Infantry should also be here as well as a Troop of Horse."[27] This was April 3, 1843. The Lieutenant for the county, Lord Rossmore, backed Shirley in his request, adding that "a similar event having taken place last autumn upon a neighbouring estate in the adjacent County seems to lead to the inference that this has not been an isolated movement taken up at the instant, neither is it connected with sectarian feeling nor resulting from the oppression of Middle Men."[28]

The Under Secretary, Edward Lucas, immediately sent troops from Dundalk to Carrickmacross, where the detachment was promptly paraded. The next day Shirley sent his thanks to the Castle, adding that it might be necessary to keep the troops there for a while "as it will not be wise, however desirous we may be for peace, to *give way* to the wishes of a mob or to be forced to comply with the demands of a numerous tenantry when urged on such a violent manner."[29]

The issue quickly found its way to the press. The conservative *Northern Standard* of Monaghan took the tenantry to task for their conduct, citing that Shirley had made many efforts, "with a strong sense of duty, imparted by religion" to improve their lot.[30] But a pro-tenant newspaper in County Down imputed other motives to Shirley and Trench, implying that Trench had been told that "he could rule the people of Farney with a 'sally switch' provided he first acted the despot toward them." Commented the paper caustically, "no doubt the aching in his bones at this minute convinces him that the 'sally switch' is less likely to be effectual in the Black North for the exaction of rent than the 'yellow stick' proved to be in one of the Hebrides to effect a change of religion."[31] Perhaps the issue would have died away had it not been picked up by the London papers. But the incident soon was spread over their pages, and the influential London *Times* editorialized: "What, then, we ask, must be the condition of that country, in which thousands of men can be collected at any one point to make war upon property, under pretense of redressing grievances which they have never felt? And what must be the moral condition of these multitudes, when the objects of their attack are inoffensive men, kind men, or men who have expended their money and their time in enlarging the labour fund of the country."[32]

Shirley now found himself uneasily cast in the public role of defender of the landlord interests all over Ireland. His actions no longer just affected Farney. On all sides Shirley was exhorted to "stand up to the challenge" and not to give way to pressure. His lawyer in Carrickmacross mirrored the landholders' sentiments in a letter of advice: "Whenever open and effectual resistance has been given to the recovery of a rent or tithe, any delay in asserting the rights of the landlord or tithe owner strengthens the opposition and makes the people begin to think they could be successful. They have time to make the combination more general and complete and to arrange plans of resistance and mutual cooperation."[33]

Shirley finally agreed to meet a deputation of the tenantry to discuss their grievances. At the meeting Shirley, according to a sympathetic journalist, first reproved the delegation "in strong but temperate language"[34] for their conduct toward Trench. But in an effort to meet the tenants half-way, Shirley agreed to reduce bog rents and lime prices, to assume the entire first payment due under the new Poor Law, and to eliminate the practice of the late agent of "raising the coppers"—always raising rents that totaled to the odd penny to "the even shilling." Shirley made it clear, though, that the rents for the farms were to be maintained, and that he would use "all lawful means" to collect them if tardy.

Were the rents too high? Evidence is conflicting, but tends to support the tenants' case. The entire estate had been re-evaluated in 1834 and at that time a general analysis of rentals was made. They varied widely depending on the type of land—substantial numbers of acres carried rents of from fourteen shillings sixpence to fifteen shillings per English acre, but some meadowland went as high as twenty-four shillings and rocky land as low as four or five. The yearly income, assuming all was paid, was £24,607 (including bog rentals). The acreage was just short of 30,000; the average rent per acre was therefore a bit over fifteen shillings. The valuation of 1834 by Richard Griffith was £20,372; so the rentals exceeded the valuation by twenty-one per cent.[35] In the spring of 1843, after the Trench incident, Shirley's lawyer asked Griffith for an opinion concerning the fairness of the Shirley rents. Griffith was painfully honest in comparing Shirley to other landlords: "I have frequently found that the rentals of great landed proprietors who deal liberally with their tenants are nearly at or very little above the scale of the general valuation."[36] But Shirley felt that he had made as many concessions as he could, and held fast to the established rentals.

Further trouble soon broke out. One of Shirley's bailiffs was assaulted while posting a reward notice (for the Trench incident) on the wall of one of the parish chapels. Trench ran into increasing difficulty collecting the rents and Shirley authorized "driving," that is, impounding of tenants' cattle for nonpayment. The tenants first met these efforts by hiding their cattle in the cottages or off the property. When the drivers became more aggressive, the tenants began assaulting them physically. Anonymous notes were attached to the drivers' doors threatening them with "instant death" if they persisted. Shirley nervously appealed to Dublin Castle for additional troops and the assignment of a stipendiary magistrate, "an old and experienced one," to supplement the local magistrates. Trench himself appeared to be wavering; at least Shirley records in his diary (April 19, 1843), "Had some talk with Mr. Trench who I thought seemed dissatisfied with his position as agent here."[37] Adding to the confusion, Daniel O'Connell (sensing the opportunities present in the Farney agitation) appeared at Carrickmacross on April 25 for a Repeal meeting and 20,000 people turned out for it. O'Connell commented that "he was in a barony where such tyranny as he had alluded to flourished, alas, to a lamentable excess."[38] He also made a strong plea for the tenants not to resort to Ribbonism in retaliation. But the appearance of the revered "Liberator" at this critical time only served to stir up passions.

Trench's assistants, the bailiffs and drivers, now found themselves in a precarious position. Every time they moved out on the estate they were followed by large and threatening mobs, sometimes just the men but often augmented by women and children. One of the bailiffs commented, "I was afraid of the women and none of the others; they were very violent and I did not know any of them . . . the women threw stones after I left the bog."[39]

Trench's bog bailiffs were supposed to issue bog tickets and supervise the collecting of bog rents. After the riot of April 3, increasing numbers of unauthorized turf cuttings were noticed. Finally on May 9 an anonymous note was posted exhorting *all* the tenants to move out to the bogs all over the estate at one moment to cut turf in concert. The notice ended with the threat, "Let there be a water pool ready for the bog trotters." Trench was powerless, for the bogs were scattered out over 30,000 acres and it would have taken hundreds of bailiffs, probably backed by additional hundreds of militia, to prevent the invasion. But the police did succeed in arresting fourteen of the hundreds of tenants involved, and quickly brought them before the local magistrate where they were summarily tried on May 12 and fined thirty shillings each, in spite of the protestations of the defense attorney that no actual cutting was done by any of the fourteen. Seven could not pay their fines and were marched off to Monaghan gaol.

Now the pace of resistance stepped up. The following day a notice was posted threatening the drivers that "we will dissect you alive—life is sweet."[40] A week later one of the Shirley process servers giving notice to a rent defaulter was assaulted by a mob of men with faces blackened and dressed in women's clothing. It was at this point that the soon-dreaded name "Molly Maguire" made its appearance in Farney. Trench graphically described its use: "These 'Molly Maguires' were generally stout active young men, dressed up in women's clothing, with faces blackened or otherwise disguised; sometimes they wore crape over their countenances, sometimes they smeared themselves in the most fantastic manner with burnt cork about their eyes, mouths and cheeks. In this state they used to suddenly surprise the unfortunate grippers, keepers or process-servers, and either duck them in bog-holes, or beat them in the most unmerciful manner, so that the 'Molly Maguires' became the terror of all our officials. At last neither grippers, process-servers, nor keepers could be got for love or money to perform any duty, or to face the danger of these dreaded foes."[41]

"A council of war was held," continued Trench. "It was agreed on all hands that the 'Molly Maguires must be put down.' " But how to do this was not so readily solved. One magistrate proposed that "we should lie in wait, and fire on them with light shot or 'sparrow-hail' in our guns." But when it was announced that the "Molly Maguires" carried pistols under their petticoats, and if provoked would most certainly use them, this design was abandoned as untenable. Finally Shirley's lawyer appealed to Dublin Castle for additional troops, implying that there was a "regular conspiracy" among the tenants, who even had a defense fund collected by a known dissident of the estate. The lawyer particularly wanted the troops to aid the Shirley bailiffs in serving notices for ejectments. Dublin Castle had attempted in the past to keep troops out of what was essentially "landlord business"—they were not to be used for rent collections or evictions. But the borderline between civil disturbances and tenant disturbances was a misty one, and in this case troops were finally authorized for protection of bailiffs posting ejectment notices.[42]

The use of the troops brought immediate retaliation and on June 4 the famous "battle" of Magheracloon resulted.[43] This incident, though more serious than the riot, again could hardly justify as much notoriety as many others of the day. But the Farney situation had firmly captured the public eye, and the "battle" was magnified all out of proportion.

So far as one can tell from police reports and the other available sources, an eighteen-man company of troops escorting a Shirley bailiff marched toward the church at Rock Chapel, where the bailiff was to post a notice of ejectment on the chapel wall (which, by the concept of "substitution of service," then made it official). They were met by a howling, hooting mob of such size as to persuade the magistrate in charge of the police to order a strategic withdrawal. Returning to Carrickmacross they obtained eleven more men and set out again in wagons under the leadership of the sub-inspector. Although followed by the mob (who stayed up in the hills along the road), they were able to post the notice at Rock Chapel. But at the next objective, Magheracloon chapel, the mob moved menacingly down to the road and intercepted the police contingent. The sub-inspector remonstrated with them to no avail, then formed his group into three sections and read the Riot Act. The troops fixed their bayonets, moved forward, only to be met with a shower of stones. The events of the next moment were very confused—several of the uniformed men were hit with stones and at the same instant the entire contingent discharged one round each from their guns into the crowd. The crowd backed off. The sub-inspector, fearful of a greater slaughter, called his troops back to their carriages and they beat a speedy retreat, followed all the way by angry remnants of the mob. And back in the road in front of the chapel a young servant boy lay dead.

At the inquest the next day the exact basis for the volley was widely disputed, the sub-inspector averring that he did not order the shots and that only after several of the company were hit with stones did the firing occur. The boys who drove the police wagons were all interviewed and told conflicting stories, one admitting that "I was in such a confusion that I did not see any more of what the people did."[44] Two days later the coroner's jury (composed of six Protestants and thirteen Roman Catholics) held that as it was not known whose shot had killed the boy, no responsibility could be assessed. But the jury pointedly commented that "it has not been sufficiently proved to us that at the time of the firing the party of Constabulary were in imminent risk of their lives."[45] And the pro-tenant paper headlined the story "Rent Slaughter."[46]

Incidents continued through most of the remaining months of 1843. Bog bailiffs were beaten, turf was destroyed, houses were attacked. In July, Trench's sub-agent filed a libel suit against the pro-tenant paper, the *Newry Examiner*, accusing its editor of implying that he was a "mercenary underling" using his part-time job as owner of a grocery business as a club to force tenants to trade with him. He won the case and was awarded one hundred thirty pounds damages.[47]

Shirley and Trench realized that unless active steps were taken to mitigate tenant complaints they might well be faced with a general uprising. Though rents were continued at the 1834 levels, Trench actively entered into a campaign to help in all ways possible any tenant who was willing to work. Trench and Shirley held long meetings in August 1843 and discussed the methods of the previous agent. The espionage system was central to many of the complaints; the late agent had often sent bailiffs directly to the houses of defaulting tenants, and had them searched from top to bottom. The system was successful in obtaining the rent—the tenant would do almost anything to keep the bailiff outside the house—but the threat of search was a hated club. Trench recommended that the system be dropped and Shirley readily concurred. Trench and Shirley also worked out a new system for an improvement fund, half to be paid by the landlord and half by the tenant. A campaign was launched to encourage better windows and doors for the cottages. As Trench frankly put it, they could progressively eliminate the indolent and reckless by giving preference to the better tenants "who have something to lose; we thus act on the principle of 'divide and conquer.'" Lastly, they decided on an active campaign to eliminate the destitute cottiers on the estate. Notices to quit, and ejectment, were to be widely used, with crops to be seized if necessary to clear the debts. But in all cases efforts were made to aid the ejected to emigrate, the cost (about three pounds per person) to be met by Shirley.[48]

Both Trench and Shirley now spent many hours moving about the estate, encouraging the working tenants and actively eliminating the marginal. The volume of memorials and petitions to Trench and Shirley vastly increased, evidence both of better relations and the vast accumulation of tenant problems. These petitions, found among the Shirley manuscripts, eloquently chronicle the problems of estate living.

The energetic efforts of Shirley and Trench soon strengthened bonds with the better tenants. The marginal tenants were being actively forced out of the estate. By the spring of 1844, one hundred forty adults and forty children had been aided in emigration, costing Shirley three hundred fifty-six pounds.[49] This was not the total number of cottiers severed from the estate. Some were unwilling to emigrate, and others were not aided by Shirley because they lacked legal status on the estate. Trench maintained a cottiers' register and any additions were to be cleared with him. Few petitions for new cottiers were allowed after 1843, and some small tenants let cottiers settle on part of their property without authorization. When detected by Trench, these were summarily ejected.

In 1845, Trench tendered his resignation and Shirley appointed his own cousin, George Morant, as agent. Morant, like Trench, actively involved himself in estate management. Shirley's son, Evelyn Philip, had now married and returned to Lough Fea as a part-time resident, and was taking considerable interest in the estate.

The efforts of the Shirleys and Morant might have eventually brought the estate to some prosperity. The population still remained excessive, the holdings still widely subdivided. The Shirley plan of aid to tractable tenants, combined with vigorous efforts to eliminate the small holder, was, in terms of estate management, a logical course. But a terrible event intervened and shattered these plans irrevocably. The famine hit Farney in August 1846.

✣   ✣   ✣   ✣   ✣

Evelyn John Shirley was at Lough Fea when the blight struck the potato. The years of personal involvement, particularly since 1843, had quickened Shirley's reactions and he attacked the famine problem in the most effective way he knew—aid for the tenant so that the tenant could help himself. He hired a professional agriculturalist, who traveled around the estate with the new agent, George Morant, attempting to push the tenants into activity. The famine brought little actual starvation to Farney, but the combination of low diet and fear of the future seemed to breed a feeling of helplessness and lethargy (a manifestation noted all over the country during the famine years). The agriculturalist circulated a handbill which began, "Having now gone over a considerable portion of the Estate, I see the fields of many of you totally neglected, where you planted your potatoes last season nothing is yet done for a coming Crop."[50] Morant was even more pointed: "As you love your Children, your Homes, your Country, be up and stirring! . . . lose not another hour . . . rouse yourself from the lethargy into which the loss of your favourite root has thrown you. Remember that lethargy FOR A FEW WEEKS PROLONGED will be to many of you the Sleep of Death."[51] Though

Morant and the agriculturalist encouraged any planting, even potatoes, they also pushed diversification. Turnips were emphasized, and
a quite advanced explanation of the concept of crop rotation was
handbilled to all tenants in 1847. Even the Shirley prize contest
shifted to put emphasis on diversified crops. But success was modest.
The innate conservatism of the Irish farmer made it difficult to im-
plant any new idea; new ideas often frightened uneducated peasants.

Shirley's involvement in the tenants' problems was, as always,
honest and with the best of intentions. But his unfortunate failing of
often sounding sanctimonious and paternalistic again caused him to
fall off the pedestal he deserved. In September 1846 he put the following on a handbill:

It becomes the duty of all classes, under this affliction of Divine Providence, to exert themselves to alleviate the distress occasioned by the
awful dispensation; the poor to exert their patience and to calm their
fears; the rich, to aid in devising the best plan to secure food for those
whose means will soon be exhausted . . .

Meanwhile, let the tenantry take advantage of the blessed weather, by
increased exertion in securing, threshing, and selling their corn while the
market is high, and paying their rent, aiding the landlord to help the
distressed . . .

Let us by cheerfulness and firmness soothe the timid and encourage
the active and industrious; remembering that this affliction is intended as
a trial for our good, and must be borne with resignation to the Divine
will. But above all things avoid the counsel of those bad men, who, with
their rents in their pockets, delay in paying it, while they endeavour, for
their own selfish purposes, to increase the alarm in the minds of the
poor and weak.[52]

Again his words fell into unsympathetic hands, and again it was
the London press that pushed him unwillingly into the limelight.
This time it was the most severe of all satirists, *Punch:*

PUNCH'S PRECIOUS LANDLORD

Great is the blessing of a good landlord to his tenantry at all times.
Doubly great the blessing of such a landlord in Ireland. Trebly great of
such a landlord in Ireland, at the present terrible crisis.

Honour and laud, then, to Mr. Evelyn John Shirley, M. P., one of the
largest proprietors in the county of Monaghan!

The poor on his large estates are starving. His tenants, in dismay looking round for help and comfort bethink them of their landlord . . . Mr.
Shirley sends back—money?—himself with his means and experience?

—a cargo of meal?—directions to his agent to set the poor to work?—a remission of rent to the sufferers?—No: but a letter of advice—and such a letter! . . .

Read it, starving cottier; dwell upon it, ruined tenant; learn the true division of responsibilities at such a moment, and, above all, rise from it impressed with the binding—the sacred—the awful duty of paying your rent! . . .

Mark Mr. Shirley's division of duties. That of the poor is "to exert their patience and to calm their fears," i.e., to be patient under starvation, and calm their fears as they loathingly swallow their last fetid "lumper." That of the rich is to feed the poor, to give them meal, money, work? No: *"to devise the best plan* to secure food for those whose means will soon be exhausted . . ."

A division, beautiful, equitable, and pleasant for the landlord. Something like the monkey's, when he swallowed the oyster, and awarded a shell to plaintiff and defendant . . .

And this is Mr. Shirley's letter to his starving tenantry!

Pay your rents, and be patient! Noble, disinterested, unselfish, pious, high-minded Mr. Evelyn Shirley! You shall sit on our right hand, with the proud title of—*"Punch's* Pet Landlord!"[53]

The article was greeted with indignation, not only by Shirley's friends but also by some of the skeptics. Caught for once with its facts wrong, *Punch* printed an "Amende Honorable" noting all of Shirley's efforts. But it couldn't resist a last dig: "Mr. Shirley acts like a good landlord but writes like a bad one. *Punch* judged him by his writing, not knowing him by his acts. If he be what our informant describes him, he does his duty. The rare discovery of a good landlord in Ireland reconciles *Punch* to the still rarer discovery of a harsh judgment in himself."[54]

Nevertheless, the wide circulation in Farney of the original *Punch* article laid new seeds of discontent. As he left for England and the relative peace of Ettington, Shirley penned a handbill to the tenants that plaintively began, "I must again address a few lines to you before I leave Ireland; and I hope no Editor of a Public Journal will trouble himself to notice what one of the large body of landlords thinks fit to say to the Inhabitants of the family Estate."[55] He went on to compliment the tenantry on their "perfect harmony" and to urge them toward greater individual efforts.

In 1847, Shirley felt particularly strongly about the relief program of that year. The British government had recognized the ravages of the famine (belatedly, thought many) and had set up a scheme involving two alternatives. On the one hand, the benefits of the Public Works Act could be requested by a relief aspirant, who, if he qualified, could obtain work on various public works programs. Most of these were for road improvement and road extension. This cost the tenant nothing; in fact, he made a nominal salary. His other choice was the Drainage Act. Here both the conditions and the objectives were different. Essentially it was a land reclamation act. If a tenant elected to utilize it on his own property, he had to pay part of the cost. In turn, he would become more productive through improved land.

It was clearly to Shirley's advantage to push the Drainage Act option, and he argued vehemently for it in his always blunt manner. But if Shirley stood to benefit by better abilities to pay rent, he was also dead right as economist. The barony needed new roads far less than it needed better land. Farney had wet ground, and reclamation could pay off handsomely. Post-famine evaluations confirmed Shirley's thesis. Farney suffered far less than some other baronies, and contemporary experts attributed some of this to the extensive reclamation accomplished.[56] Over 1200 acres were brought to new cultivation. But these same experts also pointed to the still-serious problem of overpopulation. And it was precisely here that Shirley encountered the most severe ill feelings of his lifetime.

Shirley's decade-long attempts to hold rents at the level of the more prosperous 1830's had already caused him difficulties in the Trench period of 1843 and 1844. Any hope he may have harbored that business conditions—and rent payments—would be bettered were now dashed by the famine. The separate ledger of "Arrears" kept by Morant quickly grew, each followed by Morant's cryptic comments concerning possible collection ("Sick, has a cow to sell"; "This is a very bad case, greatly in debt"; "Paid nothing, house burnt"; "Broke his word"; "Press payment of this immediately").[57] Perhaps if Shirley's tenants had all been "improving" tenants with holdings of reasonable size, they could have held on through the famine. But the vast overpopulation on the estate, the subdivision down to miniscule plots and the large amount of "conacre" and outright squatting swelled the numbers of impoverished small holders.

Early in 1847 Morant issued a handbill strictly forbidding *any* conacre and followed this with explicit new rules concerning subdivision and cottiers. All subdivisions, sales, mortgages, and exchanges had to have his personal approval, and no tenant holding under 20 acres could henceforth have any cottiers. Still rent receipts declined. On January 1, 1848, Morant warned all the tenants that "whilst liberally rewarding those who deserve his approbation, the Landlord is determined to enforce exactness and punctuality in the payment of Rent. Those who decline attending to this caution will have to blame themselves for the consequences which will inevitably follow this neglect."[58]

Most of the tenants "declined." There was practically no cash left on the estate, and what crops or cattle did remain were desperately guarded against distraining by the Shirley bailiffs. Cows and pigs could be hidden. But the crops presented a more difficult problem. If they could be harvested during the night and spirited across the county line to a friend, the bailiffs could be frustrated. This was always difficult to do.

Morant's threat of inevitable consequences soon was fufilled. In mid-1849, at the height of the famine, Shirley made his move. Morant's process servers appeared all over the estate, carrying in their hand the dreaded "notice to quit." Shirley's patience had run out—mass evictions were to be the "consequence."

The economic logic was sound. Overpopulated estates led to inefficiencies. The famine had accentuated these, and landlords who formerly had absorbed the losses now found themselves forced closer to bankruptcy by the almost complete unproductivity of their land. A great many estates went under during this period. Viewing the situation from the landlord's side, the need for wholesale clearances of marginal tenants was apparently the only possible alternative. There was now a Poor Law and workhouses—the desperate conditions appeared to be beyond the powers of estate owners to solve. In their view, poverty and overpopulation were public problems, and the only salvation of the estate was realignment of the tenantry toward higher productivity.

But in the tenants' eyes this was hitting far below the belt. For the small cottier or the conacre holder, the alternative to holding his land was disaster. The workhouse was believed a ticket to degradation, starvation, and death. There were no possibilities of obtaining land elsewhere, for landlords all over the country were evicting. Short of emigration—an often terrifying alternative—the only hope appeared to be holding the land by any means possible. And this is precisely what happened at Farney.

Shirley had never evicted more than a dozen or so families per year in all his years at Lough Fea. But now the scale changed. The number rose from eight in 1846 to one hundred seven in 1847, dropped to only four in 1848 and then rose to three hundred seventeen in 1849.[59] It was this last year that again brought Shirley into the public press and again cast him so unwillingly in the role of the landlord "exterminator" par excellence. Shirley now experienced real difficulties in actually getting the people out of the cottages, and turned to wide use of "wrecking," pulling the houses down by crowbar and battering ram. Two cases particularly excited public indignation. A Dublin periodical, *The Nation*, summarized them both on September 22, 1849. The first was as follows:

The Case of Bridget Wright

The case of Bridget Wright has been already before the public. The facts are briefly these: She was ejected for one year's rent, and had her house unroofed. She got a shed thrown up against one of the remaining walls, and lived in it for nine or ten days, until the bailiffs came round again, for the purpose of completely levelling the house. It is a fact, that they used considerable personal violence in ejecting her from this hut, at one o'clock in the day, and that she was dead before twelve o'clock the same night. The clergyman who went to attend her could not reach the place in sufficient time to administer the last rites. The following extracts from the *Newry Examiner's* report of the Carrickmacross Board of Guardians, will fitly conclude this case:

Mary Wright, a wretched looking woman, applied to the board for a coffin for her mother. She said, "We were turned out this day fortnight. The house was tumbled—and my mother died yesterday evening. I have no money to bury her; I have no coffin."

Mr. Morant—Where was she?

Mary Wright—She was in a shed for nine or ten days, sir.

Mr. Shirley (Evelyn Philip)—Why did she not apply to come in here? [That is, to the poorhouse. E. P. Shirley, the son, and Morant, the agent, were members of the Carrickmacross guardians of the poorhouse.]

Mary Wright—She was very old—so she was—and she had a smothering in her, and she thought she might as well die outside.

The Chairman—Do you mean that she threw the sticks up against the house and made a shed?

Mary Wright—Yes, sir. She only owed a year's rent.

The Chairman—I made two attempts to induce her to come into the house; but she said she was afraid she would not live if she did so.

Mr. Minnet—The change from landholding to the poorhouse is so great they do not like to come in at first. It takes some time to do away with that feeling.

Mr. Shirley (addressing Mary Wright)—If you don't come in you will die too. If you don't come in you will deserve to die. You will kill yourself.

The guardians having no power to order a coffin from the rates, subscribed among themselves a sufficient sum to purchase one. For this purpose Mr. Shirley gave a shilling. I continue from the *Examiner's* report:

Mr. Shirley (addressing Mary Wright)—You have killed your mother. That is the fact. I do not doubt but you intended her kindness; but you must now see what you have done.

Mary Wright (crying)—When I had it I did more for her than was in my power. God knows I can't say I killed her—I can't; indeed, I can't. The neighbours were very kind to us; God bless them, they were very kind to us.

Mr. Morant—Does this woman apply to come in now?

The Relieving Officer—Not yet, sir.

Mr. Shirley (addressing the woman)—I hope you will think better of the matter, and come into the house.

Mary Wright—Oh, yes, sir. When she is buried I will come in—for I have no place under heaven to go to now. You know the house is down, sir.

The unfortunate woman then left the room, weeping bitterly.

The second case, as described in the periodical, was briefer but hardly less pathetic:

Mary Connor (Carickarthur), a widow with five children, and her father, an old man, dependent on her, was ejected last week. The whole family had had fever, but were nearly recovered from it, except two children who were lying dangerously ill. Those two children were carried out by the bailiffs and left by them lying *absolutely naked* on the ground. The mother was either too ill herself, or too overwhelmed by her misfortunes to take any care of them, and they lay there wholly uncovered until some charitable passers by extricated from the house, then in process of demolition, some bed-clothes to cover them with.

The elder Shirley was particularly stung by the outcry of criticism in this second case, and penned a letter to the Carrickmacross guardians of the poorhouse: "I beg leave to state that the head bailiff of the Shirley estate had always received positive instructions to defer ejectment in cases of fever . . . In the case of widow Connor the bailiffs state positively that the children were not ill, and that the woman stripped them naked for the purpose of exciting commiseration. This statement I have reason to believe to be perfectly true, and consequently the account of the relieving officer was erroneous."[60] But at the next meeting of the guardians the case was again debated (and duly reported in all the Dublin papers). Though Morant and the younger Shirley were members of the guardians, most of the rest were anti-landlord. The anti-Shirley chairman questioned one of the guardians, one McCabe, who had been present at the eviction:

Mr. McCabe—I went into the house of the widow Connor, and I saw the children on a bed or wad of hay or straw. Part of the house was then down. The woman begged of me for God's sake to do something for the poor children. She told me they were lying in fever. I went in to the house, and I saw the two children myself, lying in the corner. I told her to carry out the children, or that the house would be down on top of them.

The Chairman—You said there was some part of the house down then?

Mr. McCabe—Yes; about one-fourth of it was down at the time. There were eighteen bailiffs there. The woman carried the children out to the side of the ditch, which was near the house. I asked a woman who was present if the children had no clothes, for the mother was so much distracted with grief that she did not know what she was about. I got some old clothes which a woman brought out of the widow's house, and I covered the children with them. The mother carried out one child, and someone else the other.

The Chairman—Did you see the mother stripping off their clothes?

Mr. McCabe—No; I did not—they were naked when I saw them, being in bed. I felt the children's pulses, and they were very weak.

Mr. Kelly—Did you ask if they had a medical attendant?

Mr. McCabe—I did, and I found there was not.

Mr. Kelly—Did you report the case to any medical man?

Mr. McCabe—I did not; unless I paid a medical attendant myself, I had no power to send one to them from the guardians.

Mr. Ward—Are the children there still?

Mr. McCabe—I was there on last Saturday, and their mother told me that they were still in the same state as when I saw them. Some of the neighbors gathered on Sunday last eight days, and built a shed for them against the ditch.[61]

The case soon became famous, with the papers losing all restraint in their descriptions:

There in the dank ditch. There is his wife, who has passed from the fresh bloom of young matronhood to a gray, wrinkled, sere, and shrivelled old age in one month of hunger and one week of fever. There. The young child's bleeding lips tug in vain at those barren breasts. Under the scrogs there, these two poor young things, the boy and the girl, naked, the red spots of the sickness over them—stark naked, there the young wasted bones, that you fear to see bending lest they cut the skin through, covered with the horrid fur of famine—then their thin eye-lids dosing in the sleep that will be wakened by the hymns of young Angels.

Round the road, with drunken roar and ribald song, comes the Wreckers' car. Which side are the drivers today? Down goes Atty MacMahon's thatch over his head. The widow Wright died last week of the treatment they gave her: (more betoken Shirley gave a shilling to bury her.) Mary Connor's children died of the fever, after being shovelled out naked. The Guardians are making room for a thousand paupers. All Shirley's work![62]

There seems to be no evidence other than this lurid acount that the two children actually died. In any case, the Shirley tenants now began to fight back, resisting the evictions:

Excitement now ran high as it was known that the next tenant to be ousted would defend his home . . . All the approaches to the house were filled in with bushes, and against the door was a pile of some tons of stones which were liberally sprinkled with slush from an open cesspool . . . It was decided to effect the break at the back of the building . . . As soon as the inlet was made the tenant appeared at the window, and threw out a copious supply of boiling water, before which the bailiffs quickly beat a retreat. Mr. Hamilton warned the man to desist or he would be arrested, but the man for some time continued to throw pailfuls of hot water at the bailiffs, each discharge being greeted with loud cheers by the people . . .[63]

But face-to-face defiance was a weak weapon, and the tenants finally fell back on the secret society as the only effective way to counter the landlords' power. Ribbon attacks broke out all over the county, pushed along by the inflammatory newspaper articles. The Dublin *Freeman's Journal*, one of the most widely read papers in the country, set the tone: "Is it wonderful, however blameable it may be, that the people form combination? We may condemn—we may regret—we may strive to stop it, but we cannot feel surprised that the peasantry . . . combine illegally and resolve not to remain apathetic."[64]

The landlords were truly frightened this time, and appealed to Dublin Castle for additional troops. The county was "proclaimed" under the "Act for Preventing Crime and Outrage in Ireland," and a grudge battle was set in motion that again followed the age-old pattern—mob beatings and killings, followed by harsh retaliatory actions by the police. The situation in Monaghan so disturbed the people in England that even Queen Victoria, in her annual message to Parliament, felt it necessary to single the area out for censure:

While I have observed with sincere satisfaction the tranquillity which has prevailed throughout the greater portion of Ireland, it is with much regret that I have to inform you, that certain parts of the counties of Armagh, Monaghan and Louth have been marked by the commission of outrages of the most serious description. The powers of the existing law have been promptly exerted for the detection of the offenders and for the repression of a system of crime and violence fatal to the best interests of the country. My attention will continue to be directed to this important object.[65]

For the remaining famine years the Shirleys bore the burden of a public censure that their actions did not completely warrant. As dogmatic (though necessary) as was Evelyn John Shirley's decision to clear the marginal farmers from the estate, he still tempered his efforts with honest attempts to persuade the remaining tenants to become more productive. He continued his practice of agricultural prizes, and used the Great Hall for annual tenant dinners, where frugality and industry were preached.

Tenant opinion was divided on these dinners and their concomitant rewards. Those sympathetic to the family—generally the more successful and most often the larger holders—reacted favorably both to the prize competition and the tenant dinner. A substantial portion of the tenants had agreeable relations with the Shirleys, as evidenced by the turnout at various Farney functions.

However, there is no doubt that another substantial group felt a hostility toward the family that increased over the lifetimes of Evelyn John and Evelyn Philip Shirley. Some people were not even invited to the dinners—mainly the cottiers, who lacked the legal status of tenants on the Shirley rolls. But many tenants who were invited refused to attend. Some of these were unsuccessful farmers (unsuccessful either through sheer circumstances or because of laziness and indolence) who would have received, at best, a grudging dinner and at worst a lecture as to why they weren't more effective. And some of the adamant ones were farmers, both successful and unsuccessful, who objected to the whole notion of a tenant dinner as smacking of feudalism and patronization.

In the years before the 1843 rent troubles and the 1849–1850 evictions, the character of the dinners was straightforwardly agricultural. But as the family found itself under attack—for reasons they felt were so unjust—the dinners became forums for justification of the family's actions. By the time of the dinner of October 10, 1850, in the midst of the most extensive evictions conducted so far, the toasts and speeches were pointedly defensive.

The evening began with a toast to Evelyn John Shirley, "the Lord of the Soil," after which, according to a pro-Shirley newspaper, son Evelyn Philip rose

to return them his heartfelt thanks for the toast . . . He had heard with disgust the abominable attacks (cheers)—that had been made on him at some Tenant League meetings by some wandering Tenant League agitators (cheers) . . . Nothing such men could do would set him against the tenantry, and he thought he might venture to say that nothing they could do would ever set the tenantry against him (Loud Cheers) . . . Was he a man then to be held up to the aim of the assassin because through the failure of the potato crop, the abolition of the corn laws, and other causes, their tenant right, which had always been acknowledged on that estate—(cheers)—had been so far reduced that it could not find a purchaser? Was it his fault, when they were so far sunk that they could neither support themselves nor pay any rent, he should relieve them by sending them abroad, at vast expense . . .[66]

It was an evening of "unalloyed enjoyment," said this paper, the *Newry Telegraph* in nearby County Down. But by this time the *Dundalk Democrat* was publishing in nearby County Louth; and, if the *Telegraph* was overly sympathetic, the *Democrat* was overly vitriolic:

Two of the tenants, we are told, sung Irish songs to the delight of everyone present . . . As the names of the songs which they warbled in the hearing of the company are not given, we suspect that they were abusing Shirley [the elder] and his "brigade" before their faces. Ten to one that the songs were recently composed on the exploits of the "Shirley Brigade," for Farney abounds with Irish poets . . . When the muse is in an angry mood, her denunciations of tyranny and tyrants are awfully grand . . . Mr. Shirley said it was forty years since he came amongst them, and in the course of that time he had seen great changes for the better . . . How these landlords do look at matters! Shirley sees thousands of acres on his estate without a tenant, houses without roofs, and misery on all sides of him; and yet he says that he has seen great changes for the better! There is no use arguing with a man of this kind.[67]

The following year the family presented, with the prizes, a small medal with a facsimile of Lough Fea house engraved on it. The *Democrat*, always ready to embarrass both the family and the rival *Telegraph*, caustically commented, "Was there ever greater delusion practised on an unfortunate people than this farce enacted at Shirley Castle? A medal given to encourage people to starve themselves and pay an enormous rent! The medal should represent Mr. Morant dressed in his shoot jacket and fancy hat, and moustaches combed and oiled, with stick in hand, commanding the Crowbar Brigade at full work demolishing a cabin; with Carrickmacross Workhouse in the distance, and on the obverse side 'Ruin to Farney' which is unfortunately no legend but a reality." The *Democrat* continued its attacks on the Shirleys and, particularly, on the institution of the dinner, calling it "degradation that none but the meanest would endure" and "a mockery in having them summoned from their cold and gloomy homes to witness how they lived on the fruits of the unfortunate farmers' toil." Thus the paper used the dinner as a club to lambaste the Shirleys.[68]

Shirley continued to aid tenants to emigrate, paying a substantial part of the crossing money. For this was the period of the great Irish movement across the seas—to Australia, to Canada, to the United States. Even for these efforts Shirley was needled by the press. A writer in the Monaghan *Northern Standard* used Farney as an example of the ills of emigration:

The men who can view the men, women and children on their estates to be an overstock to be reduced, as surplus population to be exported— anywhere, anyhow, to stagnate in putrescent, contagious idleness in our lazar poorhouses—to die by our roadsides—to manure with their bones the already over-fertile plains of the Mississippi and enrich with their labour what seems the refuge of our people—the forests of Canada and the savannahs of the Far West . . .

. . . The poor, quarter-civilised Farney men that used to crowd the streets . . . the men whose fagot votes, created to subserve family interests, turned the scale at every contest . . . have been alternately humbugged and trampled on—bamboozled and cheated—caressed and spat upon—made use of while useful, and now when used up and useless, regarded as overstock . . . although these men are of a different race—of a different language—of a different creed, and even garb; yet, they are fellow men—not WHITE NIGGERS.[69]

Shirley indignantly replied that he had personally paid for the emigration of 939 people.[70] (This was November 1849; he aided many more after that date.) But the public image of Shirley as the "exterminator" was far too entrenched, and skepticism greeted every effort he made to help the evicted tenants. Shirley continued to try, in his English way, but the ill-will generated in this period remained to trouble the family for many years.

✤   ✤   ✤   ✤   ✤

Still to come in Ireland were countless additional agrarian crimes, continuing harshness in English administration, effort upon effort in the political areas to bring about Repeal of Union, self-administration, independence. Still to come were the Tenant League and Land League agitation in the period 1850–1880, the Phoenix Park murders in 1882, Easter Week 1916, and the internecine Civil War in 1922. For eighty-odd years after the "Molly Maguires" first appeared on the Shirley estate, Ireland would continue to feel the effects of the great land war that had occupied the country's energies for so many centuries before. One of the saddest sagas in modern Western civilization had yet a great many bitter chapters to run.

But, for the hundreds of thousands of Irish who were to give up their native land for a new world in America, for the many thousands of these who were to find their way to the coal regions, the famine was the great watershed. Those who remained alive were left, if possible, more destitute than they had ever been before. By the hundreds of thousands the survivors walked to the ports all around the coast of the island, got passage in whatever vessel they could find, and emigrated. And they carried with them the accumulated grievances of hundreds of years of serfdom, ill treatment, and degradation. They brought with them deep, bitter, black resentments, resentments that could only be erased by time. And, before they were completely wiped out, these resentments were inexorably destined to come to the surface again.

Part Two ❖ *The Reading Fights the Union*

Chapter 4 ✦ *Black Gold and Irish Green*

*W*HEN Irish emigration soared in the nineteenth century, England and Scotland had first call; there were almost half a million Irish in the two countries by 1841.[1] All through the large industrial centers of England, "Little Irelands" proliferated. Frederick Engels, writing about the working class of 1844 in England, described Manchester's Irish as "having grown up almost without civilization, accustomed in youth to every sort of privation, rough, intemperate and improvident, bringing all their brutal habits with them among a class of the English population which has, in truth, little inducement to cultivate education and morality."[2] The Irish took the meanest jobs, and were accused of depressing the existing wages by their eagerness to accept bare subsistence rates. But not all were unskilled laborers—in Wales the Irish became coal miners and were as adept as the Welsh with pick and powder charge.

Irish emigration to the United States was large from the start of the century. In the 1820's almost 52,000 of the 135,000 who entered the United States as immigrants were Irish—over 38 per cent. In the 1830's it was 170,000 of 538,000—31.6 per cent. In the six years 1840–1845 it was 226,500 out of 513,300—over 44 per cent. And the climax came in the famine years 1846–1854, when, of the 2.8 million immigrants from all over the world, over 1.2 million came from Ireland—again an amazing 44 per cent.[3]

Stories of the immigrant crossings to North America are classics, and have been evocatively told elsewhere.[4] The agonies of the forty to seventy days at sea were beyond endurance for many. The steerage was terribly crowded; ventilation was almost non-existent; and both problems were accentuated by the lack of sanitary facilities. Food was often bad, water scarce. And disease stalked many a vessel; frequently entire families were wiped out before reaching the United States.[5] The Irish as a group experienced some of the worst conditions of all who crossed. A large number were penniless, and many others tried to appear so, hoping to beat their way as cheaply as possible (for the Irish peasant was highly secretive about his personal finances). In 1834, a writer in a Baltimore periodical reported:

We have frequently heard the character of emigrant ships from Ireland declared to be worse than that of those concerned in the slave trade of Africa [and] the "Thomas Gelston," from Londonderry, substantiates this opinion . . . The number of passengers was somewhere from 450 to 517. They were nine weeks, and suffered much from want of water and provisions. Besides two tiers of berths on the sides, the vessel was filled with a row of berths down the center, between which and the side berths there was only a passage of about three feet. The passengers were thus obliged to eat in their berths, each of which contained a great many persons, say five and upwards. In one were a man, his wife, his sister and five children; in another were six full-grown young women, while that above them contained five men, and the next one eight men.[6]

When the famine struck in the late 1840's, the frenzied rush to get to port and take any ship westward soon brought conditions more horrible than could have been imagined. Boats that had never before handled passengers now were stuffed full of people. Typhus was ravaging Ireland, and it was inevitable that sick members of families would be spirited aboard, in spite of efforts (often desultory) by the ship captain to start out with a healthy ship. The worst of the famine years, so far as the conditions of emigration were concerned, was probably 1847. A contemporary traveler later wrote concerning his voyage:

Who can imagine the horrors of even the shortest passage in an emigrant ship crowded beyond its utmost capability of stowage with unhappy beings of all ages, with fever raging in their midst? Under the most favourable circumstances it is impossible to maintain perfect purity of atmosphere between decks, even when ports are open, and every device is adopted to secure the greatest amount of ventilation. But a crowded emigrant sailing ship of twenty years since, with fever on board!—the crew sullen or brutal from very desperation, or paralysed with terror of the plague—the miserable passengers unable to help themselves, or afford the least relief to each other; one-fourth, or one-third, or one-half of the entire number in different stages of the disease; many dying, some dead; the fatal poison intensified by the indescribable foulness of the air breathed and rebreathed by the gasping sufferers—the wails of children, the ravings of the delirious, the cries and groans of those in mortal agony![7]

*   *   *   *   *

The sentiments in the United States toward this precipitous influx of Irish soon became painfully clear. Almost all the Irish immigrants were Roman Catholic, and latent religious tensions from long-past "Old Country" attitudes came rushing to the foreground. A convent was burned in Massachusetts in 1834, and in most of the larger cities anti-Catholic demonstrations increased. The difference between the Irish as an ethnic group and the Irishman as a practicing Catholic was soon lost—Irishmen were "Papists" all. Further serious riots in the 1840's (the worst in Philadelphia in 1844) were abetted by scurrilous writing in newspapers and books that often reached the depths of obscenity, bigotry, and pornography. Especially vicious were "exposés" of alleged sexual excesses behind convent walls, as exemplified by the famous book, Maria Monk's *Awful Disclosures*, first published by Harper's in 1836 (and used as late as the political campaign against Al Smith in 1928).[8] There was an epidemic of rabble-rousing in the 1850's, with anti-Catholic forces now organizing politically to form the Supreme Order of the Star-Spangled Banner. This polyglot group of nativists soon was dubbed the "Know-Nothings," although they preferred Native-American as their party name. After some startling successes in the elections of 1854 and 1855, they declined as a political force. But bigotry against the Irish Catholic continued through that decade. (The immigrant German also felt the antipathy of the nativists, the animosity being aimed largely at the refugee radicals from the 1848 revolution, who were accused variously of being "agnostics," "freethinkers," "atheists," "socialists," and "communists.") There were pitched battles between Irish and Know-Nothings in Philadelphia, Newark, Brooklyn, St. Louis, and the Massachusetts towns of Chelsea and Lawrence. Baltimore became known as a "mob town." Cincinnati experienced a serious election-night battle between Germans and the Know-Nothings. Louisville had a "Bloody Monday," when Irish and Germans fought nativists; the nativists set fires, looted houses, taverns, and stores, and so terrified the populace that many of the Irish and Germans subsequently moved from the town.[9] Though America was becoming more tolerant religiously, the anti-Catholic bigotry before the Civil War remains one of the serious blots on the history of the country.

The Irish fought back vigorously. And in the forefront of the fight were the Irish-American societies.

Earlier varieties had been beneficial societies, aiding the newly arrived immigrant (often indigent) to get settled, sometimes providing burial benefits, and acting as a hub for revered Irish practices—parades, outings, wake celebrations. The Friendly Sons of St. Patrick, founded in 1771 in Philadelphia, had allegedly numbered among its members George Washington himself.[10]

But with the increased tensions, the Irish-American societies reverted to time-honored defensive maneuvers and became again secret societies whose aim was protection of the Irish and aggressive attack on their enemies. The Know-Nothings were both secret and aggressive; it was inevitable that the Irish societies would retaliate. The pattern was too firmly established in Ireland to have had it otherwise.

The attitude of the Catholic Church in America toward secret societies had many parallels to that of the Irish hierarchy. The secret societies in Ireland, though falling increasingly under the ban of the Church, nevertheless stemmed from such basic causes—the landlord-tenant hiatus and the attitude of the English Protestant Ascendancy toward the Irish Catholic—that the Church was forced to act warily in its attempts at suppression. Pragmatically, the secret society seemed to be the only short-term way to mitigate the excesses of landlordism and militant anti-Catholicism. Those excesses were equally an anathema to the Church, and though the Church might take a strong stand concerning means, it was wholeheartedly sympathetic to the ends. Since the peasant Irish Catholic could seldom make the rather subtle distinction between illegal means and lawful objectives, the Irish bishops were constantly faced with the practical problem of trying to bring more ethical methods into play, while at the same time treading gingerly lest they lose influence with their lay members. In spite of Bishop Doyle's vigorous denunciation of Ribbonism in 1825, and similar efforts by other Irish bishops, substantial numbers of Irish clergy throughout the first half of the nineteenth century had neither the belief that secret societies should be vigorously extirpated nor the nerve to try it.

These very pressures were heightened in the United States. The American bishops often denounced secret societies, whether anti-Catholic or otherwise. In their very first meeting in America in 1810, taking their cue from the condemnation of the Freemasons in 1738 by Pope Clement XII, they cautioned their priests to avoid any connection with Freemasonry.[11] The Odd Fellows (founded in 1819) and the Sons of Temperance (1842), both secret, oath-bound societies, came under the same ban. The Fourth Provincial Council of Baltimore in 1840 repeated earlier warnings against secret societies, and the Fenian Brotherhood had solid opposition from the American bishops long before its decisive condemnation by the Vatican in 1870.[12] But it was one thing to condemn such patently anti-Catholic groups as the Masons and such openly revolutionary fringes as the Fenians, and quite a different problem to treat fearlessly the wide range of "fraternal" and "benevolent" societies that mushroomed among the Irish wherever they settled in America. For these societies stood as a practical bulwark against vicious American forms of anti-Catholic bias.

With "Irish" and "Catholic" practically synonymous, most antagonists made no distinction and flailed both with equal fervor. Squarely in the middle stood the Catholic Church. When Bishop John Hughes stressed in a pastoral letter in 1842 that any oath-bound society was illegal, he was challenged in the press as a bigot, and ended by backing down concerning the Masons and Odd Fellows.[13] Cases like this taught the bishops that it was best not to name any society, but merely to issue sweeping denunciations of amorphous "oath-bound secret societies." In 1865 the Holy See ruled that no condemnation by name could be made by any bishop or priest until it had been interpreted by Rome. In doing this, the Vatican was attempting to prevent hasty condemnation of suspected groups that were merely secret, but not "anti-social." Although all secret societies were forbidden to Catholics under pain of sin, the bishops could not apply the extreme penalty of excommunication unless Rome had explicitly ruled so. The effect of this ruling was aptly illustrated in a decree issued by the Second Plenary Council of Baltimore in 1866. In the process of reviewing the ban on secret societies, it forbade any cleric to condemn *any* society unless he held it "certain and beyond any doubt" to fall directly under a papal pronouncement.[14] Few priests would have had the presumption to be so unequivocal.

Prior to the Civil War the Church had not seen fit to make any specific pronouncement concerning unions, although many individual churchmen were deeply concerned with the uplift of the workingman. After the war, a few bishops began to make cautious statements in the direction of drawing a distinction between unions and secret societies. The Baltimore Plenary Council of 1866 went so far as to state that, "after carefully considering these things there appears to be no reason why the prohibition of the Church against the Masonic and other hidden sects should be extended to those associations of workmen which evidently have no other purpose than mutual help and protection in exercising their trade."[15]

But secrecy, so often a bitter necessity for the early trade unions, brought disapproval in many other cases. James Roosevelt Bayley, the Archbishop of Baltimore, warned his diocese in 1868 that although "it is true that those which have been formed in this country have not as yet adopted the harsh rules and sanguinary penalties of the secret societies on the Continent, and the labour combinations in England, . . . the principle is bad and 'no bad tree can bring forth good fruit.' "[16] The Pennsylvania anthracite region felt the whiphand of the Church long before the Molly Maguire incidents; John Siney, president of an early coal union, in 1874 bitterly denounced the attitudes of many of the priests in the region: "We have been called 'agitators,' we have been called 'demagogues,' because we have counseled the members of the organization to try and secure those objects. In some places even the clergy have placed their anathema upon the society, and why? Is it wrong to teach men to seek a higher moral standard? If so, let them vacate the pulpits . . ."[17]

So the Church's attitude toward labor unions appeared to be one of "watchful neutrality." If the union had anything approaching an oath, it could expect censure from the Church. If it was merely a secret organization but not oath-bound, it could expect ambivalence from the Church, depending upon the attitude of both the parish priest and his bishop.

Nevertheless, there were a few strong-willed bishops in the United States who called their shots on secret societies with unmistakable emphasis. One in particular—James Frederic Wood—stands out over all the rest as the pre-eminent example in America.[18]

For, in speaking strongly against secret societies, he lashed out vehemently at the Molly Maguires and in the process became inextricably enmeshed in the Molly Maguire saga.

Wood had been born and reared as a Protestant. Of English ancestry, he was sent to England at age eight to attend grammar school. Returning to America at fourteen, he entered business in Cincinnati, first as a bank clerk, then as "individual bookkeeper and discount clerk," and finally as cashier. But at age twenty-five he suddenly decided to become a Catholic, and immediately upon his conversion entered the priesthood.

Historians have inferred many motives for Wood's conduct from this background. One biographer succinctly noted that "as a convert, he was rather rigorous, over-zealous, and probably unsympathetic to the Irish."[19] The English Protestant background and the years in business must have colored Wood's attitudes, he concluded.

Wood rose rapidly in the hierarchy and in 1857 was made Bishop of Philadelphia. It was a demanding diocese. Not only did the city itself range from the "Main Line" to Philadelphia's own version of "Little Ireland," but the diocese extended northward to include the anthracite fields. Anthracite—"hard" coal—was found, with minor exceptions, only in one part of the United States, the wild region between Pottsville and Scranton, Pennsylvania. Four separate fields extended along the sharp mountains characteristic of this area—the "First" or "Southern" field running through Pottsville; the "Second" or "Mahanoy" field, a little to the north; the "Eastern Middle Basin" in the Hazleton region; and the "Northern Basin" running through the region of Wilkes-Barre and Scranton. The first two, by both their pattern of development and their transportation outlets (south to Philadelphia), had common interests and a common trade name for their coal ("Schuylkill"). The miners in both of these areas thought of themselves as "southern" miners. Generally the miners from the eastern middle basin (trade name "Lehigh") aligned themselves with the northern (trade name "Wyoming") miners. The two "southern" districts were in Bishop Wood's diocese, and remained so after the other anthracite fields were put into newly formed dioceses in 1867. And it was in these two southern districts that the Molly Maguires were to flourish.

Thus the two southern fields, which are mainly in Schuylkill County (see map), are the locale of our story.

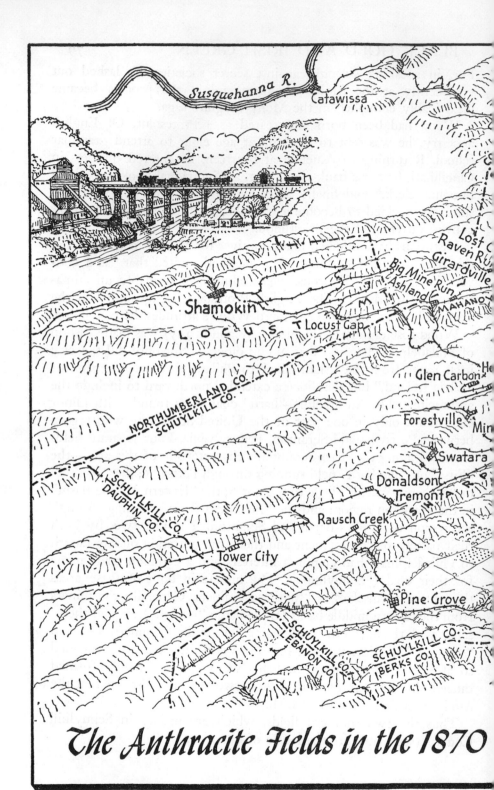

The Anthracite Fields in the 1870

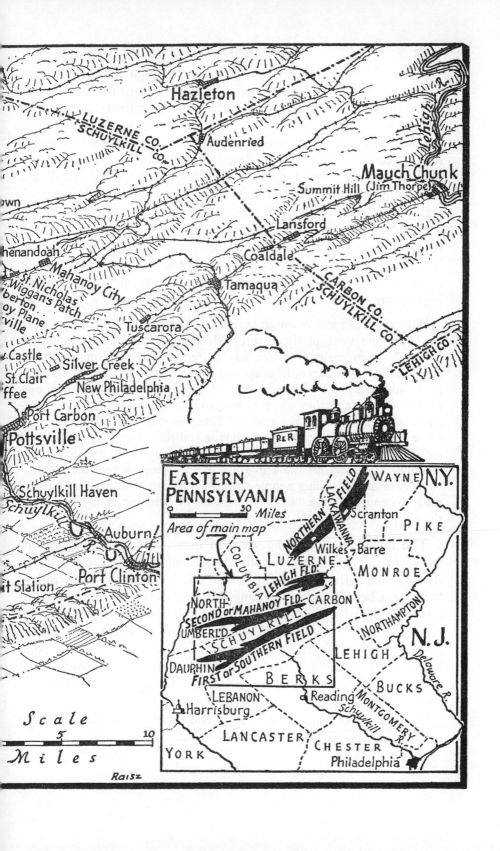

Hazleton

LUZERNE CO.
SCHUYLKILL CO.

Audenried

Mauch Chunk
(Jim Thorpe)

Summit Hill

Lansford

Coaldale

henandoah

Mahanoy City

St. Nicholas
Wiggan's Patch
berton
oy Plane
ville

Tamaqua

CARBON CO.
SCHUYLKILL CO.

LEHIGH CO.

Tuscarora

Castle

Silver Creek

St. Clair
ffee

New Philadelphia

Port Carbon

Pottsville

Schuylkill Haven

Schuylkill

Auburn

Port Clinton

t Station

Scale

5   10

Miles

P&R

EASTERN
PENNSYLVANIA

30   Miles

Area of main map

NORTHERN FIELD

LACKAWANNA

WAYNE   N.Y.

Scranton

PIKE

COLUMBIA

LUZERNE

Wilkes - Barre

MONROE

LEHIGH FLD.

NORTH
SECOND or MAHANOY FLD.

CARBON

UMBERL'D

SCHUYLKILL

NORTHAMPTON

N.J.

DAUPHIN

FIRST or SOUTHERN FIELD

BERKS

LEHIGH

BUCKS

Delaware R.

LEBANON

Harrisburg

Reading

Montgomery

Schuylkill

LANCASTER

CHESTER

Philadelphia

YORK

Raisz

Anthracite had been known for some time, but its extraordinary effectiveness in an open grate was not known until the first decade of the nineteenth century. Combustible qualities proven, it quickly became prized as "Black Gold," just waiting to be dug out of the ground. The whole anthracite region was seized with speculative fever. "Rumors of fortunes made at a blow, and competency secured by a turn of the fingers, come whispering down the Schuylkill and penetrating the city," noted one observer in the 1820's ("the city" was Philadelphia). "The ball gathered strength by rolling," he continued. "Young and old were smitten by the desire to march upon the new Peru, rout the aborigines, and sate themselves with wealth. They had merely to go and play the game boldly to secure their utmost desire."[20] C. K. Yearley, in a recent study, wrote the following account, containing quotations from an 1852 book by Eli Bowen.

Villages spread and towns appeared literally overnight . . . Into these places came a vital, predominantly white population "in no mood for trifling." "Immense crowds" of adventurers, along with an assortment of ex-farmers, townsmen, laborers and clerks, anxious to play their cards right, initiate a "spec of some magnitude" and make their killing: meantime "what though they slept in layers on the sanded floors of Troutman's and Shoemaker's bar rooms." Scruples went by the board; "the grave Quaker, the ejaculating Methodist and the sober Presbyterian" all sat at the same bargaining tables using their ingenuity to outwit one another. Hovering on the fringes of these groups were the miners— "hordes of tartar looking people cohabiting together in shanties or tents" ready to engage in the "laudable business of penetrating the bowels of the earth."[21]

The first mining was the work of local amateurs, who dug out small amounts from outcroppings and shallow shafts. It was clear, though, that anthracite mining was a skilled and demanding business. "We have been bungling, making shift and skimming the surface of our coal field long enough," cried the Pottsville *Miners' Journal* on June 16, 1827, as the editor noted the arrival of the first sixteen English miners "together with suitable picks and shovels." Soon large numbers of skilled English and Welsh miners were flowing into the coal fields, encouraged by the optimistic reports of high wages and great opportunities in America.

The Irish, too, found their way to the Pennsylvania fields in large numbers. There was some tradition of Irish coal mining experience in the Welsh and Scottish mines—very little, though, in Ireland, for the few mines there, mostly in County Kilkenny, were marginal. But mining also had many unskilled jobs to be done. Each miner had one or more laborers assigned to him, and there were other underground workers (mule drivers, railroad operators) and a host of unskilled jobs above ground (pickers and sorters—mostly boys— in the breakers and other outside jobs). The total of these far exceeded the skilled positions.

The Irish were further drawn to the coal fields because the coal "patches" (the small towns that grew around the many mine shafts) gave the sense of close-knit community so desired by the Irish as they came to other lands. This is one of the main reasons why they did not pursue farming very much in the United States. In spite of the fact that eighty per cent had farming backgrounds, only about six per cent settled on farms in the United States. Having very little capital, with only the marginal farming experience of growing potatoes, they were used to the communal life bred by the conacre and cottier system and were fearful of the isolation and loneliness of Western farming. On the other hand, though the Irish recognized that the coal mine was dangerous and the coal patch often depressing, anthracite mining appealed to them.

These mining "patches" were most often on land owned by the coal operator. The miner could build his own home, and pay a modest ground rent to the company. But most miners were in no position to afford this, and were required to rent, either from the company or a local owner. Here the charges were often high. The typical house was a duplex, each side having two rooms down and one up. Generally it was made crudely of hemlock boards, with weather stays over the cracks and no plastering, no ceiling, or wallpaper. A rough bedstead and a table with four chairs, all crudely made by the colliery carpenter, composed the furnishings.

The miner's provisions were obtained in many cases from a company store. This much-maligned institution had its brutal abuses not only in this earlier period but far later in the modern-day coal fields. The miner often had little choice in its use. If the operator decided to run a store himself, and to require trading at this store as a condition of employment, the miner had no other choice than to move away or trade on the operator's terms. Certainly little doubt was left in the miner's mind by the following notice, posted by one Pennsylvania operator:

You will, therefore, please understand, one and all, that from this time henceforth we shall take particular notice who deals at the store and who does not. And as the time is near at hand when we shall reduce the number of our men, just such men as have no account at the store will be dropped, and those who have shown the sense to deal justly will be retained at work so long as it is in our power to keep them. After the spring run is over, and the dry season sets in, it is our purpose to employ from 40 to 50 men at each works, and they will most certainly be selected in the manner we have above noted. We have started this store for our mutual benefit, and we intend to run it; and although our people have not given it that support due from them, after a fair, honest trial, we are now determined that it must be done, and that the store shall receive the patronage of all our employees, without one exception—not through any force or compulsory measure on our part, but only by keeping such men as will do so of their own free will.

(Signed) Joseph Walton & Co.[22]

The practical effect of trading at the store, whether in cash or scrip, was often a ten to twenty per cent reduction in salary. A "bob-tail check," was possible—where the cumulation of rent and the cost of powder, oil, and groceries would add up to the total of wages due, leaving the miner with nothing to show for his work.

But the issue is not clear-cut. Many operators, unable to persuade an independent store operator to come in, were forced into the store business. And there was no guarantee that even if obtainable an independent storekeeper would be scrupulous. The opportunities for taking advantage of an immobile buyer were tempting. The system itself was ripe for exploitation. Thus the miner's appellation—the "pluck me store."

Another pervasive institution of the coal patch was the tavern. Any rough, frontier-type community has its full share of drinking and drunks. But the amount of drinking by the miner is emphasized by observers all through this period. Up until the 1850's liquor was sold at many collieries, but public pressure (especially from miners' wives) finally brought prohibitions there.[23] The dangers of a drunken miner below ground were patently clear to all concerned. But the tavern continued to loom large as a social force, and it figures importantly in the Molly Maguire story.

✤   ✤   ✤   ✤   ✤

If the Irish had harbored any hopes that ethnic tensions had been left back on the shores of Ireland, they were quickly disabused of these notions. The English and Welsh held most of the skilled jobs; the Irish were relegated to the low-status positions. All the past hatreds and slights came welling up again, and the mining patches were quickly divided, physically and socially, along ethnic lines. Soon the Irish turned to protective societies.

As far back as the 1830's these began to make a noticeable impact on the life of Schuylkill County, especially around St. Patrick's Day. In 1832 the Society of St. Patrick, established, according to the Pottsville *Miners' Journal*, "on principles of benevolence and generosity affording relief to suffering countrymen wheresoever exiled,"[24] paraded prominently on the patron saint's day, and, editorialized the writer, "with decorum." He hinted that this had not been true in past years. By 1838 the major group in the county was the Hibernian Benevolent Society of Pottsville. Each succeeding year's St. Patrick's Day parade found the societies more numerous and membership larger. And, it seemed, each year the county held its collective breath until the day was over, hoping that, as editor Benjamin Bannan put it, "the brawling, noisy reveler—who flourished his stick and shouted the name of his patron saint," would not be found too frequently. In 1841 the editor noticed "with pleasure in the procession a *Temperance Banner* with an appropriate inscription. The Temperance Society has completely revolutionized the habits and character of our Irish citizens."[25]

But the Irish societies were often less well-behaved, and fights and brawls were common. In the Irish tradition these were frequently individual or faction fights among themselves, but others were against the age-old antagonists. The English and Welsh miners had their own organizations, and clashes with the Irish were inevitable.

The heavy influx of Irish into the anthracite region from famine-ridden Ireland compounded tensions. What had been a minority ethnic group now became a majority. This brought changes in attitudes toward the Irish, and "native-Americanism" became the fashion here along with the rest of the country. In Schuylkill County, Bannan's *Miners' Journal* began to shift its views, first subtly, then baldly. By the mid-1850's the paper gave wide circulation to anti-Popery blasts and began to feed the fast-rising anti-Irish antipathies in the county. By 1857 the St. Patrick's Day paraders were startled to see an effigy of the saint hung on a telegraph pole with a string of potatoes around its neck. And it was this year that the name Molly Maguire first appeared in print in Schuylkill County.

Benjamin Bannan was one of those who ascribed great political power to the Molly Maguires. He reported that no less than fifty-five indictments had been found by the Grand Jury of Philadelphia against inspectors of the 1856 U.S. presidential election, for frauds in office. Then he asserted:

Every one of these inspectors were Irishmen, belonging no doubt to the order of "Molly Maguires," a secret Roman Catholic association which the Democracy is using for political purposes. The Philadelphia *Transcript* says this Association commenced in Boston and now extends all over the country, controlling all the nominations of the Democratic Party in our cities and in some parts of the country . . .

So powerful and notorious has this Association become, that no less than two Catholic Priests in Philadelphia have called attention to it.

The honest thinking citizens of all parties ought to unite in putting down such a "secret association" as this—and the Democratic press, which has been so horrified at secret "Know-Nothingism" will, of course, lead off in its denunciation.[26]

Rumors persisted throughout the 1840's and 1850's that a secret society was operating in the coal fields. But the first allegations linking the name "Molly Maguires" with terrorism come with the Civil War. Here the relation of the Irish to the Democratic Party becomes important.

Secession placed many Pennsylvanians in an honest dilemma. Southeastern Pennsylvania—Philadelphia in particular—had always been a focal point for interstate trade. Pennsylvania businessmen were fearful of the effects of stopping this trade, and the ties of Pennsylvanians with their southern neighbors were strong enough to bring widespread Copperhead sentiment in the southern part of the state.[27]

The governor, Andrew Curtin, was a Republican, staunchly pro-Union. But the Democrats were strong in many parts of the state, and in general they took a more conciliatory position toward the South. In the coal regions the Democratic Party had come to rely on the Irish miners for support, and party officials found their constituents expressing widespread antagonism toward the war.

The disenchantment of the miner with the war and its attendant difficulties was brought to a head in mid-1862. Before the war was a year old, authorities in Washington realized that voluntary enlistments, even when stimulated by cash bounties, could not keep the army up to necessary strength. Accordingly, Abraham Lincoln and his cabinet introduced an unpalatable step: conscription. In August, Lincoln ordered a draft of 300,000 militiamen. The actual procedures were to be left to each state.

Governor Curtin faced a formidable job in Pennsylvania. If the draft further alienated the conciliatory segment of the population, anarchy could result. Alexander McClure, a colonel in the state militia, was appointed to draft the 17,000 Pennsylvanians requested. In Philadelphia his quota was 3,000. But he could not meet it. The resulting failure had to be covered by trick bookkeeping for fear of the political implications of not enforcing the draft to the letter.[28]

But, to McClure, writing forty years later, this "hesitating, doubting sentiment was not the most to be feared. In several mining districts there were positive indications of revolutionary disloyalty, and it was especially manifested in Schuylkill, where the Molly Maguires were in the zenith of their power."[29]

McClure's doubts about the miners' reaction to the draft were well-founded. Labor all over the country was suspicious of the war, as being "a rich man's war and a poor man's fight." Pushed along by Copperhead propaganda, workingmen began to really believe the insinuations that they were fighting the war "to enable abolitionist Capitalists to transport Negroes into the northern cities to replace workers who were striking for higher wages."[30]

In Schuylkill enlistments were far below expectations. Benjamin Bannan commented, "All through the County these propagandists of mischief have secretly urged men not to go to fight in an abolition war."[31] The Pennsylvania plan called for a census of each household, after which a quota for each county was to be set. The quota could be reduced by a record of substantial previous enlistments. In Schuylkill County, where the commissioner of the draft was Bannan, the census was effected with only moderate trouble. But when the list of conscripts was finally picked on October 16, pent-up feelings exploded.

The plan called for the conscripts to go immediately to the county seat, Pottsville, to entrain for Harrisburg. But large crowds of men quickly gathered and traveled from patch to patch in the county, persuading miners to quit the collieries and join the mob. They first visited a liquor store in Swatara and, at gun point, according to Bannan's paper, "left the proprietor high and dry." After carousing about, they summoned enough nerve to stop a train filled with recruits. "Those who want to go, can," the leaders were quoted as saying, "but we will protect those who don't."[32]

Bannan immediately sent word to Governor Curtin. The governor was terribly upset and excitedly telegraphed Secretary of War Edwin Stanton, asking for armed help. Stanton promptly authorized the use of the regular force "and any other military force in your State." But Curtin soon found that persuading the preoccupied field commanders to relinquish battle troops for an internal police action was more easily discussed than accomplished. He again took his troubles to Stanton: "Major Ward telegraphs me that he is ordered to Kentucky . . . We all think that the resistance to draft is the first appearance of a conspiracy, and, unless crushed at once, cannot say how far it may extend. We know there are 5,000 men in the league in three counties, and all work is interrupted by them. I do not wish to magnify, and hope I am not alarmed . . . With 1,000 men, who have been in actual service, with our force, we can put it down." By now Stanton became alarmed himself, and hurriedly took the problem to Lincoln. Both the President and his Secretary realized the implications of insurrection, and Stanton's reply to Curtin mirrored the consternation: " Your telegram of this date has been submitted to the President and General-in-Chief. The General Government will exert all the means at its command to support you. The Anderson Cavalry will be retained for your service. The regulars cannot be taken from General McClellan's army, but one or two regiments that have served through the war can be sent from here upon your requisition. General Wool has been ordered to confer with and aid you."[33]

Governor Curtin apparently lost his nerve at this point and telegraphed Lincoln, giving his views of the peril of provoking the rioters. The next day, according to Colonel McClure's later account, the President sent a message that he "was desirous to see the law executed, or to at least to appear to have been executed." McClure immediately got in touch with Bannan. "Lincoln's message was well understood," McClure relates. "Bannan was most desirous for a peaceful solution of the problem, and he said that the draft could not be executed in Cass Township without a bloody conflict with the Molly Maguires, and he could conceive of no method by which there could be given the appearance of executing the law. I told him that there was but one way in which it could be done; that several districts in the State had shown conclusively that their quota had been entirely filled by volunteers, some of whom had enlisted in county towns or in the cities and had not been properly credited to the township as the law required. Where the facts were made clear I had at once revoked the order for the draft, and I said that only in that way could the Cass Township problem be solved if it were practicable."[34]

On the following evening Bannan was back in Harrisburg with a large number of affidavits executed before a justice of the peace proving on their face that the quota of Cass Township had been filled by volunteers, chiefly by men connected with the mines who had enlisted from the towns where regiments were being formed. The affidavits were carefully tabulated and they made the quota of Cass Township entirely full. "They were undisputed," McClure continued, "and I at once issued the order releasing the conscripts of Cass Township from reporting for duty because the quota had been filled with volunteers. Commissioner Bannan did not proffer any explanation as to how the affidavits had been obtained, nor did the Governor or myself make any inquiry." The law appeared to be executed, although the affidavits were fictitious. "But it was an imperious necessity to avoid a conflict between the Molly Maguires and the troops," concluded McClure. The troops were at once ordered back from Pottsville.[35]

McClure and Bannan had a powerful assist from Philadelphia. Bishop Wood made a special trip to Pottsville during this week of unrest, meeting with the priests in the patches and with some of the miners. Bannan commented, "he taught them their duty under the laws, as good citizens," and Curtin reported to Stanton that "the presence of Bishop Wood, who kindly went up when requested, has relieved us all."[36]

And the fact was lost on no one that the great majority of the rioters were Irish. Several papers back in Ireland made pointed reference to the coal field disturbances; the influential *Cork Examiner* put it bluntly:

Our countrymen have played the part of the dwarf in this war, to the giant—the native Americans—the Know nothings—the abolitionists. They have fought the battles, got the blows, and bear the wounds while their companions receive the glory and the plunder. For the latter are the colonelcies and the generalships, the army contracts, and all the other sources of honor and profit to which a great war opens to the unscrupulous. Our countrymen seem to be getting tired of this state of things. In Lauserne [Luzerne] County, Pennsylvania, a number of them resisted the draft. The military . . . shot four or five. The effect of this tragical incident . . . should be an opening of the eyes of our countrymen to the recklessness of the faction for whose interests they are flinging away their lives.[37]

This was a garbled account—the disturbance was not in Luzerne County and the military did not shoot four or five—but it accurately reflects the attitude of many Irishmen toward the Civil War and conditions in the coal fields.

✽   ✽   ✽   ✽   ✽

If rebellion was not carried to fruition in the 1862 draft disturbances, other events of a more local nature came closer. The early war years produced violence in the coal fields on an unprecedented scale, with the undercurrent of Molly Maguire terrorism woven through it. If the actual existence of the society could not yet be proven, the legend was mushrooming by the day.

Though later writers with benefit of hindsight attributed to the Mollies a dozen or more murders in the coal fields in the 1860–1862 period, the first case actually figuring in later Molly trials occurred in June 1862. And at that time it was not linked directly to the feared secret society.

The scene was Carbon County, which lies immediately northeast of Schuylkill. At a public meeting held in Audenried to prepare for the 1862 Fourth of July celebration, a group of miners began expressing Copperhead sentiments. A young miner, John Kehoe, allegedly let his antipathy push him into spitting on the American flag. F. W. Langdon, a mine foreman, then denounced the dissident miners. Kehoe in turn (it was later alleged in court) snapped "You son of a bitch, I'll kill you." [38] Other miners with Kehoe echoed the threat. As soon as Langdon was isolated from his friends, he was attacked and severely stoned. He died the next day.

Langdon was alleged to have been unpopular with the miners— his job included the hated task of checking miners' coal loads to determine if the refuse content was too high. The motive for the crime was probably simple revenge. At any rate it remained unsolved and later provided a dramatic highlight in the Molly Maguire trials.

Meanwhile resistance to the draft continued, and in July 1863 it took on an ominous new dimension. By this time state conscription had miserably failed, and Congress, in March, had passed a national Conscription Act. In New York City, the first day of conscription, July 13, was a signal for revolt, and for five days the city was besieged by armed mobs. Conscription offices were destroyed, the mayor's residence attacked. Venting their fury not only on Unionists but on the Negro, the mob pillaged, burned, raped, and killed. Not until troops had raked the streets with cannon was order restored. The number of rioters killed in the bloody week was variously estimated to be from 400 to 2000; the exact number could never be known, for the rioters retrieved their dead at night and buried them secretly in the backyards of slum rookeries.[39]

Because of the New York riots, draft authorities all over the country were apprehensive. General William Whipple, in charge of Schuylkill County affairs, had a particular right to be uneasy. For the antagonisms of the previous fall appeared ready to break again into the open. His first report to Washington, on July 23, 1863, outlined his plight:

First, the miners of Cass Township, near Pottsville, have organized to resist the draft, to the number of 2,500 or 3,000 armed men.

Second, they drill every evening, and are commanded by returned nine-months' men and discharged three-years' men.

Third, it is positively known that they have two pieces of light artillery, and it is rumored that they have seven.

Fourth, they threatened to burn down the houses and coal breakers owned by Republicans. They have served cautionary notices upon three citizens, Messrs. Bannon [sic], Robert Morris and another.

Fifth, the U.S. force, commanded by Major Dayton, is stationed at Pottsville, and consists of two companies of the Invalid Corps. Three days ago the force had only twenty rounds of ammunition.[40]

Whipple pleaded that the draft be suspended in Schuylkill, or that a large contingent of federal troops be assigned if conscription was to be enforced.

The Provost-Marshal-General in Washington, James Fry, instructed Whipple not to try to force the issue. Additional troops were soon sent, under a charge from Fry that "if the miners resist the law forcibly, I hope you will make a severe example among them." General D. N. Couch, leading the new forces, reported, "You may be assured that sending troops to Pottsville and Scranton has had a good effect." He said "the ignorant miners have no fear of God, the State authority, or the devil. The Democratic leaders have not the power of burnt flax over them for good. A strong military power under the General Government alone keeps matters quiet."[41]

Couch began enforcing the draft in what he termed "the very worst districts" with outward success. But the fear of an uprising remained. When asked if he could safely withdraw, Couch replied strongly in the negative—"Order off these, you may have Pottsville laid in ashes and a thousand barbarities committed . . . "[42] Finally, in late August, the draft was completed and the forces withdrawn. But hatred among the miners was fanned by the peremptory handling of the affair.

The hatred soon spilled forth in new violence. On the night of November 5, 1863, again at Audenried in Carbon County, an armed band of men with blackened faces invaded the home of George K. Smith, a mine owner and operator, and in full view of his family and an employee, killed him instantly with a ball through the head. Smith was generally considered a fair employer but a hard taskmaster. Further, he had let his sympathies on the draft be known. Just a few weeks before he had entertained a group of soldiers in the area to enforce conscription. Several men were arrested for the shooting but were forcibly released several days later when the sheriff was accosted by a large mob of miners. No trial was held— thereby saving the whole case for a date fourteen years later when the killing would be linked with the Molly Maguires.[43]

This was the high point in a pattern of widespread violence—for there had been three other murders in the Audenreid area alone in a five-week period. The officials were grim. The Pottsville officer in charge of the militia, Captain C. Tower, when learning of the Smith killing, immediately dispatched a long, rambling letter to Washington, suggesting that "the flag of the United States should be raised at once on the house of Smith, and a sufficient force be quartered there to keep it flying and overawe all the rebels." One of Pottsville's eminent citizens, General Charles Albright, even penned a letter directly to Abraham Lincoln.[44]

A month after the Smith murder, violence in Cass Township erupted again with a series of beatings and wild shootings, caused, according to Benjamin Bannan, by "some Buckshots not having work enough in Cass to employ their time."[45] ("Buckshots" was an alternate name for the Molly Maguires.)

At this point, in January 1864, Bishop Wood again intervened. His visit the previous year had apparently not been enough; now he would use a bigger stick. He composed a pastoral letter, and required it to be read from the pulpit of every church in his diocese. His theme was secret societies. "It is a fact too well known to need any proof at this day, that the Catholic Church, through her revered Head, the Sovereign Pontiff, has again and again censured all secret societies." Yet "most insidious efforts have been, and are being made, in many parts of our Diocese" to entangle unsuspecting parishioners "in the meshes and shackles of these unlawful and forbidden societies." Not only the Masons, Odd Fellows, and the Sons of Temperance, "about whose condemnation no doubt can exist," but also new organizations must be prohibited. The National Brotherhood and the Fenian Brotherhood must now be added.

"And, in addition to these," Wood concluded, "the Molly Maguires, Buckshots and others" must be condemned. He said their "spirit is equally objectionable" and their names "seem to be selected rather to conceal than to indicate the object of their association."[46]

✽ ✽ ✽ ✽ ✽

With the release of pent-up wartime tensions after Appomatox, the anthracite fields were again shocked by violence and murder.

David Muir, a Schuylkill County mine superintendent, was ambushed in broad daylight two hundred yards from his office on August 25, 1865. Early the following year the murder of Henry H. Dunne, a prominent Pottsville mine superintendent, outraged the populace. A ground swell of public indignation led to efforts to bring more rigorous law enforcement. Bannan was particularly critical of the local law enforcement, and advocated aid from the state: "The curse of Schuylkill County is miserable, inefficient officials, who are either afraid to, or do not know how to discharge their duties. The fact is that we must turn from the imbeciles here to the state for protection from the bands of secret assassins that infest the County."[47]

In this one county the first three months of 1867 brought five additional murders, six assaults, and twenty-seven robberies. The *Miners' Journal* reported further that there had been fourteen murders in 1863, fourteen in 1864, twelve in 1865, and six in 1866—all unsolved.[48] Public feeling was finally pushed to a fever pitch after the killing of a popular superintendent, William Littlehales, on March 15, 1867. The motive was clearly robbery, for Littlehales carried the payroll funds out to the mine each week. But the attendant circumstances provided enough pathos for everyone in the region to wallow in grief and hand-wringing. Just two weeks before, Littlehales' young son had fallen under a railroad car and lost a leg by amputation. In Bannan's words, "the scene at the house of Mr. Littlehales on the evening of that fatal day was most distressing. On one bed lay the mutilated child, on another Mrs. Littlehales in a hysterical condition from the terrible shock of the murder, and on a third the disfigured corpse of the murdered husband and father. It was a sight to touch the hardest nature, and to bring tears to the eyes albeit unused to the melting mood."[49]

The aroused citizens appealed to Harrisburg for relief, and a "Court, Police and Jury Act" was passed by the state legislature.[50] A new court district was set up to include Schuylkill and three adjacent counties, two new jury commissioners were provided, and, more important, a Marshal of Police was appointed (by the Governor) to head a force of police up to a limit of one hundred men. Whether for this or other reasons, violent crime decreased remarkably in the late 1860's.

The Molly Maguire legend, however, was firmly planted in the minds of the people. Not one of the crimes had been solved; not one person was publicly linked to the feared secret organization. No one yet knew if such an organization actually existed, or, if it did, what its purposes and functions were. But few in the region could have been convinced that the whole story was a myth—a fabrication. There were too many murdered men already in their coffins.

* * * * *

Coal mining was a "boom and bust" industry. Civil War needs, for example, pushed anthracite production to all-time highs. Army enlistments by miners and reduced immigration soon dried up the pool of underemployed and brought a sellers' market for mine labor. Mining wages soared spectacularly. One historian commented, "The anthracite laborers, who at the beginning of the decade were as poorly paid as any in the United States, had become [by 1864] perhaps the best paid."[51] But, with the return of peace, the stoppages of iron work and the general stagnation of business caused coal demand to fall sharply. Prices dipped to ruinous depths; wages were dragged down with them. Laid-off miners were augmented by hordes of war-weary veterans returning to the fields. And those who were still at work resentfully tried to make both ends meet on their dwindling pay.[52]

With the market glutted in late 1867, the operators held a mass meeting to discuss possible wage cuts. Though many of the operators refused to cooperate—the coal fields were characterized by extreme individualism—those in the area of St. Clair, in Schuylkill County a few miles north of Pottsville, decided upon a ten per cent cut at the Eagle Colliery as a trial balloon. The four hundred miners retaliated in January 1868 by striking. The operators couldn't afford to allow their competitors to continue to sell, and rescinded the cut.

It was a small strike, but it produced two important results. First, a new coal union was founded in April—"The Workingmen's Benevolent Association of St. Clair." Second, a new leader emerged —John Siney. Both were destined to play major roles in the Molly Maguire story.

There had been earlier unions in the coal fields. Boatmen on the Schuylkill River and its canal, transporting coal to Philadelphia, formed an ominous-sounding "Committee of Vigilance" and struck in 1835. After what the *Miners' Journal* editor, Benjamin Bannan, called "a reign of terror" (but which consisted mainly of a few peltings of strikebreaker boats with rotten eggs and stones), the group disbanded.[53]

Now the miners tried organization and struck in 1842 when a Minersville group protested being paid in scrip redeemable only at the company store. This time roving bands of strikers beat "black legs" (strikebreakers), and posted coffin notices at mine breakers where men refused to join the strike. But the operators held out and the strike was lost. Bannan probably mirrored the feelings of the townspeople of the region (as opposed to the miners) when he commented, "we are pleased to learn that the operators generally manifest a disposition not to employ any who took a prominent part in the late difficulties."[54] It was a harbinger of later, widespread black-listing for union activity.

In 1849 a union led by an Englishman named John Bates also struck over the company-store issue, and again had little success. By this time, though, Bannan did admit that the men had a right to strike "if the movements go no further than an honest, prudent effort to better their conditions."[55] But the notion that a committee should be allowed to speak for the miners—perhaps even tell the miners whether or not they could go back to work—still rankled Bannan: "It would be better to let all our Collieries *rot* and our region become wilderness than such tyranny should be engrafted on the business of this region by a few restless spirits." He said that if the operators were to give in, "they had better emigrate to Russia as suitable materials for making good serfs under that despotic government."[56] With this attitude predominating, John Siney's success with the Workingmen's Benevolent Association in the Eagle Colliery strike is more noteworthy.

Siney's qualifications hardly made him an expert on mining.[57] Born in Ireland but reared mainly in England, he had miners in his family but he was a cotton spinner (from age seven). After losing his job in an English mill, he briefly worked in a brickyard, organizing a small local union and becoming its first president. In 1862, when this job, too, went sour, he migrated to St. Clair, Pennsylvania, to work as a miner on contract. Illiterate and relatively inexperienced, he was hardly a candidate for leadership in the rough-and-tumble coal fields. When quizzed at a later state investigation as to whether mining was his trade, he replied, "No, I have no trade."[58] How, then, could such an unlikely candidate achieve the reputation he later did?

Part of the answer lay in Siney's background. His father, Patrick, when an Irish tenant farmer, had become widely known as a rebel—openly against the landlord and the English. His dissidence became so pronounced that he was finally evicted from his land in 1835, and it was this that brought about the family's emigration to Wigan, in Lancashire. John was then just six years old. When he went into the textile mill, several of his brothers began working in the Lancashire coal mines, at the time when Lord Ashley's Parliamentary Inquiry chronicled the miserable conditions in the English coal industry. Wigan was highlighted in the report. And Siney also witnessed the intense militancy of the Lancashire cotton spinners, which was later to become world-famous.

In Pennsylvania, Siney soon consolidated the gains he made in the Eagle Colliery strike of 1868. In June of the same year he spearheaded a county-wide strike in Schuylkill to hold total wages firm in the face of a cut in hours. But Siney's success in persuading Schuylkill County miners to turn out was not enough. If strikes were to be effective, *all* anthracite miners should go out. Here an important facet in the make-up of the anthracite region intrudes.

As the southern strikers moved in bands into the northern Wyoming Valley fields, they found decreasing cooperation. Mechanics and miners in the Wilkes-Barre area turned out, but a large delegation from Carbon and Schuylkill Counties, numbering several hundred, had little influence on the Luzerne County miners in the Scranton fields. Unless the northern fields joined, the strike was doomed. The northern miners remembered that the southern group had failed to support them in a local strike in 1865; now the tables were turned.

Excesses by the roving bands as they moved up the fields complicated the picture. "Contributions" of food and drink were exacted from farms, stores, and taverns. Finally, the southern strike leaders were forced to send money northward as restitution and eventually to send men after the more vociferous of the travelers to force them to return.[59]

Failure to persuade the northern miners to join broke the strike. By late August the men were back at work. But the attempt had two results: The chronic glut was at least temporarily brought under control; and area-wide unionism was at least a glimmering hope. While the strike was still in progress a mass meeting of all the miners and laborers in Schuylkill County was called at Mahanoy City. The turnout dumbfounded all; the number was estimated at from twelve to twenty thousand. Siney was elected president, and the charter of the Workingmen's Benevolent Association—the W.B.A.—was amended to extend to the entire county.[60]

Through the fall of 1868 Siney vigorously organized with good success in Schuylkill County—and no success in the northern fields. To a derogatory article by the editor of the *Scranton Morning Republican,* Siney replied, "He must have based his information on something he has read in times gone by about 'Molly McGuires,' 'Buckshots' etc. etc. never once giving us the credit that our Association is not yet nine months old; and further that it is not responsible for the action of the whole community. By the rules of the Association all acts of violence are strictly prohibited."[61] Siney promised that the W.B.A. kept "strict adherence to social law and order," but the preachments appeared to have little effect. Not only the Philadelphia papers but large sections of the coal regions began to associate the W.B.A. with the still-unknown and feared secret society. Their inability to distinguish between the two would increasingly haunt Siney and his aides in the future.

There were solidly grounded reasons for the antipathy between the northern region (the "Wyoming" and "Lehigh" fields) and the southern region (the "Southern" and "Mahanoy" fields). Both regions mined and marketed anthracite coal, but there the similarities ceased. The southern region was characterized at this time by a large number of individual operators, each competitive in the labor market and sales field with all others. Although in November 1869 most of these operators banded together in an employers' organization—the Anthracite Board of Trade—even this did not bring unity. The northern region, by contrast, was dominated by large operators. The history of the Wyoming field was heavily intertwined with the history of its two transportation kings, the Delaware & Hudson Canal and the Delaware, Lackawanna & Western Railroad. Both had outlets east to New York City, a tremendous advantage over the Philadelphia & Reading Railroad and the Schuylkill Canal companies of the southern region, whose outlets were only south to Philadelphia. The middle "Lehigh" field around Hazleton was even more fortuitously situated, for the Lehigh Valley Railroad had outlets to both Philadelphia and New York City, as did the Lehigh Coal & Navigation Company's canal.[62]

But the differences were not in marketing alone. More important for Siney and the union was the pattern of ownership of the coal lands. Three of the four transportation companies in the middle and northern fields already owned vast tracts of coal land and were the dominant operators there. The fourth, the Lehigh Valley Railroad, had just begun buying up land in self defense, since the other three companies were expanding their holdings so rapidly in the postwar period that it seemed there might soon be no independent operators left to ship their product over the Lehigh.

These four companies, together with a fifth important anthracite operator, the Pennsylvania Coal Company, of Pittston, set the pattern of working conditions in the middle and northern fields—the northern region. Their labor policy was the acme of absolutism. Brooking no interference on the part of their employees, they set wages according to a sliding scale based on the selling price of coal. Wages were advanced a specified percentage when the price of coal on board vessels at Elizabeth Port, New Jersey, increased, and were reduced when those prices fell.[63] Unions were not tolerated.

Indefatigably Siney tried to meld the dissident voices of the various regions. Late in March 1869 a convention was held in Hazleton and a "General Council" was organized—on paper. Delegates came from all the anthracite counties, and it was agreed that subsequent representation was to allow one delegate per one thousand miners. All agreed, for the moment, that whenever four counties voted a work suspension, *all* the counties would suspend as one.[64] The promise of unity was there, but what of the reality?

Siney soon learned the answer to this question. Glutting continued, and the limited economic reasoning of the union officials called for only one course. On May 1, the W.B.A. announced that as of May 10 all districts would suspend.

A war of nerves began. The idea of a suspension to correct a market imbalance was not in principle foreign to the operators. Often they had resorted to just such a strategy to maintain profits. Many of the southern operators at this time even tacitly agreed with Siney's plan. But they were also convinced that the rampant individualism within their own ranks would not allow any employer unity at this time.[65] Better to let the miners do it for them.

The individual miner also had his misgivings. How nice it would be to let the other fellow walk out in order to reduce total supply, but for *him* to stay on the job drawing a paycheck. And the individual operator—thinking to himself—came to the same conclusion. "Let George do it!"

Personal selfishness won handily. Important segments of the northern miners—abetted, probably, by the companies—dragged their feet on the suspension. A Scranton union official pleaded, "We are not strong enough yet. We are not satisfied that Schuylkill will do the fair thing with us . . . Suppose we suspend and Schuylkill obtains their Basis, are they going to share their money to help us live?"[66] While piously going on record for unity, they voted to "delay" their own suspension.

Other issues besides the glut became enmeshed in the case. The union from the start demanded a minimum wage. The miners wanted a floor on the selling price of coal at the ports, below which the operators would automatically suspend, and they wanted a minimum wage to be established in accordance with this "basis" price. In effect, it was the equivalent of the modern-day "escalator clause," with a floor on downward movement.

Unexpectedly acting together, the southern operators now embraced the concept of the sliding scale. But they would not agree to a minimum. They proposed that the price of coal at Port Carbon (just outside Pottsville) be used as a base; when coal sold there at three dollars a ton the men would receive their base pay. This base pay varied according to difficulty in mining, and whether the miner worked on day work or piece (contract) work. Most were on piece work, receiving a stated amount for a wagon loaded with coal or for a cubic yard dug. From this pay were deducted the wages of the laborer (his loader and helper) and charges for powder and oil used. The sliding scale then provided that these wages would be advanced—for each price advance of twenty-five cents per ton at Port Carbon, an advance of fifty cents per week for day workers and five cents per wagon, with cubic yardage rates in proportion. Similar reductions were to be made as prices fell.[67]

Siney carried the proposal back to the Schuylkill County miners, and after bitter discussion it was accepted.

So the first "General Suspension" ended without gaining support throughout all the region; the northern miners remained uninterested in unity. Chortled one northern-district paper, "The Lackawanna companies can grow rich on a fair basis and starve and bury Schuylkill while doing it. To be sure, there is something rather savage to such vengeance, smacking of fire, faggot and scalping knife, but it is human nature, in corporate bodies, and of course it will be done . . . The Lion and the Bear fought for a carcass until both were exhausted when the Fox slipped in and carried it off unchecked."[68]

Chapter 5 • Gowen Declares War

A NEW CHARACTER now enters the story. And both in union-employer relations and the Molly Maguire saga he will be the most important influence of all. This man is Franklin Benjamin Gowen, the newly elected president of the Philadelphia & Reading Railroad.

If, in 1828, the Schuylkill area "was in a state of nature, and afforded retreats for panthers, wolves, bears, deer and other animals,"[1] within a few years the influx of men drawn by high speculative profits from coal mining must have scared away some of the more timid of these animals. By 1842 the region was sending half a million tons of coal south to Philadelphia, all by the Schuylkill Canal. A number of local railroads—of varying capacities, states of repair, and even gauges— had honeycombed the area. But in January 1842, the canal's exit monopoly was rudely torn asunder with the opening of the Philadelphia & Reading Railroad from Pottsville to Philadelphia. The canal's tonnage soon stabilized at about a million tons, but the railroad passed this in 1844, and by 1855 had hit two million.

The Reading (as it was popularly called, and as it now is officially named) was technically efficient and had marketing strengths, but these blessings were not matched by profitability. The company's credit was poor, since it was well-known that the cost of the road had exceeded the original estimate several times over, and its ability to earn fixed charges on the watered capital was not yet demonstrated.

The history of the Reading's early financial tribulations and shenanigans are too doleful and drawn-out to hold us long here. In the 1848–1850 period, the railroad almost incurred complete disaster but was bailed out by a combination of manipulation of the capital accounts and improvement in business conditions. One of the side effects of this brink of danger, though, was a pooling agreement with the canal in 1849, the first such formal transportation pool in the country, according to one authority.[2]

A bit more conservatism in both operation and finance in the early and middle 1850's kept the company in the black, and now expansion was financed in spite of high dividends. But the Panic of 1857 slowed all of this down and the railroad headed into the 1860's in fiscal peril again.

Up to this time the company had depended largely on privately owned feeder lines within the fields. (It owned only one of the five key lines.) As long as these short lines remained independent, there was always the danger that traffic might be stolen away by another line—and there had been persistent rumors that such outside competition might come in. A new management entered with the election of Charles E. Smith as president of the line in 1861. And with the new management came a new policy of securing by lease or purchase the control of the lateral roads.[3] Smith soon involved several reluctant feeders, as well as the canal, in a tonnage war. By 1863 the canal had capitulated—the Reading leasing its key feeder. According to one historian, "it made the Reading dominant in the Schuylkill field, and the canal was never again considered a serious competitor."[4] (The Reading finally absorbed the canal in 1874—not because of its competition, but merely to eliminate it as a rate-cutter.)

The Reading made enormous profits in the closing years of the Civil War, but, according to Benjamin Bannan, did not pass any of this prosperity to the coal operator. This was a gross oversimplification—mining profits had always been heavy in prosperous periods, and had, in fact, led to the chronic overproduction characteristic of the whole anthracite region. However, there were seeds of truth in Bannan's accusations, for the transporter held a whip hand by the nature of the pattern of business organization in the southern region. The coal-carrying segment of the railroad had consistently shown an extraordinary spread between railroad cost and the rate paid by the operator, with commensurate windfall profits to the railroad. The profits from merchandise and passenger traffic alone were by this time sufficient to pay the interest and sinking fund on the debt, leaving the large earnings from the coal traffic for dividends.

Perhaps this pay-out would not have rankled Bannan and others in the district if substantial amounts of stock had been held within the district itself. But almost all was held by "absentee owners." Worse yet, the biggest of these blocks—a controlling interest, in fact—was held by a firm of British financiers, McCalmont Brothers,

& Company. All the insular spleen that Bannan heaped on the "outsiders" in nearby Philadelphia was doubly vented on these truly foreign interests. More dispassionate analysts have minimized the influence brought to bear by the McCalmonts, particularly after Smith took over.[5] But the notion of passing windfall profits—presumably extracted from the region's pockets—to Englishmen three thousand miles away was galling.

As long as there was prosperity, mutterings were carried no further. However, when depression struck in the chaotic period immediately following the Civil War, the bitterness of the region toward the Reading exploded. Bannan—as the self-styled spokesman for the region—reiterated, over and over, that "so long as the monopoly remains, the power to 'turn the screws' exists and while the 'English Bankers' control this power, we are simply the geese which lay the golden eggs, and may at any time experience the sad fate of our celebrated prototype. Monopolists are always extortionists."[6]

The cumulative effect of these attacks led Smith to take a "leave of absence" on April 28, 1869, because of ill health, and he left for an extended vacation in Europe. His successor was Gowen.

Franklin Benjamin Gowen was just thirty-three years old when this awesome responsibility fell upon his shoulders. But into this short number of years he had already crowded several careers.

Gowen was of Irish descent. His father, James Gowen, had migrated to Philadelphia in the pecuniary state of most from Ireland—penniless. But the immigrant's profession of weaving got him a start, and his forays into groceries, wine and liquor made him a wealthy man. An Episcopalian, he nevertheless was intensely interested in the Irish immigrants, who were predominantly Catholic, and he served for years on prominent posts in the Philadelphia Hibernian Society for the Relief of Emigrants from Ireland. Further, he was a Democrat.

Franklin, his fifth child, who was born in Philadelphia in 1836, must have been profoundly influenced by this "hot-tempered, domineering old Irishman" (as Gowen's biographer put it),[7] and undoubtedly influenced, too, by his stint in school—at the famous John Beck's Boys' Academy. Here came the sons of Virginia planters, Lancaster County iron masters, Philadelphia bankers. Most of the first families of eastern Pennsylvania were represented on the rolls of the academy. Gowen learned rapidly under the strict discipline and rich curriculum. Here he developed his facility with figures, his familiarity with history, and his beautiful, flowing penmanship. And a bit of the patrician probably rubbed off from his fellow students. But when Frank reached age thirteen, his father concluded that such training would suffice and sent his son out into the business world—with a Lancaster County merchant.

Gowen's ambition would not long stand still for the mundane tasks of measuring muslin, weighing vegetables, and deferring to picky housewives. He first joined with his older brother, Thomas, in a coal retailing company at Shamokin, and in 1858 went into a partnership in a coal mine at Mt. Laffee, just north of Pottsville. The year was a poor one for mining, and by 1859 Gowen had to dissolve the company, with the sheriff selling off all the property. Gowen learned a bitter business lesson.

He was an incurable optimist, though, and was soon launched on a new career—the law. Two older brothers already had become barristers. After reading law during the winter of 1859–60 in a Pottsville lawyer's office, he was admitted to the Schuylkill County bar just a few months later.

Here was a career cut out for him. The law training had been short but the concomitant histrionic needs of the new job were not. Gowen had already exhibited that brand of gusto and flowery speech so prized by the nineteenth-century barrister. When he had first come to Pottsville he and his brother had taken active roles in forming the Pottsville Literary Society; at its first meeting he had recited Poe's *Raven* "effectively and with a just appreciation of the author's sentiments."[8] He had followed this with a lecture on "The Triumphs of Genius" at the second meeting, and at the third was a resounding success on the negative side of a debate, "Was the execution of Charles I justified?" By 1859 he was popular enough to be elected to the presidency of the Society. His inaugural address inspired the usually critical Bannan to some flowery words of his own: "Touching and truthful, at times his remarks revived associations, mournful as when the wind sweeps over the aeolian lyre, starting amid the dirge-like music, the involuntary tear, anon depicting with a masterly hand, local pictures." The fledgling lawyer drew upon this reservoir of rhetoric for a speech he was asked to give for the July 4th celebration in 1861. Bannan reprinted the speech in full, commenting that it was "a chaste and eloquent address—sparkling with beautiful sentiment and classical references."[9]

A closer examination of this "beautiful sentiment," however, discloses some rather harsh words, even for that emotional year. In Gowen's denunciation of the men of the Confederacy might be detected a note of sanctimony and self-righteousness, not uncommon during this period. He exclaimed, "How much cause of thankfulness have we in comparing our condition with that of the people now suffering under the baleful influence of those misguided men who 'would rather rule in Hell than serve in Heaven.'" He said these men had "forfeited all claim to a share of our common inheritance of glory: and as if aware of their degeneracy and exulting in their degradation, the legislatures of some of their States have stricken the Anniversary of the Declaration of Independence from the list of national holidays."

Bannan's enchantment soon disappeared. In 1862, Gowen, now twenty-six, was nominated for the job of Schuylkill County district attorney on the Democratic ticket. The editor, now county chairman of the Republicans, pulled all stops out in his efforts to defeat the opposition party. The Democrats were considerably more pro-South than their opponents; Bannan blew this up into a real Donnybrook. Calling the opponents the "Pro-Slavery" ticket, he vented all of his regional and political partisanship against the Democratic ticket. To be sure, Bannan was kinder to Gowen personally, calling him "a young gentleman of ability, without experience and in bad company."[10]

But the "bad company" prevailed, and the entire Democratic ticket won a resounding victory at the polls. Gowen ran ahead of all but one member of the ticket. He served as district attorney for two years, resigning in November 1864 to devote full time to his expanding private law practice. What was his success as district attorney? The answer—little—is an important additional clue to Gowen's actions later in the Molly Maguire incidents.

The assaults and murders of the 1862–1864 period, during the draft riots and labor troubles, were punishable crimes. But in the overwhelming majority of cases no one was prosecuted. Few arrests were made. There were no convictions for major crimes throughout Gowen's term. How can we explain Gowen's lack of diligence?

One of the strongest influences must have been the fact that the Democratic officeholders were elected primarily by the Irish vote.

And the Irish were heavily involved in most of the crimes. The party simply could not afford to offend its own constituents.

Bannan, always ready to blame the Democrats for any ills in the county, attributed the lawlessness in this period largely to failings in prosecution. After a killing—unsolved—in October 1864, he railed, "thus is another life sacrificed in accordance with the teachings of the Copperhead leaders." He wrote that "the murders will probably go unwhipt of justice, as many here have gone heretofore," and that "this is society in Schuylkill County under Democratic rule."[11]

Before painting Gowen too heavily with the brush of opportunism, we must consider the difficulties faced by any law enforcement officer at this time. With much of the crime centered within the Irish groups, the age-old desire to protect members of the clan came into play. The fact that false swearing for alibis was perjury was little or no deterrent, and any accused Irishman could depend on his friends for whatever testimony was needed to absolve him. Coupled with this was a marked reluctance on the part of the populace to testify against an Irishman for fear of reprisal. Already the name "Molly Maguire" struck fear in the hearts of many—an unreasoning fear that stopped not to ask whether there was in fact such a secret society. There were enough instances of coffin notices, mob action, and ambushes to give a ring of truth to such allegations.

Gowen, then, showed a singular lack of diligence in his term as district attorney. Whether this was due to a lack of fortitude, to political expediency, or to plain neglect we cannot fully determine. But later events will give partial answers.

❧ ❧ ❧ ❧ ❧

Soon after Gowen gave up politics he managed to make a fortuitous connection—an appointment as head of the legal department of the Reading Railroad. He moved back to Philadelphia to take up this new career.

His success at protecting the legal rights of the railroad was as good as the times allowed. The railroads were fighting not only each other but the public as well, for the cry of monopoly was getting stronger. Gowen won his biggest case in 1866, when the Reading and the Pennsylvania Railroad were litigants over certain east-west connections. Appearing before the Supreme Court of the state, Gowen employed all his talents to put forth a brilliant performance. Drawing upon not only legal citations but maps, humorous stories, classical quotations, and even a toy train exhibit, he charmed the justices and the case was tipped to the Reading. The Reading's management was so impressed that they had the speech printed for distribution to the public.

There were a number of reasons why Gowen was a logical choice as president to replace the embattled Smith in 1869. Gowen combined legal skill with knowledge of railroad finances—he had been boning up on the Reading's over-all problems for several years. He was a man of good appearance and commanding presence; his considerable charms at rhetoric might well be quite handy in dealing with unimpressed stockholders. And, equally important, he was a former Pottsville resident, friend of the Irish, a well-known local booster. Even Bannan had acknowledged grudgingly that he was a smart man. And if Bannan's vitriol could be contained, so much the better for relations of the railroad in the coal regions.

For the railroad a serious problem still remained—Mr. Siney's union and its resistance to the mine operators' desire for a wage cut. It was not long before Gowen and Siney began to match wits.

By late 1869, retail coal prices had fallen to $2.89 a ton. The operators argued for a wage cut, holding that the basis should be two-way. The newly formed operators' association in the two southern fields, the Anthracite Board of Trade, met late in December and proposed a change in the basis from $3 to $2, a reduction of one third. Day-work miners would start at this basis with a base rate reduced by twenty-five to forty per cent below that of 1869. Contract miners were to take a flat forty per cent cut.

The W.B.A. saw the operators' proposal as a declaration of war and adamantly demanded the old three-dollar basis. In January 1870 the operators attempted to enforce their demand by suspending operations. But the solidarity of the operators, too, was not yet effective enough. Several important companies continued working and the Board was forced to rescind its plan.

The operators came back in February with a modified offer calling for a basis of $2.50, with higher base rates. But it was too late. The union met in convention at Summit Hill and rejected the compromise summarily. The operators reacted angrily and, in the largest meeting of anthracite operators ever held, gave the union an ultimatum to accept the compromise or face a suspension on April 2.

The union remained obdurate and the suspension began on schedule. It was the most effective shutdown ever promulgated in the Pennsylvania anthracite fields up to that time. While the northern regions remained at work—stealing away southern markets day by day—the southern production fell to a trickle. By July 1, the distress in the coal patches was acute—the miners were in imminent danger of being starved into submission.

Siney now found himself trying to manage a Frankenstein monster. In spite of the public denunciations of Siney as arrogant and unbending, in truth he was much less sure of the miners' ability to resist the operators' proposal than were most of his lieutenants and members. As early as May there had been intimations in the *Miners' Journal* that Siney had written a secret letter advocating that the miners accept the compromise. And his resolution appeared to waver more and more as the specter of starvation began to loom over the region. Although he remained convinced of the justice of his position, he now began preaching that "half a loaf is better than no bread."[12]

Meanwhile, Franklin B. Gowen was concerned over the strings of idle coal cars on his sidings. Except for mine suspensions, when Gowen surveyed his railroad domain he saw excellent prospects. His first annual report to the stockholders in January 1870 had begun on an optimistic note: "The results of the business of the past year . . . cannot but be gratifying to the stockholders."[13] Tonnage had been over four million, the second highest in the history of the road. On a gross income of just over $11 million, the road had made a profit of $3.2 million (and even this was understated by the accounting convention in those days of charging much capital equipment as expense). Results, then, were heart-warming; prospects for 1870 potentially even rosier—except for one thorn.

Having successfully taken over the Schuylkill Canal and the feeder lines, the Reading Railroad now had a virtual monopoly of transportation out of the region. But it still had no direct control over production. If either miners or operators embarked upon a suspension, the Reading's coal cars sat idle, only to be forced into overtime work when the suspension ended. Although the 1869 suspension had lasted only five weeks, Gowen foresaw that interruptions would be frequent as long as the union insisted on power to control production and the operators insisted on trying to hold coal prices up to three dollars a ton. If coal prices could be brought down to $2.50 a ton, and production stabilized, the Reading would have more coal to carry. Gowen was unwittingly formulating the very economic concepts—high volume and low prices—that were soon to carry America to the highest standard of living in the world.

Short of direct ownership of the mines, Gowen's best approach in the 1870 situation appeared to be in the role of mediator. The grapevine confirmed that Siney was receptive and that the operators were nervous about the suspension and anxious to settle. Benjamin Thomas, one of the more restive operators, conferred individually with Siney in mid-July and returned to Philadelphia with a proposal to Gowen to act as a mediator. Sensing that settlement was imminent, Gowen accepted. After conferring with the Anthracite Board of Trade, Gowen traveled to Pottsville and met with the union officials. Gowen commented afterward that "we talked the whole thing over," that "there was no starvation there," that "the men told me they would stand out until they got their rights," and that "the men treated me well."[14]

And in his pocket Gowen brought back a new proposal—the soon famous "Gowen Compromise." It provided that when coal sold at three dollars, wages would be as in 1869. Further, if coal prices rose, for each increase of twenty-five cents wages would go up eight and one quarter per cent. But—if coal prices dropped, for each decrease of twenty-five cents wages were to be *reduced* by eight and one quarter per cent. And this reduction would continue until the price of coal reached two dollars. In essence, the union took a major gamble—a gamble that coal prices would remain at three dollars or higher. If they fell instead, the union would be hit with a wage cut, possibly up to thirty-three per cent. The upward provisions of the new proposal were much more liberal for the miner than the earlier operators' demand—it looked here as if the union had won a major victory. But if prices fell the wage cuts would be huge, for the new floor—inserted by Gowen—would be far below any union conception of what a minimum wage should be.

Gowen warned the miners that he expected coal to average considerably below the three-dollar figure. But he did agree to lower freight rates immediately, thereby indirectly raising the price received by the operators. (He had boosted freight rates fifty cents a ton earlier in the suspension, purportedly to put some pressure on certain operators who wanted to undercut the combined employer effort by going back to work.) The miners were jubilant; Siney told the men that the railroad president "was with them."

The operators were much more reluctant, at first voting down the proposal 38 to 4. But when Benjamin Thomas said he was going back into operation anyway, they rescinded the vote and agreed to the compromise. Hoping to eliminate some of the misunderstandings of previous years about the terms, the operators voted also to sign a contract with the union—the first signed joint agreement in the anthracite fields and one of the very early examples in the entire country.[15]

Bannan was suspicious of Gowen's motives in proposing the compromise, and commented in his newspaper:

. . . hereafter we would advise the parties interested in selecting an umpire to select one who has no personal interest in the matter. We have great respect for Mr. Gowen, the President of the Road, and no doubt he done all he could under the circumstances, but he is an interested party, and his interests as President of the Road must clash to a certain extent with the interests of the producers . . . We have the most unbounded confidence in the honesty and capacity of Mr. Gowen as an individual but as President of the Road we would always treat him as President of the Road and an interested party . . . The present adjustment permits hostile interests to force both prices of coal and labor below what they ought to be.[16]

And the miners soon echoed these feelings, for Gowen's popularity melted away on the first pay day. Instead of the increase they had expected, the miners found their wages docked eight and one quarter per cent. Once the mines were back in operation, the old fear of overproduction had rapidly forced the price of coal downward. By September their wages had dropped by sixteen and one half per cent, in November by twenty-four and three quarters. The miners accused Siney of a "sell-out," and the union officials found themselves rapidly losing the prestige and power they had so avidly sought.

The stage was now set for a conjuncture of events that would finally push the Molly Maguire shadow out into the light of day.

❖   ❖   ❖   ❖   ❖

It started out well enough when the W.B.A. officers sat down with a committee of the Anthracite Board of Trade in early November 1870. The two groups quickly found a meeting of minds, and a contract was drawn up and signed, to be effective when the union and operator members ratified it. In its total effect it was substantially the same as that for 1870.

The unexpected harmony was further enhanced when the two groups called upon Gowen to request a freight-rate reduction as part of the agreement and found Gowen sympathetic. "I congratulated them upon it," he said, "and told them it was perfectly fair, and I thought we would have no further trouble."[17] The foxy Gowen refused to be committed to a particular figure for the reduction, saying only that the tolls would be reduced "very considerably."

The question quickly became academic. An unexpected force from outside the southern region intervened, blasting all hopes for an amicable settlement. The culprits: again the miners in the northern fields.

During all the 1870 suspension the northern companies had continued working. The northern members of the W.B.A. had swallowed feelings of loyalty and eagerly embraced the high wage rates that the northern companies had been willing to pay to continue operations (and to usurp the markets of the southern mines). This worked well during the suspension days. But the economics fell apart as soon as the suspension was terminated. The chronic glutting, painful enough for the southern operators, worked with doubled intensity on the northern companies. In December the northern companies announced a drastic wage cut—amounting up to thirty-four per cent for contract miners. The northern W.B.A. members struck.

With the shoe on the other foot, the northern miners had no alternative but to appeal to Siney's group—the very group with which they had twice previously broken faith—for support. Twice in the last two years the southern miners had been betrayed by their northern counterparts; twice during these same years the southern miner had borne the brunt of idleness while his northern neighbor had reaped windfall benefit from the artificially lowered coal supply. Here was a ready-made opportunity for retaliation.

The call for suspension was put before the union's general council and brought to a vote. Siney and the other Schuylkill County delegates registered against suspension, but were outvoted. The suspension was approved by majority vote. The long-sought vision of a unified labor movement for all the coal regions proved to be a stronger force than the ready-made chance for retaliation. Siney agreed to commit the Schuylkill miners to the suspension, and so informed Gowen.

Gowen was embittered. Just when it appeared that he had a working arrangement with the southern miners—an arrangement that suited his own plans—an outside force had intruded. More importantly, this defiance must have signaled to Gowen that the control that he presumed he held over the union was largely illusory. At some moment during this period the thought must have finally become imbedded in Gowen's mind that the union could not be held in bounds. For a new Gowen now begins to emerge—with traces of the old desire to compromise and to manipulate, but with increasing efforts to break the union.[18]

At some time during this period there was a turning point—a turning point that set in motion a campaign against the W.B.A. that soon was to become part of a death struggle between Gowen and the Molly Maguires.

✤   ✤   ✤   ✤   ✤

The strike began as scheduled on January 10, 1871, with the entire anthracite region shut down. By the first week in February the entire region was in pain from loss of paychecks. The *Miners' Journal* editor wrung his hands in horror, describing in detail the "Destitution and Death" that was being visited upon the area. Reports were filtering in that "men, women and children are suffering from lack of clothing and food, and especially children, among whom many deaths are occurring from being insufficiently clad and from hunger."[19] Taking into acount the bias of Bannan, one must suspect that his forebodings of doom were a bit exaggerated. But it is true that the miner was especially vulnerable to poverty at that point. This was the third year running in which a suspension was endured; and the chronically low wages were short of providing ample sustenance even when the mines were working.

Late in January a new issue was introduced when the Schuylkill W.B.A. demanded the 1869 basis, thus abrogating the November agreement. Gowen, thoroughly disenchanted, now began to bring his powers of persuasion into play upon the operators. He called a mass meeting of all Schuylkill owners on February 2, and laid before them a plan for concerted action against the miners—and against any operators that desired to deal independently. He proposed to force the union's surrender by making it impossible for any mine to operate on the union's terms.

The plan he proposed came none too soon. The second month of the strike brought many operators to the verge of bankruptcy, and soon there were rumors that some were willing to sign on the union's terms. The W.B.A. officials rejoiced and voted to return to work for any operator so willing, as of February 15. Several operators agreed.

At this point Gowen's bombshell was exploded. When the operators who had started up offered their coal for shipment by the Reading, they found to their consternation that the freight rates had been raised—not a mere fifty cents as in the previous year, but an astronomical rise of 100 per cent, from two dollars a ton to four dollars a ton. The rates were prohibitive. Since no other means was available to ship to market, production by anyone in the region was as effectively terminated as if the mines had been temporarily flooded. His move was followed by similar raises by the other railroads (after a secret meeting in New York), and work in the region remained at a standstill.[20]

The miners were aghast. When they countered with a compromise proposal for settlement, they were curtly informed by the head of the employers' group that he was not authorized to deal with them. The union paper, the *Anthracite Monitor*, lamented, "Franklin B. Gowen . . . has made good his threat that he would make open war upon the organization."[21]

Gowen's boost of the freight rate now pushed what had been a localized strike into the national limelight, and triggered a series of recriminations. Philadelphia and New York newspapers began to cover the strike in detail, and generally took the consumers' side in deploring the action of the railroad and the operators. Some papers even intimated that the operators and *union* were acting in concert against the consumer. This might have sounded plausible in earlier suspensions, where it sometimes seemed that the operators were tacitly approving a "strike" in order to stimulate the flagging demand by artificial shortages. But this time such a notion was patently false.

The issue now was that of power—who was going to rule the coal fields?

Even more disturbing were stories that the Molly Maguires were again active. Bannan had kept the name alive in the papers during the last three years with stories variously titled "A Molly on the Rampage," "Atrocious Outrage by the Molly Maguires," "Molly Beating," "Molly Coffin Notice." Now the stories cumulated.

And a new editorial voice had been added in mid-1870, a voice that was to exert a profound influence in the Molly Maguire story. A brash young journalist, Thomas J. Foster, began publishing a newspaper in Shenandoah, a mining town a few miles north of Pottsville that was subsequently to figure prominently in the Molly incidents. This was the *Shenandoah Herald*. Unlike Bannan, Foster was highly sympathetic to the W.B.A. But, perhaps feeling that he needed a circulation booster, he became a relentless enemy of "The Mollies." In his maiden issue he reported in flaming prose of a "Highway Robbery and Attempt at Murder," and added a postscript to the story that soon snowballed on him: "We can hardly find language sufficiently strong to condemn this fresh outrage. Crime is getting to be as common in this county as in California, in the days of Vigilance Committees." He added that "perhaps, if things continue this way long, the talk of them here, a few weeks ago, may prove to be something more than mere talk." Foster backtracked a week later, advocating that "what we need is a good, effective Detective Police Force [or else] fifty citizens might be murdered in a single month."[22] The seed of vigilantism had been planted in print, though, and this seed was to produce bitter fruit.

In that same summer of 1870, Bannan, in the *Miners' Journal*, vented his anti-Irish bias. The *New York Herald* had printed a series on crime in New York City, part of which was composed of statistics on crimes and pauperism. The Irish ranked at the top in both categories. Bannan eagerly picked up this story and tied it to the current campaign against immigration of Chinese. He editorialized that perhaps it was the Irish that should be excluded, rather than the Chinese, for "if the Chinamen are Pagans, we may convert them to Christianity and mere Paganism cannot have a more demoralizing effect upon the country than the crime and pauperism of the Irish."[23]

Though Foster clearly distinguished the Mollies from the W.B.A., Bannan did not. When the 1871 suspension became national news, the *New York Herald* ran a series of stories on certain shootings at

Mt. Carmel, northwest of Pottsville. Bannan did not like these stories, particularly with respect to the relation of the union to the Mollies:

He says that the Molly Maguires do not belong to the W.B.A. This is not true; they all belong, because they could not get any work whatever if they did not. There are but two classes in this Region—members of the W.B.A., or what they term blacklegs. The correspondent says: "the 'Buckshots' and 'Molly Maguires' are the self-constituted detectives and judges for the Workingmen's Benevolent Association, although not members of the order." This is true, so far as the acts of these persons are concerned, and it is also this class that the quiet and orderly men dread so much, and always obey when ordered to stop work; but when the writer says that they are not members of the organization, he states what is absolutely false. They are the Danites of the leaders, and whenever the *Monitor*, the organ of the leaders denounce any person, the Danites are ready to execute the order.[24]

Foster, too, was disturbed by the Mt. Carmel incidents and cautioned the W.B.A., "The affair at Mt. Carmel of Saturday demands the most energetic action on the part of the officers of the Workingmen's Benevolent Association. The matter should be immediately investigated and the skirts of the Association cleared of any responsibility."

The miners commanded a certain political power in the state legislature, and they now demanded that the whole freight-raise question be investigated. The miners were not alone in their fear of the newly invoked power of the railroad corporations; the public's concern for the large corporation's ability to dominate economic life was already being voiced throughout the country. If the railroad's manipulation of rates could be used against the union, could not it be also used against the shipper? The Harrisburg *State Journal* commented: "If a railroad company can advance and lower its charges for transportation at will, then there is not an industrial operation in the State that may not be destroyed in a month."[25]

The pressures for action poured in on Governor John W. Geary. When first questioned about conditions in the coal regions, he showed a singular lack of awareness of the issues. But the combined pleas of both operators and miners, abetted by the press, soon awoke him to the political implications, and he asked a legislative committee —the Senate's "Committee on the Judiciary, General"—to investigate.

The miners were jubilant. The shattering turn of events resulting from the surprise freight raise had convinced many of them that there was little hope of winning, but now it seemed that Gowen was on the defensive, the union on the offensive. The few who had advocated early settlement on the operators' terms now were easily persuaded to continue the suspension. When the investigation opened at Harrisburg on March 8, 1871, the union's hopes were high.

But they were to be shattered quickly. Gowen seized the initiative on the first day and persuaded the Senate committee that the question of the freight raise was a narrow point of law—a point that inevitably would be decided in favor of the railroad. Dismissing the legal question under examination with a single sentence, he declared that the railroad had the right under its charter to charge whatever rates it pleased. The important question, Gowen maintained, was the power of the union to damage the coal business by its intemperate actions. Within the first five minutes of his testimony his true objectives became apparent, to indict the union as the prime, if not the sole, cause of the anthracite troubles: "Our object was to rescue a great industry . . . from the control of an association that had almost destroyed it . . . I think, when you have heard what I have to say and what the witnesses have to say, you, gentlemen, will agree with me."[26]

Gowen then proceeded graphically to describe the tyranny and lawlessness of the miners' combinations—and the union that prevented men from working, forced prices to heights that the poor could not pay, and repudiated contractual agreements. He described the chronic conditions of overproduction and surplus labor and laid at the door of the W.B.A. the entire responsibility for the depressed conditions of the trade. He deftly intimated, without actually making an accusation, that the recent murders of strikebreakers could be traced to the union. Without mentioning the Molly Maguires by name, he so associated the W.B.A. with this shadowy secret society as to leave the impression that they were the same:

I do not charge this Workingmen's Benevolent Association with it, but I say there is an association which votes in secret, at night, that men's lives shall be taken, and that they shall be shot before their wives, murdered in cold blood, for daring to work against the order. At Trevorton, six or eight weeks ago, a man, working outside of this organization and against their order, who was sitting quietly beside a sick neighbor, was shot and killed by a bullet through the window of the house. Last week there was an attempt to kill a man working outside of this organization, by igniting a keg of powder under his house, and he was then shot. *I do not blame this association*, but I blame another association for doing it; and it happens that the only men who are shot are the men who dare disobey the mandates of the Workingmen's Benevolent Association.[27]

When Gowen had finished, the union was so busy defending itself it was never able to turn the questioning back to the original issue of the rate boost. By the time John Siney was called to the stand the damage was done. Siney was repeatedly questioned about his $1500 salary and expense account, and about rumors that he had sold out the union. The democratic processes of the union were attacked, and the economic reasoning of the union subjected to scorn.

This contest of 1871 was an unequal match from the start. The famed Gowen rhetoric was at its peak; Siney did his best, but was inept. By the end of the investigation, Gowen had taken over the function of a quasi-prosecutor and Siney was the defendant. Even Siney's protestations of complete lack of knowledge of the Molly Maguires were made to have a hollow ring:

By Mr. Petrikin.—Q. Do you know of the existence of a secret society, in Schuylkill county, amongst the miners?

A. [by Siney] I wish to be placed upon my oath. As workingmen we are stigmatized as a band of assassins; anything coming from our lips is supposed not to be believed; I know of none; I have heard say that such a thing is in it; I do not know a solitary man belonging to it.

Q. Is it generally believed there is such a society in that region?

A. It has been taken for granted that there has been, long before this organization was organized; we are an organization; we were first chartered by the county, next by the Legislature; to-day we have neither sign, password, oath nor pledge, and we do not know each other when we meet in the streets.

By Mr. Gowen.—Q. Have you not always heard, ever since you have been in Schuylkill county, that there were secret societies that committed outrages?

A. Yes, sir.

Q. Have not you heard three times that attempts have been made to throw our trains from the track?

A. Yes, sir.

Q. Have not you heard that a man, at Trevorton, was killed in this way, eight weeks ago?

A. Yes, sir.

Q. Have not you heard that a man at Mt. Carmel was shot and his house blown up in the night?

A. Yes, sir.

Q. Don't you know that the offence of those men was working outside of what other men thought was right?

A. I do not know, but I have seen it in the *Miners' Journal*.

Q. Do you know any other reason why these men were killed than that they had been working outside of what other men thought was right—did you ever hear anybody charge them with other crimes?

A. I have heard members of the association say that they were not members of the association; it is the current report, in papers, that these men were not members of the association; but that is not in the county which I represent; Schuylkill has been made the butt in this connection.[28]

The investigation was a total defeat for the union. The committee gathered much valuable information on the industry, but in its final report merely stated that it was powerless to interfere without legal authority for rate setting. As to the question of whether the railroads had illegally combined to raise rates, the committee held that this was a matter for the courts to decide. The committee closed its investigation with a proposal for arbitration of the dispute.

The number of violent incidents quickened, as in the latter stages of previous suspensions. Again the disturbing notion of vigilantism was mentioned in print, this time by Bannan in the *Miners' Journal*. Bannan first advocated that the suspension be called to the attention of the April grand jury. His proposed instructions to the jury are interesting—Bannan wanted action: "The Jury need not go into an investigation of the causes but the fact is apparent. Let them so declare and recommend that the authorities act." If this failed, there was a more awe-inspiring alternative: "Nobody can justify Lynch law, except under very peculiar circumstances but such circumstances sometimes occur," wrote Bannan. "It did in San Francisco, and a number of scoundrels were tried on the spot, and hung by a Vigilance Committee. Under the circumstances, it was the only remedy that would remove the evil and every honest man throughout the whole country justified the act, because it did remove the evil and caused peace and quietness ever since."[29]

The union, now realizing that it had been fooled in its hopes for the investigation, scrambled about for a means of settling the suspension. With the warmer weather of April, the fears of fuel shortages disappeared and the public quickly tired of the battle. Governor Geary met with Gowen and two of the union officials on April 5, but there were no results. The governor acted more decisively a day later, calling out the state militia when a massed mob of strikers shot three men near Scranton. The governor testily issued a proclamation castigating both sides.

The repeated suggestions for use of a new concept—arbitration—finally took effect. By agreement made in early April, arbitrators were selected from both sides for Carbon, Luzerne, Schuylkill, Columbia, and Northumberland Counties. Judge William Elwell, of Columbia County, was elected impartial chairman. Unfortunately, the wage issue was not at first made a part of the award. Elwell rendered a decision on April 19 that dealt primarily with the rights of the union to interfere with the working of mines, the union's policy toward non-union men, and the treatment accorded the union by the operators. The rule of exclusive control by the operators was established, and the right of the union to refuse to work with non-union men was scored as "subversive to the best interests of the miners."[30]

The wage issue remained unsettled. Though the operators had been willing to submit wages to arbitration, the union had balked. Now the Schuylkill operators decided to undercut the union by making a direct wage proposal to the men. Siney was caught flat-footed. He tried to counter the move by printing cards attacking the operators' efforts, but pressures for settlement were too strong. The northern miners had already gone back to work on the operators' terms—having again parted company from the southern miners. The southern miners soon pressed Siney to accept arbitration on the wage issue, and Elwell, now arbitrating only for the southern region, on May 17 split the difference between the $2.00 minimum basis insisted upon by the operators and the union's demand for a $2.50 minimum.

In all, the union had suffered badly. The period had been decisive for all concerned. Just how decisive was not fully apparent, though, until one further event became public knowledge. From shortly after the first of the year, Gowen had been pursuing another plan—but pursuing it privately and under cover. Now that the suspension was settled, interest was finally focused on this amazing development.

In historical perspective it was to become much more important than any of the suspension issues: Gowen was buying coal land.

✣   ✣   ✣   ✣   ✣

For years Bannan had been harping on the hope that a rival railroad might be built into the southern region both to break the Reading's monopoly and to link Pottsville with New York City. The chances of a brand-new line were really slim—the area was already honeycombed with facilities and railroad construction costs were heavy. A more realistic possibility was the movement into the area of an already existing outside line. To make this feasible, it would be necessary to guarantee that a reasonable supply of coal would be forthcoming. Rumors were flying that both the Lehigh Valley and Northern Central railroads were buying large tracts of land just north of the Reading's territory, and that the Lehigh Valley, the Central Railroad of New Jersey, and the Delaware, Lackawanna & Western were joining together to build a line directly into Tamaqua, in the heart of the Reading domain. To do this, they would need coal lands.

The railroad and canal companies in the northernmost (Wyoming) field were holders of large tracts of coal land—but only because their original charters allowed them to buy it. The Lehigh Valley had obtained its rights of purchase in the district around Hazleton only by purchase of defunct corporations already having such rights. For coal lands to be purchased by a railroad in the two southern fields, specific legislation had to be passed by the legislature. The Reading's charter, alone of the six big transportation companies, gave it no rights for such land ownership *anywhere*.

When Gowen became president, the cumulating pressures from the competitor railroads, the individualism of the Schuylkill operators that precluded regulation of supply, and the newly evidenced strength of the W.B.A. all pointed to one clear lesson—supply had to be secured.

But, first, the legal roadblock had to be removed. It would probably be dangerous, he rightly assumed, to ask that the Reading charter be amended—too much public protest might be aroused. Better to obtain a charter for a corporation with some innocuous name, but with a proviso tucked away in the small print allowing the Reading rights.

His first effort misfired. When a bill to incorporate the Franklin Coal Company came innocently before the lawmakers in January 1871, Senator Esaias Billingfelt, a stony-hearted foe of monopoly, asked what company was backing the bill. The Gowen-primed senator who introduced the bill first limpingly said it was handed to him by "a friend who is engaged in the anthracite coal business in the county of Schuylkill"[31] but under repeated questioning he finally allowed that it was Gowen. The Senate struck out the clause that Gowen needed and the bill became useless.

But Gowen had no doubts about the eventual outcome of his effort. Pending the capitulation of the legislators, he now quietly approached friends of the Reading with the proposal that they personally buy up Schuylkill coal lands. He promised them that the company would take the properties off their hands at cost, plus six per cent interest, as soon as he had hoodwinked the legislature. He also bought land under his own name with funds furnished by the London stockholders.

Interestingly, this was the very period when the famed legislative investigation of the Reading was being pursued. In the course of the hearings, Gowen was asked a direct question on the rumors that coal land was being bought by Reading interests. His reply was notable for its lack of candor:

Q. Did you purchase the Trevorton tract?

A. Not for the Reading company; I have bought, lately, as counsel, a large amount of lands, but that does not concern this matter; it was business for private individuals.

Q. I desire to know whether these purchases that have been made lately of large bodies of land are not indirectly for the Reading railroad company?

A. They are not; because the Reading railroad company has no right, I think, to hold those lands, and the lands have been paid for by private individuals.

Q. Is not your company interested in a bill now before the Legislature to incorporate the Franklin coal company?

A. The people owning these lands are interested.

Q. Are not they stockholders of the Reading railroad?

A. Some are, and some not.

Q. Are not the large mass of them?

A. Yes, most all; this is a matter in which I act for private individuals, and I claim that I have no right and ought not to speak of it . . .

Q. Are the persons for whom you are agent, attorney or trustee not stockholders in the Reading railroad company?

A. Some of them own stock; I think some do not.

Q. I would like to know how many do not?

A. I decline to answer any question that has no reference to the Reading railroad company, and seeks to make public a private transaction between myself and my clients.

Q. Is the Reading railroad company interested in any coal operations in Pennsylvania, other than in transporting coal over its road?

A. Not in any matter except as transporters of coal . . .

Q. Who purchased the Trevorton lands?

A. I purchased them myself for a gentleman in England; the Reading railroad company has no connection with that.

Q. Are those gentlemen stockholders in your company?

A. I decline to answer any question in regard to clients of mine for whom I transact business.[32]

On the day the legislative investigation adjourned, March 28, 1871, Gowen's allies were again approaching the legislature, and again through the back door. The "front" company this time was to be the Laurel Run Improvement Company. Which Laurel Run was to be improved, if any, was not specified. The obtuseness of the bill allowed it to slip through the House without changes, although one legislator commented, "here was a bill that took in the Island of Black Susan and Sandomingo, and not a word was said against it."[33] But the vigilant Senator Billingfelt was not so easily fooled. In the Senate the Reading's vested interest was brought out in the open and the bill's key clause was stricken by a vote of 17 to 15.

But, while the Senate was adjourned for lunch, Gowen had an opportunity to work a miracle of conversion. When the Senate reconvened, three of the bill's opponents were conveniently absent, and another had changed his mind. On a motion to reconsider the morning vote, Senator Billingfelt fought a valiant delaying action, but his cause was lost, and the vital section went back into the bill. Gowen was accused of bribery, but no one could make the charges stick.[34]

The bill passed and went to Governor Geary for his signature. Bannan's Harrisburg correspondent must have had his mind elsewhere, for his column to Bannan failed to connect the Reading to

Laurel Run. When the governor signed the measure, Bannan was taken completely by surprise. For two successive weeks the *Miners' Journal* devoted its first page to the "Revolution in the Coal Trade of This Region." Lamenting that "the bill was put through without the people knowing much about it, in fact we never heard of it until after it was passed," Bannan lamely commented "this was certainly rapid work." The articles blamed the W.B.A. for bringing the development about, and echoed Bannan's old feelings about large corporations: "The Reading Railroad Company are now masters of the situation. They now control every thing. No rival road can now come in while they control the product."

But Bannan was willing to be charitable to Gowen, perhaps in anticipation of increased Gowen influence in the county. "The business men generally have accepted the situation, and so long as Mr. Gowen controls the road, we feel confident that he is disposed to give this Region all the facilities he possibly can." Bannan said Gowen "understands this business, and acts fairly to all, and above board." Bannan then spelled out just what this "understanding of the business" should be. Discussing at length the clannishness and dislike of authority on the part of the foreign populations of the area, Bannan hoped that Gowen would leave "little foothold for agitators, lazy folks, and those who care more about creating difficulties on which they may thrive without earning their living by the sweat of their brow." Even the self-possesed Bannan could not know at this time how prophetic he was.[35]

Certainly no one at that time had any conception of the scale Gowen was to give to his purchases. The time was singularly unpropitious for the accumulation of a coal estate for permanent investment. The legacy of war demand had kept mineral land values high, in spite of the recurrent suspensions. Further, the country was on an inconvertible paper basis, and coal lands bought at greenback prices would have to be paid for by the scale of bonds payable in gold, thus raising the real cost of the investment.

Even the eternally optimistic Gowen must have realized the difficulties here. But analysis of Gowen's actions during the period of *sub rosa* land purchases raises some interesting speculative questions. Gowen presumably made his decision to buy coal lands shortly after the first of the year 1871. Though his early steps in that 1871 strike clearly were designed to resolve the argument and get the miners back to work, his later tactics were just as clearly not. When the suspension had dragged on for many weeks, not only were the miners in serious financial straits, but also many operators. Some were close to bankruptcy, and many seemed eager to get back into operation, even at the expense of employer solidarity and capitulation to the W.B.A. At precisely this point, Gowen jacked his freight rates to their prohibitive heights. The suspension was forced to continue and many of the operators must have then been close to the wall. These were the very operators then being approached by Gowen emissaries to sell! It was a neat trick; publicly the savior of the employers, Gowen was privately undermining their interests for yet-unknown Reading purposes.

In Gowen's defense two factors should be noted. First, even if it were not the most propitious time to buy, Gowen must have felt that buy he must if the railroad were to survive. Business conditions were generally good, prospects for coal trade appeared excellent. The union was beyond control when dealt with at arm's length—better to be actually the miners' employer. Second, the actions of all parties concerned must be measured against the times. Even so, one might well hold that the widespread chicanery in others during that period neither justified nor required Gowen's methods of doing business. But one would have been hard pressed to prove to Gowen—in his new and unsettling role as president of an embattled railroad—that modest and openly conceived efforts would win out.

Even without criticizing Gowen on his underlying motives, we can take him severely to task in his business judgment.

On June 1, 1870, the Reading Railroad had less than six million dollars of mortgage bonds outstanding; an additional set of debentures and real estate mortgages brought the total long-term debt to an amount less than eleven million dollars. Even by today's standards, this was a conservative financial position, for Reading common stock was worth over thirty million dollars, and profits were adequate in 1867 and 1868 and substantial in 1869 and 1870.[36] The ability of the road to earn enough to provide decent dividends seemed unquestioned. Certainly the improved financial position of the railroad over that of its early history justified the considerable reputation that the stock of the company enjoyed in the securities markets.

But the satisfying debt position of the company was quickly altered by Gowen's amazing purchases of coal land. For these purchases were not modest by any scale of value. Rather than carrying through a planned, selective approach that would pre-empt the best tracts, Gowen appeared compelled to purchase every bit of land he could possibly obtain. By the end of 1871 the railroad, through its Laurel Run satellite, held 65,605 acres of coal land. In 1872, despite Gowen's assurance in the previous year that all needed lands had been acquired, an additional 15,000 acres were purchased. And even this was not enough for Gowen. By the end of 1874 the Reading coal lands consisted of over 100,000 acres, more than double that owned by any other corporation.

How much business judgment was exercised in these purchases? The average price paid per acre for the first large bloc of 65,000 acres was $293.22, probably well in line with the then-current prices.[37] But subsequent purchases were not so sound. In later testimony before a United States Congressional committee, Gowen's land agent was questioned concerning these prices:

Q. Was there much competition by the persons seeking to purchase these lands?

A. I do not think there was much competition. There was competition as to some tracts. For instance, there were efforts made for the Mason and Williams land by the Northern Central, and it put up the price for that land . . .

Q. Did the Reading Company buy these lands with a view of heading off other people from securing them . . . other railroads coming in there?

A. The purpose was, as I stated, to secure their tonnage against some road coming in there . . .

Q. Hence they wanted to control the lands?

A. They wanted to control the lands for the purpose of controlling the tonnage.[38]

The land purchases required financing on a scale never before attempted by the railroad. First, in 1871, a new consolidated mortgage of twenty-five million dollars was authorized, and over eleven million worth of six and seven per cent bonds were sold immediately. A new issue of convertible debentures at seven per cent was sold to stockholders in 1872, and a ten-million-dollar improvement mortgage issue at six per cent was sold in London in October 1873. The latter was effected at the height of the panic following the failure of the Jay Cooke banking house, and in spite of it brought healthy proceeds, attesting still to the good credit rating of the road.

But this credit reputation was on more tenuous ground than most thought, for disaster was not far ahead. To get funds needed for reorganizing the mining operations on a large scale, Gowen marketed a new loan—sixty million in mortgage bonds—on July 1, 1874. Some of this was to be used to retire previous debt, the rest for further expansion. By the end of 1875, the bonded debt was over sixty million, and in addition the company had guaranteed over fifteen million in bonds of its coal and iron subsidiary. This subsidiary by now was no longer the Laurel Run Improvement Company; it had been renamed the Philadelphia & Reading Coal & Iron Company.

But the chronicle of what happened to the railroad under this crushing burden of debt must be delayed for the time being in order to record a parallel story. For Gowen next turned his attention to the Molly Maguires.

Part Three ✦ *The Pinkertons At Work*

Chapter 6 • Alias James McKenna

*A*T *SOME TIME* before the middle of October 1873, Detective Allan Pinkerton made a special trip to Philadelphia from his Chicago headquarters to see Franklin B. Gowen. At this meeting decisions were made that set in motion a chain of events leading to the downfall of the Molly Maguires. For Gowen and Pinkerton agreed to use the resources of the Pinkerton's National Detective Agency to obtain legal evidence of Molly crimes.

If we knew exactly what transpired in that meeting many of the remaining puzzles of the story would be solved. It is an unrealistic hope, though, for no record of such secret planning was kept. There are several versions of the meeting. Pinkerton himself described it in his famous semifictional account, *The Mollie Maguires and the Detectives* (one of a series of popular Pinkerton-authored books on the exploits of the detective agency). In writing this, Pinkerton unwittingly telegraphed Gowen's underlying reason for fearing the Mollies. "The Mollie Maguire wields with deadly effect his two powerful levers: secrecy—combination," Pinkerton reported Gowen as saying. Gowen was then purported to have continued, "Men having their capital locked up in the coal beds are as obedient puppets in his hands. They have felt they were fast losing sway over that which by right should be their own command."[1]

"Combination" generally meant unionism. The "right of command" aptly expressed the rampant individualism characterizing the nineteenth-century business leader. Was Pinkerton hired, then, as a strikebreaker?

Some analysts imputed even more diabolical motives. The official history of the Ancient Order of Hibernians reported the "actual words" of Gowen as:

I control the means of communication and transportation to and from the district. I want you to send a man into Schuylkill County to join the Mollie Maguires and become its leader. I want this man to gain the confidence of the Irish miners, become an officer of their organization and start them out on a crusade of crime. I want him to precipitate strikes against the several mines and make the lives of the mine managers a burden. I want him to lead bands against the English, Welsh and German miners and mine bosses, beat them and kill them off, until the collieries will be unable to run for want of competent men. That course will force the rest of these independent operators to sell out to me at my own figures. Finally, I want this man whom you will send to turn informer on his associates, hand them over to the authorities—and I will do the rest. With the execution of these fellows two results will be accomplished: I will be looked upon as a savior of the coal region—the supreme preserver of the peace—and organized labor will be given a black eye from which it will never recover.[2]

Antiunionism in the 1870's included such devices. Gowen's private motives were such that, given certain circumstances, he could well have countenanced violence.

But his true motives were never completely clear. Already his life was full of contradictions. He was of Irish descent but a Protestant, a long-time resident of the coal regions but now its absentee master—holding in his power as president of the rail and coal companies the economic life of the region. As district attorney of Schuylkill County, he had a conspicuous lack of success obtaining convictions in the face of extensive criminal activity. His Democratic political leanings seemed to align him with the working class, but his attitude toward unions was negative. And many outside forces operated upon him. The English stockholders may have entertained antiunion attitudes, which were prevalent in Europe at this time, although no direct evidence exists that they brought any pressure on Gowen here. Gowen was a pragmatist. Any indication that a campaign against the union would backfire would undoubtedly have changed his course.

For the moment, then, it is safe to posit that Gowen looked to the Pinkertons to bring the depredations to a halt, and entertained residual hope that a corollary would be a more tractable—and non-union—work force.

✤   ✤   ✤   ✤   ✤

Allan Pinkerton brought to the case a new set of precepts and principles. We must analyze these carefully, for they vitally affected the final result of the Molly Maguire story.

Pinkerton was born into police work; before his teens he had seen first-hand the dangers of matching wits with criminal elements. His father, William, was a sergeant on the police force in Glasgow, Scotland, where Allan was born in 1819. When Allan was ten, his father was so seriously injured in one of the brutal Chartist riots that he was never able to walk again; he died four years later. The young son, forced to support the family, was apprenticed as a cooper at age twelve and became an independent craftsman at nineteen.[3]

Incongruously for a budding capitalist, he became an active supporter of Chartism. In the 1842 disturbances he was so deeply enmeshed that he prudently decided flight was better than arrest and left for America, stopping only long enough to marry his Glasgow sweetheart. Perhaps the statement of one writer that he was "fleeing from arrest as a social revolutionist and an active agitator in the proletarian movement"[4] overdoes his early role as a liberal. But Allan Pinkerton not only observed but actually participated in radicalism prior to his flight to the United States.

He took up his old trade of cooperage in the Scotch colony of Dundee, Illinois, outside of Chicago. His coopering brought him back to police work in a strange way. While cutting hoop poles on an uninhabited island in a river near Dundee, he chanced upon a rendezvous for a gang of counterfeiters. He hastened back to town, organized and led a posse and captured the gang. Other similar successes in free-lance local detective work soon brought him enough renown to be tendered in 1846 a deputy sheriff's post for Kane County. Again success followed, and when officials of Cook County appointed him deputy sheriff he moved his family to Chicago. After brief service he was made a detective, one of the first in the world to hold such a position. In 1850 his penchant for working on his own, coupled with the promise of commissions from several railroad companies, took him out of public service, and the private detective agency he had dreamed of for several years became a reality. His spectacular and widely reported success in solving several Adams Express Company robberies brought him national fame, and soon Eastern accounts were obtained.[5]

In 1861, while investigating threats by Southern sympathizers against the Philadelphia, Wilmington & Baltimore Railroad, Pinkerton uncovered what appeared to be a plot to assassinate President Lincoln in Baltimore on his way to Washington to his inaugural. Just exactly what was involved here has never been fully documented, and historians have battled over the years as to the veracity of the plot. Majority opinion today would probably back Pinkerton's claim. At any rate the authorities put enough credence in the probability to reroute Lincoln, and Pinkerton was himself involved in the altered plans.[6]

George B. McClellan had employed Pinkerton for investigative work when McClellan had been president of the Ohio & Mississippi Railroad. When the railroad president was appointed General in charge of the Ohio Department, he engaged Pinkerton for secret service work in the Union forces. Pinkerton, temporarily leaving his agency, took the name of Major E. J. Allen and became widely known throughout the forces as a counterespionage officer. When McClellan was asked to resign in 1862, Pinkerton loyally followed suit, and spent the rest of the war as a private citizen investigating claims against the government.

After the war Pinkerton reactivated his agency, adding offices in Philadelphia and New York. Work for the railroads and for express companies proliferated, and a number of notorious criminals were tracked and captured by Pinkerton's men. In 1869, Pinkerton, now fifty, contracted a disease, brought about, he believed, by the rigors involved in a particularly difficult criminal case he had personally conducted. It left him partially paralyzed and forced him to conduct most of the field work vicariously through agents. He bitterly missed the thrill of the actual chase, but when his two sons entered the agency (the elder, Robert, heading the New York office and William, the younger son, working with him in Chicago), this somewhat compensated for the loss. Another calamity came in October 1871, when the great Chicago fire swept through his office building, incinerating many of his valuable records. Files and "rogues galleries" on many contemporary criminal cases were lost, as well as Pinkerton's vast secret-service files on the Civil War (which, he reported to a friend of his, were about to be sold to the Secretary of War for a tidy sum). In all, Pinkerton claimed he lost $250,000 in the fire, a serious setback for the firm.[7]

It is at this point in the chronology of the agency that we can take a closer view both of agency management problems and the personal characteristics of Allan Pinkerton himself. Fortunately, we have some helpful Pinkerton publications, and besides, Pinkerton left his personal letterbook covering this period.[8] In it the agency and its founder exhibit the characteristics that made their involvement in the Molly Maguire incidents so interesting, yet so difficult to assess.

❖   ❖   ❖   ❖   ❖

General Principles and Rules of Pinkerton's National Police Agency was the rather imposing title of a small guidebook that Allan Pinkerton published for his organization in 1867. In it he demonstrated his accurate assessment of the dangers such an agency faced.[9]

The concept of a professional detective agency was new; past practices were almost universally of a shady nature. Pinkerton described them:

It has hitherto been held as the leading canon of detective practices that a "thief only can catch a thief," and, to a very great extent, this has been acted upon, not only by the Police of America, but of all the world. Nearly the whole detective force of Paris are men who have themselves either been convicted of Crime, or who have committed it, and whom the Police are ready at any time to pounce upon, whenever the Mouchard fails to do his duty . . . The same principle has also prevailed in the "Stool Pigeon" system of England and America.

Thieves have been employed by the Detectives, and have been allowed to commit Crimes with such impunity, and with so free a license, that they have outwitted the Detectives, and only occasionally shared with them their ill-gotten gains.

They have furnished them, likewise, with information in regard only to the smaller and less important thieves, who would from time to time be arrested by the Detectives while the great Criminals went free, and, so long as they acquired a newspaper notoriety, which kept them before the public, and so long as the Detectives received their wages, it mattered little to them who escaped from justice, or who was punished.

But "crime itself has become more scientific," Pinkerton continued. "It is, to many, a matter of study how they can possess themselves of the property of others." He added that "many men have entered upon a course of crime powerful of mind and strong of will." To meet these new challenges a new detective must emerge, "of a high order of mind." Pinkerton sketched his qualities thus: "The profession of the Detective is a high and honorable calling. Few professions excel it. He is an officer of justice and must himself be pure and above reproach. The public have a right to expect this from their officers, nay, more they have a right to know that their lives and property are to be guarded by persons . . . of whose integrity there can be no question." A detective must be a man "of considerable intellectual power," he continued, and possess such a knowledge of human nature "as will give him a quick insight into character." Further, "a keen analytical mind—as well as large powers of combination—so that he might be ready for any emergency."

Above all, Pinkerton insisted, the detective must recognize that secrecy is the prime condition for success—"It is the chief strength which the Detective possesses beyond the ordinary man." Indeed, he went on, "It frequently becomes necessary for the Detective, when brought in contact with Criminals, to pretend to be a Criminal; in other words, for the time being to assume the Garb of Crime." Pinkerton recognized that this was one of the most sensitive of all his principles. He said it is "unfortunately necessary to resort to these deceptions." He explained that "the Detective has to act his part, and in order to do so, he has, at times, to depart from the strict line of truth, and to resort to deception, so as to carry his assumed character through."

"Moralists may question whether this be strictly right," he continued, "but it is a necessity in the detection of Crime, and it is held by the Agency that the ends being for the accomplishment of justice, they justify the means used." The operative, when the ends of justice were accomplished, would "return, of course, unblemished by the fiery ordeal through which he has passed, and take his place once more in society."

Pinkerton faced up to the inconsistencies involved in certain questionable means, particularly, for one, the loosening of tongues through liquor:

While associating with Criminals, the Employes of this Agency must abstain from using intoxicating liquors, except when it is absolutely necessary; and never, except by direct orders from their superior Officers, must intoxicating liquors be used to such an extent as to influence the mind of the Criminal . . . The Detective must not do anything to further sink the Criminal in vice or debauchery; but, on the contrary, to win his confidence, by endeavoring to elevate him, and to impress him with the idea of his (the Detective's) mental and moral superiority. The use of liquors for the purpose of stimulating the mind of the Criminal must only be used in extreme cases . . . when on account of the settled habits of the Criminal, it is impossible to keep his company without using more or less liquor.

Once the criminal was convicted, sentenced and confined to the prison cell, "it ought to be the duty of those brought in contact with him to do all in their power to elevate and ennoble him." It was true that the detective "can do but little in any way to reform the Criminal, because, after his condemnation, he seldom sees him, and, in many instances, the mind of the Criminal would be so poisoned and embittered against him that he would be loath to believe that anything good could emanate from him." Nevertheless, "kindness and justice should go hand in hand, whenever it is possible, in the dealings of the Detective with the Criminal."

In particular, Pinkerton emphasized impartiality. "The Detective must, in every instance, report everything which is favorable to the suspected party as well as everything which may be against him. The object of every investigation is to come at the whole truth." He said "there must be no endeavoring therefore to overdo or exaggerate anything against any particular individual . . . His data should be founded upon knowledge only, and if upon hearsay, the same must be fairly expressed. All suspicions must be verified by facts." "Actions alone are amenable to law and justice." "These are fundamental axioms of this Agency and must be borne in mind by every Detective who is attached to it."

Allan Pinkerton apparently sensed that only through such a self-conscious set of goals and precepts could a detective agency achieve a lasting reputation. Through his lifetime he pursued these ends with a fervor and personal dedication that bordered on fanaticism. He was careful to keep the agency out of dubious cases, particularly those involving marital indiscretions. His agents were always compensated on a straight salary basis, never allowed to share in rewards. He appeared to be personally incorruptible, and his tenacity in following a criminal for years and "to the ends of the earth" was widely acclaimed. The agency truly merited its reputation as the greatest in the nation.

But, too, these were rough times—and rough methods were used by both pursuers and pursued. Crime was widespread in the post-Civil War period. Economic conditions were difficult, especially after the spread of the depression beginning in 1873. And Pinkerton practices did not always match Pinkerton principles.

One of the most difficult problems facing Pinkerton was finding the right man for an agent, and then training him well enough to keep him on the narrow tightrope between ineffectiveness and over-zealousness. The very nature of detective work, in which the agent was in the field working on his own and adapting himself to rapidly changing circumstances, required an extraordinary degree of decentralized decision-making. Pinkerton was never comfortable in loosening the reins of control. He was a marvel of meticulousness; his detailed written instructions to his agents were masterpieces of planning. But, particularly after the paralysis hit him in 1869, the execution of plans was left to the agent. Good men were difficult to hire. Practices inherited from the older days of detection persisted; that is, agents knocked down money on the side by demanding blackmail payments, or by illegally selling off clients' goods. Pinkerton seemed to have inherent distrust of agents; in 1872 he told George Bangs, his general superintendent, working out of the New York office: "Mr. Watson has said that his experience has led him to believe that there are but few detectives that are honest and reliable and such has been my experience through life." He said that "detectives have got to be watched," and that "they are willing to make money in any way and are totally devoid of principle." Pinkerton continually exhorted his key men to upgrade the ethics of the agency. In the same letter to Bangs he said, "I have never been willing to stoop to any of that kind of business," and ended in a typical manner: "Let us keep head and shoulders above everyone until someone again comes and exclaims, 'Excelsior, higher still higher.' "[10]

But his exhortations did not prevent slips. When these occurred, Pinkerton became highly agitated and seemed to take the falls from grace as personal affronts. When a shadowing job had been mishandled by one of the New York agents, Pinkerton bitterly wrote Bangs:

Oh! Great God! Was there ever such a bungling as this . . . was there ever such a bungling piece of business done by one of my men, my face is reddening with shame that I have to say that these are my men following in my footsteps and let Mrs. Chapman [the suspect] slip through our fingers.

I need not say more . . . I am mad, so devilish mad that if swearing could do any good for the wooden heads of my Superintendents, then I might swear at them, but there is no use, for my God! I am so mad, I cannot go farther . . .[11]

One of Pinkerton's greatest difficulties with his agents was their drinking on the job. There were circumstances where imbibing was a natural accompaniment to obtaining information (as Pinkerton recognized in his "General Principles and Rules"). But the line between business and pleasure was very thin. After one of the Chicago agents came to the office drunk, Pinkerton said in a private letter to his son Robert: "I can't do without Fitzgerald, for when he is really sober he is the best man. But every day, drinking, drinking, drinking . . . Oh God, everything is on fire, I cannot stand it." His frustration poignantly came to the surface in the last sentence of this letter: "I wrote to you because I must write to someone . . . I have always told you this mind must have vent. Not that I am expecting you will do me any good, but only as I said to vent my feelings."[12] Often this frustration shortened his patience so severely that he struck out blindly, even at his sons. Apologies were then necessary: "These matters have worried me a great deal and I have not been able to dictate of late . . . When I am cross do not think I have any feeling against you, but I shall take pride in you as my own son—you have done well, I never could have done it better."[13]

Pinkerton reserved special vitriol for his superintendents, whom he thought weak and vacillating in personnel relations with their agents. When a New York agent was again caught drinking on the job, Pinkerton demanded his removal. But Bangs demurred. Pinkerton, railing, penned a letter to his younger son, William: "I have given Mr. Bangs strict orders to discharge him, yet he does not do it."[14] When William was to be sent to England to bring back several suspects in a bank robbery, Pinkerton dispatched minute instructions for the entire trip. But Bangs handled certain parts his own way. Pinkerton was beside himself: "I have written Mr. Bangs upon the necessity of having more identification . . . but he and the bank authorities are indifferent. Well! I can't do any more than I have done."[15]

As if the peccadilloes of the agents themselves were not enough, Pinkerton heard in 1875 that Bangs himself appeared to be drinking on the job. Pinkerton immediately wrote his older son: "With regard to my order to you requesting you not to pay any money to Mr. Bangs except his salary. I shall adhere to it; I shall not relax any. This must continue until we understand each other better. This thing has almost driven me mad ... Write me anything you can learn, be it good or bad, I want to know the whole."[16]

The problem of drunkenness had varied dimensions. Beyond the damage done to the public reputation of the agency, it was frequently the catalyst for leakage of secret information. Pinkerton constantly feared that a loosened tongue would let information slip out that would endanger the work, and perhaps the lives, of the men in the field. In 1873 the Philadelphia office files were broken into by "counterspys" (apparently the Irish janitress and her son) and Pinkerton was apprehensive that the stolen plans were destined for a gang of thieves the agency was then pursuing. Pinkerton couldn't find out just how much had leaked out, and wrote Bangs, "I believe I shall be half crazy until I do know, still I feel sure the thieves don't know much we have been doing, except that Willie is in London sometime ago."[17]

A more serious case the following year involved two drunken agents (one each in Chicago and New York), and, again, possible leakage of information. But in this case, the potential recipients were the vicious gang led by Jesse James and Cole Younger. Pinkerton wrung his hands. "Oh! It's horrible to think that any moment will bring me news of the murder of my own men. Oh! God it's awful."[18] As three Pinkerton agents were eventually killed by the gang, his concern was not based on fancy. Divulging of any agency business became an anathema to Pinkerton. Even when his old friend General McClellan asked to see the remaining Pinkerton Civil War files, Pinkerton demurred. He said that although the General "of course, can be trusted to a certain extent," nevertheless "it won't do—the General will have another one, or two, or three, or four, or a dozen [collaborators] and away goes all the secrecy."[19]

Pinkerton always demanded to know all that was going on in the various offices—immediately and in detail. Bangs was particularly slow in replying and evasive when he did. In a touchy case in 1872, concerning an embezzlement in the New York office by one of the agents, Bangs failed to notify Pinkerton until after Pinkerton heard of it directly, and then Bangs wrote only a thirty-two line letter, sketchy and defensive. Pinkerton replied: *"My God! George* do you realize that I am in misery, misery from this whole concern." "Tell me all, black as you please. I will be satisfied if I know the worst. But *Good God*—Nothing. I ask you, George, is it fair? All I ask is to know all."[20]

This case aptly illustrates another fundamental dilemma faced by Pinkerton. The operative who had embezzled the agency funds was assigned to a particularly sensitive job for the Erie Railroad—undercover observation of train conductors to see whether they were embezzling rail fares. Premature disclosure of the fact that a check was being made would spoil months of work. Fearing that the agent, if summarily fired, would immediately sell secrets to the conductors, Pinkerton was forced to retain the man until a more propitious time for removal. Thus the problem of disciplining agents for wrongdoing was tremendously complicated by the fact that the agents frequently knew too much for Pinkerton to incur their hatred. Lurking in the background in some of the cases was the possibility that the agent if fired would attempt to blackmail Pinkerton for some of the excesses the agency occasionally slipped into. One of these will occupy our attention in a later chapter.

Pinkerton's close surveillance of agency activities also covered financial matters. The "General Principles and Rules" exhorted the agents to deal carefully with agency funds; the agent was to "economize money, and be economical in all his habits," for "there is no occasion for them to resort to the higher class of Hotels, nor is there very much necessity for their riding in stages or omnibuses."[21] A thorny problem here was Pinkerton's son William. After a series of what Pinkerton thought were high bills, he wrote Bangs, "I have had my attention called to my son William's having charged enormous bills . . . If any bills of the kind have been presented to you and you allowed them to go without cutting down, you will be liable for them yourself . . . I want you to act with him fearlessly."[22] When a woman agent in the Philadelphia office appeared to be squandering her money on clothes, Pinkerton wrote, "I am afraid to trust you with money, I am afraid you have got into the habit of spending your money for trivial matters . . . I will not allow you to borrow money from any person whatsoever, either in my employ or out of it . . . I don't like to see anyone who is obliged to borrow money, no matter how small the sums may be."[23]

Pinkerton appended an interesting postscript to this letter that illustrates the dimensions of his concern for his employees' morals: "I would like to say to you, without injuring your feelings, that card playing is bad and I would advise you to discontinue it at once and forever. I think it leads to many things which are bad. You will please me very much indeed if you will promise not to play cards any more with any person."

Employing women as agents caused Pinkerton many headaches. He had long felt that for certain types of detection a woman was best fitted. But the possibilities of public misinterpretation were sizable. Even within the agency, Pinkerton was a target for innuendoes about the woman agents. When he proposed in early 1876 to establish a "Female Department" in Philadelphia, his son Robert and Benjamin Franklin, the Philadelphia superintendent, objected, implying that it was at least undignified and perhaps immoral. Pinkerton was outraged, feeling that this amounted to a direct challenge to his authority as "Principal." He commented in a letter to his New York superintendent, "I intend to use females whenever it can be done judiciously. I must do so or falsify my own theory, practice and truth." As Mrs. Franklin had evidently egged her husband on to make the complaint, Pinkerton continued: "I cannot tolerate that a female should be consulted about this, and under no circumstances will I allow any argument to be brought up on the subject . . . I will allow no compromise whatsoever. I am right, I will stand the consequences as come what may."[24]

Pinkerton's moralistic and sometimes self-righteous attitudes toward his employees even extended to religion, but in a rather surprising way. Hearing that some of the agents in the Philadelphia office were attending revivalist meetings, Pinkerton wrote Franklin he was "shocked" that "the evil preachings that are spread through the U.S. at the present time by Moody and Sankey" should have penetrated the agency. "On Sunday," Pinkerton continued, "where they are on special duty they are to give their whole time to my business without any reservation whatever." Pinkerton then made his point crystal clear: "Page 11 of the 'General Principles and Rules' speaks broad and wide enough for anyone. It simply asks all the employees to speak the truth; is not that sufficient, is not that religion enough without hypocrisy?"[25]

Pinkerton's most abiding concern during this period was getting and keeping business. The agency had prospered in the 1860's, but the impact of the 1871 fire, coupled with a marked decrease in business activity, had, by 1872, seriously alarmed Pinkerton. The tone of urgency in his letters heightened, though the type of exhortation varied according to the recipient. To his younger son, William, he always remained the optimist; even in late 1872, in the face of impending financial disaster, he wrote, "don't be alarmed . . . I will come out all right bye 'n bye." "You see, Willie, my idea is never lose heart, never think a moment of giving up the ship. I am bound to go through sink or swim . . . Hold your head up, don't be afraid. I will back you at all eternity."[26] But such optimism did not match the facts, and Pinkerton's letters to Bangs and the elder son, Robert, reflected the distress he felt concerning business developments in 1872.

New business was increasingly difficult to obtain. By summertime, business was turning downward; even under the best of conditions such a new concept as private detective work was hard to sell. But this always troubling problem was compounded by serious difficulties in collecting accounts for work already done. By August, the credit position of the firm was precarious. The individual superintendents made the collections, and Pinkerton desperately pleaded with them to bring in some money. On August 15 he wrote to Bangs: "I suppose there is no hope for anything paying in New York. God knows what I am to do two days from this date."[27] A letter the same day to his Chicago superintendent repeated the theme: "We are in great want of money, on every hand I am in debt, yet I cannot get any person to help me, but everyone whom I owe a shilling to are calling on me for it . . . It is nearly Saturday and you know I have to pay everyone. I must have money for they must have money. I would not for anything allow them to go without their wages, but how am I to get the money unless you and others do your duty and bring in the money?"[28]

Money dribbled in, but not enough to turn the tide. By mid-October, Pinkerton, sensing the impending financial panic of the country, wrote Bangs: "I now say to you collect all your Bills without one moment's delay, as things are coming right on us. *Let business stand for the moment*—go to work and collect Bills, sacrifice everything to get money, discount at any price . . . any day whatever there may be a crash around us that we little suspect."[29]

But, by November, Pinkerton was forced first to borrow from employees, and then to mortgage some of his property and pledge a substantial block of his personal railroad stocks for cash loans to finance a new job the agency had obtained with the Atlantic & Great Western Railroad. This was galling to a man who had preached so long to his employees to keep their lives on a cash basis. His creditors soon became—he said—"abusive." The largest loan had come from Henry Sanford, general superintendent of the Adams Express Company, an old friend who now "has insulted me in every way lately."[30]

The loans tided the agency over into the new year, but this was to be the famous year of the failure of banker Jay Cooke, the "crash of 1873," and the beginning of one of the most serious of all American depressions. By May, Pinkerton wrote Bangs, "I scarcely can tell which way to go and many a time I am perfectly bewildered what to do . . . I am afraid." Though the agency still had a number of accounts, he continued, "business will be failing I fear very fast unless in some way or other we can get it roused up."[31]

It was precisely at this point, and under these desperate conditions, that Pinkerton's involvement in the Molly Maguire movement began. For Pinkerton, in the same letter, instructed Bangs to "go to Franklin Gowan [sic] occasionally, see how he feels, bring up A. C. Gowan's matter, and see how he takes it. I am talking about him and writing to Robert and Mr. Franklin. Suggest some things to Mr. Gowan about one thing and another which would be feasible and I have no doubt he will give us work."

❖   ❖   ❖   ❖   ❖

Gowen and Pinkerton had done business before. The Reading, like the Erie, had used the agency as an independent check on the honesty and competence of his railroad conductors. Gowen had received a letter from a customer in January 1870 complaining that he had been cheated by a conductor. Sensing a more widespread pattern of peculation, Gowen hired Pinkerton agents to ride the line anonymously, reporting on any irregularities. By 1872 the agents had uncovered many examples of kiting or pocketing of fares, failure to collect fares and other petty slips. These were reported in great detail to Gowen. For example: "Bought of a man 5 ft. 8 inches high,

40 years, dark complexion, black hair, bald on top of head, full black whiskers and mustache, peculiar accent. Feb. 4th, #11 Phoenix-ville to Ringgold, $2.10." And, illustrative of Pinkerton's concern for the full truth, the reports also detailed fair and honest operations of other conductors—even to praise for the way some called their stations.[32]

The early months of 1873 brought increased turbulence in both the rail and coal domains of Gowen. These incidents took a serious turn—beatings of mine supervisors, derailing of railroad cars, burning of coal tipples. Gowen's concern heightened.

Bangs, under instructions from Pinkerton in his May 18 letter to "suggest some things to Mr. Gowan about one thing and another," must have found a receptive audience. Through the following months the Pinkerton operatives turned their attention to the broader pattern of crime. In September several blatant incidents near Glen Carbon, a few miles west of Pottsville, culminating in the burning of a large Glen Carbon coal tipple, persuaded Franklin, Pinkerton's Philadelphia superintendent, to concentrate the agents there. And there, for the first time, the Pinkertons linked the name "Molly Maguire" to the depredations—as relayed by Franklin to Gowen in the following report: "The operatives report the rumored exist-ence at Glen Carbon of an organization known as the 'Molly Maguires,' a band of roughs joined together for the purpose of instituting revenge against any one of whom they may take a dislike."[33]

The rash of depredations was apparently serious enough to war-rant the face-to-face meeting of Gowen and Pinkerton in Phila-delphia. Whether Gowen instigated this meeting (as implied in Pinkerton's *The Mollie Maguires and the Detectives*) is unclear. But the results of the meeting *were* clear: Franklin reported to Gowen on October 29, "my operatives are now turning their atten-tion to learning all possible information in regard to secret organiza-tions inimicable to the interests of your company."[34]

Pinkerton, feeling that his operatives in the coal fields could not fully handle the responsibilities of the new assignment, decided to bring a new man on the scene. Four years later Pinkerton told the story of how he described this yet-unknown agent to Gowen: "It is no ordinary man that I need in this matter. He must be an Irishman, and a Catholic, as only this class of persons can find admission to the Mollie Maguires. My detective should become, to all intents and purposes, one of the order, and continue so while he remains in the case before us. He should be hardy, tough, and capable of laboring, in season and out of season, to accomplish, unknown to those about him, a single absorbing object."[35] This was written in hindsight with perfect vision. Whether Pinkerton really sensed at the first meeting with Gowen that he was entering one of the agency's most sensitive cases is problematical. The assigning of a young and relatively untrained man did not match with Pinkerton's usual meticulousness in such matters.

Pinkerton described a richly imaginative process of racking his brain to find this paragon—how he mentally discarded employee after employee, and how he suddenly was struck by the eminent qualifications of one young agent when he happened to see him on a streetcar. The agent at that time was working incognito as a conductor, carrying out a routine check. His name: James McParlan.*

McParlan fitted Pinkerton's description well. He was a native Irishman, born in County Armagh in the province of Ulster in 1844 (thus was twenty-nine when he began the Pennsylvania adventure). Prior to coming to America in 1867, he worked in a chemical factory in Durham, England, and in a Belfast linen warehouse. After immigrating he took a job in a New York City grocery, then another in a dry goods store in Medina, New York. A year later he had his first taste of detective work when he was employed by a small Chicago detective agency as a "preventive policeman." This was a springboard to the Pinkerton Agency, which he joined some time in 1871.[36]

McParlan must have had misgivings about accepting the Molly assignment. For, in addition to danger (natural enough in detective work), he was to be, quite simply, an informer. Much detective work must of necessity be "informing," often by adopting a disguise and gaining the confidence of the party involved. In this case, though, McParlan was asked to inform on his fellow countrymen, people of his own ethnic and religious background. No other person in all of Ireland was more hated and despised than the informer. Many years later, Robert Pinkerton, commenting on the case, said, "It

* Often spelled "McParland," even by members of the Pinkerton organization. But his own signature was without the final "d" during this early period of his life. Later he, too, added the "d"! Also, the name "Molly" was often spelled "Mollie," though the former seems to have been the preferred version.

required something more than mere pecuniary reward to secure the right sort of person for this task. The man had to feel that he was serving his church, his race and his country; otherwise, it would be impossible to get anyone to undertake a work which invited death by assassination."[37] Such a sanguine view of the detective was not shared by all; a later anti-Pinkerton version held:

The famous detective had in his employ many hundreds of men, in many different cities, yet he had difficulty in selecting the man wanted by Gowen. Many thieves and assassins on his payroll were marshalled before his mental vision—men whom he knew would slay and rob without compunction—but he doubted their utter heartlessness. This anthracite case was one that required the services of a being that had touched the nethermost depths of degeneracy—of a man whose hands were red with the blood of victims and whose nature was incapable of remorse. An extraordinary criminal was needed—a prodigy in fiendishness—and at last the detective found his man. In Chicago there was a young man, not many years from Ireland, who was known as a good man on any job of depravity and who was as wily as a serpent. This man was Detective James McParlan.[38]

Pinkerton first assigned McParlan the task of researching secret societies in Ireland, so that Pinkerton could both inform himself and check out McParlan's abilities. The young detective quickly came up with a remarkable document. The request had come on October 8; on October 10 he gave Pinkerton a very long letter that tells a great deal about McParlan's intellectual caliber and his understanding of the Irish.[39]

He documented the northern Irish secret societies reasonably well, but seemed to have little knowledge of the south of Ireland. After discussing Orangeism and the early Ribbon groups, he chronicled the famine, and at this point analyzed the Molly Maguires:

Some of the people in the provinces of Ulster and Connaught resolved not to starve as long as there was any food stowed away in the public markets or warehouses or any storekeeper who might have a supply of stock on hand. They immediately organized under the name Molly McGuire. The objects were to take from those who had abundance to give to the poor who were then dying by hundreth with hunger. They seldom ever at this time compelled a man who they might visit to give them money. But of course would not refuse it if offered to them. Their mode of operation was to have there leader dressed up in a suit of womens clothing to represent the Irish Mother begging bread for her children under there disguise. The leader or Molly as she was called went to the storekeeper provided she knew he was pretty well off and demanded of him the amount levied on him in the shape of meal flour and general groceries. If the things were not forwarded at the time and place designated by Molly in the limited time she provided her men immediately visited the store or house and after securing the Inmates they immediately proceeded to help themselves to everything in the shape of provisions on the premises taking with them all they could possibly carry. They then released the Inmates of the said house giving them to understand that if they said anything which might lead to their detection and punishment they would again visit them and for every one of them that were arrested they would make at least three of the said household suffer.

Such romantic, "Robin Hood" activity on the part of the Irish secret society was possible, but police reports during the famine period do not chronicle just such a case, nor does the concept "take from the rich—give to the poor" truly represent the Irish secret society. McParlan was clearly falling victim to hearsay here.

But, according to McParlan, in the postfamine period the Molly Maguires, in "performing the simple Act of taking from the rich and giving to the poor," began to change character, "something after the fashion of the Ku Klux Klahn . . . but as they had no Negroes to kill they commenced by shooting down Landlords, Agents, Baliffs or any unoffending neighbor who might not coincide with their views."

Because of a number of trials and hangings, McParlan continued, "the Ribbonmen . . . Emigrated to England and Scotland, had formed a new society and being the name Ribbonmen or Molly McGuire was now considered treason, this society adopted a new name which was called the Ancient Order of Hibernians." In order to join the society, McParlan stated, one had to be a Catholic of Catholic parents, and had to swear allegiance to the Board of Erin, "which as far as I can learn sits in Dublin," and which sent forth signs and passwords every quarter. McParlan's reason for this was interesting:

Being that it is a secret society it debars its members of the previlidges of the Confessional. Then when any of its members wishes to avail themselves of that previledge they got nothing to do but resign for a month at the commencement of each or any quarter of the Year and then when asked as to whether they belong to any secret organization they can state they did formally but not now as it is not a sin in reality but the mere fact that belonging to any secret Order deprives them of this so claimed benefit.

McParlan then concluded his document with a footnote to Pinkerton, "I presume by the time you have got this read you will get tired of most of it or in fact all of it. May not be interesting to you, nevertheless it is a brief sketch of Irish Societyism."

This document speaks to both the abilities and disabilities of McParlan. He had a comprehensive knowledge of Ireland, far more than that available from the books on Ireland in that period. The greater part of his knowledge and experience was of Ulster, and he tended to view the Irish secret society much more as a clandestine religious institution than as an economic protest. As an Ulster Catholic he tended to view Orangeism as the key factor, not the landlord-tenant relationship. And as an Ulster Catholic he would seem to be heading for a particularly ambivalent position in his proposed assignment. His treatment of facts should give us pause, although it must be balanced against the fact that this long and comprehensive letter was almost an overnight job. The letter is intelligently written for the most part, though, and must have impressed Allan Pinkerton.

Satisfied with his choice, Pinkerton set the plans for McParlan's entry into the coal fields. McParlan was to tell his fellow employees at the agency that Mr. Pinkerton had kindly sent him to England for his health, and was to leave immediately for Philadelphia for a briefing session with Superintendent Benjamin Franklin. Only the three Pinkertons, Bangs, and Franklin knew of his assignment. His identity was even kept secret from Gowen, only his initials being used in reports going forward to the railroad. On the 27th of October he left for the anthracite regions, attired as a tramp and going under the assumed name of James McKenna, surely not realizing at that moment that his exploits would become so well-known in American history.

❧ ❧ ❧ ❧ ❧

Exactly how do we know what McParlan did during his two and a half years in the coal fields? Up to now the reconstruction of his activity has depended largely on his public testimony at the trials in 1876 and 1877, embellished by the flamboyant and lurid account published by Allan Pinkerton in 1877. A very small number of the actual detective reports had trickled out, covering only a few of the thirty months involved. In total all of those fragments were slim evidence to establish the true story, but, in spite of this, many "definitive" accounts have been attempted.

Now, with the availability of the Allan Pinkerton letterbooks, much more can be known of the agency and its founder. And with the opening of the Reading Railroad files, the same is true of McParlan's field work.

As valuable as these are in coming closer to a clear understanding of the facts, certain inherent weaknesses in each must be understood. First, the letterbooks are all "one-sided," for they chronicle only Allan Pinkerton's letters *to* correspondents. No records to date are available of letters *from* correspondents. Second, the McParlan reports are still incomplete, and there are significant gaps where only Pinkerton's book and the trial records remain. Further, all but one set of McParlan's reports are secondhand in that they are handwritten summaries of McParlan's communications prepared by Benjamin Franklin in the Philadelphia office and sent to the railroad president. Franklin gave the same treatment to the reports of Captain Robert J. Linden, who joined the case in 1875. Exactly how much editing of the original reports was done by Franklin is unknown, although the few checks possible seem to indicate that the documents were largely direct transcriptions from what McParlan and Linden wrote. And, of course, the fallibility of the two agents themselves must be considered, for it is more than a possibility that, either for reasons of personal prestige or by instruction of Pinkerton or Franklin, certain things were overemphasized or omitted. The reports, then, must be used with great caution.

Fortunately, one additional set of papers now available from the Reading manuscript collection adds a gratifying control. During a substantial part of the period McParlan's and Linden's expense accounts, detailed according to all expenditures for each day, are available.

In the following chapters careful distinction will be made between those periods still illuminated only by the trial records and published books, and those periods now embraced by the new evidence. For the sake of initial perspective, the Allan Pinkerton and Reading Railroad sources are laid out in the accompanying table.

TABLE OF ALLAN PINKERTON AND READING RAILROAD RECORDS ON MOLLY MAGUIRES

A. ALLAN PINKERTON LETTERBOOKS (in Pinkerton MSS, Library of Congress)

    Vol. I—August 25, 1872, to August 20, 1875

    Vol. II—September 2, 1875, to November 12, 1883

B. PINKERTON DETECTIVE FIELD REPORTS (in Molly Maguire Papers, Reading Railroad, Philadelphia, unless otherwise noted)[a]

Year	From James McParlan		From Robert J. Linden	
	Reports	Expense Accounts	Reports	Expense Accounts
1873	*None (entered coal fields in October)*		*Not yet assigned to coal fields*	
1874	Jan. 1 –Jan. 25 Jan. 26 –May 3[b] Aug. 27–Oct. 21 Nov. 13–Dec. 6	Dec. 21 –Dec. 31	*Not yet assigned to coal fields*	
1875	Jan. 23 –Feb. 16 Feb. 17 –Feb. 26 Mar. 6 –Mar. 30 Apr. 13–May 12 July 1 –July 10 July 15 –Aug. 2[c] Aug. 21–Sept. 2[c] Oct. 12 –Dec. 26	Jan. 1 –Feb. 13 Feb. 16 –Apr. 2 June 30 July 19 Aug. 11–Oct. 5	May 6 –May 22 May 24–June 14 July 15 –Oct. 20	Apr. 28 –July 31 Aug. 28–Dec. 31
1876	*None (out of coal fields after Mar. 1)*		May 20–June 11[c] Aug. 6 –Aug. 30[b]	Jan. 1 –Feb. 5 July 31 –Sept. 23 Oct. 23 –Nov. 18

[a] All of the Reading Railroad's Molly Maguire Papers have heretofore been unavailable to scholars. The series marked "b" and "c," which are in other repositories, have been available, though not all have been used in published works. The Reading Railroad's Molly Maguire Papers contain, in addition to the reports covered in this table, various memoranda and other manuscript materials. Among these are extensive field reports of other Pinkerton agents during the period 1870–1880 inclusive, some of which bear on the Molly Maguire investigation, especially those of detectives P. M. Cummings from November 1874 to February 1875; William McCowan from February to June 1875; and "W. R. H." (never further identified by name) in February 1875.

[b] Molly Maguire MSS, Historical Society of Pennsylvania, Philadelphia.

[c] Kaercher MSS, Mrs. George Keiser, Pottsville, Pennsylvania.

Chapter 7 * In Search of Murder

> Loveliness
> Needs not the foreign art of ornament,
> But is, when unadorned, adorned the most.

WITH THOSE LINES Allan Pinkerton began his account of James McParlan's detection in the Pennsylvania coal fields. "For," he continued, "the detective's adventures . . . are sufficiently romantic and attractive, if properly related, to satisfy the most exacting reader, without the author having recourse to the smallest amount of extraneous matter, employing any of the powers of the imagination, or the tricks of the professional novel-writer in enchaining attention."[1]

We must tread warily in accepting Pinkerton's pious declaration. Just how much of the derring-do in *The Mollie Maguires and the Detectives* really happened will never be known. McParlan was on his own; the main links were the reports going back to Benjamin Franklin in the Philadelphia office. In spite of Pinkerton's protestations of being "in daily contact" with McParlan, the files show McParlan only reporting every other week or so, sending his accumulated daily reports for the period covered. Pinkerton, waxing mysterious, implied an alternative plan, "not necessary to be divulged, arranged by which all interruptions through the mails would be prevented." This was most likely the local telegraph company, for it was owned and operated by Gowen's railroad. A simple code system was probably arranged, and contact could have been made. Nevertheless, the amount of independence invested in McParlan is remarkable.

*   *   *   *   *

On October 27, 1873, James McParlan left Philadelphia for the coal regions. James McKenna, an itinerant tramp, stepped off the train at Port Clinton. A two-and-a-half year stint of double life began.

Arthur Conan Doyle creates appropriate atmosphere for this day in his Sherlock Holmes novel, *The Valley of Fear*. Doyle met William Pinkerton during a transatlantic crossing shortly after the turn of the century, became intrigued with Allan Pinkerton's account of the Mollies, and constructed the American portion of *Valley of Fear* as almost a paraphrase of the actual story. "Jack McMurdo"—Doyle's name for James McKenna—is staring moodily out of the train window.

Through the growing gloom there pulsed the red glow of furnaces on the sides of the hills. Great heaps of slag and dumps of cinders loomed up on each side, with the high shafts of the collieries towering above them. Huddled groups of mean, wooden houses, the windows of which were beginning to outline themselves in light, were scattered here and there along the line, and the frequent halting places were crowded with their swarthy inhabitants . . . The young traveller gazed out into this dismal country with a face of mingled repulsion and interest . . .[2]

Facing the "repulsed" but "interested" McParlan when he got off the train were certain critical necessities. First, he had to familiarize himself with the region and choose a base of operations.

Certain spade work had been accomplished by other Pinkerton detectives before he arrived. But this was small help. In McParlan's day, travel in the anthracite region was difficult. The many small hamlets, or "patches," were isolated from each other both by the mountains and by patch customs and friendships. The two southern fields, where McParlan was to concentrate his efforts, lay in long, narrow valleys separated by mountain ridges. (The whole anthracite region, when viewed on a topographic map, looks very much as if Gargantuan men had laid their hands side by side into soft clay.) As the railroad spurs, taking the lines of lesser resistance, ran along the individual valleys, communication and travel was much easier in a particular valley than from valley to valley.

McParlan came up the Schuylkill River, stopping briefly at Port Clinton and Auburn before reaching the southern boundary of the first Schuylkill field at Schuylkill Haven. (His travels can be traced by the map on pages 80 and 81.) His first major trip took him out the western extension of the field—to Swatara, Tremont, Rausch Creek, Donaldson, and Tower City. The gregarious "tramp" made many acquaintances in the taverns and "shebeens" (the unlicensed shops located in private homes) and heard many stories of the Mollies' awesome power. Apparently there were no Mollies in the western end, but the detective picked up veiled references that they were scattered along a line running northwest from Pottsville to Girardville and then east through Shenandoah, with a special concentration in Mahanoy City. Moving back eastward, he entered Pottsville, the county seat of Schuylkill County.

Here he first met Pat Dormer. Pinkerton's book describes the man and his place:

The Sheridan House, Patrick Dormer, proprietor, situated in Centre Street, Pottsville, was somewhat celebrated in annals of the town, and its reputation among the inhabitants by no means doubtful or uncertain. While in some regards the tavern boasted entire respectability, in certain others it bore a name far from enviable. Its isolated honors were due to Mrs. Dormer; its many dishonors to her physically gigantic but morally erratic lord and master, and the calling he followed. Many were the drunken brawls and midnight orgies transpiring beneath its steep roof and within its tawny brick walls; but against the lady of the house nothing could be truthfully charged—except she was Dormer's wife. The edifice was neither private residence nor hotel, but a compound of the two. Three stories in height, having a long low extension in its rear, lighted by a sky light, and in which was located the well-patronized ten-pin alley; the basement of the main structure was employed as dining room, kitchen, and laundry, and the first, or business floor, front, for saloon purposes. Just back of the latter was a card playing and bagatelle division . . .[3]

Warned by a chance acquaintance of the persistent rumor that Dormer was a "Sleeper" (an alternate name for Molly Maguire in Schuylkill County), McParlan jumped at the chance to visit him. He planned his entrance carefully. Lurching through the Sheridan House door in feigned drunkenness, he launched into a skillful Irish jig to the accompaniment of a fiddler who had been desultorily strumming away in a corner of the tavern. According to Pinkerton, the initial hostility of the patrons and Dormer soon melted before the lilting tap of heel and toe. After receiving both the plaudits of the crowd and a reinforcing shot of whiskey, the detective next exploited another soft spot in the Irish temperament with a song. His choice was quite calculated—it was the famous Molly Maguire ballad of Donegal (quoted in an earlier chapter) concerning the murder of the land agent Bell by Pat Dolan's Mollies.

The amenities of dance and song out of the way, McParlan was next asked to visit the back room for a game of euchre, Dormer honoring the detective by choosing him as his partner. After first winning, Dormer and McParlan began to drop more and more hands. The reason soon became apparent; McParlan suddenly grabbed the arm of one of his opponents, exposing the fact that the man had six cards instead of five. The man loudly disputed the accusation of cheating, words became more angry, and McParlan was finally challenged to a fist fight, to be held forthwith in the center of the barroom. And, so Pinkerton's story goes, the detective handily whipped the cheater in five rounds, after which he called all to the bar "to join us in drinkin' confusion to all mane scuts and chates."[4]

Dormer was won over. Calling his new-found friend to a private table, he proceeded to quiz the stranger, giving McParlan his first real chance to paint the image of "James McKenna." The immediate past and the potential future of this living phantom (as McParlan carefully developed during this evening and over the succeeding weeks) was as follows: McKenna was not really a tramp, but a criminal on the "lam" from a killing in Buffalo, New York. He had also lived in Colorado, and had been with the Union forces as seaman with the Navy on the Mississippi. His apparently inexhaustible supply of money to stand for drinks in his night-by-night whiskey bouts, he explained, came in part from a government pension (which he sometimes hinted had been fraudulently obtained). But the main device through which he kept his pocketbook full was by peddling counterfeit money—"shoving the queer." Dormer and his friends were impressed by this, for when McParlan showed them examples of this "bogus" money, it looked to them to be just as good as real money (which, of course, it was).

But the crucial point which McParlan had to establish—a point in which he could afford no slips—was his presumed past membership in the Ancient Order of Hibernians (AOH). The Molly Maguire song at Dormer's that first night, the carefully planted offhand comments he made in subsequent days, all cumulated to build up the image that he had been a member of the organization before coming to America. Pinkerton's book quoted McParlan, "In Ireland, once, sure an' I had a little of what ye might call exparience in that line . . . It's been such a long time since I heard anything, or thought anything, of the order, that, as ye might say, I'm almost as ignorant as if I niver had seen the inside of the affair, an' I belave, until I am once more initiated, the best thing I can do is to say as little about it as convanient!"[5]

At times he also implied that he had been a more recent member—alternately naming New York, Buffalo, and Chicago as the locale. This was a dangerous avenue, though, for the immediate reaction was often the demand to produce a "traveling card," a device used among the various lodges in the United States. (Whether there were actually traveling cards issued by the Ribbon lodges in Ireland for a member emigrating to America is unclear; there probably were some.)

McParlan, on shaky ground here, countered the demands by cautioning that any check in these towns might alert the police to his whereabouts and thus bring his arrest. Some of the more fanciful stories of McParlan's exploits have built up many wild legends of the lengths to which the Pinkerton agency went in aiding McParlan to establish his hypothetical past. Many tell the story that the agency sent in agents disguised as New York police to inquire ostentatiously about McParlan, thus supporting the detective's story of being a fugitive and giving his new "Sleeper" friends a psychological tie to him by allowing them to provide an alibi to the "policemen." An even more astounding story has appeared in some accounts in recent years that McParlan, having learned that a mine watchman was singled out to be killed, promised to take care of the job himself. He soon reported to his friends that he had beaten the man to death and thrown his body down a mine shaft. This was confirmed, so the story runs, when the local police reported finding the body, and McParlan and several "Sleepers" were then actually reputed to have attended the funeral. But, report these writers, this was all an elaborate hoax devised by McParlan and the agency—the mine watchman was paid to leave the county and to allow his "death" to be reported.[6]

There is no record in the available detective reports of any of these elaborate devices. Perhaps it would have been a simple matter to send in agents pretending to be police. The mine watchman hoax, though, stretches our credulity; few people would be willing to go to such lengths unless compensated quite substantially. And there is no evidence that Pinkerton, at this stage of the investigation, saw in this case the major publicity potential that later developed. More likely, McParlan was charged to depend on his own wits, with a little help from the Philadelphia office.

McParlan knew that if he initiated questions about the Mollies or the AOH he would immediately fall under suspicion. But an unexpected break, occurring just as he entered the fields in October 1873, aided him in bringing up the subject. The *Boston Globe* printed a long letter from an anonymous individual in Mahanoy City about the "reign of terror of the Molly Maguires." Probably this would have come to nought had not the *Pilot*, the official Catholic paper of the Boston diocese, picked up the story and reprinted it in its entirety on October 18. The *Pilot* was one of the most influential Irish-oriented papers in America and was avidly read in any district peopled by the Irish for its extensive coverage of happenings back in Ireland and for its Irish-American news. As soon as the Molly story appeared in the *Pilot*, its shocking allegations became the talk of the coal regions.

The author of the letter used his best poetic license in building his story of violence, citing the "murder and plunder" done under a "regular system of Ku Klux messages and signs used to intimidate people." He quoted a particularly brutal coffin notice—"what is known as a Mollies' notice to quit"—and described in flaming prose several fresh outrages. But his intended punch line in the letter—his promise to expose who the Mollies were—proved to be a fizzle. Calling them the "Modocs" (he was quite incorrect, as the Modocs were Welsh and German miners), he added veiled references to a headquarters near Locust Gap, "two dark-looking places in the Broad Top Mountain."

This was no more than had been written countless times over the last fifteen years in the *Miners' Journal* and the Philadelphia papers. But a real shock came three weeks later. An anonymous reply, penned to the *Pilot* just after the first article, was published by the *Pilot* on November 8. Its author came immediately to the point:

Their headquarters are not in this country, nor in the coal regions at all, the President of the "Ancient Order of Hibernians" in New York is the direct leader of the Society . . . If, therefore, you wish to know all about the "Molly Maguires" you must look to the "Ancient Order of

Hibernians," for in that Society you will find everything of "Molly Maguireism" that has made the coal regions so famous for lawlessness . . . The members have been publicly excommunicated and the Society proscribed by the Bishop of Philadelphia, Scranton and Harrisburg . . . The subject is of greater importance to the Church than at first may appear to your readers . . . I hope you will take hold of and follow up the subject until this "Ancient Order of Hibernians" has been shown in its true colors. You exposed the "Mechanics"—don't spare the "Hibernians."

This article brought immediate reaction. "A Member" of the AOH wrote the *Pilot* that it was "a violation of the Constitution of the AOH and an utter impossibility for a man to belong to said Order and be guilty of the crimes mentioned." He said, "The Order is founded on the three principles of 'Friendship, Unity and True Christian Charity.' " Soon other letters poured in, largely indignant that the AOH had been so accused. A "Hibernian" from West Virginia also seemed to be astounded at even the possibility that a member could commit a crime, insisting that "a section of the Constitution reads as follows, 'If any member of this Order be convicted of robbery, perjury or any other atrocious offence, he shall be excluded from the Order for life.' " Another attack on the AOH was made after this letter, emphasizing that the order was secret and therefore "no one so circumstanced is, or can be, a good practical member of the Church."[7] There the *Pilot* allowed the issue to die. But the notoriety given to the AOH in the coal regions had had its effect. The issue was debated in taverns all over the anthracite district, giving McParlan ready-made conversation. Though the detective was still unclear as to just what the relationship was between the Molly Maguires and the Ancient Order of Hibernians, the *Pilot* articles warned him to be observant whenever either was mentioned.

By watching carefully in his nightly tavern bouts, McParlan soon discovered—according to Allan Pinkerton's book—that secret signs were seemingly being flashed at him. But, realizing that a slip here might crumble the whole structure of fabrication, he was careful to imply that he knew the password and sign system but was not familiar with the current versions. Once during these early weeks he was challenged by one member to produce more specific evidence and was forced to feign a drunken stupor to avoid exposing his lack of knowledge.

According to Pinkerton, on whose chronicle we must depend for these episodes before the end of 1873, the psychology that McParlan planted within this disguise was ingenious. He was a criminal—a counterfeiter and murderer—thus encouraging any of the "Sleepers" who had crimes on their conscience to confide them without fear of exposure. McParlan always had money for treating, thus giving him an opportunity to be popular with the nightly barroom crowds and to aid in loosening their tongues via intoxication. (Thus he violated one of Allan Pinkerton's "principles.") And being an Irishman—a true-blue singing, dancing, brawling broth of a lad—gave him entree to any gathering of the Irish in the area. Too, he was a Roman Catholic, but the implications of this must be held in abeyance for the moment.

The giant Dormer was completely won over by McParlan's story. Here was not only a rollicking addition to his tavern—singer, dancer, and story teller—but also a man with plenty of money. Fortunately for McParlan, any notion that Dormer might have had of checking the details of this alibi was submerged under the cascade of new money flowing over the bar.

The contact with Dormer was McParlan's first break. The tavern was a mecca for the "Sleepers" of the Pottsville region, and, through Dormer, McParlan met not only Pottsville's "true-bred" Mollies (an expression McParlan himself was to use[8]), but also the frequent visitors from "over the mountain"—the area of Mahanoy City and Shenandoah beyond Broad Mountain. Almost everyone agreed that those two towns were the real hotbeds of the Mollies. Dormer was temporarily under a cloud with the organization, having been accused of being a member of the Odd Fellows, the natural enemy of the Mollies. McParlan feared the possibility that he might have to take sides against Dormer, and decided to move up the line to the two "hotbeds."

His first stop was Girardville, just over Broad Mountain, where he apparently met John Kehoe, known to us already as the young miner in 1862 that had spit upon the American flag and subsequently threatened the mine boss Langdon moments before Langdon was killed by an unknown party of assailants.

Kehoe is one of the key figures in the Molly story, a man to whom the newspapers subsequently gave the dubious sobriquet "the King of the Mollies." At this time he was the successful owner of one of Girardville's taverns, the Hibernian House. Kehoe, now in his early forties, was a native of County Wicklow, Ireland. He was married to a Mahanoy City woman who was related to several leading trouble-makers of that town. As Pinkerton put it, "she was the sharper member of the hymeneal firm, and fully in accord with her husband on the Mollie Maguire question."

Hindsight worked wonders for Allan Pinkerton in his book, and he went to great lengths to set up the image of Kehoe as a diabolical mastermind. Here is his description of Kehoe's appearance:

> There were some impressions of crow's feet at the outer corners of his small, sharp, light-blue eyes, occasionally a grey hair among the plentiful brown ones of his head and in the equally dark, full whiskers and mustache. The beard was noticeably lighter in color at the far ends, as though somewhat faded. The eyes were set too close together to give a square, honest look to the face, as a whole which was slightly cadaverous . . . The nose, unnaturally sharp, as though pitted by small-pox, assisted in forming for Kehoe a fox-like and cunning look . . .[9]

Allan Pinkerton's interest in physical features is noticeable throughout his writings, and mirrors his great interest in phrenology, one of his hobbies and apparently a device he sometimes used for judging a man's character. (He objected to a man who wished to marry his daughter, "Pussy," on the grounds that his head was too small for him to be intelligent.) But whether McParlan recognized Kehoe as an important figure at this time is doubtful. Pinkerton proceeds to tell an enigmatic story of a trip that Kehoe and McParlan took around Girardville during which they met the local priest, Father Bridgman, and heard him roundly denounce the Mollies. The effect on Kehoe was amazing—"the color of his face changed a little and his legs quivered perceptibly . . . His small eyes wandered from object to object, however, resting on nothing long. He was wounded by the imprecations of his clergyman, yet could find no means of escaping their weight." But, if this signified guilt, McParlan did not stay long to find out. For the next day, on January 1, 1874, he went to Mahanoy City.

It is at this point that we pick up the first thread of documentation via McParlan's "daily reports" to the Philadelphia office. Undoubtedly Pinkerton and others have embellished the adventures to here. But it is clear that McParlan had succeeded by this date—just over two months after leaving Philadelphia—in insinuating himself into the lives of many of the men later publicly named as Molly

Maguires. His report of his first day in Mahanoy City, as edited by Franklin, confirms his success in establishing himself at Dormer's: "The detective met a number of his acquaintances who all recognized him as having been a member of the Molly Maguires." It must have been quite a party, as the following day's account succinctly sums up—"Hangover." But the next day, January 3, produced a real scare. He was spending the evening in McDermot's Tavern among a large crowd of miners, "all thoroughbreds," when one of them again threw him a sign—putting his right forefinger to his ear. Nonplussed for a moment, McParlan regained his composure, smiled and shook his head and replied mysteriously that "he had seen the day." Questioned sharply about what he meant, McParlan answered that "he knew as much as the doctor." To his relief, his circumlocution was once again accepted, and he immediately launched into the Molly Maguire ballad, "which had the effect of getting all the old men down on their knees praying in a most fervent and fanatical manner."[10]

McParlan spent a week in Mahanoy City, and concluded that it was the most riotous and "Godforsaken" place he had ever seen. The town was really one long street at that time, running down the narrow valley. Half the town was Irish, the other half Welsh, English, and German. The center of the main street was the dividing line and woe to either group if they crossed to the other side at night. McParlan now experienced firsthand the violent antipathy between the Irish and the Welsh, between the Irish and the English, and, to a lesser degree, between the Irish and the Germans. He sent the Philadelphia office a list of nine presumed Mollies in Mahanoy City, three of them saloon keepers.[11]

Next the detective went to Tamaqua, up the eastern finger of the Schuylkill field. He reported that he "visited the different Irish saloons."[12] He found the town (according to Pinkerton) "a centre of attraction for a flock of unemployed stragglers, discharged men from adjacent collieries, tramps and other reprobates. Liquor flowed unrestrainedly, and was largely consumed in the various saloons and taverns. A storm of wind, rain, and sleet prevailed, and the streets wore a deserted appearance, while the grog shops and gambling rooms were all crowded and in full blast . . . Tamaqua was filled with excited men and exciting whiskey." Idleness was prevalent because of a local suspension in the mines; thus, Pinkerton lectured, "an idle brain is the devil's own workshop." But after spending a few days in this turbulence McParlan came to the conclusion that in spite of this there was little actual Molly activity. After briefly calling at the tavern of Alexander Campbell, whom he called "a 'Bos' in the MM's," the detective returned to Pottsville.[13]

Back among Dormer and his friends, McParlan resumed the nightly drinking bouts in the Sheridan House, avidly welcomed back by the partakers of his liberal offers to treat. One of the more extravagant imbibers, "Bushy" Deenan, offered to take McParlan over the mountain to Shenandoah, for James McKenna "was just the kind of company he wanted—there was to be a big spree on." The detective was led to understand that "spree" meant an attack of some sort. But McParlan was dubious, for Deenan was "making a sad hand of himself, being continually drunk," and "some of the MM's are speaking threateningly against him." A better contact had appeared to be materializing when McParlan met Chris Donnelly, a miner from New Castle, a mountain patch above St. Clair, which is just north of Pottsville. Donnelly, in Pottsville to purchase green ribbon and fringes for the upcoming St. Patrick's Day parade, was introduced to McParlan as a prominent member of the Mollies and a "butty master" (bodymaster or head) of the New Castle group for the past six years. That evening a terrific spree ensued, where, McParlan reported, "they all became too drunk to know anything," and "they walked the streets flourishing revolvers, shouting and hurrahing." Donnelly stayed for several days, and finally asked McParlan if he would like to march with them in the parade. This was as far as the detective got, though, for Donnelly returned to New Castle without mentioning any further relationship.[14]

With all the talk of "sprees" and intimations of crime, McParlan had yet to hear of anything that went further than barroom bragging. In late January the area was thrown into excitement by the murder of a miner named Bradley in Minersville, just west of Pottsville. McParlan, sensing a possible break, immediately left for the scene of the crime. But it turned out to be a drunken grudge fight, and he reported to Philadelphia that he "was satisfied that the MM organization had no hand in it whatever."[15]

Though McParlan's circle of acquaintances was growing by the day, he still had received no tenders for membership in any of the local lodges of the AOH. Until he could get this close, he was doomed to operate on the periphery. Had it not been for Dormer's difficulties with the Pottsville lodge, he might have been able to join there. But Dormer did succeed indirectly in meeting this critical need by introducing McParlan to Michael Lawler.

"Muff" Lawler, a man who bred fighting gamecocks as a hobby, was a Shenandoah tavern keeper who also doubled as a contractor for employment in the mines. As McParlan had needed an excuse for traveling all over the region, he had pretended to be searching for a job in the mines, hoping privately that the slack in work would save him from coming actually face to face with a miner's pick. Lawler visited Dormer's in late January. After the burly Pottsville "Molly" introduced him to McParlan, the detective's first evening with Lawler produced an interesting quotation, duly forwarded to Philadelphia. An item had appeared in a local paper that day hinting that the railroad intended to import five thousand raw men into the fields as strikebreakers. Lawler was incensed, and McParlan reported his comments thus: "If President Gowen undertakes to do this—in place of requiring the state militia to protect those new men in the mines and protect his breakers, shafts and depots from the torch—he will require them all to protect his own life."[16]

Lawler was friendly to the man he knew as McKenna and asked him to come to see him in Shenandoah. When Dormer told McParlan that Lawler was a "butty master" there, and that he would ask Lawler to get McParlan into the AOH there, the detective needed no further urging. On January 30, 1874, he arrived in Shenandoah, which was destined to be his home for the remaining period in the coal fields.

✤   ❖   ♣   ♣   ❖

"A rather prepossessing personage, something past forty in years, above medium height, heavily but not clumsily built—yet more fleshy than the generality of miners—with black hair and heavy side whiskers of the same color, the chin being shaven; eyes a deep hazel, and withal, 'Muff' was slightly bald at the crown of the head . . . " There, in Pinkerton's words, was Michael Lawler.[17]

Quickly McParlan insinuated himself into Lawler's graces, and moved right into Lawler's small combination house and tavern midst the family of eight. Lawler had promised McParlan work, and

McParlan was hired as a coal loader at one of the Reading's mines at ten dollars a week. As the reporting date was several days off, the two men relaxed into the tavern rounds, and McParlan rapidly widened his acquaintance. "This locality is full of MM's," he reported. One night several miners threw McParlan signs, but Lawler extricated him by explaining that the operative "was as good as any of them but had 'been lost' for sometime past."[18] But McParlan's oblique suggestions that he be asked to join the Mollies brought a rejoinder from Lawler that this might be possible provided McParlan was working. This was a strange request, seeming to imply that the organization was a rudimentary trade union. Subsequent events belied this; nevertheless, McParlan could afford no slips, and he faced up to the fact that he would have to go down in the mines.

The reckoning day came, and McParlan staggered up to the surface after a full day loading coal cars, his hands well blistered after "the hardest work he had ever done." Five days later his inexperience showed through. A slight accident—a fall of coal—mashed his hands and he was temporarily incapacitated.

This day, February 17, also produced another incident, of far more fundamental import. Sitting around the table with Lawler and several of his friends, McParlan learned that a man had been shot and killed in Centralia, a patch half a dozen miles west of Shenandoah. The Molly group spoke in bitter terms of the murder, for the victim was another Molly, "the stuff," said Lawler. Though the assailant was still unknown, the Molly group was convinced the deed had been done by a member of a group called the "Chain Gang."

McParlan was startled at this new piece of information, for his image of the Mollies had been that they were an anti-employer, anti-English-Welsh organization. Now the first overt act he had dug up turned out to be something quite different, for the "Chain Gang" was Irish, too. McParlan found himself right in the middle, not of a class war, but an Irish faction fight.

The "Chain Gang" (so named from the old Irish defensive maneuver of walking in single file) had several other names—the "Iron Clads," the "Iron Shields," and sometimes the "Sheet Iron Gang." McParlan's reports for several weeks were filled with further information about the shadowy opponents.[19] He was never able to document fully its membership, for it was apparently far more loosely knit than the AOH group, but his conclusions reached at this time were probably close to the facts. The "Chain Gang" appeared to be composed of an assortment of dissidents—men who had been dismissed from the Molly Maguires, "young Irish-Americans," and, lastly, a large majority of the men who had come from County Kilkenny. It was not that County Kilkenny men were inherently more clannish than the rest, for all the counties tended to maintain their identities in the coal fields. But Kilkenny was the seat of the only coal mining found in Ireland; those coming from there were about the only skilled coal miners among all the Irish. They undoubtedly got the cream of the jobs in the mines, and would have resented any man from another part of Ireland getting ahead on the job. It seems likely also that they might have teamed up with the Welshmen, who would also be experienced miners, and that other Irishmen would have resented this.

This guess seems confirmed by the alternate name used for the "Chain Gang" by its opponents—"soup drinkers."[20] In nineteenth-century Ireland, when all shades of evangelical Protestant groups set about proselyting among the Catholics, they had a habit of testing their converts by making them eat meat or take soup on Fridays. The name "souper" came to be applied generally in Ireland to all Catholics who turned Protestant.

There is no such proselyting evidence in the coal fields, even so mild a variety as that practiced by Evelyn John Shirley at Lough Fea. If there were any lapsed Catholics among the Kilkenny men, it was likely by personal choice alone. The chances are greater that it was mere association with the Welsh that brought the acrimonious nickname.

But the rival faction was bitterly hated by the Mollies, and greatly feared, too—one Molly in this period actually fled Schuylkill County because he had heard that his name was on a list of seven men marked for death by the "Chain Gang." A fresh shooting of a Molly on March 19 brought a comment from Lawler's close companion, Frank McAndrew, that the feud was on the verge of breaking into open warfare.[21]

After reporting this shocking piece of new information, McParlan turned his attention back to the effort to "join the ring." Mrs. Lawler had taken ill, and McParlan had moved to the house of Fenton Cooney nearby. But he still saw a great deal of Lawler, McAndrew, and the others. Two more small accidents in the mines soon brought the detective up to the surface for good, thus freeing him for the incessant tavern rounds, now extended to the days, too, because of a strike in the town's collieries. It was a rough, very often brutal environment. Cheap (and often bad) liquor was consumed in large quantities, and there was incessant betting—on cockfights, on dog fights, on footraces, even on the frequent barroom fights. Though almost all of the Irish were Roman Catholics, McParlan's friends could be considered only nominally so. In one of his early weeks in Shenandoah, the detective went to church with Lawler; the parish priest, Father O'Reilly, read from the pulpit the pronouncement of Bishop Wood against secret societies. Lawler commented that O'Reilly did this every week, but he, Lawler, "didn't care a damn."[22]

In the almost total absence of moral sanctions, violence lurked near the surface. Most of the men he met, commented McParlan, were armed—with a revolver if they could afford it; if not, with "billies" or steel knuckles. Lawler's young nephew, Ed, who often accompanied the crowd, was rumored to have already shot and maimed four or five men. He was just twenty-one.

Quarrels and fights—even shootings—were seldom settled by processes of law. Direct retaliation in kind, either on a personal basis or through the secret societies, was preferred. Ed Lawler had shot and wounded an antagonist shortly before McParlan arrived in Shenandoah; after threats had been exchanged between the two families involved, Michael Lawler had obtained a "settlement" by paying twenty dollars to the injured man.[23]

McParlan's increasingly friendly relations with the Lawlers soon began to bear fruit. "Muff" Lawler often asked him to cockfights as Lawler's "second," and seemed to have implicit trust in McParlan. Each week brought renewed promises to get McParlan "in the ring." The detective's confidence was shaken in late March by Frank McAndrew, who confided that Lawler was under suspicion by the membership, and was being accused of being an Odd Fellow. McParlan began to wonder if he had put his money on the wrong candidate. Careful observation in succeeding weeks disclosed a power struggle behind the scenes between Lawler and McAndrew. Fortunately for the detective, however, the private battle did not come to the surface, and both men wanted the detective in the society.

On April 14, 1874, McParlan was asked to appear at Lawler's house. Lawler was there, together with McAndrew and three other miners. McParlan was asked to remain downstairs with McAndrew while the others went upstairs for a conference. (Allan Pinkerton's account implies that McParlan thought he might have been discovered as a spy, but nothing in the detective's report supports this.) Soon the two were called upstairs, McParlan was asked to kneel, and Lawler read the purposes of the organization. McParlan reported these purposes in his lengthy account of the evening: "to promote friendship between Irish Catholics and to assist one another at all times, to keep all things secret connected with the workings of said society." An oath was then administered, McParlan paid his three-dollar initiation fee, and the current sign and passwords were given him—and duly noted in the detective's report.[24] McParlan was a member! A "final triumph," the detective called it. Pinkerton, in his book, edited this to "So you see victory is won at last."

What was the real nature of this triumph? McParlan was now a member of the Shenandoah lodge of the Ancient Order of Hibernians. It was clear to the detective that Lawler, McAndrew, and the other members were using the names "Molly Maguire" and "AOH" synonymously. But the bold talk of the power and influence of the Molly Maguires (McAndrew had said several weeks earlier that they "were 200 strong" in that area alone) were still not substantiated. Five days after he was initiated, the detective attended his first meeting. There were just seven others present. Lawler, the bodymaster, after calling the meeting to order by blessing himself, stated its purpose to be "to organize and see where they stood." The lodge, he said, was in danger of being cut off from the national AOH "for want of organization." Lawler admitted that a great many members had dropped out because of the pressure of the Church, but promised that most of them were planning to come back "after having 'gone to their duty to the priest (communion).' " The most immediate problem was the pressing need to pay a nine-dollar assessment that had been made on each lodge in Schuylkill County in order to send Barney Dolan, the county delegate, to the state AOH convention at Pittsburgh and the national AOH convention at New York City. Lawler admitted that the treasury of the Shenandoah lodge was nonexistent, a former member having absconded with all funds. But he pleaded that the eight present "come formal" and pay up their dues (they were thirty-five cents a month), and after some coaxing he collected seven dollars. The cases of two members, one a constable and one a policeman, were then discussed. Having failed to pay their dues, the two were suspended for one year. The meeting then adjourned to the bar, where they, in McParlan's words, "cemented the brotherly bond with bad whiskey." During the course of the evening, one of the self-styled "senior" members warned McParlan not to trust too fully the three younger men, as they were "green hands still." Certainly the awesome reputation of the Molly Maguires must have been substantially deflated for McParlan that night.[25]

But over the succeeding weeks McParlan's first views of the organization were rapidly modified. Now the detective was able to talk AOH secrets with the members, and soon was forwarding to Franklin many details of the organization's methods of operation. He traveled to Pottsville late in the month; now he was able to talk with his old friends, not as an outsider, but as a fellow member. On April 28, he forwarded the names of twelve of the bodymasters in Schuylkill County. And on April 30 he summed up what he had learned from talking with these bodymasters. It was startling information.

The meetings of the Molly Maguires were generally held in taverns, because large groups could congregate there without suspicion, "halls being out of the question." (That several of the bodymasters and other influential members owned these very taverns makes one suspicious that there were pecuniary motives, too.) "After taking a drink and looking around," the report continued, "they quietly and singly drop out the back way—either up stairs in a bedroom or down into the cellar, so that any stranger in the saloon would never suspect . . ."

But the next piece of information was clearly the most important of all McParlan had learned, for it documented for the first time the actual relationship between the Mollies and the AOH: "When there is a job to be done (men to be beaten or murdered) the question or matter is never brought up in open Lodge—but the Bodymaster receives the grievance and complaint and appoints the man or men privately and secretly notifies them of what they are required to do and then the 'job' is done, and the very members of the Lodge are never made aware of the transaction or who the 'avengers' are, which must be kept a profound secret . . . If any member is caught in a fuss and arrested, he can always prove an alibi."[26]

There was, then, an "inner circle," composed of AOH body-masters and other officers, who acted sometimes singly, more often in concert, to settle grievances privately. The AOH membership probably knew in a general way that such a system existed, but were not made privy to the plans. The name "Molly Maguire" was used by most people as synonymous with the AOH lodges in the anthracite region. But the "Molly Maguires" that struck fear in the coal fields, the group which, McParlan reported on April 30, "are held in such terror that all the office holders and politicians are on their side and they can always command both money and influence," was the "inner circle"—the bodymasters and county officers. These men, McParlan now knew, were the particular Mollies he was after.

❖   ❖   ❖   ❖   ❖

But if the microscopic vision of McParlan magnified the eight-member Shenandoah lodge of the AOH to a picture of Molly Maguire terror, the macroscopic view of Franklin B. Gowen, taking in the whole of the two Schuylkill coal fields and their manifold problems, was too preoccupied for the moment with the broad picture to be much concerned with the reports he was receiving from Benjamin Franklin. For the Reading had decided to rule the coal fields—and the Reading was Gowen.

Gowen's purchase of the coal lands (60,000 acres in 1871–1872, an additional 40,000 by 1874) had appeared to be a shattering blow to "individual enterprise," the institution that had been particularly hallowed in the southern fields. But the mournful prognostications of the "antimonopoly" forces (always abetted by the vitriol of Benjamin Bannan's pen) were not, in the early 1870's, borne out. Instead, Gowen confounded his antagonists by leasing back most of the Reading's acreage to individual prospectors, and further surprised everyone by making loans to colliers, advances on mortgages, renovations of old collieries and construction of new ones, and in general being a champion of better mining techniques. One of Gowen's favorite whipping boys, Schuylkill's "dirty coal," was aggressively attacked by the rail president; and by both exhortations and penalties against the colliers' pocketbooks (through rigid inspection), he substantially upgraded the reputation of the county's coal.[27]

But even Gowen's dramatic efforts could not overcome all the heritage of wastefulness, of poorly financed organization, of lethargy and ultraconservatism. Mines still went bankrupt, and when they did, the Reading eagerly gobbled them up at distress prices, to be worked more rapidly than even the miners desired, said Bannan in January 1873. But three weeks later the usually fiery editor admitted that although "things were not quite as the *Miners' Journal* might like them to be," nevertheless there were positive values in Gowen's new role, especially because the stability might "draw a good class of miners around them." Perhaps, too, the fire had gone out of Bannan; a month later he sold his remaining half of the *Journal* to Colonel Robert H. Ramsey (who had purchased a half interest in 1866). Bannan did continue to edit the "Coal Trade" column.[28]

This oversimplifies Gowen's new role. The shining armor that he turned to the face of the region cloaked a still-abiding drive to secure a monopolistic hold on the coal trade. The 1872 "basis" had been settled amicably (but harshly, with wage reductions all down the line). After the tactical losses suffered in 1871, the Workingmen's Benevolent Association was in no position to dictate. With the nation at the height of its postwar prosperity, demand was high. But the production potential of 1872—freed of the strikes that had occurred in each of the five previous years—was even higher. Under the pressure of this imbalance, prices plummeted. By March, coal fell to $2.25 a ton, about the cost of getting it to the consumer; by August this was depressed to a shattering $1.92 and many collieries shut down rather than lose so heavily.[29]

The reason was clear: lack of control of production, and, particularly, of the marketing of the product. Production in the two Schuylkill fields was at least potentially under control—Gowen owned most of the mines. Control of its marketing was not, for here the impact of the other anthracite regions was strong. Gowen also saw clearly what was needed here.

First he trained his sights on the coal "factors," or middlemen, in Philadelphia, whom he had characterized as "sitting at the water's edge like leeches, sucking the lifeblood of a healthy trade."[30] By setting up a direct sales system, he revolutionized the retailing structure in Philadelphia. The factors were outraged, of course, but the remaining independent producers in the county generally supported Gowen.

This solved only a small problem; the big problem was control of the amount sent to the market. And here the New York market had a direct influence. Unless the coal from all three anthracite regions was controlled, any region could undercut the others. Gowen knew this, and did something about it—a revolutionary move that was to have profound implications on the entire American economy for many years into the future. In mid-January, 1873, Gowen traveled to New York to meet his rail-and-coal-president friends who had been involved with him in the freight embargo of 1871. They were Asa Packer of the Lehigh Valley, Thomas Dickson of the Delaware & Hudson, George Hoyt of Pennsylvania Coal, and Samuel Sloan of the Lackawanna. A newcomer, the president of the Central Railroad of New Jersey, joined them. Out of this came an agreement to fix prices at an average of five dollars a ton wholesale in New York— the first industry price-fixing device in United States history.

The group first felt that because demand appeared so high in 1873, there was no need to have a complementary control of production; but second thoughts on this led them to meet again a month later and establish a tonnage limitation on the amount that each company shipped to competitive markets (though each could mine all it wished). The Reading was to have 25.85 per cent of the market, the Hudson 18.37, the Jersey Central 16.15, the Lehigh 15.98, and the Lackawanna 13.80. The Pennsylvania Coal Company, though not formally a party to the arrangement, agreed to abide by a quota of 9.85 per cent. America's first major pool was born.[31]

The year 1873 proved to be a profitable one for the anthracite producers. Despite the panic devastating other industries, demand for anthracite stayed high, production reached record heights, the price fixing arrangements held up (and, therefore, wages, still on the sliding-scale, remained adequate). Trade was more stable and peaceful than it had been for years.

But many smoldering resentments lay just under the surface. The union—the W.B.A.—had still been forced to accept a basis below what it felt entitled to, for it knew it was weak and unable to effect any real pressure on Gowen for the moment. Furthermore, local conditions contradicted the industry's surface calm. Whereas in previous periods prosperity often brought a slackening in crime, in 1873 both rose together.

Ramsey, the new editor of the *Miners' Journal*, was alarmed at the incidence of prostitution. "There were too many young girls walking the streets Saturday night," he said May 3. "They are taking the first downward steps! Mothers, keep your girls at home." With the lack of concern for libel so characteristic of this period of country journalism, he even named names. One of his favorite targets was the "infamous Continental den" on the main street of Pottsville, and his crusading zeal spread out over the area. A sample on August 1:

There is now in Shamokin a girl, aged only sixteen years, who is determined to become one of that innumerable throng of miserable women who tread the path whose only ending is in hell, and who go from their graves to collect the wages of their sin. More than once she has been rescued from houses of ill repute in Reading and Pottsville. Each time she has announced her invariable determination to return in spite of the most zealous watchfulness. Less than a fortnight since she was taken by Chief Smith from a brothel on Bunker Hill. Poor fool, God help her! Else the devil will take her.

"What is the matter with the people?" demanded Ramsey in that same issue. "Are they losing their brains through drink?" Though liquor licenses had decreased in Pottsville, intemperance continued unabated. The *Journal* reported on October 19 that there were eight illegal grog shops in tiny Lanigan's Patch alone, one specializing in "hell-fired leniment."

And the incessant brawling diminished not at all; assaults filled the pages of every issue of the *Journal*. In the month of September 1873, alone, reported the editor on September 26, over three hundred pistols had been sold in Mahanoy City. Many of the beatings and shootings resulted in death, and most of these were attributed to "the Mollies."

The Irish were not always on the antagonist's side. On August 11, 1873, an Irishman, Edward Cosgrove, was murdered in Shenandoah, and a young Welshman, Gomer James, was arrested and tried. James was acquitted, later to figure in one of the most sensational of the Molly Maguire crimes.

Even the shiny façade of the pool and the temporary halo of Gowen slipped in 1874, after he tightened the controls because of worsening business conditions and persistent rumors that "outside interests" were attempting to break the combination. The wage basis in the two Schuylkill fields was being negotiated, and though Gowen proposed that last year's basis be used again (except for a small cut

in contract wages), there were widespread fears that Gowen intended to manipulate prices so that wages, under the sliding scale,
would go down. The *Miners' Journal* reported in January that the
New York Times accused Gowen of attempting to precipitate a
strike in order to be able to raise prices, and that another New York
paper, the *Commercial Advertiser*, said, "altogether, it is about one
of the most thoroughly organized schemes for a 'corner' that we
have ever contemplated." The New York papers represented the
consumers' attitude, and the producers' point of view in the *Miners'
Journal* was much more sympathetic. But Ramsey also pointed out
that "the companies are now masters of the situation" and cautioned
that their power could be used evilly as well.[32]

In the face of this power, the W.B.A. was in a poor bargaining
position, and in spite of the *Miners' Journal* report on January 16
that the men "are in a good condition, as they have not been
squandering their money and say they can easily hold out for six
months," the union backed down on a show of power and John
Siney, the W.B.A. president, wrote the railroad combination a formal
letter accepting the 1873 basis again. The fear of the unilateral power
of the combination remained, and there were mutterings through the
region about the dismal prospects ahead. On May 31, 1874, at a time
when Detective McParlan was busily collecting information for the
Reading Railroad from his observation post within the AOH, the
Miners' Journal printed a petulant but prophetic letter from Siney's
union, saying that "all workingmen must lend us their assistance in
repelling the onward march of this oppressive Company. For where
they succeed in crushing the manhood out of our miners and deprive
us of our independence, then will come the day of retribution for the
rest of the citizens everywhere that they rule supreme."

Gowen was master of the situation, and all waited with apprehension to see what he would do with his power.

✤   ✤   ✤   ✤   ✤

John Siney would have been doubly distressed had he known that
one of the new miners in the area, P. M. Cummings, was not only
a miner. Cummings had arrived in St. Clair, Siney's home town, just
as the negotiations had begun. Cummings told Siney he was looking

for work, having lost his job in the Illinois coal fields because of his union activity. Further, Cummings purported to have been an officer of the union there, and an acquaintance of the general secretary of the new Miners' National Association in Cleveland. Siney was very active in that union (and would soon leave the Pennsylvania fields to become its national president). He immediately took a liking to Cummings. Cummings seemed to be always around, and Siney found himself increasingly taking his new friend into his confidence. But what Siney did not know was that Cummings was a Pinkerton detective.

Gowen, evidently not wanting to depend on McParlan alone, decided early in 1874 to hire another Pinkerton man to infiltrate the W.B.A. itself. Allan Pinkerton found Cummings in Pinkerton's former residence of Dundee, Illinois, and dispatched him east on February 20, 1874. So, during most of the same period that McParlan was in the coal fields, Pinkerton also had a man deeply entrenched in the W.B.A. hierarchy—for Cummings became a member of the St. Clair district committee of the union.[33]

*   *   *   *   *

James McParlan ("James McKenna"), a few weeks after his AOH initiation, attended another meeting that became the direct cause of much personal misery for the detective. There is a gap in his surviving reports from May 3 to August 27; therefore, for the events of the summer of 1874, we must depend largely on the less precise account of Allan Pinkerton. The gathering in question was another initiation meeting (to bring a young Irishman into the fold), and was held outside "on the mountain." The weather was raw, and McParlan contracted a cold which soon turned into something more serious. McParlan's nights of dissipation and this spell of sickness took heavy toll on his constitution, so that he became, in Pinkerton's words, "thin and cadaverous." Worse still, he lost most of his hair and began to wear a wig.

The bout with sickness gave him an excuse, though, for not working in the mines again. Pleading the need for rest, he prevailed upon Lawler to give him a "traveling card" (duly authenicated by a secret mark from the county delegate, Barney Dolan) and left on a trip to the northern fields. Among AOH members there, he found considerable antipathy to the Schuylkill lodges. He is also said to have attended a venomous meeting between six Roman Catholic priests, headed by Bishop O'Hara of Scranton, and a large group of bodymasters of the AOH in various coal counties. O'Hara had not yet taken the final step of excommunication that was so aggressively expounded by Bishop Wood of Philadelphia, but did lay down an ultimatum to the lodge leaders that major changes would have to be immediately effected lest he follow the path of Wood.[34] Back in Shenandoah, McParlan found both the local lodge and the county amalgamation in a high state of agitation—over, respectively, their two leaders, Michael Lawler and Barney Dolan. The internecine in-fighting for the positions of power was rapidly coming to a head. Lawler's case was first.

After Gomer James, the tough young Welshman, had been indicted for the 1873 killing of Edward Cosgrove, there were whispered threats of revenge, for Cosgrove had been a member of the AOH. With James out on bail, walking evidence of defiance to the Molly Maguires, a group of Mollies decided to kill him, according to Pinkerton's book. Lawler evidently chaired the meeting (again our evidence is lacking) but equivocated in appointing the killer. Other lodges in the county knew about the plan, and as the weeks passed without action by Lawler, pressures were exerted for his removal. Finally, Barney Dolan was sent for, and Lawler was forced to resign as Shenandoah bodymaster.

With the leadership of the Shenandoah lodge now ready for grabbing, Dolan excited the membership by proposing "James McKenna" as bodymaster. The detective was worried, for leadership would force him to plan and execute crimes himself, rather than be a mere observer and witness of crimes. Some versions of McParlan's adventures boldly accuse him of being an "agent provocateur," originating and actually committing crimes in order to gain convictions. John O'Dea, in the official history of the AOH, went quite far on this point:

To keep the movement active, and to prove to his employer that he was earning his pay and making progress, McKenna led most of these attacks in person. Occasionally he persuaded his dupes to branch out and engage in highway robbery, and in these affairs he invariably participated, both in the execution of the deeds and in the enjoyment of the profits. At last he reached the summit of his efforts—the chief object of his mission—by persuading and assisting in person, two or three of the men to commit the crime of murder . . . Astute lawyers and sagacious criminologists have declared that there were at least three men who met their deaths . . . after McParlan's arrival who were undoubtedly killed by the detective.[35]

These are serious accusations, and later we must make the best judgments possible, on the basis of the facts available, as to their merit. But reflection on the role McParlan had set for himself tells us that at this particular time, whatever his future plans might be, it would have been unwise to accept leadership of the lodge.

At any rate, after a long (and quite drunken) meeting on July 15, Frank McAndrew was elected bodymaster. And because McAndrew was illiterate, McParlan was given the newly created post of secretary, an ideal spot for him to be able to cover up his reporting to Superintendent Franklin under the guise of "lodge business."

Shortly after this, Barney Dolan's case became active. Again we depend on Pinkerton for the story. The often tipsy Dolan was in trouble with his fellow Mollies on two scores—first, for incurring a public censure from a local priest for publicly cursing the Church, and, second, for misappropriating AOH monies. A special meeting of all Schuylkill County bodymasters was called by the state delegate from Pittsburgh, Captain John Gallagher, and Dolan, too, was removed from his office, further suffering a lifetime dismissal from the AOH and being fined five hundred dollars. Dolan now drops out of the AOH hierarchy. But his successor as county delegate was crucially important in subsequent events. The new man was John Kehoe.

All signs pointed now to renewed AOH activity. There was wide interest in the coming Pennsylvania state and county elections, and political alliances—both open and secret—were avidly dispensed, promises for political patronage were marketed, and there were even rumors that political payoff money was changing hands. Kehoe, as AOH county delegate, saw an opportunity to move into state politics; McParlan reported a visit of Kehoe to Shenandoah to "get him [McParlan] to speak favourable of Laville, the Candidate for State Senator," among the Shenandoah Mollies.[36]

Molly activity in faction fights and tavern brawling stepped up. In September one of the Shenandoah Mollies, James McHugh, got drunk after a wake and tried to shoot a saloon keeper and a liquor dealer who was visiting the saloon. Jailed, he was bailed out by McParlan himself, who reported to Franklin that "the MM's say if McHugh was in jail for any great offence they would take him out and not ask anyone to go his bail." Almost every day brought further reports from McParlan about faction brawling, some very graphic: "In the evening the Operative went to the Chas. Hayes Saloon and found Hayes and all the boarders drunk. Mrs. Hayes said they had been quarrelling among themselves all day and had whipped a Welchman who had come around to whip Kelley. Hayes said he had been around to whip a man named Buffy who had made the assertion that he had helped to dip an Irishman in Blood at Wales . . . Buffy is the same man that Lawler shot last March."[37]

But the fight that proved to have the greatest repercussions involved Lawler. When deposed, he had resigned from the lodge in a huff. But finding himself on the fringe (and perhaps losing tavern business in the bargain), he soon let it be known that he was ready to return to the fold. Unfortunately for him, the rest of the membership did not see it this way. McAndrew was adamant that Lawler was not to be given the new "goods," and the ostracized tavern keeper rushed about among the membership attempting to find an ally that would support his candidacy. He concentrated his efforts on McParlan, and the detective had to disavow his friend in order to stay on the side of power. Early in September, Lawler visited Kehoe in Girardville to plead his case, but the new county delegate told him he would have to clear through the state delegate, Gallagher, in Pittsburgh. He finally persuaded Kehoe to give him a card, but when he returned to Shenandoah (as reported by McParlan) "McAndrew would not accept the card, as he said too many in the Body were opposed to Lawler coming in." Lawler then pleaded with McParlan to "take his card in," but McParlan refused because he feared he "would be expelled for life."[38] How far the former bodymaster had fallen!

But worse was in store. Three days later Lawler was waylaid by McHugh, accompanied by other Shenandoah Mollies, and beaten unmercifully for his failure to have Gomer James killed. The next day Lawler plaintively told McParlan that "it was not his fault that James was not killed, as Cosgrove's own Cousin backed out, when he was one of the men appointed to do the deed, and of course after

Cosgrove's Cousin backed out all the others would not do it."[39] But the tavern keeper was fighting mad now, and threatened vengeance against McHugh and his friends. Lawler attempted to join the Mahanoy Plane lodge in order to be able to bring charges against McHugh before the county committee, but the Mollies there would have no part of it. If McHugh had known then how Michael Lawler was going to re-enter his life at a later date, he might have welcomed being able to have the case treated privately by the county committee.

If the hardening of grudges within the lodge boded increased trouble, a new hardening in attitude by the Church now provided the most serious shock to the AOH since the detective had entered the case.

Though the Mollies appeared unconcerned about the antagonism of the Church in their bluff boasts along the tavern bars, this did not mirror the true feelings of most of them. All were Catholics, and the patent violation of basic precepts of the Church that was entailed in AOH business greatly troubled them. Finally, in late September, all the Schuylkill lodges banded together to try to do something about it. Each lodge was assessed five dollars to defray the cost of a trip by Captain Gallagher to Philadelphia to see Bishop Wood, to attempt to persuade him to lift his ban against the AOH. Gallagher went off in high hopes; but to no avail. Wood refused to reconsider, and the lodge was now in a worse position than before.[40]

Perhaps the issue might have stayed below the surface had not a group of Schuylkill priests chosen this precise moment to take a public stand. As had been true through the long history of Ireland, the local parish priests generally tended to be less decisive in taking stands against secret societies than their superiors higher in the Church hierarchy. Caught in the middle between trying to hold to broad Church doctrine and still being able to retain the loyalty and friendship of their parishioners, they often felt it necessary to equivocate on certain local aberrations. The priests in the coal regions were in daily contact with the miserable living conditions, the degrading treatment of the Irish miners, and the anti-Catholic feeling of the area. The provocations were so strong for secret-society action that they must have felt great sympathy for the objectives, if disturbed by the methods in the process. As a result, though most of the local priests in the county had obediently read the Wood pronouncement from the pulpit and inveighed against excesses, most also condoned at least the need for organization itself.

But the cumulation of excesses, the drunkenness, brawling, fighting, even murdering, went beyond such bounds as even a highly sympathetic priest could tolerate. And at the very time that Gallagher was attempting to calm Wood, a group of influential Schuylkill priests came out publicly, and with finality, against the AOH.

The lead in this effort was taken by a young, dynamic, and respected priest from New Philadelphia (a small mining patch just east of Pottsville), the Reverend Daniel McDermott. On October 3, 1874, the New York *Freeman's Journal and Catholic Register*, one of the most influential Catholic papers in the country, published a diatribe he had delivered in New Philadelphia entitled, "The Church and Forbidden Societies: The AOH and the EBA." (The EBA was the Emerald Brotherhood of America, another Irish organization.) It filled seven full columns of the paper. In a very literate and reasoned way, he strongly attacked the AOH as being opposed to basic precepts of the Church, and backed his argument with specific Catholic teachings that left not a shred of doubt that he considered secret societies in general and the AOH in particular wholly and completely anti-Church and extremely pernicious for any Catholic.

As impressive as this piece was (for it was the first time that a truly detailed and reasoned analysis *in print* had hit the coal fields), the trump card was still to be played. An AOH defender could have said that Father McDermott's article was "one man's opinion," but the following week (October 10) the same Catholic paper published an editorial supporting the article, and also printed a "Declaration of Seven Pastors," signed not only by McDermott but by six other priests in six key parishes of Schuylkill County. They bluntly accused the AOH of being run by "men of notoriously infamous character" and that evidence "sufficient to convince the most skeptical has come to light that works forbidden by the Commandment, *Thou shalt not kill*, are traceable to the AOH." It was vain, they felt, to eliminate "the objectionable features from the letter of the laws of such a society" while the same spirit and traditions remained and "the same men control it." In short, there was no hope that the AOH could be reformed.

The "Declaration" was widely circulated in the county, and brought consternation to the lodges. On October 21, Kehoe received a letter from Gallagher saying that Schuylkill County would not receive any passwords, and the lodges found themselves fighting for existence. If the "Declaration" had meant only that the lodges would lose their national affiliation, this would be serious but not disastrous. But if it meant also that each member could expect to lose automatically all ties to the Church—even to be excommunicated by name publicly from the pulpit—this was a deadly blow.

The issue seemed to be joined. The Shenandoah local, under instructions of Kehoe, began to make plans to salvage the organization by having the body "suspend" all but six men, with the suspended members taking their cards to Luzerne County lodges for temporary affiliation. Presumably, the six who remained would take the final step by cutting themselves completely away from the Church. McParlan wrote to Superintendent Franklin that he hoped to be one of the six—a remarkable determination when one realizes that the detective had been a loyal Catholic all of his life.[41]

But the plan was abandoned, because a final decision of the state AOH officers to cut off Schuylkill County never materialized. Perhaps they feared the loss of income or thought that such a step would prejudice the case for a secret society that could stay within the Church. At any rate, they failed to act, and thereby helped to keep the Molly Maguire legend alive. The Church, too, apparently could not push its decision to full reality. Some local priests stayed loyal to the AOH lodges, and the continuing animosity of the "Seven" became just one of several alternative Church positions available to Schuylkill miners. Perhaps the Molly Maguires were now too strong—politically, economically, and personally—to be brought to their knees by any single action, no matter how decisive it might appear. The "moment of truth," when Molly Maguireism might have been dealt a death blow, had come and gone. Left, instead, was a potential for further depredations. And the potential was now to be realized.

Chapter 8 • The Long Strike

A STARTLING new killing now provided fresh evidence. Faction fighting in Mahanoy City was its cause. The "Modocs," a loosely organized gang from among the rougher elements of the Welsh and the Protestant Germans, had formed a fire brigade. The Irish had their own. Each served its own side of town. But a fire in the center of town was often answered by both; and, when this happened, tensions and excitement engendered by the fire almost always spilled over into personal combat—usually, but not always, after the fire had been put out. (And there is clear evidence that some fires in the period were purposely set in order to bring fire companies into firing range; Pinkerton detective P. M. Cummings reported from Mahanoy City in November 1874 that "another fire will be gotten up by the Sheet Iron Gang, at which they will go around and clear the MM's out."[1])

On October 31 a fire in the center of town brought the two companies face to face. The fire amounted to nothing—but the ensuing melee did. A general fight broke out, shots were exchanged, and several people were injured. Finally George Major, the chief burgess, stepped out into the street to attempt to bring order. Major angrily pulled out his pistol and shot a dog along the sidelines, whereupon one of the mob retaliated by lodging a bullet in Major. Before the officer fell, he succeeded in firing two more bullets. Whom they hit soon became a matter of great interest. For a young Irishman, Daniel Dougherty, was quickly arrested as the assailant of Major, having himself been shot in the head. Major, mortally wounded, corroborated that it was Dougherty, and died the next day.

Feeling ran high. Dougherty's Molly Maguire friends (for it turned out that he was a member of the AOH) insisted that he was seriously wounded, could not be interrogated, and, further, was innocent of the shooting. The other side was equally vehement concerning his guilt. Robert Ramsey wrote in the *Miners' Journal* that Dougherty was "taken red handed" and was not in truth badly injured, for "our representative and Dr. Carpenter visited him and found he was only shamming." Not content with this, Ramsey went on: "Are the days of the Molly Maguires and the Blood Tubs, of Pat Hester and the 'Flour Barrel Hotel' coming upon us again? It seems like it." A "carnival of crime" was raging in Schuylkill County. "Let us learn from the apologue of the old man, who, when he found he could not dislodge a boy from his apple tree by flinging grass at him changed his tactics and knocked him out with a stone." The article concluded that "one good, wholesome hanging, gently but firmly administered, will cure a great deal of bad blood, and save a great many lives in this community."[2]

This at best condemned Dougherty before trial, and came perilously close to being an incendiary invitation for mob violence. Vigilantism was already near the surface, thanks to the provocations of Thomas Foster, editor of the *Shenandoah Herald;* now a blood bath hung in the balance.

Fortunately, Dougherty was removed from the Mahanoy City jail to the better protected one at Pottsville, to await trial for the murder of Major. This trial (when finally held in April 1875) with its subsequent recriminations became one of the key events in the Molly Maguire saga. For the moment, though, we must leave Dougherty behind the bars of the Pottsville jail and pick up the trail of disorder that came on the heels of the shooting.

The AOH closed ranks behind Dougherty, and began a canvass through the various lodges to raise a defense fund. Kehoe was in charge, aided by several of the rougher members. One of them, Thomas Hurley, brought in twenty-five dollars in one night, and McParlan's report the next day accuses him of "plundering"— Hurley had evidently stolen some clothing and sold it illegally. By November 29, the day Dougherty was supposed to be tried, over six hundred dollars had been contributed, "with several places yet to be heard from," McParlan reported.[3] The trial was postponed, though, by efforts of the defense attorney.

November was full of outrages—beatings, slashings, a killing—and more fires. In Mahanoy City an attempt was made to fire the Catholic Church; the *Miners' Journal* called it "A Riotous Night in Mahanoy City," begun when a "party of roughs" from Jackson's Patch challenged the Modocs, "a party of Mahanoy roughs." Father Charles A. McFadden, the local priest, apparently knew who attempted the arson, but, according to McParlan, would not tell because "it might make trouble."[4] McFadden was no apologist for the Mollies, but was sympathetic to the AOH as an institution and attempted to exert his influence privately with them rather than publicly from the pulpit or courtroom.

Given the predilections of journalists, these outrages were soon reported in fulsome detail in the Philadelphia and New York newspapers. In the eyes of many in the county these reports were overdone. Editor Ramsey of the *Miners' Journal* was a carbon copy of his predecessor Bannan in prideful provincialism and reacted to these "big city editor" reports with indignant outrage. Just five weeks after having sprinkled the pages of the *Journal* with purple prose on the Dougherty case, Ramsey took the New York papers to task on *their* reports of the incident: "We have contended all along that the false reports of lawlessness in the Pennsylvania coal regions, spread broadcast by New York papers, are calculated to injure our good name and change our reputation." He said that "all over the Union Schuylkill county is looked upon as over-run by a species of Ku-Kluxism which goes by the name of Molly Maguireism," but "as a rule Schuylkill county is quiet and dull and it is only now and then that here and there law is broken."[5]

A careful reading of the *Journal* by an unbiased party might have led him to ask who was misrepresenting what, for the "here" and "there" seemed to blanket the county. But it does appear that Schuylkill was achieving a distant reputation far beyond even the seamy facts, for McParlan also cautioned in one of his reports in November that some of the depredations mentioned in the Philadelphia and New York papers "are purely false." Even the careful Father McFadden, who had not reported the attempted burning of his own church to the authorities for fear of offending, felt moved to write the *New York Herald* on an AOH article he felt was garbled.[6]

❖   ❖   ❖   ❖   ❖

Pinkerton operative P. M. Cummings was also active during this period, late 1874. The bargaining on the 1875 wage basis was supposed to begin. John Siney had resigned the W.B.A. presidency so that he could pursue his efforts with the Miners' National Association. John F. Welsh, a forty-year old Irish Catholic, a native of County Down, Ireland, had replaced him.[7] Siney, however, remained active in Schuylkill union affairs, helping the union he had headed so long and attempting to persuade it and other W.B.A. branches in the anthracite fields to amalgamate with the national union, which had achieved some success in soft-coal organizing in western Pennsylvania, Ohio, and Illinois. Cummings stuck close to Siney whenever the labor leader was in the area, and duly reported Siney's personal views to Gowen. Siney knew that the anthracite union was hostile both to him and to the national union. Many miners believed that Siney had run out on them by getting involved in the national—there was little contact between the anthracite miner and the bituminous miner. The national had found itself attacked through bitter antiunion devices, particularly the use of strikebreakers. Siney reported to Cummings that in the West many employers were infiltrating spies into the union "but the officers of the National Union were not asleep and are making all arrangements to hunt these men to death—revenge was sweet." If this harsh statement from the usually mild-mannered Siney troubled the detective he did not show it, for Cummings that month was elected vice-president of the St. Clair local. Cummings also reported Siney's all too prophetic statement that the W.B.A. would be broken by any strike for the 1875 basis that lasted over three months.[8] Although McParlan was now no longer seeking work, nevertheless the pervasive interest in the bargaining for the basis infected him, and he, too, went to several meetings of the Shenandoah branch of the union.[9]

The situation facing the union in the basis negotiations was alarming. At the beginning of 1874 the coal operators, having standardized the port arrangements, had agreed to hold wages at approximately the level of the previous year. Though this appeared to be a tactical victory for the union, the realists on both sides knew that it had just postponed an inevitable show of power until 1875. Now, toward the end of 1874, the operators were in an even stronger position. Gowen had organized most of the independents in Schuylkill County into the Schuylkill Coal Exchange, to carry out the pooling system in allocating production within the county. The operators' bargaining power, already high, was further enhanced by a spurt in production during the fall that built up the stocks above ground to a level high enough to meet the demand through most of the winter. Through the coal fields the rumor spread that the companies were planning to precipitate a strike. And when the operators' basis proposal for the whole anthracite region was made in December, the rumor became a reality.

The terms were harsh. Cuts in day rates ranging from ten to twenty per cent were proposed for miners and laborers. Further, the previous practice of a minimum or floor on the "sliding side" was to be abolished; the men were to be cut one per cent for each three cents coal fell below $2.50 a ton. The operators adamantly cried, "No maximum, no minimum," a motto deliberately designed to goad the union.[10] And, as an insult to the union itself, the operators made it clear that these terms were not subject to discussion with the union —the miner himself could unilaterally accept or be out of a job. It was clear that the operators were committed to reducing wages and breaking the union in the process.

The always troublesome competition among the anthracite areas quickly came into play. The northern "Wyoming" miners, largely nonunion, accepted the cuts and stayed at work. The Lehigh group and the miners of the two southern fields, now held tenuously together by the union, believed they had no alternative but to strike. Mines began to shut down in November and December. By the first of the year the two areas were almost fully suspended. A critical strike had begun. With both miners and operators prepared and determined, it was clear that many weeks of inactivity would have to ensue before a climax of desperation would finally force a settlement. A collective shudder must have gone through the coal fields as 1875 arrived.

❖   ❖   ❖   ❖   ❖

The AOH lodges were on the periphery. Many of the lodge members were miners. Most of these were members of the union and deeply concerned with the progress of the strike. But lodge atrocities went on, independent of the crucial economic forces operating about them. If anything, the tensions brought by the strike intensified the brutalities within the lodge. Bitterness, hunger, and inactivity were driving forces for further factionalism, internal power struggles, and furtherance of personal grudges.

Shortly after the first of the year—probably on either January 4 or 5, 1875—the AOH lodges of Schuylkill County were called together at Girardville by John Kehoe to meet with important outside visitors. These visitors turned out to be several state officials of the AOH, accompanied by two men from the national headquarters itself. McParlan's reports for this period are missing, and we depend here on his sworn testimony at a later Molly Maguire assault trial (on August 10, 1876).[11]

The subject of the AOH meeting was the earlier trial of Barney Dolan for embezzling the Schuylkill lodges' funds, which Dolan was now appealing. The appeal itself is unimportant except as evidence that both the state and national organizations took a responsibility for local AOH affairs (Dolan was presumably acquitted at the appeal but told he could not hold an office[12]). But what McParlan reported as happening after the meeting is of interest (as given in his later trial testimony):

Q. Was there anything spoken about murder or crime or anything at that meeting when these men were present?
A. No; there was this spoken of—
Q. Just give me an answer first and you can explain afterward.
A. Yes; there was a little spoken about crime.
Q. What was it?
A. There was a national delegate that was present there.
Q. Who was that national delegate?
A. His name was Campbell [n.b., the "National Delegate," or president, of the national AOH at that time was Patrick Campbell]; and a Mr. Reilly was there that represented the President of the Board of the City and County at New York at that time. He was the representative of it, but I believe he was not the man that should have been there as I heard. After those men had given their decision in the Dolan case, Mr. Campbell made a kind of a speech to the parties that were present; to the convention. He stated that there had been some outrages committed, that men had got shot and men had got beat through the coal regions, and that it had given them a very bad name, and Barney Dolan replied that some fellows had to get a little beating once in a while to make men out of them. It seemed to be pretty well taken. The old man Campbell, himself, said, in a kind of a way, "Well, I don't know." He thought if a man would oppose him he would jump up and fight himself. The old man was right, too, in that respect. That was the only thing about beating and killing.

This revealing statement reportedly made by Campbell shows, first, a much deeper awareness by the national AOH concerning Schuylkill affairs (including the violence) than subsequent disavowals both at the time of the Molly trials and in later writings would imply. Further, it illustrates again the difficult dilemma faced by so many of the parties to the Molly story. The national AOH leadership, realizing the bitter anti-Catholic, anti-Irish attacks in the coal fields, could not come out foursquare against even the excesses without losing for their constituency one of the very few friendly (and powerful) forces available.

Although we cannot document this enigmatic meeting directly through McParlan's reports, another independent check helps us— McParlan's expense statements.[13] These are available for most of the remaining period, and in their limited way help to authenticate certain facts. Through them we can trace McParlan's day-to-day location, for each trip away from and back to Shenandoah is duly recorded as to destination and fare. On both January 4 and January 5, McParlan did record a round-trip fare from Shenandoah to Rappahannock Station (Girardville). And his expenses for "treating," that is, buying drinks for his friends, were substantial for each of these two days—$2.75 on January 4 and $3.75 on January 5. But even these were not as large as that of January 11, on the occasion of a county AOH convention in Pottsville to plan the St. Patrick's Day parade. McParlan spent $6.20 that day—an astronomical amount of whiskey at the prices then in effect!

These expense statements are sometimes tantalizingly uninformative, too. For example, on January 18 there is a charge of sixty cents for a "telegram." This is the first time that the last-resort communications device appears in the reports, and although in later months the stepped-up tempo brought it into play many times, there is nothing in any of the reports around January 18 to indicate any need to communicate by such a potentially dangerous method. What compelled McParlan to send this telegram? We will probably never know.

The January 11 meeting, as McParlan reported it, provided an interesting example of the "coffin notice." After the meeting had adjourned, a Molly of St. Clair, John Regan, gave Bodymaster McAndrew "a threatening notice to put up in front of the long shute at Turkey Run Colliery." McParlan explained in his report that it was aimed at intimidating "the Cornishmen," the English miners that favored Anglo-Irish Union, so that they would quit the W.B.A. and allow Regan and his brother to take over their jobs. McParlan stated its substance as being, "to the Union men now in the union. I would have you take your tools out of this place. This is my first notice but, if I have to come back again, it will be a different requisition." The detective did not say whether the threat was actually posted, but the use of an AOH meeting to transact union affairs, albeit illegal ones, is noteworthy.[14]

The union was continually harassed by being linked with such unauthorized acts. After a rash of "coffin notices" in January, the officials of the union felt compelled to pass a formal resolution, duly published in the *Miners' Journal*, disavowing "the mean and cowardly act."[15] But try as it might, the union was never able to disassociate itself from such random fringe violence.

McParlan's reports at this time began to contain more information on the union and the strike. There is little indication in any of the detective's reports that he had a deep interest in the progress of the strike and its relation to Gowen. Nevertheless Gowen was beginning to obtain useful insights from McParlan. As all the parties to the strike now realized that this was no ordinary suspension—that the course of the strike would probably establish patterns that would stand for years—the information going to Gowen took on more significance. During this period Gowen seemed to be increasingly convinced that the union could be beaten decisively. And sometime in this same period Gowen also appeared to realize that violence connected with the strike could be meshed with the violence long attributed to the Molly Maguires, and the two tied up into a neat package for clubbing all union activity under the guise of preserving law and order. Thus, in the first months of 1875, Gowen began to appreciate more readily the potential of McParlan's role.

By this time Gowen had at least four more detectives at work in Schuylkill County (and perhaps more, for strange initials occasionally appear in the agency billings to the railroad that cannot be traced to any of the four; some of these agents worked in other parts of the Reading system).* The differences between what was reported by

---

* A full set of billings from Pinkerton's National Detective Agency for the work done for the Philadelphia & Reading Railroad is available in the Reading Railroad's Molly Maguire Papers. These are both instructive as to the total amount billed and enigmatic as to exactly what was done. McParlan's work was always separately reported; all other work was listed in one large billing. We will look closely at these totals later in the book, but for the sake of perspective now, here is a summary of the billings for the early months of 1875:

McParlan:

Salary, January 1–April 10, 100 days @ $6.00		$600.00
Expenses		242.50
		$842.50

Other agents P. M. C., W. McC., R. J. L., G. E. J., D. P., C. A., T. A. P., J. O. B., J. F. O. B., T. G. for period January 1–July 1 — $4465.99

McParlan and by the other four are substantial. The other four were instructed to infiltrate the union, P. M. Cummings in St. Clair; William McCowan in St. Nicholas and Shamokin; operative "W. R. H." (never further identified by name) at Frackville; and H. B. Hanmore at Pottsville. Hanmore was not a Pinkerton man, but a newspaper reporter from Newburgh, New York, who had personally contacted Gowen with an offer to report privately on what he saw. Gowen sent him an occasional lump-sum check and Hanmore, in turn, wrote letters directly to Gowen. Cummings and McCowan were by now officers in their local union branches, and were able to report on private union affairs.

Particularly strong during this period were the bitter feelings against Siney. Even the officers now turned against him. The prophet was now without honor in the very area for which he had labored so hard. Of course Siney was now preaching a form of dual unionism, for he desperately wanted the Miners' and Laborers' Benevolent Association (as the old W.B.A. was now called) to affiliate with the new national. But he further rubbed salt in wounds by speaking out against strikes in general and thereby undercutting the Schuylkill strike. In January, when the news was published that Siney had made a speech in Swanton to this effect, Cummings reported that "English, Irish, Dutch and Welsh are cursing Siney."[16]

Cummings, McCowan, and "W. R. H." all reported that times were hard, credit at the stores tight, and internal dissension in the union endemic. In contrast, McParlan reported all through January, February, and March, 1875, that spirits were high, credit readily obtainable, and the strike attitude very positive. Some part of this discrepancy can be attributed to the point of perspective. The others were inside the union, while McParlan was seeing the union largely through its public face—the bragging in the taverns and the rumors flying up and down the patch streets. H. B. Hanmore was equally far out of touch and apparently much less able to differentiate between bragging and actual threats. His letters to Gowen kept saying Gowen was imminently in danger of assassination, a barroom boast heard frequently but apparently having little substance at this time.[17]

Though McParlan was not very close to the strike, his reports are far the most detailed. Through them, Gowen was able to learn a good deal about general attitudes of the populace. The detective reported that a fire in a colliery of the railroad in East Norwegian township in February, which the papers implied was Molly Maguire terrorism, was believed by the people to have been set by the railroad itself to prevent the state legislature from having any sympathy with the miners in an upcoming antimonopoly legislative investigation in Harrisburg. Another act of vandalism in early March, blamed on the Mollies, McParlan attributed to a local faction fight, and the substantial damage to railroad property at Summit Station, also considered to be a Molly outrage, he placed on the doorstep of the union itself.[18]

In February he reported that the strikers would rather deal with the railroad, bad as it was, in preference to the apparently untrustworthy "independents." But a month later he pointedly reported that "all classes of people in the coal regions are very much embittered toward your Company and openly denounce the course you have pursued," and that "the enmity seems to be so universal that there is danger of depredations being committed upon your road at any time." The operative also reported a few days later, "any violence against the owners was praised by all miners, whereas in earlier periods it was condemned by most." So McParlan apparently reported what he saw and heard with respect to the strike, without concern for whether it would be palatable to Gowen.[19]

His most active interest, though, was in the affairs of the lodges of the Ancient Order of Hibernians, and the bulk of the information he sent was on that subject. His entry of March 9 said the AOH had only about 450 members in Schuylkill County, and "about 400 of them belong to the W.B.A." The AOH plans for the St. Patrick's Day parade of March 17 moved forward; substantial money was spent on preparations, especially regalia—McParlan charged the expense account $9.85 for his on March 14. But a dark cloud hung over an otherwise happy prospect. It had always been customary, although not required, for the Irish lodges in the various towns to check their plans for the parade with the local priest. Though the parade was not church-sponsored, the day itself was the greatest of Irish national celebrations, and with Know Nothingism still lurking under the surface the priests realized that it was *de facto* a day for Catholicism to blossom forth. The AOH lodges, knowing this, had decided to make a formal approach to the priest of the town where the parade was to be held, Father Charles A. McFadden of Mahanoy City. Kehoe, together with Chris Donnelly (the county treasurer of the AOH), McParlan, and one other member, called on McFadden in mid-February. As McFadden had at least been sympathetic to the AOH as an organization—if not to the Schuylkill branches—their hopes were high for approval. But McFadden quenched these hopes rapidly. As Bishop Wood had pronounced against the AOH, he would too. The parade was to terminate at the church, but the AOH would not be allowed to come inside in regalia.[20] Pinkerton quotes Kehoe as saying they would march if necessary over the priest's dead body. The threat may have been an idle one, but the lodges did decide to go ahead.[21]

As the day approached, other quarters were heard from about the lodges' defiance. Father O'Reilly in Shenandoah, McParlan reported on March 14, said concerning the AOH that "he was glad the MM's were in the parade, as he would have the opportunity to see all the cutthroats in the County," adding, for good measure, "God's curse and his curse on the Molly Maguires and their families and anyone who goes to Mahanoy City to see them parade."

The hallowed day, March 17, 1875, arrived, and Kehoe was in full command. Gathering the members together, he laid down the fiat that no member was to appear in the parade drunk or otherwise misbehaving—if anyone did, Kehoe would personally and publicly strip him of his insignia. "Let's show the clergy and the public we don't deserve our bad name," McParlan quoted him as saying.[22]

The day went off without incident. Though another Catholic group also paraded in the same town, no fights broke out. But the members were quickly disabused of any notion that their mild actions in the parade had won them any more acceptance by the priests, for Father O'Reilly read a long list of names of AOH members from the pulpit the following Sunday and asked the congregation to pray for their lost souls. Though far short of a formal excommunication, it was still a startling experience for the members involved. And James McParlan, sitting in the church that Sunday, heard his alias—"James McKenna"—near the top of the list.[23]

In spite of the AOH setback, John Kehoe's personal star was on the way up. His power in his home town, Girardville, was growing by the day. In the local elections in February, he had easily won the post of High Constable, running on the Democratic ticket. This gave him, according to Allan Pinkerton's book, "the power of arrest and charge of the municipal prisoners," and "if the latter chanced to be of the Order, they were handled tenderly and fared sumptuously. If of the Chain Gang, the Modoc, or Sheet Iron sort, he bundled them into jail without gloves and fed them upon whatever might be cheap and unsavory."[24] McParlan reported on March 16 that the Shenandoah lodge was assessed eight dollars to send Kehoe to the AOH state and national conventions. Kehoe was King. (None of the extant records authenticate this trip, and it would be interesting to know if he actually went.)

As the strike dragged on with no apparent signs of a break, tensions mounted and the pace of violence increased. Soon McParlan himself came perilously close to involvement. A group of Shenandoah Mollies, together with other dissident miners, had determined to blow a key railroad bridge on the Catawissa & Williamsport branch of the Reading (north of Shenandoah) to thwart the shipping of nonunion coal southward. The leaders approached McParlan with a request for more men, and they proposed to include the detective himself. McParlan felt he would be in danger of exposure if he did not go along with the plans—the most dedicated of the group were leaders in the lodge, including McAndrew. As McParlan himself related in his old age (Pinkerton's version seems excessively flamboyant), the conspirators met on the mountain on the night of April 6 to make the final plans and at this meeting the detective was able to have the attack postponed. He informed the group that he had "absolute knowledge" that a group of coal and iron police were stationed in the valley for just such a contingency.[25] But it was a close call for the detective and brought home to him again the bogeyman of exposure and the difficulty he had in communicating threatened violence to Philadelphia.

A few days later, on April 13, 1875, a car loaded with iron slag became mysteriously uncoupled on a siding that ran into "Heckshers Breaker." It rolled down the siding and out onto the main track, then sped toward a passenger train unsuspectingly plodding toward it. At Top Creek, railroad employees saw it looming in the distance and were able to shunt it to a side track at the last moment. A major tragedy had barely been averted. McParlan reported to Franklin the next day that this had been the night when two Shenandoah Mollies had threatened to overturn a rail car in this same area. McParlan had overheard them plotting, and thought he had talked them out of it, but, he reported, "they probably proceeded with the job through spite." McParlan's ego showed through in the last line of his report: "Under these circumstances the operative feels it will be somewhat difficult to prevail on them to admit that they committed the outrage, but he feels equal to the task.[26]

Over the next few days McParlan diligently questioned the members about the case, gaining McAndrew's aid by pointing out that the two men were in charge of the lodge "and could expel them for life if they offended them and it was best to have the men afraid of them." Their efforts paid off. One of the participants "owned up to the whole affair" and implicated the other man involved. McParlan had solved his first Molly Maguire crime.[27]

But of what use *was* this? Perhaps McParlan and McAndrew could hold it over the men's heads and thereby increase their fear of the two leaders. But could the new knowledge serve as the basis for any action by the railroad or the authorities? If McParlan could be put on the stand, a legal case might be made. But this was patently unrealistic. First, Pinkerton had exacted a promise from Gowen when he first took the case that none of his detectives would be forced to break their disguise by appearing in court. Moreover, there was little use in having McParlan break his disguise at this early date, even if Pinkerton had been willing. Further, the difficulty of getting a conviction in the face of false alibis and perjury had already been made uncomfortably clear in the many previous cases. There was an inherent flaw in the plans for McParlan's use—he did not have anyone whom he could reach quickly (even a telegram to Superintendent Benjamin Franklin and a return telegram to the fields took many hours) nor anyone who could corroborate his findings. If crimes committed were to be pinpointed and the culprits tried, and if threatened violence was to be prevented, something further was needed.

McParlan had mentioned his plight to Franklin on a short visit to Philadelphia at the end of March. Now, with an apparent breakthrough in sight, Pinkerton made a new move. The agency head came to Philadelphia on April 28 and met with Franklin and Gowen in the agency's offices. Fortunately, we have a record of this meeting, as set down by Franklin.[28] Though Pinkerton's book flatly states that McParlan was also there, Franklin makes no mention of his name, and McParlan's reports continue from Shenandoah all through this period. McParlan had apparently yet to meet Gowen.

According to the Franklin memorandum, Pinkerton proposed to Gowen that a "flying squadron" of police be set up immediately to rove the fields. They would ostensibly be "coal and iron police," but would actually be composed of five or six men from the agency and an equal number of picked men from the railroad, all to be under the charge of a Pinkerton lieutenant. The latter would be put in direct touch with McParlan, and the two could deploy the forces so that they could be on the spot when a crime was being committed, thus gaining legal evidence for a conviction. Pinkerton implied that this group was not to be "preventive police" to forestall crime, but "convicting police" able to make a case out of the crime, and, in Franklin's report of Pinkerton's words, "there would be but little difficulty in breaking up this association and when the arrest of a gang was made, the names and localities of all the known MM's in the County should be published and thus strike terror within their midst."

Here is further evidence to aid us in eventually making one of the knottiest analytical judgments required in the Molly story—to what extent, if any, did McParlan, under instructions of Pinkerton and/or Gowen, actually fail to prevent crime but, instead, allow the crime to be perpetrated in order to obtain evidence? Circumstantial evidence is strong, in the report of this meeting, that both Gowen and Pinkerton felt that the only way to bring order to the coal regions was through well-publicized convictions. Hopefully, these might be convictions for *past* crimes; but in the spring of 1875 this remained to be seen.

With the new plan agreed upon, Pinkerton immediately sent for one of his most trusted lieutenants, Robert J. Linden. Linden had been with the agency since shortly after the Civil War. After working a while in the Philadelphia office, he had been made assistant superintendent of the Chicago office in 1871. Pinkerton described him as "about forty years of age, tall, powerful in frame and physical organization, with black, close-curling hair, whiskers and mustache of the same texture and color, blue eyes, which were expressive of confidence—just the kind of orbs to win the confidence of others."[29]

Linden hurried east, and, after a brief meeting with Pinkerton and Franklin in Philadelphia, went to the coal fields on May 3, 1875. He first stopped at Schuylkill Haven, where he was met by McParlan. The two operatives had a drink and cigars together in a tavern (twenty cents for the drinks and the same for the cigars, Linden said in his expense account), and set up their plans in regard to mode of contact and probable locations.[30] The next day, in Pottsville, Linden was formally inducted into the Reading's Coal and Iron Police as a captain. This private police force was commanded by General Henry Pleasants. Within it was a "flying squadron," consisting at first of a seven-member group of Pinkertons (though not publicly known as such) headed by Linden and a seven-man non-Pinkerton group headed by Captain W. J. Heisler. The Heisler segment was detailed to several company locations at Locust Run. Linden and his six Pinkertons left for Ashland.

It was at that point that the Daniel Dougherty case came to its climax. The unfortunate Irishman, still bearing in his head the bullet that had struck him the night George Major had been killed in Mahanoy City, had been in the Pottsville jail since November. Finally, on March 28, his case was called in Pottsville. Feelings were intense—both for and against him—and special trains were run between Mahanoy City and Pottsville. After a panel of jurors had been called, the defense startled the crowd by demanding a change of venue, citing the high feeling in Schuylkill County and the inflammatory statements against Dougherty in the press. The judge promptly agreed and the case was transferred to Lebanon, in Lebanon County, southwest of Schuylkill.[31]

It was late April by the time the case came up, and again large crowds came from Mahanoy City. The prosecution paraded a long line of witnesses, all swearing that they personally saw Dougherty shoot Major, after which the defense paraded an equally large group who swore that it was another man whom they identified as John McCann. (McCann was reputed by this time to have escaped back to Ireland.) Clearly, someone was lying. As the case for the defense was not overwhelming, Dougherty's attorneys finally decided it was necessary to extract the bullet from Dougherty's head in order to prove that it did not come from the gun of George Major. The painful surgery was accomplished, and the bullet apparently did not match George Major's pistol. This was enough to satisfy the jury of Dougherty's innocence, and he was acquitted. The verdict was greeted with jubilation by Dougherty's friends, and a rowdy demonstration broke out, only to be quelled by the judge's threat to cite the participants for contempt of court. The question of perjury was widely debated. The *Miners' Journal* quoted with disapproval a comment in the *Lebanon Courier* that "if this is the character of testimony that prevails in the Schuylkill County courts, we do not wonder that there are no convictions for murder." The Pottsville editor replied that "the *Courier* is guilty of a great inaccuracy in alluding to Schuylkill as place 'where murders are almost everyday occurrences.' " He said "there are more than enough but not as many as all that."[32]

But Dougherty *was* innocent, and our authority for this is none other than James McParlan, in a revealing bit of testimony at a later Molly trial. The Dougherty case was resurrected by the defense in an effort to raise doubt in the jurors' minds about McParlan's ethics. McParlan was being cross-examined by a defense attorney named Martin L'Velle:

Q. From information you received since then, you say that Dan Dougherty was not the man that shot Major?

A. Yes, sir.

Q. How soon after the alleged shooting did you ascertain this fact?

A. I ascertained that fact upon a Monday.

Q. The following Monday?

A. Yes, sir.

Q. You were aware of the fact that Dan Dougherty was indicted for the murder of Major?

A. Yes, sir.

Q. And on trial in Lebanon for the murder?

A. Yes, sir.

Q. And you knew of his innocence?

Mr. Hughes [prosecution]. He did not say that he knew of his innocence.

Mr. L'Velle. He swore it was not Dan Dougherty.

The Witness. I had positive information that it was not Dan Dougherty.

Q. You knew he was in prison charged with that murder, you also knew he was on trial for his life, charged with murder, and yet remained silent?

A. I also knew Dan Dougherty was apprised where John McCann was, and could get out at any time. The idea was that Dougherty was innocent, and knew where McCann was, and he would be tried, knowing he could be cleared, and meanwhile McCann could escape.[33]

L'Velle felt that he could exploit this story as evidence of a major moral flaw in McParlan's character, and hit heavily on it in his final summation to the jury. At that time McParlan had been revealed as a detective, but the lawyer called him by his fictitious name.

Yet with this information in his bosom, James McKenna never raised his voice to avert the conviction . . . McKenna tells you that it was in order that McCann should escape that Dougherty undertook the hazard of his conviction and the surrender of his life. What a fallacious pretext! What an apology to offer in a court of justice! Is that the man to whom was confided the detection of crime, and the bringing of criminals to justice, and, as an antithesis to that, the safety of the innocent . . . Yea, he would have permitted him to go to the gallows and be hung like a malefactor though an innocent man . . . Would you conceal in the recesses of your heart, in the secret cells of your bosom, the knowledge of a murderer who had confessed himself a murderer? Would you keep that knowledge in your hearts and permit an innocent man to go to the gallows? Ah, foul would be the heart, infamous would be the intent, dishonest would be the purpose, unworthy of credit would be the assertation of any man . . . that would conceal such a crime and see an innocent man go to the gallows.[34]

L'Velle's accusation poses again the fundamental dilemma inherent in McParlan's role. By May of 1875, as the "Long Strike" dragged into its fifth month, the need to break the back of the violence by equally decisive countermeasures—if possible a series of public trials for either past or future murders—seemed clear to Pinkerton and Gowen. To do this, McParlan would need to keep "within his bosom" both confessions of past crimes and potential plans for future crimes until that moment when, in one fell swoop, the authorities could move in for arrests. Premature disclosure of his role, even indirectly, could bring down the entire structure of plans. Yet it can be argued that because of this withholding of information, Dougherty came perilously close to being hanged. Had McParlan passed his knowledge concerning McCann to the police, his carefully built role would have collapsed. It is interesting to speculate on what McParlan would have done had Dougherty been found guilty in Lebanon. McCann was evidently far away by this time. Perhaps McParlan would have been the only person whose testimony would have been given enough credence to overturn a guilty verdict. Fortunately for Dan Dougherty this was never tested.

But if Dougherty felt himself snatched at the last moment from the jaws of death, it was not to be his last brush with premature eternity. Late in May he was returning home through a patch of trees when he was suddenly confronted by two men armed with pistols. Both fired, and the bullets actually pierced his clothing. But

Lady Luck had not abandoned him—he was unscratched. Nevertheless, it appeared that the Major adherents still felt him to be guilty.
The *Miners' Journal,* which had dropped its vindictiveness toward
Dougherty after the trial, promptly excoriated the attempted assassination as "a dastardly act that no decent man can fail to condemn."
Still, threats continued, and Dougherty's attorneys finally took the
unusual step of making a public statement emphatically affirming
their belief in his innocence.[35] But poor Dan Dougherty was still not
finished with involvement in violence.

❖   ❖   ❖   ❖   ❖

Meanwhile the "Long Strike" of 1875 brought increasing stories
of distress bordering on starvation. The spectacle of poverty and
famine was fit game for the Philadelphia and New York papers,
which in hair-raising terms told the nation of the "anarchy in the
coal regions." *Frank Leslie's Illustrated Newspaper* on March 11
printed a poignant picture of a miner's wife cooking "the last loaf"
in an outside fireplace amid the snow, surrounded by her starving
children, while her drunken husband and his drunken companions
cavorted in the background.

The miners' traditional ability to get provisions "on the tick"—
buying on credit from the storekeepers—had always been counted
on to get them through a strike, and in the past it always had. But as
the storekeepers' credit balances rose higher and higher, their fear of
insolvency also rose. The storekeeper had always accepted the credit
risks in a strike as a normal part of business, and had shrewdly warded
off the probable losses by charging high enough prices to come out
ahead. Now the scale of credit began to terrify even the most stal-
wart, and some began to refuse further credit.

One storekeeper, in a letter published by the *Miners' Journal* on
April 2, said that although up to then "the fear of losing what I have
already sold" had kept him going, he had finally decided that even
this loss was not as great as continuing. "I am going to stop selling
goods and shut up," he announced. His plight was understandable.
John Welsh, Siney's successor as president of the union, had persuaded each local of the union to pass a resolution that shopkeepers
would be paid back as soon as the strike was over; but this, in spite of

good intentions, was becoming unrealistic. The letter to the *Journal* pointed this out with irrefutable logic—how could even a working miner making ten to twelve dollars a week, and supporting a family, lay aside any substantial sum for repayment? The answer was that he could not. The letter must have encouraged others to make the same decision, and for the remainder of the strike, provisions were more and more difficult to obtain.

Under such conditions of frustration, inaction, and fear, the tendency toward excess infected more and more of the people. Gowen had asked the resident engineer of each station to keep him informed of any acts of vandalism against railroad property. His office was flooded with reports of damage, most of it minor but some of it more serious. The coffin notice was now epidemic, and each crudely scrawled message was duly forwarded. Sometimes there was even a humorous side to the incidents; the district mine inspector at Shamokin reported on an attempted opening of the Greenback colliery that "forty union women from the patch met them and commenced stoning them, making it generally unpleasant for them to attempt starting work—the husbands of the women were in the woods enjoying the scene."[36]

The continued operation of the mines in the northern district, once again devastatingly undermining the strike in the central and southern fields, had renewed the old bitterness between the northern and southern miners, and lead to increasingly scurrilous attacks by the southern group. The *Scranton Times,* an advocate of the northern district, put the issue frankly on the line: "Giving up one's daily bread for the benefit of another is loving one's neighbor better than oneself, which is more than we are required by scripture to do."[37] Interestingly, though, the Scranton miners continued to contribute to a relief fund for the strikers, in spite of the continuing animosity.

The tensions put a real burden on the AOH leadership in Schuylkill County. Most of the lodges had an element that was impulsive under the best of circumstances, almost uncontrollable under conditions of stress. Kehoe, as county delegate, was faced with a dilemma. On the one hand he wanted to keep the lodge respectable enough to hold on to its state and national affiliations and pious enough at least to keep the Church from excommunicating its individual members. On the other hand he wanted to keep the lodge powerful enough to be a force in politics (Kehoe certainly saw new vistas for himself here) and able to defend itself against its enemies —Modocs, Sheet Irons, and employers. The power came from both membership numbers and membership willingness to flex its muscles. Kehoe was easily re-elected to his AOH post at a county convention on April 29, but McParlan reported that Kehoe was having difficulty preventing new outbreaks of violence that did not fit Kehoe's personal plans. However, as McParlan reported on May 6, though "Kehoe was also opposed to anything of the kind, at the same time if Cannon [an AOH bodymaster] wanted men Kehoe would be compelled to send them."[38]

And the detective himself soon was forced into a precarious position by these same pressures for action. On May 10, three Shenandoah Mollies, John Gibbons, Thomas Hurley, and Michael Doyle, brought the startling information that the Reading's coal and iron company was planning to open its West Shenandoah colliery in spite of the strike (there had been intimations that many miners were ready to become "black legs" if the company would furnish them protection). The three men were notoriously volatile and already had been involved in private vendettas. Now they baldly proposed to McAndrew and McParlan that the lodge arm itself and "destroy" the "traitors" and their homes. McParlan was put directly on the spot, for, as he reported to Franklin, he was "well known to all parties . . . and did not dare attempt to do anything to halt the plans." He decided to appear to fall in with those plans. Hurley and Doyle reappeared that night with their revolvers. McParlan, sparring for time, treated the group to drinks, had several himself, and fell into a drunken stupor. Having already established a reputation for heavy drinking, his inebriation was accepted by the rest of the group, "and they left him in care of the saloon keeper." As soon as the men had gone, McParlan lurched out of the tavern and—at least according to his report—immediately sent word to Linden.[39] (The fact that Linden was then in Ashland, ten miles away, raises doubts as to the effectiveness of such notice, even if it arrived.)

The next day Gibbons reported that "all was a failure," but intimated that there were "a few jobs to do tonight" and again invited McParlan to go along. The detective "pretended to be very sick so staid at home."[40] But it was questionable just how long he would be able to elude the conspirators through his repeated defaulting.

At this point—May 12, 1875—we lose our inside information from McParlan via the reports and once again are forced back into secondary sources. McParlan, according to Pinkerton, felt he was all too close to being forced into action, and decided upon a short side trip to Northumberland County (northwest of Schuylkill), at the moment the scene of considerable strike activity. Needing an excuse, he professed to have become enamored of the young daughter of Patrick Hester, a prominent Locust Gap AOH official, when he had visited there on an earlier trip. Now, he said, he wanted to see her again. We depend on Pinkerton's fertile pen (and possibly his fertile imagination) for the love interests of McParlan; a later romantic attachment of McParlan, according to Pinkerton, plays a profound part in the rounding up of the gang. At any rate, McParlan probably did visit Hester's house, but whether we can accept Pinkerton's slyly suggestive story of McParlan's evening with Maria Hester and her sister is less certain: "When two games of euchre had been finished, and success was about equal on either side, the house was closed, and all, excepting McKenna and the young ladies, retired. It was not quite morning when this trio separated, mutually pleased with each other and the manner in which they had passed their time."[41]

A few days later McParlan returned to Shenandoah, to be faced with a disconcerting new development. Bodymaster McAndrew, having been promised work in the northern district, let it be known that he was leaving immediately and would turn over the leadership of the lodge to McParlan until he returned. McParlan must have been upset at this. And he was even more disturbed when John Gibbons and Michael Doyle, together with two other Mollies, immediately took advantage of McAndrew's absence to propose the effecting of the long-awaited "execution" of Gomer James. Again McParlan was squarely on the spot. As Pinkerton put it, "to show cowardice or hesitation under the circumstances would prove sure if not immediate death."[42]

Unfortunately, we have no direct authentication for this period. McParlan evidently did fall in with the plot, hoping that he could forestall it by some ruse. Two abortive and almost comic attempts were made to kill James, both without McParlan's being present. At any rate, James was not "executed" at this time, and temporarily left the county.

But we do have an independent check on some of McParlan's activities during this month (May 1875) through the daily reports of Linden. Again it is a comedy of errors, but useful. On May 14, Linden stoically reported that he was not having much success in gaining information and "can only wait patiently for business." But "business" quickly came, for three days later McParlan sent him information of a plan to derail a train near Locust Gap. Linden gives us a detailed description of what was done about it. McParlan's tip came by letter, arriving at 4:30 p.m. the day the outrage was planned, and McParlan gave explicit details as to where to station the police. On the basis of this, Captain Linden immediately wired General Pleasants: "Can I get lease today?" Pleasants replied, "I will be at Ashland at 7 p.m. this evening and you can see me about lease." Captain Heisler arrived with an augmented group of the flying squadron at 7 p.m. The total of twenty men—Linden's and Heisler's—were deployed by running them down the track on a Reading engine and dropping a man off every forty feet. Three strangers came walking along the track, "but did no harm" and the train passed through without incident.[43]

Over the next two weeks there were almost daily contacts from McParlan in respect to proposed violence—plans to burn breakers, "capture mines," derail trains, blow up stations. In every case they failed to materialize, but Linden, ever the meticulous planner, always took these threats at face value and set up elaborate countermeasures.

If these nightly chases came to nothing for Linden and McParlan, they help us to judge the type and quality of the contact between the two men. The system appeared to be reasonably speedy, yet still secure from exposure. Sometimes McParlan was forced to use a letter, rather than the telegraph, but this seemed to be fast enough to arrive in time for deployment of the men. It is interesting, though, that all the threatened violence during this period was directed against *property*, and for this McParlan and Linden were indefatigable in leaving nothing to chance. But in the one case where a threat had been made against a person—Gomer James—the message had not arrived in time to prevent murder attempts. It is true that James understood he was being threatened and decided to leave the county, and Pinkerton claimed in his book that McParlan did get a message through and that the Reading had warned James. But the information could have come to him through any number of sources. It is hard to accept Pinkerton's statement that James was warned by the Reading. The danger of losing the carefully built security system would seem to have been too great.

✤   ✤   ✤   ✤   ✤

The strike now was breaking apart. When it had officially begun in January, the operators had made it clear that their new and lowered wage terms were being proposed unilaterally—the miners could take it or leave it, but the operators would not bargain with them. Having tried a rudimentary form of collective bargaining in previous years, the operators had decided that whatever value this method had was overbalanced by the disadvantages. And they stuck to this thesis throughout the "Long Strike." The "bargaining," such as it was, was carried out through the public press, and the chief voice, the Pottsville *Miners' Journal,* became increasingly antiunion as the weeks went by with no settlement. If Gowen was a prophet with some honor in the eyes of editor Ramsey, his monopolistic predilections caused a number of papers outside the coal region to support the strikers. The *Harrisburg Patriot* on April 17 paid the union a left-handed compliment in the process of sending off a diatribe against the company: "The miners' union, pernicious and arbitrary as are many of its rules, is necessary to defend them against monopoly. It enables or greatly assists them to obtain their share of the profits that are paid by the consumers. They might with as much reason and justice ask the Reading Coal and Iron Company to abandon its own organization in their behalf."

The year 1875 was marked by industrial strife all through the country. The depression had deepened; wage cuts and dismissals were widespread. On May 29 the *Pilot,* the Catholic periodical in Boston, defended strikes in a ringing editorial and took as examples the weavers' strike at Fall River, Massachusetts, and the anthracite strike in Pennsylvania. The *Pilot* insisted that "the system of strikes is a phenomenon worth observing: it is one of the great signs of the times—the sign of a transition period in American history." It added that "trades unions may be a mistake; but they are an absolute necessity." *Frank Leslie's Illustrated Newspaper* on June 12 attempted a more balanced economic interpretation of the anthracite strike, and held that it was the competition from bituminous coal that forced the operators to attempt the wage reduction which had precipitated the strike.

Thus at various levels of sophistication the coal strike was debated in the public press through the country. But the needles stuck into the body of the coal operators' combination had little effect in changing its stand on the strike. The union had long since become nervous over its deteriorating position, and when an important northern group at Hyde Park had voted in early April not to join the suspension, President John Welsh had realized that the time had come for some sort of union action. We have a revealing view of his dilemma in a private letter circulated to all the Schuylkill County locals on April 10. Though Welsh said in a wistful postscript, "It is hoped that this circular will not be shown outside of the Union," it was immediately forwarded to Gowen by one of the Pinkerton men! In the letter Welsh reported that the Hyde Park men "are prepared to divide their work with Union men," and advocated that "some means be devised for sending a number of our people to places where mining is now being done." Those willing to go but not having the money would be supported with "as much money as can be had and which is not absolutely needed to buy bread." He also proposed that the men who could get work with the independents should accept this work at the 1874 basis, pending settlement, and that even the Reading mines should be worked, provided no shipments were actually made. But Welsh seemed to recognize that he was barking at the moon on this latter point, for he continued, "Mr. Gowen may be stubborn and I have been told by those operators who are in the Coal Exchange will not take advantage of the offer for fear of not getting cars."[44]

This was what happened. Gowen was adamant, and none of the independents could afford to stand against the combination—Gowen had all the trump cards. In spite of Welsh's pleading exhortation that "we must maintain a bold front, we must not permit ourselves to be frightened or cajoled," the union's cause was rapidly slipping through his fingers. On April 21, the union proposed arbitration, the cure-all so enthusiastically advanced by the operators in 1871, but the operators did not even deign to reply. Finally, on May 14, a committee of the Schuylkill operators agreed to meet with union representatives. The union, desperate to find a face-saving alternative that would not have the appearance of capitulation, came to the meeting with a startling proposal—that all sliding scale and contract wages be eliminated in favor of a single flat rate of $15 for a week of six eight-hour days. The operators, sensing imminent victory in the strike, quickly rejected the offer.

This was the last meeting ever held between the Miners' and Laborers' Benevolent Association and the operators. Late in May the operators decided to reopen the mines unilaterally and offer the 1874 basis to whoever would come to work. Further, they made it clear that they were prepared to provide protection for those who did come.

This opened the flood gates. There were many miners who had been willing for several months to return; their ranks were swelled daily by additional men who had either lost faith in the union or who were in such desperate straits that they had to have money. When the Reading opened the huge West Shenandoah colliery on June 1, 1875, the final nail was apparently driven into the union's coffin.

But was it? McParlan did not think so, for he sent word to Linden that day that a raid was to be made on the "black legs" who had come to work at West Shenandoah.[45] Linden and Heisler knew that although this might be a dying gasp, it could be serious, for this was the bellwether mine of the area. Both went immediately to the mine, taking eighteen of the "flying squadron." Nothing happened at first, and Linden on June 2 was preparing to leave the scene, keeping only a token force at the mine, when a messenger ran to him to say there was a large group of marching men who had just persuaded the Lost Creek miners to quit work, and that it was rumored they planned to march on Shenandoah.

The rumor was true. On the night of June 2 a group of miners gathered on "Number Three Hill" for what was billed as a "labor picnic." But it turned out to be part bacchanale (drinking was very heavy, most of the miners sleeping the stupor off right on the hill) and part mob excitement. At 7 a.m. on the 3rd a crowd began to gather at Heckshers Colliery—"their drums were beating as early as 5:00 a.m."—and began to move toward the West Shenandoah colliery. Linden and Heisler had about twenty-five men "and 15 guns," and formed them "about two feet from the top of the slope on a piece of ground, about 100 feet square." Heisler rushed back to Shenandoah for reinforcements. Soon the shouting miners, accompanied by loud drum beats, appeared in sight. Linden counted 613 men. In the front ranks, wild-eyed and shouting, was "James McKenna," "carrying a large hickory club, and beneath his long, patched grey coat he had two revolvers tucked in his belt. At his side was his bulldog, looking as tough as its master."[46] As the mob surged forward, Linden ordered his men to level their rifles at it. For one precarious moment it appeared that the order to fire would have to be given. Pinkerton gives us his always exciting version:

> "Halt," shouted Linden.
> "Forward," commanded Walker [the "marshall," according to Pinkerton].
> But few obeyed Walker's call—and they stepped back hastily, as though they had blundered, when, at a signal from Linden, a score of Winchester rifles promptly came to the shoulders of as many hardy and resolute men, ready for the expected order to "fire."[47]

The resolution of Captain Linden and his force was greater than that of the mob. The hesitation revealed who was victor. The mob drew back and soon disappeared into the woods.

Probably the will of the crowd was broken at that point; but trouble was to die hard. The miners went from Shenandoah toward Mahanoy City, taking out the men from three small collieries along the way. When they arrived in Mahanoy City, they were greeted noisily by a large group of Hazleton strikers who had taken out half a dozen mines on their way down. The mere presence of that many people in the town—there were well over a thousand by now—intimidated the local merchants, and almost all of them closed up and stayed home behind locked doors. The tavern keepers, though perhaps equally faint-hearted, could not resist the unexpected windfall, and stayed open through the day and night.

A minor skirmish soon occurred between the local sheriff and a part of the mob attempting to close Little Drift Colliery. At this point authorities put in a call for help. The state militia was already deployed nearby—Governor John F. Hartranft had called them out in mid-April to control the miners' rioting in the Hazleton area—and a contingent of armed troopers came to the scene. But they did not have to take any action—their mere presence seemed to signal that the final nail really had been driven and the union coffin was ready for burial. The mob dispersed, and the following day all the collieries that had been closed were reopened.[48]

On June 8 the union's executive board, making a desperate stab at salvaging the organization, announced that it would make a direct appeal to Gowen for a compromise. But the triumphant rail president scotched the plan before it had a chance to reach the miners in the patches. He addressed a devastating letter to Welsh the next day and had it published in the *Miners' Journal* on June 10, 1875. Readers had to go no further than the first paragraph:

I notice by the newspaper reports of the proceedings of your Association at Pottsville yesterday, that a committee of which you are a member, was appointed to confer with me about tolls, price of coal, etc., and to inquire whether it is not possible to make some compromise upon the rate of wages. I have of course, no further information than that contained in the newspapers, and assuming it to be true, I think it is my duty to the workingmen to protect against the use of my name for the purpose of prolonging the strike. I am not a member of the committee of the Coal Exchange, appointed to take charge of the subject of wages, and therefore I cannot consent to have any conference whatever with your Association upon that question.

The last hope died with this uncompromising refusal, and on June 14 the union capitulated—but not able to resist firing a final volley which was printed in the *Journal* of June 17:

BROTHERS: For now more than five long months you have struggled with a courageous determination almost unprecedented against the enforcement of a most unjust edict, issued, it is true, in the name of the operators of the Schuylkill region, but inspired and upheld almost exclusively by the half dozen well-known Autocrats of these anthracite coal fields . . . They had never once, since the beginning of the contest, taken the trouble to call the members of the Coal Exchange together . . . but after consulting with the King of the ring, they had taken it upon themselves to respond . . . with contemptuous silence or shameful misrepresentation of facts . . . And now Mr. Gowen and the operators of Schuylkill c. have the satisfaction of knowing that as a county organization we can continue the fight no longer . . .

Gowen, then, was widely believed to be the villain, the Mephistopheles who had personally manipulated the destruction of the union. He became a permanent symbol—the king of the robber barons—and his name was preserved in the oral traditions of the miner:

> But don't think, Stranger, we make all the strikes,
> There's Mr. Gowen makes one when he likes.
> To him they don't say BAH about the thing;
> But see the difference—He's a Railroad King.

> And then again, this Mr. Gowen's sly
> And makes the people think the reason why
> The mines have stopped, is that the men have struck
> For higher wages—darn the fellow's luck![49]

The strike was lost, and everyone knew it. As another miner put it in the ballad, "After the Long Strike,"

> Well, we've been beaten, beaten all to smash
> And now, sir, we've begun to feel the lash,
> As wielded by a gigantic corporation,
> Which ran the commonwealth and ruins the nation.[50]

Gowen's biographer largely absolves him from this role of master manipulator: "It appears likely that he was not responsible for the harsh wage terms; it was said that he had never seen them until after they were drawn up. His only public action during the entire strike was his letter of June 9 . . . "[51]

The evidence is not clear-cut on that question. It is true that Gowen had many other problems on his mind during this period. A very substantial legislative investigation of the Reading had again been mounted at Harrisburg late in April, initiated by the union and presumably spearheaded by the Philadelphia coal dealers who had been so badly hurt by Gowen's elimination of the middlemen. (Gowen, incidentally, was not sure himself who was behind the investigation and used three more Pinkerton detectives to find out who was responsible![52]) Railroad shipments, of course, had fallen off badly during the strike, and Gowen was being pressed by the London stockholders. General labor problems were only part of his over-all concern. When an embryonic organization of mechanics on the railroad itself got into a wage hassle with the company in early 1875, Gowen wrote the lawyer representing it that he had referred the whole question "to Mr. Wooten, the General Superintendent of the Road, who has entire charge of all questions connected with the men in his department. I must therefore refer you to him as my engagements are of such a character as to prevent my giving any personal attention to the matter." And even in a private letter to Superintendent Wooten, Gowen merely stated, "The whole matter is therefore referred to you."[53]

But on the basis of our rather more intimate view of Gowen via the Pinkerton reports, it seems that such detachment was not present in the case of the coal dispute. The Schuylkill Coal Exchange was a captive organization, for the Reading not only owned most of the mines involved but controlled *all* of the shipping. Gowen took the initiative and acquainted himself intimately with the progress of the strike; most of the reports were directed personally to Gowen, rather than through railroad and coal-and-iron company channels.

It is fair to say that Gowen broke the strike, and killed the union in the process. But he had not yet killed the Schuylkill AOH.

Chapter 9 * The Summer of 1875

*L*OSS OF the "Long Strike" was felt for years afterward. Impoverishment from the idleness, fanned by the bitterness of the battle, left searing wounds. But the desperate need to get back to work—under any conditions—dictated the swallowing of pride, the hiding of antipathy under a mantle of subservience. On the surface, the miners' will was broken.

John Kehoe's was not, though. Nor were those of his immediate Molly Maguire intimates.

Most of the members of the Ancient Order of Hibernians were miners, with substantial stakes in the strike. It was hard to be much interested in lodge business and faction fighting when families were near starvation. But the leadership were only on the fringes of mining. Kehoe and some others were saloon keepers; the idleness actually increased the consumption of their wares. (It probably increased their cash intake, too, for there is no evidence that they faced the same severe credit pinch as did the storekeepers; ordinarily, whiskey was cash, provisions "carry".) Many other Molly leading lights were idlers and roughs, more concerned with internal squabbles than with mining. The violence of the latter stages of the strike gave them an excellent outlet for pursuing personal vendettas. The end of the strike meant less to them than to most of the miners.

On May 26, 1875, McParlan visited Girardville to see John Kehoe. He was with him most of the afternoon. Here he learned of—and became deeply involved in—a Kehoe plan for murder. The progression of this plan became the basis, the following year, for one of the most sensational of the Molly Maguire trials.[1] We depend now on McParlan's sworn testimony at this trial, for the daily detective reports are not available for this period.

McParlan found Kehoe bitter about the attempts to assassinate Dan Dougherty. According to McParlan, Kehoe "told me he had been to Mahanoy City . . . and that things were in a bad state, that the Modocs were raising the mischief, and that he calculated to call a meeting of the Ancient Order of Mollie Maguires of the county to arm themselves and go to Mahanoy City and challenge them to a fight and shoot them down in the daytime."[2] In attacking McParlan's testimony at the trial, the defense insinuated that McParlan himself had gone to Girardville and initiated the plan, but McParlan replied that "I did not know there was such trouble as he represented to be at Mahanoy City at that time."[3] (This was shading the facts a bit, for McParlan had reported an attempt to shoot Dougherty to Superintendent Franklin on May 9.[4]) Kehoe told McParlan that he had sent for Dennis Canning, the Northumberland County delegate and the bodymaster at Locust Gap, and an important meeting would be held on June 1 at Mahanoy City. He asked McParlan to be there to represent Shenandoah, as Bodymaster McAndrew was still working in the northern district.

McParlan could see that something substantial was brewing, and on May 28 he went to Mahanoy City to investigate. Calling on Michael O'Brien, one of the AOH'ers there, he found that Kehoe's plans had become more specific: "to get about six good men, armed with Navy revolvers, and he would send a man around with those men, and this man would point out to those strangers who would come who he wanted shot, and that they could do it all in one night."[5]

With plans moving so rapidly, McParlan decided to see Kehoe once again before the June 1 meeting, and went back to Girardville on the 30th. Again he, Kehoe, and John Regan, bodymaster of St. Clair, spent the afternoon discussing the case. This second meeting at Kehoe's led (at the trial) to a strange disclosure of Kehoe's mentality. That very day Kehoe's wife had given birth to a child, and the youngster was born with a harelip. While McParlan was there, two doctors came to the house to see the mother and child. Neither saw McParlan, who was sitting downstairs in the bar, and the defense attempted to shake the detective's story of even being there; but the attempt proved to be weak, for the doctors admitted being preoccupied.[6] Kehoe did not let the matter of the birth deter him in his planning, according to McParlan. While the doctors were upstairs he appealed to McParlan to give him some men from Shenandoah who were "good on the shoot" for the approaching battle. McParlan demurred, saying that his men were young and inexperienced, but did promise to be present at the June 1 meeting.

The day came—June 1, 1875—the same day when the West Shenandoah colliery was reopened and the "Long Strike" was almost over. When McParlan arrived at the rendezvous in Mahanoy City, he found Kehoe and seven other AOH'ers assembled.[7] It was an imposing lineup of AOH officialdom. Those present, in addition to the two county delegates (Kehoe of Schuylkill and Dennis Canning of Northumberland), were the county treasurer, Chris Donnelly; the county secretary, William Gavin; the Mahanoy City bodymaster, Michael O'Brien, and secretary, Frank McHugh; and two other bodymasters, James Roarity of Coaldale and John Donahue of Tuscarora.* McParlan described the meeting's progress:

When I got in the room, Kehoe was the President and kind of opened the meeting, and told them he supposed they knew the object that they had been called there together for, and I believe gave a description that the Modocs had tried to shoot Dan Dougherty and commit some crimes of that kind.

Then Christopher Donnelly objected to Frank McHugh. He asked what fetched him there. Michael O'Brien said that he was his secretary, and he wanted him to be there. So Francis McHugh stayed there.

Christopher Donnelly then made a motion that the convention should procure some stationery; that is, some pens and ink and paper, and for Frank McHugh to write a kind of minutes, or what purported to be minutes of the meeting, so that if any trouble should arise from the convention, they could produce those minutes to show that they had met there on legal society business. This paper was got.[8]

Apparently Kehoe planned to run the "convention" as a quasi-trial (the age-old pattern in the secret societies in Ireland), for he next sent out for Dan Dougherty:

Dougherty was fetched into the room. There were two who went out after him. I forget now who they were. They got him in his boarding house. He showed us one or two bullet-holes in his coat, somewhere up by the shoulder, and stated that he believed that Jess Major was the man that shot him, and he had come to the conclusion that the probabilities were that the Majors were going to kill him anyhow, and he thought that if the Majors and Bully Bill were put out of the way he would have peace.[9]

* One of the interesting problems in the Molly Maguire story is that of keeping the names straight, for the spellings varied within a single trial record. For example, Roarity was often spelled without the "i"; Donahue was sometimes written Donohue. The dangers of mistaking identity are sizable for researchers but were even more important for the law officers, judges, and juries at the time.

"Bully Bill" was William M. Thomas, a Mahanoy City Welshman whose past scrapes—beatings, robbery, drunkenness—had apparently richly earned him his nickname. "The Majors," Jesse and William, were also Welshmen, kinsmen of the late George Major. Dougherty's statement was enough "evidence" to convict the three men, and, after asking Dougherty to retire, the members immediately got down to the business of effecting the "executions." The two Majors were temporarily absent from Mahanoy City, mining a vein near Tuscarora; so Donahue and Donnelly agreed "to take care of their side of the mountain if we—referring to O'Brien, Roarity and I—would take care of ours." Canning offered to send some men from Northumberland—the old Irish device of "trading jobs"—but Donnelly "stated that the job was a light one, and that we could do it ourselves." He was not implying that the Majors would be any less dead! It was "light" because the Majors were working in an isolated section, where identification and assassination would be easier.

The group next took up the Bully Bill plans. "Kehoe then turned around and stated that it was now devolved on O'Brien, Roarity and I as to how we would dispose of William M. Thomas or Bully Bill—he advocating that the best plan was to get a couple of men well armed, and go right up to him on the street and shoot him down in daylight."[10] O'Brien objected to the plan as too dangerous, and argued that two outsiders from another lodge be brought to Mahanoy City and housed via AOH funds at a boarding house, to await a good chance to waylay Thomas between the town and Shoemaker's Patch, where Bully Bill lived. Again Canning offered men, but Kehoe said it wasn't necessary, and, instead, instructed McParlan and Roarity to call meetings of their respective lodges, set up tentative plans, and then check with him. All (including McParlan) agreed, and the meeting was terminated, the plans for the "light jobs" being well under way.

But what was McParlan's AOH position—official or otherwise—at this meeting? And what was the precise nature of his commitment at the end of the meeting? These questions were bitterly debated at the various trials, and served to raised the issue, over the succeeding years, of whether McParlan was, in fact, an *agent provocateur*. These questions have never been satisfactorily answered—and very likely are unanswerable. Nevertheless, the trial testimony is revealing, and we should pause to analyze it before moving on to settle the fate of Bully Bill.

Was McParlan at this time actually the *de facto* bodymaster of the Shenandoah lodge, fully responsible for its role in the affair? And had he not agreed to plan *and execute* the killing on his side of the mountain? The Molly defense attorneys attempted to implicate him in this way; but McParlan disagreed:

Q. You went home, and you called your meeting in Shenandoah?
A. I went home, and notified some of the members just as I met them.
Q. Whom did you notify?
A. I notified Edward Monaghan.
Q. One.
A. I notified John Gibbons.
Q. Two.
A. I told Thomas Hurley and Michael Doyle.
Q. Did you fix a time for that meeting and tell them where you would meet them. Recollect now that you were the chief man; you are body master from this time out?
A. That may be your impression, but I did not even fix the time. I had not the authority even for that.
Q. Yes, you had. You told us in your examination-in-chief that Kehoe told you to go and call a meeting?
A. I told you . . . that Kehoe told me to go home and notify the members.
Q. Yes, that is it?
A. Well, notifying the members and calling a meeting are not altogether the same thing. I had not the authority to call a meeting.
Q. You said that when you had the authority of the county delegate you could act as body master in the absence of McAndrew and you got the authority of the county delegate to call this meeting?
A. I did not fix a place. There is a gentleman sitting right behind you, Mr. Gibbons, that fixed the place of the meeting and named the bush.
Q. Mr. Gibbons was not body master there, was he?
A. No, but he was in company with Kelly and Doyle.[11]

McParlan was obviously on thin ice here; in the eyes of Kehoe and the Shenandoah Mollies he appeared to be the leader. In light of this, the key question is what he did with this leadership power. Notification was actually made by someone, and a small group of the Shenandoah lodge met on the mountain on the night of June 4, 1875. Thomas Hurley, Michael Doyle, and John Gibbons decided to go to Mahanoy City the very next day to carry off "the job." They asked McParlan to accompany them—and he accepted. Ques-

tioned about this, at the trials, the detective vowed that he had not
urged his own assistance, but when the men had asked him point-
blank to go, he had replied that he was "as brave as any of them." It
would seem he could hardly have replied otherwise and still have
maintained his pose.

Perilously close to being forced into actual crime, McParlan contacted Benjamin Franklin on that same night of June 4 (he did not
know Captain Linden's whereabouts). He testified he "reported the
fact that I expected to be on that committee and that I was satisfied
that I could postpone it until perfect arrangements were made to
catch them all in the trap."[12] Asked at the trial to expand on the plans
for this trap, McParlan stated, "We wanted to catch these men right
in their tracks. We could not arrest them for what we knew they
were going to do, unless they did it, and we wanted to take them
right in the act."[13] Presumably the hope was that Bully Bill might
be saved in the process, but the defense later attacked Thomas'
character and implied that he wasn't much worth saving anyway.

McParlan's sanguine belief that he could hold the attempt for a
more propitious time proved correct. He met the other three in
Mahanoy City the next day; all four were armed. But this was the
very period when the troops had been sent in because of the threats
to the collieries by the union mob, and McParlan was able to persuade
his fellow conspirators that action in such a hornet's nest would be
suicidal. "Any one of us is worth fifty of Bully Bills," he told them.

A few days later McParlan again became quite ill, and was confined to bed. But the fortunate return of Frank McAndrew roused
him, and he accompanied McAndrew to Girardville the next day to
see Kehoe. The county delegate questioned the two as to whether
anything had been done, and, when told of the lack of progress,
sharply told McAndrew to "attend to this business," and to expel
any member who fell down on the job. McParlan pleaded that he
was too sick to be involved, and Kehoe apparently accepted his
excuse.

The matter was now out of McParlan's hands, and McAndrew
moved quickly. Three days later (June 27) McParlan was sitting
on his porch in the evening, when Hurley, Gibbons, John Morris,
Doyle, and McAndrew came up. As the conversation progressed
(all this is from McParlan's testimony), it became clear that an
attempt was to be made on Bully Bill's life the following morning.
Plans were made for providing substitutes for Morris and Gibbons

in the mines that day (the substitutes to be paid for by AOH funds). Hurley was in shirt sleeves and asked McParlan if he could borrow his coat, after which the conspirators broke up.

At this point it would seem to have been imperative that McParlan immediately contact Franklin or Linden. McParlan did not do so. He was questioned very closely about this:

Q. So you had kept Captain Linden posted with every step that was taken until the very last step . . . ?

A. That was the straw that broke the camel's back, and when that step was to be taken I was not able to notify him. I was not able, and it might be right for me to state that even if I had been well it would not have been possible that I could have left the house on that evening to have seen Captain Linden . . . I had a man there with me up to half-past 11 o'clock that night . . . It was as much as my life was worth to have communicated the facts to Captain Linden.[14]

In Allan Pinkerton's book McParlan's attempts to spring loose from his companion of that evening are expanded in almost comic-opera fashion. Pinkerton went to some length to establish that McParlan was desperately attempting "to save Thomas or have the assassins arrested in the act." Pinkerton continued, "the only plan, therefore, possible of accomplishment, was to send off a cipher dispatch to Mr. Franklin. In default of that he must try and deposit a written message in the post office . . . The letter must naturally be too late, still it would show that he was trying to do his duty by the man whose life stood in jeopardy."[15]

Though Pinkerton does seem curiously defensive on this point, this probably mirrors only an attempt to counter the widespread allegations that the agency instigated crime, rather than an attempt to cover up a deliberately planned act by McParlan. Lack of notification would seem to forestall one of Pinkerton's key hopes—to catch people in the act. And one can sympathize with McParlan's unwillingness to tip his hand in any way—for life was appearing cheaper by the minute among the Mollies. Even the defense attorneys could not bring themselves to the conclusion that McParlan actually wanted Thomas killed in order to make a "case," although they went to some lengths in their charge to the jury to plant seeds of doubt:

The flimsy, trifling reason which was given by McParlan was, that he was unable to inform anybody, that he was suspected of being a traitor,

and that it would have been unsafe for him to have conveyed the information of the intended outrage . . . As to why he did not stay the hand
that was raised to strike down this man, he does not explain in any
satisfactory way. He did not answer that question as an intelligent and
candid man would have answered, but he answered it in a manner that
clearly shows he designed to evade all questions as to the motives which
prompted him upon that occasion. If, then, it would amount to nothing
to catch them in the act, with McParlan's lips sealed, unless they were
caught after the murder was committed, then the arrangement McParlan
swears to about catching parties in the act, was to let them kill their
man first, and then arrest them afterwards. This would seem too inhuman
to become the subject of a contract, and I do not believe such was the
intention.[16]

Early in the morning of June 28, 1875, McParlan was in his room
completing a report to Franklin (so he testified) when Michael
Doyle came in the rear door and up to the room. Quickly locking
the report in his valise, McParlan accompanied Doyle up Ringtown
Mountain, and soon came upon Morris, Gibbons, and Hurley, sweating and exhausted but highly excited. Bully Bill had been killed!
Tom Hurley further described the triumph: At daylight they had
lain in wait at the stables in Shoemaker's Patch. William Thomas
came in to saddle a horse. Hurley walked up to the door and fired.
Thomas threw his hat in Hurley's face, but Hurley was able to get
another shot off, after which John Gibbons was able to get in and
fire two shots. Morris followed with several more shots. Thomas by
this time had fallen to the floor under one of the horses (Hurley
believed that they had probably killed one or two horses, too).
Doyle somewhat sheepishly admitted that the one or two shots he
had fired had been fired outside the stable. At any rate, though,
Bully Bill was out of the way.

McParlan went back down the mountain, found Bodymaster
McAndrew and came back up, McAndrew with ham, bread, and
cigars, and McParlan with a pint of whiskey. The four assassins
repeated their story, essentially the same as their first story to McParlan. Gibbons seemed the most agitated, stating that "he was afraid
to show himself; that he was remarkable; that he was afraid of being
detected"[17] and vowed that he was going to clear out. He stated
his intention of going to Kehoe for some money (which he later
did, receiving a paltry $1.50), and also asked McParlan for an AOH
traveling card. The detective said Kehoe could probably supply

this, but if not, Gibbons could write him and he would send one along. With this settled, the group broke up, Gibbons to fly and the rest to return to their homes believing that a "clean job" had been done.

They were wrong. Bully Bill Thomas had been desperately wounded—one bullet had gone completely through his neck, a quarter of an inch from the jugular vein, and another into his side, off a rib and out again. Miraculously, he lived to testify against the men who had conspired to kill him.

But exactly one week after the shooting, another assassination was attempted. And this time there was a corpse. It happened at Tamaqua, a dozen-odd miles east of Shenandoah. McParlan knew nothing of the planning, nor, at this time, any details of its execution.

Ordinarily quiet, Tamaqua on the night of July 5, 1875, was still stirring with the excitement of the national anniversary celebration the day before. There were many people on the streets, among them several strangers.

The police of the town consisted of only two men, Benjamin Yost and Barney McCarron, the former of German and the latter of Irish descent. Yost had experienced considerable trouble with James Kerrigan, an unemployed Irish miner who was the Tamaqua Molly Maguire bodymaster. Yost had arrested Kerrigan for drunkenness several times, and had at least once used his club to subdue Kerrigan. McCarron, too, came in for his share of ill will among a certain element in town. But it was Yost, with his German parentage, that was especially disliked. Several times he had been threatened with violence, but being an old soldier and a veteran of many battles, the policeman laughed it off and kept on with his job.

In addition to regular patrol service, it was the duty of the two officers to extinguish the gas street lamps. Before doing this on the 5th, they checked at James Carroll's tavern, which was still open, and then stopped at the hotel. There they had a drink with Kerrigan. The last light that they were to shut off was the one in front of Yost's house. Yost climbed the ladder, but his hand never reached the light. Two shots—and Yost fell to the ground.

McCarron, a few yards away, turned just in time to see the shadowy forms of two assailants. He chased them and emptied his pistol, but they escaped.

Yost lived through the night and in his moments of consciousness said the two men were strangers he and McCarron had seen at Carroll's tavern before their drink with Kerrigan. Both Yost and McCarron clearly absolved Kerrigan of the shooting—the body-master was very short and would have been easily identifiable.

Seven hours after he was shot, Yost died. As the news traveled about the town, frequent accusations that it was "a Molly job" were heard.[18]

The killing brought a wave of indignation, not only in Tamaqua but all over the Schuylkill fields. This was no idler from one or another Irish or Welsh clan, gunned down in a private faction fight, but a respected officer of the law. The funeral was attended by a huge number of people, business in Tamaqua being "entirely sus-pended for the afternoon," and there were bitter mutterings about "the brutal manner in which he was hurried into eternity."[19] Some-body had overstepped a boundary line in distinctions among murders —this was too much. And this "somebody," most people believed, was a "Molly." Editor Ramsey's comments in the *Miners' Journal* were inflammatory—the assassins should be "remorselessly hunted down."[20]

McParlan's reports now begin to include increasing references to the widely held belief of the Mollies that there was a hardening of public attitude toward them, and even that some of their members were traitors, giving information to outside parties. McParlan and McAndrew had gone to Girardville on July 4; McAndrew was looking for a Molly from another patch to do a "job" for him—to kill a mine boss, "Fresythe" (Forsythe?), for discriminating against the Irish when the mines reopened after the strike. The Irish were now direct recipients of the bitterness of the suspension; jobs were scarce and anti-Catholic feelings were strong. It was not entirely a matter of injustice, though—the Irish were combative and undisci-plined after six months of idleness, and many of the "discriminations" were for cause. Even the hot-headed Tom Hurley disagreed with McAndrew about Fresythe; on the way to Girardville he argued that "Fresythe had discharged Garvey for insolence and was justified."[21]

McAndrew, though, was in a bitter state of mind; just the previous night he had lashed out at Mike Doyle, telling him that "he was a coward and did not do half his work on the Thomas case." Now he turned on Larry Crean, Kehoe's bodymaster in

Girardville. "McAndrew got very angry, told Crean that he kept traitors around him and that it was two of his men who betrayed Kehoe and caused Father Bridgeman to publish him and Curran from the altar." In another report McParlan commented, "Considerable dissatisfaction was manifested by the Molly Maguires in regard to their state of affairs." Nevertheless, McParlan reported a little later, at least among the more reckless of the populace the Mollies were more popular than ever—"men who last winter would not notice a 'Molly Maguire' are now glad to take them by the hand and make much of them."[22]

McParlan immediately reported the Fresythe threat, and, according to Pinkerton's book, the mine boss was notified and left the area for a few weeks. The Mollies, Pinkerton reported, "were loud and vehement in execrating the ill-luck that dragged a doomed man from their murderous hands."[23] But even if the Pinkerton agency had been dedicated *only* to notifying people who were threatened so that they could remove themselves from the county, the task would soon have become insurmountable; if every muttering and every barroom bluff had been a bona fide threat, the county would soon have been depopulated of a great many people. McAndrew at this time was particularly single-minded about killing Gomer James. McParlan notified Franklin, but James was not cautioned again (he was not a Gowen employee like Fresythe).[24] And this was too bad for Gomer James.

❖   ❖   ❖   ❖   ❖

The legislative investigation of the Reading, which had begun in late April under the joint prodding of the union and the coal dealers of Philadelphia, continued in a desultory way. But the rapid disintegration of the union in the dying gasps of the "Long Strike" left the coal dealers standing alone as antagonists of Gowen. They were no match for him—this was the type of forum the articulate president handled so well. By early July it was evident that Gowen's silver tongue had again moved public opinion around to support of the railroad. By the time the committee was able to publish its report in February 1876, the controversy had subsided to minor grumblings by the dealers themselves.

Two incidents during these hearings have some connection to the Molly Maguire story, though.

The first occurred in early July 1875 when the committee decided to hold a few days of its hearings in Pottsville (soon after, they adjourned to Atlantic City's cool breezes—a coal town in dead summer was no place to conduct an investigation!). When Gowen publicized his intention of accompanying the committee to Pottsville, Pinkerton was apprehensive over the possibility that his client would be assassinated. McParlan's reports during this period, though not mentioning Gowen as a target for threats, were filled with plans against Reading mine bosses. So Pinkerton, taking no chances, assigned several detectives to shadow Gowen, apparently without his consent, during the three days in Pottsville; and he also ordered McParlan to Pottsville. The detective saw Linden each of the three days ("cigars with J. McF. [sic] for cover" reports Linden in his expense account). But nothing untoward occurred, and McParlan reported that the whole business was "humbug."[25] (Reminiscing about the Molly case many years later, though, McParlan, evidently not wanting to contradict his employer's version, was quoted as saying there was a "Molly Maguire plot" for assassination at this time.)[26]

The second Molly-oriented incident in the investigation was manufactured by Gowen himself. On July 29 and 30 he held the floor for a summation of the Reading's case. Few were Gowen's peers in such a situation. He gave the committee an histrionic bath that must have left them limp despite Atlantic City's breezes. Most of the argument was taken up with railroad issues, particularly those concerned with its alleged "monopoly," and we do him an injustice by merely summarizing his points, for it was a brilliant, if not an entirely honest, job. Gowen freely admitted the presence of the coal operators' combination, but built a plausible case that it was more stable and efficient than the competitive model. He was on shakier ground defending the coal land purchases, but managed to throw a cloak of confusion over the issue. The Philadelphia dealers, he insinuated, were not only an anachronism, but were also guilty of unethical practices. Throughout, it was a stellar performance by the accomplished thespian of the business world. And, toward the end, he made a violent attack on the union which he had so crushingly defeated at the beginning of the summer.[27]

In this attack he disavowed any animus toward "the workingman," saying, "Let him who will erect an altar to the genius of labor, and . . . I will worship at its shrine." But he hastened to point out that there was "a class of agitators—a few men trained in the School of the Manchester cotton spinner" who were causing all the trouble. He then detailed a long list of outrages perpetrated by the "atheists and infidels! advocates of the Commune and emissaries of the International!"[28] These appeared to be all the instances of violence that had occurred in the "Long Strike," irrespective of whether they were connected with the union or not. He even appended a dozen-odd coffin notices. During this stirring diatribe, he did not once mention the union by name. But the most curious aspect of Gowen's testimony is the fact that he did not mention the Molly Maguires, nor was there any reference to the presence of a secret society of any kind. Presumably his "List of Outrages" came in large part from the raw material forwarded to him by General Henry Pleasants during the strike.[29] These had originally contained many references to the Molly Maguires. But he used none of these references. This is curious, for by this time the union was, for all practical purposes, out of existence. Gowen surely was not badly worried about its possible renaissance. Perhaps he now saw the major potential of the Molly story (which he himself was later to exploit so ably) but felt it was premature to tip his hand. We see here another example of Gowen's unpredictable mind.

✣　✣　✣　✣　✣

The outcry over the Benjamin Yost murder of July 5, 1875, did not die down. The mutterings soon turned into organized action, and an ominous "Committee" was formed to track down the policeman's killers. Its two leaders were Michael Beard, a close friend, and Daniel Shepp, Mrs. Yost's brother-in-law. They recognized that this was no amateur's task and decided to employ professional help. Their choice was the Pinkerton Agency, their contact—Benjamin Franklin! This put the Philadelphia superintendent on the spot. He agreed to the commission, making clear in the process (as he stated to Beard in his first report to the "Committee" on August 5) "that our investigation would be necessarily a protracted one and probably

attended with considerable expense."[30] Although the Beard committee was led to believe in succeeding months that it was the
employer of McParlan, there is no record of an actual billing of
expenses to the committee. Franklin apparently sensed the explosive
potential for premature disclosure of McParlan's presence if the
Beard-Shepp job was mishandled and decided to keep them un-
informed as to the identity and whereabouts of the detective. At
any rate McParlan was, in effect, "hired" and told to go to Tamaqua
to investigate the Yost killing.

Needing an excuse, McParlan told Bodymaster McAndrew that
he had received bad news from his sister in Philadelphia (he had
used this fictitious relative before to explain his visits to Franklin).
The "Buffalo detectives" were, he said, on his trail again about the
murder he had committed there, and his sister had inadvertently
let it slip that he was in Shenandoah. Warning McAndrew and the
other Shenandoah Mollies to "kape dark" about his whereabouts,
he went to Tamaqua on July 15.[31] It was quite a day. Wanting to
make his entry into Tamaqua noticeable, he roistered into a total of
seven taverns, and spent $6.85 on whiskey alone. We can readily
believe Pinkerton's conclusion that the word was passed about the
city, during the evening, that "that wild Irishman from Shenandoah,
Jim McKenna, was in town again on a rousing spree, and would
probably make things uncommon lively the ensuing day."[32] He did,
too, hitting four taverns on the 16th; and his expense account for
the 17th ("Tr." means "Treated") was again prodigal:

Tr. Mainellis at Campbell's	.65
Tr. Mulhern at McKenna's	.70
Tr. Mike McKinna for information	.45
Lost playing cards at Campbell's	.95
Tr. Pat McKenna and fr. at McKenna's	.85
Tr. Mollies at Simon's "turnout"	.65
Tr. McGuire and 12 fr. at Campbell's	1.15
Tr. Pat Harkins and fr. at McKenna's	.75

McParlan's largess paid off quickly. Three of the tavern owners
were AOH officials; Pat McKenna was bodymaster of the Storm Hill
lodge (just outside of Tamaqua), Alex Campbell was treasurer at
Storm Hill, and James Carroll was secretary of the Tamaqua lodge.
By playing one against the others, McParlan soon had the Yost

story. According to McParlan's daily reports forwarded to Benjamin Franklin (and with supplementary information supplied in court a year and a half later), here is what he found out:

The policeman had been involved the previous winter in a rather unsavory incident involving James Kerrigan, the Tamaqua AOH bodymaster, and Thomas Duffy, one of the members. Duffy had gotten drunk, called Yost a "Dutch son of a bitch," and threatened to kill him. Kerrigan was along, and succeeded in dragging Duffy away. A few days later Duffy was drunk again and tried to beat up another Irishman, Flynn, right in the middle of the street. Yost and his fellow policeman, Barney McCarron, came up, and Duffy went for Yost. The unfortunate Kerrigan again happened to be with Duffy. The two policemen proceeded to beat up Duffy and throw him in jail, and Kerrigan was knifed by Flynn in the process (he later vowed that McCarron held him while this was done). Duffy had to pay a ten-dollar fine, and when he was released, he and Kerrigan visited Carroll's tavern and poured out their woes. Carroll was most sympathetic, and was quoted by Kerrigan as saying, "Never mind, we will make Yost pay for that. We will make his head softer than his arse for what he done to you."[33]

The notion of revenge planted in Kerrigan's mind by Carroll soon took root. Later Kerrigan met James Roarity (the Coaldale bodymaster who had previously promised Kehoe to take care of "Bully Bill" Thomas). Duffy was there, too, and the two Tamaqua men— Kerrigan and Duffy—offered Roarity ten dollars if he would do away with Yost. Roarity promised to either do it himself or find a couple of AOH members to accomplish it. Roarity was pressed several times about this promise (he was already dragging his feet on the Thomas plan) and finally allowed that he had two men to do the job—two young Summit Hill AOH'ers, Hugh McGehan and James Boyle. These two had sworn revenge on John P. Jones, a Lansford mine boss who had blacklisted McGehan. Roarity proposed a trade—McGehan and Boyle to shoot Yost, Kerrigan to arrange for killing Jones. The bargain was struck.

On the night of July 5, 1875, Roarity sent McGehan and Boyle to Tamaqua; they met Kerrigan and Duffy at Carroll's. Kerrigan had previously studied the terrain, had his plans set. Taking McGehan and Boyle out later that evening, he planted them in the chosen spot, and returned to Carroll's where he bought Yost a drink just before the policeman began turning out the street lamps. After the shooting, McGehan and Boyle slipped away through the route chosen by Kerrigan. Duffy and Kerrigan's Nemesis was dead and both were in the clear with well-established alibis. It was truly a "clean job."

All this was poured out to the astonished McParlan the first few days in Tamaqua. But the detective had not had corroboration from Kerrigan himself, who was absent at that time. On July 17, McParlan returned to Shenandoah and penned a long report to Franklin, including information about John P. Jones, the threatened mine superintendent. On July 25 McParlan returned to Tamaqua to find Jimmy Kerrigan. And there he met Mary Ann Higgins.

❧   ❧   ❧   ❧   ❧

McParlan's public pose as "James McKenna" was that of a young, dashing, wild Irishman, full of song and dance, ever ready for a spree or a brawl, a flamboyant character whom all would remember. His success in establishing this pose was great—McKenna was a "true-bred Molly." And it seems reasonable to think that a good part of this behavior was spontaneous, even though the image of a cold, calculating machine, deliberately building each of these facets of character, was stressed in the trials. And partly spontaneous, too, were the detective's love affairs in the coal fields—or so it seems likely. The encounter with Pat Hester's daughter two months earlier seems too transitory to have much made of it. But his "romance" with Mary Ann Higgins turned out to be not so transitory.

McParlan needed easily accepted reasons for seeing a good deal of James Carroll and James Kerrigan. The former's tavern was the natural meeting place for the Tamaqua Mollies—this posed no problem. In the case of Kerrigan, though, a better excuse was needed. On July 27, McParlan visited Kerrigan's house for the first time. Mary Ann Higgins was there. McParlan immediately recognized her—she had traded coquetry with him at a Polish wedding many months before (Pinkerton even reported that she had bussed McParlan on the cheek then). McParlan reacted to this Irish lass as fitting for an Irish lad, and from this moment and for many months after, he "sparked" Mary Ann.

Now it happened that Mary Ann Higgins was Jimmy Kerrigan's

sister-in-law; a "romance" would further the investigation. Business was to be inextricably mixed with pleasure; Mary Ann was to be a pawn in a chess game, not of amour, but of murder.

Allan Pinkerton made much of this romance in his book. So, too, have many others—the love story was an important theme in Arthur Conan Doyle's *The Valley of Fear.* Pinkerton apparently over-indulged in paraphrasing McParlan's feelings—"She's a fine girl— what a pity she is of such a family! And to think that I must get her brother-in-law hanged! Oh, I never can hope to have 'Miss Higgins' transformed into 'Mrs. McParlan!' Brother-in-law to a murderer! No! Never!"[34] In the cold, grey light of the trials, McParlan's state-ments of the relationship were much more harsh:

Q. You were cementing your alliance with that of Kerrigan about that time by sparking his wife's sister?

A. I was cementing my alliance with Kerrigan, and the balance of them . . . and trying to make good terms with them; and I did it.

Q. After you began to spark in the family, you had no reason to suspect Kerrigan had any intention to injure you, had you?

A. Well, it was not for the sake of throwing off suspicion on Kerri-gan's part that I made love to his sister-in-law, but to throw off any suspicion there might be as to my object in stopping around Tamaqua.[35]

So we will leave the more flowery parts of the McParlan-Higgins involvement to the romantically inclined reader, although Miss Higgins enters the story again in a different capacity at a later date.

McParlan's first days back in Tamaqua quickly gave him the missing links in the Yost story. Carroll's tavern being the natural watering spot for a dusty traveler, McParlan stopped by to see its proprietor and sample his wares. Carroll warned the man he knew as "McKenna" that the town had been "swarming with detectives since the murder," but proceeded to show his inability to recognize one by immediately telling McParlan that it was he himself who had lent one of the pistols—a single-shot model—to the killers. Carroll said his wife had seen him do this, but at the Yost inquest she "was most emphatically a good witness" and covered up for him. (She had been called to help establish Duffy's alibi—he was sleeping in the tavern that night.)[36]

It did not take long for McParlan to locate the other murder weapon. He himself was carrying a .32 revolver at the time. Yost had been shot by a weapon of the same caliber. McParlan pulled the gun out on his first evening with Kerrigan (July 27), and the diminutive bodymaster, not to be outdone, produced another of the same caliber—"the one that 'Fixed Yost.' " It belonged to Roarity, Kerrigan confided, and had been borrowed for Hugh McGehan's use. It was a repeating pistol, and had been the chief weapon that night. James Boyle's single-shot—the one borrowed from Carroll—had evidently not even been fired. Kerrigan, expansive under McParlan's assumed admiration, then spelled out the whole affair, and McParlan had a direct confession.[37]

But additional corroboration was needed to make the accusation stick in a court of law. Somehow, another party would have to hear the same confession. To this end, Franklin called McParlan and Linden to a conference at Glen Okono, a small town outside Mauch Chunk in Carbon County, east of Schuylkill. At this meeting a plan was devised whereby McParlan was to lure Jimmy Kerrigan out for an evening walk—the cemetery at the head of the town of Tamaqua was one of Kerrigan's favorite spots for lounging—and Linden was to plant himself behind a hedge and eavesdrop on McParlan's leading questions. This was tried several times over the next weeks, but connections always missed and all Linden got for his trouble were stiff joints from the wait. It was particularly frustrating for the two detectives, for McParlan was now being supplied with new confessions. First McGehan, then Roarity personally confided their roles in the Yost case.[38]

As July 1875 ended, McParlan was still no further in his hoped-for plan for corroboration. There was still talk of the John P. Jones affair, but no killers had been appointed. According to Pinkerton, Alex Campbell was so pleased at McGehan's "clean job" that he helped set up the young Molly in the tavern business. The new tavern opened on August 14, and McParlan helped get the embryonic entrepreneur off to a good start by treating to the tune of $2.65.[39]

But while the Tamaqua Mollies were sporting with McParlan in the new tavern, important developments were occurring back in Girardville, Shenandoah, and Mahanoy City. The 14th was pay day, and the miners celebrated the evening with an unusual spree of drunkenness. The *Miners' Journal* in Pottsville emblazoned its pages on August 20 with the results—the headline was the largest Ramsey had used for a news story in months:

A BLOODY NIGHT
NORTH OF THE MOUNTAIN

Squire Gwyther of Girardville Assassinated—Gomer
James of Shenandoah Butchered at a Picnic—Fight
in Mahanoy City and a Man Fatally Shot—"Bully
Bill" in a Row and Comes to Jail—Man with an Oyster
Knife in His Back

In Girardville, gangs of roughs flourishing revolvers had ranged
the streets "absolutely rampant and defiant of lawful restraints," the
weekly paper reported. Even though special policemen had been
deputized for the day, they were "powerless and cowed." When a
particularly flagrant assault occurred in one of the taverns, the
victim went immediately to the office of Squire Thomas Gwyther,
justice of the peace, and swore out a warrant for the assailant's
arrest. Gwyther stepped out on the porch of the office to serve the
warrant, and found a revolver leveled directly at him. His daughter
cried out, "For God's sake don't shoot father," but before she could
finish her plea the gun went off and Gwyther was instantly killed.
The killer's name was said to be Love, but when Kehoe, as High
Constable, arrested Thomas Love, the alleged murderer turned out
to be, instead, his brother, William Love, who by this time was
many miles away.

In Mahanoy City, Bully Bill Thomas, the indestructible Welshman, already recovered from his brush with death on June 28, got
drunk and got into a "shoot down" on the main street with an Irishman, James Dugan. Both fired many shots, one lodging in Bully
Bill's cheek. And one other shot had gone wild, instantly killing an
inoffensive German miner waiting on the street for his wife. Thomas
was arrested for the assault on Dugan, but no charges were brought
for the killing—it was written off as just the will of God.

The biggest news for McParlan was that Gomer James, the
Welshman who had been acquitted of the 1873 murder of the Irishman Edward Cosgrove, had finally met the fate decreed for him by
the Mollies. Again a fire company event was the catalyst. James was
tending bar at the picnic of the Rescue Hook and Ladder Company
at Glover's Grove, near Shenandoah, when a man coolly walked up
to the bar, leaned across with a revolver in his hand, and shot James

dead on the spot. In the confusion that followed, the murderer brazenly walked into the crowd and disappeared. No one could offer any description of him.[40]

But McParlan quickly learned the truth. It was none other than Tom Hurley, the ringleader in the Thomas shooting back in June. The Shenandoah lodge was having a meeting on the night of August 14 when Mike Carey, a member, rushed in to announce, "Tom Hurley has shot Gomer James." Bodymaster McAndrew later rebuked Carey for announcing the shooting before all the members, but the lodge was well satisfied that James had met his death. Hurley demanded reward money, and McParlan was asked to go to Kehoe to press the claim. The wily county leader demurred, saying that the decision would have to be made in the Schuylkill County convention on August 25, 1875, at Tamaqua.[41]

A few days later Kerrigan came to Shenandoah to press a demand for help in the killing of the mine boss, Jones. Again action was deferred until the county convention. McParlan returned to Tamaqua with Kerrigan and again attempted to lure the Tamaqua bodymaster to a spot where Linden was hiding. But the plan fell through, and Linden reported to Franklin that he "failed to accomplish this most desired end."[42]

Clearly, the county convention was to be the culmination of many plans. By the night of August 24 over one hundred Mollies were in Tamaqua, liberally imbibing at Carroll's and other taverns in preparation for the events of the next day. Campbell came in from Storm Hill, but told McParlan that, as he could not be there the following day, McParlan should personally take care of the Jones plans "as Kerrigan would not keep from drink." McParlan agreed.[43]

The convention on the 25th lasted all day. Most of the time was taken up with settling grievances between members. Several were expelled (one for tipping off Jesse and William Major that they were marked for killing); others were readmitted. The bailing of a Molly lodged in the Pottsville jail was discussed at length, McParlan finally being deputized to arrange the bail money (which he successfully did on August 28). The meeting was rowdy but routine; no past or future murders were discussed. Late in the afternoon, however, after the general convention had adjourned to the bars, an "inner circle" of bodymasters met to discuss the Hurley case. When Hurley's claim for the reward money was mentioned, Pat Butler, the bodymaster at Lost Creek, vowed that a certain John McClain of his division had shot Gomer James. Hurley was infuriated and retorted that he could produce at least ten people who saw him do it; even his own mother could corroborate it. But the committee was undecided in the face of this conflicting testimony and appointed Butler and McParlan to hear evidence and adjudicate the issue. The Jones killing was brought up again, as well as similar plans for killing two other mine bosses, Lambertson and Reese. At the bar after the committee meeting McAndrew and Kerrigan had a bitter argument; "McAndrew stated that if he saw any trade to be made *he* would provide the men."[44]

McParlan stayed in Tamaqua the next day, trying to see Linden (who had come to town after being alerted to the convention by McParlan). But Tom Hurley stuck with the detective all through the day. Finally, McParlan was able to sneak away for a brief contact. Because he was running low on money, Linden slipped him twenty-five dollars. When McParlan rejoined Hurley, he was asked if he had seen Linden. McParlan denied that he had. (Linden, of course, was by now widely known as a Coal & Iron policeman, though not as a Pinkerton agent.) Hurley vowed that if Linden "was spooking about anything not right they would shoot him on arrival in Shenandoah."[45] McParlan told Hurley he thought Linden was "all square," but, nevertheless, he hurried to tell Linden of the threat after Hurley left for Shenandoah later that night. And, to the detective's consternation, Linden had a similar morsel for him: McParlan ("McKenna") was suspected by the Welsh and English of being the instigator of murder and there were mutterings of revenge against him if anything untoward happened.[46]

At Carroll's the next day—the 27th—McParlan found an un-settling lack of candor from Kerrigan, and it seemed to him then that the whole fabric of secrecy was beginning to be torn. On the 28th McParlan went to Pottsville for the bailing task, and with this assignment successfully concluded, returned to Shenandoah to meet Pat Butler for the Gomer James reward adjudication. Butler was there, but McClain failed to show up to press his claim, and Butler and McParlan gave the dubious honor to Hurley. The detective wrote a confirming letter to Kehoe, and Hurley went off to Girard-ville to collect. (There is no record as to whether he actually did get any money.)[47]

The conversation now centered on the plan for murdering John Jones. And here, again, we have a situation in which McParlan knew of, and stood ready to participate in, plans that had murder as their expressed object. We must analyze carefully four important days in McParlan's life.

❖   ❖   ❖   ❖   ❖

On the morning of August 31, 1875 (so McParlan told Franklin in his daily report), he woke up to find Mike Doyle sleeping with him. (Doyle had roomed with him from time to time over the last several months.) On the washstand was a Smith and Wesson pistol. McParlan knew Doyle did not own a pistol and asked him "what was up." Doyle admitted that he had borrowed the pistol from Ed Monaghan and that he was going to use it that morning for a killing —he was going to Raven Run, a few miles west of Shenandoah, with three other men to shoot a mine boss, "Sanger." The three confederates were to be James O'Donnell, his brother Charles O'Donnell, and James McAllister, all of Wiggans Patch, a small mining settlement near Mahanoy City.

This seems to be the first knowledge McParlan had of the proposed assault. The detective did not know the Wiggans Patch men, nor does Sanger's name appear in any previous reports. The situation must have taken McParlan completely by surprise.

After McParlan and Doyle got up, Tom Hurley came in, and soon had Doyle involved in a demonstration of the best way to kill a man. Hurley was now quite self-important about assassination, flushed with his success at having clearly established his claim of shooting Gomer James. Doyle was nervous about the plans, but Hurley sharply told him that if he "did not do his duty," the O'Donnell crowd would shoot *him too*. James O'Donnell—nicknamed "Friday"—soon showed up, followed shortly by his brother and McAllister. Taking Doyle with them (he borrowed McParlan's coat before leaving) they set off for Raven Run. McParlan reported to Franklin, "I tried to shun Hurley and dispatch to you, as I do not know where L. is but I could not manage." (Franklin received this report of August 31 and others—covering August 25 to September 2—on September 4.)

Bodymaster Frank McAndrew, knowing nothing of the Raven Run affair, called a meeting of the Shenandoah lodge that afternoon. He had come to the conclusion, he told the members, that a mine boss, "Reese," must be shot. To do this safely, a trade must be worked with Kerrigan. Therefore, he wanted men to go immediately to Summit Hill for the Jones killing, "and no growling about it." McAndrew first turned to Mike Carey, but he refused to go. He then appointed John McGrail, a Shenandoah member, and two Gilberton members, Mike Darcy and Thomas Munley. Those two were absent; so a member was dispatched to search them out and bring them to Shenandoah forthwith.

McAndrew then turned to McParlan and ordered him to go to Tamaqua and "make things right with Kerrigan." In other words, the detective was to accompany the killers and, together with Kerrigan, plan and execute the shooting of Jones, at the same time binding Kerrigan to the assassination of another superintendent named Reese. McParlan evidently felt he had to agree, for, as he put it, "I am in the fix. I do not know where to find Linden, and it would cost me my life to dispatch, as you may also see it takes all my time to get a chance of writing, although they have no suspicion of me so far, but it don't take much to make them have one, and neither man nor woman of them will spare a man if they get a chance on him."[48]

The next day, September 1, Hurley came around very early, on edge about the Raven Run affair. At 8:30 a.m., as Hurley and McParlan sat in Muff Lawler's saloon, the Raven Run party came in, thirsty and tired. In addition to Doyle, the O'Donnells, and McAllister, a fifth man, Thomas Munley, who had just been assigned *in absentia* to the Jones killing, was along. All were heavily armed, each of the five having two pistols. "Friday" O'Donnell confirmed the morning's success; it was a "clean job" on two men, "although it was not meant for any but Sanger." Each described the shooting, telling how they all exchanged clothes before and after. All the men drank heavily, after which McAllister and the O'Donnells left for Wiggans Patch. Doyle dressed for work, and Hurley, Munley, and McParlan walked along with him to the mine. On the way they met a posse searching for the murderers, and although several eyewitnesses were in the group, "still they made no shape to identify any of them."[49]

The facts, as related by the killers, were grimly true. As the men of Heaton's Colliery lounged about at the head of the shaft in the early morning, waiting for the shift to begin, many of them noticed several strangers there. But it was a common occurrence to see unemployed miners early on the ground to make application for employment.

In a few minutes, Thomas Sanger, a boss in the mine, took leave of his wife at his cottage and left for the shaft. William Uren, a young miner that boarded with the Sangers, accompanied him.

Any complacency about the strangers' purposes was now shattered, for the five of them rushed up to Sanger and Uren and at point-blank range pumped bullets into them. Sanger died in minutes, Uren the next day. Robert Heaton, one of the owners, ran out of his house with a revolver and exchanged a volley of shots with two of the assassins. As one of them fired, Heaton got a clear view of his face. But all Heaton's shots missed. The five men melted away, leaving the shocked miners the job of trying to remember the faces to which they had paid so little attention. A wife of one of the miners, in trying to restrain her young son from going outside to the shooting, had seen one of the men pass her door, Allan Pinkerton related. "She noted each feature of the murderer's face and every peculiarity of his form, as, with head raised and defiant air, he swung his weapon over his head . . . She could never forget that man; his likeness haunted her, waking and sleeping, for many nights." But the sum total of identifications was painfully small.[50]

McParlan had no time to mull over the Sanger-Uren murders, for he was squarely in the middle of the proposed assassination of John Jones, with his own role looming terrifyingly large. He was under orders to accompany Thomas Munley, Mike Darcy, and John McGrail to Tamaqua and carry out the assignment. On the first of September, just a few hours after McParlan learned of the Raven Run outrage, Munley and Darcy found the detective again and proposed that they go forthwith to Tamaqua and shoot Jones. McGrail could not come until Friday (it was now Wednesday); McParlan tried to use this as an excuse for him to go ahead alone, "but Munley and Darcy insisted upon coming with me tomorrow morning." McParlan continued, "Well, of course I agreed to, as I had to . . . " Munley and Darcy went ahead to Mahanoy City to get their revolvers, with arrangements to meet on the Tamaqua train the next morning. Hurley and McAndrew stuck close to the detective for the evening, and he apparently had no chance to dispatch a telegram.[51]

The next morning, September 2, when the train stopped at Mahanoy City, Munley and Darcy got on, sitting in front of McParlan, but not talking with him, "as in a case of this kind we must not recognize each other except in a friend's house—meaning a Sleeper's house." Both Munley and Darcy had been drunk the night before, either in apprehension or elation over the prospect. When they got to Tamaqua, McParlan found them a room in which they could sleep off their hangovers, and then set out to find Linden, but saw him nowhere. (Linden was in Raven Run investigating the murders there.) Nor could he find James Kerrigan at his home or any of his haunts, so when Darcy and Munley woke up, he sent them home to Gilberton.

Taking advantage of the momentary freedom, he completed a long report to Franklin. In it he took the time to do a bit of philosophizing about the situation. Mentioning that plans were afoot for further killings, he continued: "Now you can see yourself how this is, and what I predicted at the time of the suspension—'that if the Union would fail there would be rough times.' The Irish know this." He said that in the days of the union "each man got his turn," "but now the Irish are discharged or if not they are put to work at some place where they can make nothing." He added that "there was very little killing a doing whilst Union stood, but now it is quite the reverse." This would certainly be unpalatable to Gowen, but Franklin duly forwarded it. McParlan ended the report with brief instructions to have Franklin contact Captain Linden so that Linden and his force could surround Jones's house.[52]

It is not clear whether McParlan also telegraphed these instructions; obviously the written report would not reach Franklin in time to alert Linden. At the trials McParlan did admit that later that night he was told by James Carroll that Kerrigan was at that moment involved in a plan of his own to kill Jones. But, from the detective's report itself, there was no indication that McParlan had any intimation of the climactic events of the following morning, September 3.

And they were truly climactic. Samuel Beard, a law student, rode the train to Lansford, half a dozen miles east of Tamaqua, and arrived just moments after a terrible tragedy. John P. Jones had been shot and killed on the station steps by two unknown assailants, who had escaped. Beard, returning to Tamaqua, quickly spread the story around the town. Knots of people gathered in an excited state. When Beard repeated his story to William Parkeman, the latter said he had just seen Kerrigan with two strange men at the west end of town. Beard and a friend immediately went to the Odd Fellows' cemetery, which was on a high hill overlooking the Panther Creek Valley. Across the valley was Sharp Mountain. They had brought a spy glass, and in sweeping over the mountain they spotted Kerrigan waving a handkerchief, after which two men came out of the bush. The three sat down, apparently eating. Beard rushed back to town and a posse was formed. By splitting into two groups the posse came upon the surprised threesome and captured them handily. They were marched down to town, protesting all the time that their arrest was illegal, and promptly lodged in the jail. AOH badges were found on the two strangers, who gave their names as Edward Kelly and Michael J. Doyle, both of Mt. Laffee. (This Doyle was in no way related to Mike Doyle of Shenandoah, McParlan's roommate.) Both were identified by several people as having been in the vicinity of Storm Hill and Lansford the previous day. Ugly talk in the crowd around the jail increased and there were threats to lynch the three on the spot. The arrival of the deputy sheriff of Carbon County (Lansford was just over the Schuylkill line) averted the threat—the three prisoners were given up to his custody and immediately taken to the Carbon County jail at Mauch Chunk.[53]

McParlan was bitterly attacked in the later trials for his actions—and, particularly, for his lack of action—during these four days. In the Sanger-Uren murder trial the defense asked him, "Tell this court and jury why you, living within three miles of the poor fellows that were to be killed, that you made no effort to save their lives?" McParlan replied that "in doing so I ran the danger of losing my life." On that morning, "Thomas Hurley was present." He continued:

I devised every plan I could to telegraph to Captain Linden, or telegraph to the Agency to find out whether Captain Linden was in Shenandoah—of course he was not, but I did not know that then. Hurley remained with me from the time we first met in the morning, and when I went into Phillips' store on the pretense of purchasing some paper to write to a friend of mine, though I went in there to dispatch to Philadelphia . . . I did not know what colliery the boss worked at, or what was the name of the boss . . . If I could have found Linden, and he had got his men stationed there, the probabilities are that the boss' life might have been saved, but those things were impossible.[54]

Given the necessity to preserve the fabric of secrecy, McParlan's reasoning here seems unassailable. Had he tipped his hand in any way, Hurley would surely have suspected something. The whole Raven

Run affair was completely new to McParlan, and even had he been able to find Linden that day, there is a real question whether the police would have been in time.

These arguments do not hold up as well, though, in the Jones murder. McParlan knew on August 31 that he and the two appointed killers, Munley and Darcy, were to go to Tamaqua to see Kerrigan "to make it straight," and ostensibly to pull off the killing either on the 2nd or the 3rd. He was alone the night of the 31st, and could have attempted a contact with Linden, but did not. This is not surprising, for he had had success before in postponing scheduled violence. When he got to Tamaqua on the 2nd and could not find Kerrigan, he was able to send the two men back to Gilberton. That night, however, when he was told by James Carroll that Kerrigan was at that moment making a plan to kill Jones, he could have attempted a contact with Linden. Again he did not. If he had, it would probably not have saved Jones's life, for Linden was by this time at Raven Run, deeply involved in the proceedings of the coroner's jury in the Sanger-Uren case, and likely would not have been willing to leave. Nevertheless, the attempt was not even made.

McParlan was castigated for this; the Molly defense attorneys bitterly denounced him as an "accessory before the fact" and baldly insinuated that he had allowed Jones to die. McParlan had said on the stand that "Jones had been notified and was on his guard." This was true—McParlan had notified Franklin on July 17 that Jones was marked for death, and extensive precautions had been taken to guard Jones's home and to stay with him during work. McParlan was queried as to why he did not communicate the threat to Tamaqua authorities the night he learned the news from Carroll, but he pointed out that he was under strict instructions to deal only with Linden and Franklin. If any other person were to learn of his presence, the secrecy would be in danger, even his life.

In retrospect, then, it seems that, given the broader goals of the case as they were perceived by McParlan, Franklin, and Pinkerton, the detective pursued the only course open to him. Three lives were a heavy cost to pay for maintaining the secrecy, but perhaps many more would have been lost had not Pinkerton handled the case the way he did.

Public outrage over the killings of Sanger, Uren, and Jones now threatened to get out of hand. The embryonic lynch fever of the

Tamaqua crowd had been forestalled by quick action in getting Kerrigan, Doyle, and Kelly to Mauch Chunk. But Thomas Foster, the editor of the *Shenandoah Herald,* had filled his columns on September 2 with less-than-veiled exhortations for a vigilance committee. There had always been a hot-headed fringe advocating "an eye for an eye"; seeing so many men wiggle out of convictions via false alibis and intimidated witnesses was infuriating. The Raven Run coroner's jury was yet another example—Linden reported the testimony in full to Franklin and ended, "most of the witnesses were evidently determined *not to know anything.*"[55]

Linden returned to Shenandoah on September 3, to find that one of his "open policemen" had attempted to question a "suspicious character," and when the man pulled a gun and shot at the officer (hitting him in the cheek), he in turn shot the stranger dead. The officer was eventually exonerated, but the incident did force Linden to disclose the fact that he was a Pinkerton employee.

The ranks of the "direct-action" advocates were growing by the hour. Even the more temperate newspapers climbed on the bandwagon of action. The *Tamaqua Courier* commented on September 4, just after the Jones killing:

The Shenandoah *Herald* comes out boldly in favor of a vigilance committee that will make it so hot for those who get the shooting done and those who harbor suspected parties that they cannot longer remain among us . . .

Much as this is to be deprecated, desperate diseases require desperate remedies . . .

What is to be done? Something that will strike terror into their base hearts and make them flee from before an outraged community . . . Who can blame the friends of the victims if they demanded an eye for an eye, a tooth for a tooth and blood for blood. Something *must* be done; that something must be *sure,* swift and terrible; but let due caution be observed that no innocent parties are made to suffer and all will be well.

Something sure, swift, and terrible?

Chapter 10 ✦ *Wiggans Patch*

*V*IGILANTISM is premature—and therefore illegal—administration of justice. But this would oversimplify the issue to many
people. Suppose law and order were no match for rampant lawlessness? Suppose innocent people were suffering because of the
absence of legally constituted processes of justice? Suppose upstand-
ing and God-fearing citizens felt that only by some action "swift and
sure" could legal order eventually be made effective?

Vigilance committees had wide use in the West.[1] They attained
the highest state of effectiveness in the San Francisco Committees of
Vigilance in the 1850's, which dealt summarily with lawless elements
brought in by the gold rush after 1849. But all through the West
vacuums in formal justice were met by so-called "popular tribunals,"
and "frontier justice" became a concept all too clearly understood
by both the lawless and their antagonists. Vigilance groups have
operated all over the country. The South Carolina Regulators, organized in the back country of that colony in the 1760's by property
holders determined to suppress outlaws, are called the prototype of
American vigilante movements. Indeed, the terms "Regulator" and
"Regulation" were widely used until the 1850's when the San Francisco citizens made the term "vigilante" famous.[2] "Judge Lynch"
himself is alleged to have been a Virginia justice of the peace, although this attribution has been attacked by several scholars.[3] As with
many such terms, it is practically impossible—and probably not very
important—to document the "first" case fully. One version has it
that the first Judge Lynch was an Irishman, James Lynch, who, as
mayor of Galway, in 1493, "hanged his own son out of the window
for defrauding and killing strangers, without martial or common
law, to show a good example to posterity."[4]

Allan Pinkerton's career had been touched by vigilante action prior
to the Molly Maguire assignment. The Pinkerton agency's reputation
had been enhanced by its success in hunting down robbers. Before

the war the rapid solution of several robberies of the Adams Express Company were valuable to the agency's public image. It was natural, then, for the Adams Express executives to call in Allan Pinkerton when faced with a traumatic attack from the underworld in 1866. The criminals used a startling new device—one destined to become so much a part of American folklore—train robbery.

The culprits were the "Reno gang," a group of brothers, abetted by a sister and supported by several toughs, who had terrorized the area around Seymour and New Albany, Indiana, for several years. According to a Pinkerton biography, the Renos were the first of America's outlaw "brotherhoods" and "set the pattern followed by the James and Younger brothers, the Daltons, the Farringtons, the Burrows, the Cooks and the Wild Bunch"—all of which, except the Daltons, were fought by Pinkerton. The Renos had so terrorized Seymour prior to the war that by 1866 they were practically in control of the entire town; it was a real-life version of the ever-popular fictional "outlaw fortress." The train robbery was pulled off by two of the Renos and a cohort, and Adams Express was many thousands of dollars poorer. The saga of Pinkerton's chase is excitement in true detective-book style, and would be a wonderfully entertaining side trip for us.[5]

But our focus here must be on one aspect, the vigilante action. The Renos' dominance had not gone unchallenged, but their repeated flaunting of the law appeared to be more than a match for the constituted authorities (many of whom were "bought" by the Renos). Finally, the citizens of the area were moved to desperate measures and formed the Southern Indiana Vigilance Committee, also known as the Seymour Regulators. In 1868, the Renos arrogantly proposed to an engineer of a train that often carried large amounts of money that he secretly join with them. A trap was set by the Pinkertons. The engineer pretended to go along with the Renos, the trap was sprung and three lesser lights in the gang were captured. But, ten days later, as the Pinkertons were moving the prisoners by train to the scene of the trial, a masked mob of over two hundred men stopped the train, disarmed the Pinkertons, took away the three prisoners and strung them up at a spot known to this day as Hangman's Crossing. A few weeks later three more of the gang were captured by the Pinkertons, but again the agency was embarrassed by having its men lose the three outlaws to the mob in the same way, while trying to transport them to jail.

None of the Renos themselves had yet been captured, but the Pinkertons soon took care of this. Simeon and William Reno were quietly taken in Indianapolis, and securely lodged in jail (later they were moved to other jails, one step ahead of the vigilantes). John Reno was captured and clapped in a Missouri jail. But Frank Reno and three cronies were still free, openly running a gambling parlor in Windsor, Canada. Allan Pinkerton himself took charge, and after many adventures succeeded in bringing Frank Reno and another member of the gang back to Indiana where they were placed in the New Albany jail along with Simeon and William.

The climax was now at hand. On December 11, 1868, a highly disciplined masked group broke into the jail, shot and wounded the sheriff who resisted them, and brutally hanged the three Renos and the confederate. (Simeon was suspended on tiptoe and allowed to strangle to death in an hour-long agony before the horrified eyes of the remaining prisoners of the jail.)

Thus ended the Reno gang. The case gained notoriety all over the country, and the *New York Times* was moved to lecture the town of Seymour: "There are few of our citizens who will regard it otherwise than as an outrage of the worst kind and as utterly disgraceful of the community in which it occurred."[6] The *Times* and other observers were concerned most about the possible repercussions in Canada, because a prisoner had been handed over via extradition, only to be lynched. When this issue blew over, the case was quickly forgotten. And the Southern Indiana Vigilance Committee dispersed, its members willing now to rely on due process of law. Here, too, the involvement of the Pinkertons had apparently ended.

But six years later, in 1874, the Reno case re-entered Allan Pinkerton's life, like a specter coming back to haunt the living. One of Pinkerton's agents, who had been a key man in the Reno case, had subsequently been fired by Pinkerton for absconding with agency monies. The agent had then gone to work for a rival detective firm. In late 1874 he was arrested for illegally disposing of certain mortgaged property. The agent was to be brought to Chicago, and the head of the rival detective agency was personally arranging to have the man prosecuted. Pinkerton was terribly upset by this, for reasons

that are not completely clear in his correspondence. He wrote
George Bangs an enigmatic letter on November 1:

. . . well, I suppose there they will attempt to break me down and
bleed me anywhere from $1 to $500,000 and if I don't "come down"
_____[the agent] will go to New Albany, Indiana and there
the fight begins. Well, George, all I have to say is that if they make
any attempt to blackmail me they are sadly mistaken if they imagine
they can make anything by the operation. My old regiment is ready to
be called out and every man is ready for action and the railroad is at our
command and if the fight has to commence once more we shall go
through winning to the end . . . I am spoiling for the fray for come it
slow or come it fast, it is but death that comes at last. I shall make no
half way fight with the crowd. War to the knife and the knife to the kill
and let the best man win. Give yourself no fear about me. I am as cool
as a cucumber and feel as light as a feather when a fight is on. I have
written to Gaither [an Adams Express executive] on the subject for the
purpose of giving him courage and keeping him cool. I have also written
to my friends in Seymour to be prepared so if anything is required we
can telegraph at once. Everything is ready. I shall be pleased to have it
begin; if it is going to be a battle then I will make it short and decisive.[7]

A number of other letters went forward during the month on the
same subject, all detailing the same thesis. A letter to an attorney in
Seymour implied that the head of the rival detective agency would
try to break the agent down, and would use certain information to
blackmail Pinkerton. If he failed to pay they would then have the
agent "go down to Indiana as a witness against myself and others
who seek, you know, to cause trouble with reference to matters at
New Albany, etc., etc."[8]

Pinkerton's letterbook is tantalizingly obtuse about whatever incident had happened that would provide material for blackmail.
Unclear, too, is the nature of the need to be prepared to do "battle,"
as Pinkerton's bloodthirsty letter to Bangs implies. The available
evidence which, it must be emphasized, is circumstantial, would seem
to suggest that the agent had cooperated with the vigilantes in allowing the Reno gang to be taken away from the Pinkertons to be
hanged. But this still leaves unexplained the need to put together a
private army for a "war." Who would be fought? Certainly not the
vigilantes, who would have had equally as much to lose if further

facts came to light on the hangings. The whole intriguing incident is mysterious. Nothing further did transpire—the agent did not confess anything, apparently no attempts at blackmail were made, and the issue disappears from the letterbook in the following months. But it gives us a fascinating additional clue to the complex psychological makeup of Allan Pinkerton, a man whose public pose was not quite the same as his private motives.

Earlier letters give us ample evidence of that. Writing to General R. B. Marcy of the Inspector General's Department in Washington in 1873, Pinkerton builds an image of himself as stern in bringing the criminal to justice but merciful in rehabilitating him:

I argue that no matter how much they were degraded there is a white spot somewhere; if a hard hearted hardened detective like myself would only reach it. Such is always my case. I am stern until the criminal can be brought to the bar of justice and then to know he is convicted. I should like to be like the genie in Alladin with the wonderful lamp. I should like to rub it up and try if I cannot bring forth good faith. I always feel that I might do much more than I am doing now. I know that criminals are all hardened, but at the same time there is a white spot. Let us put it up if we can.[9]

In contrast, his letters to his own men were much more blunt; he told Franklin in 1872 concerning an Adams Express case: "It is one of those matters in which I long to see the guilty party found and hung without waiting for the Court whenever we are sure that he is the one."[10]

Unfortunately, Pinkerton did take action in one case where he was not "sure." This occurred just after the incident of the anticipated blackmail. Here the case is well known and what happened is quite clear. For it concerned one of America's most publicized criminals— and Pinkerton's Number One Nemesis—Jesse James.

✣   ✣   ✣   ✣   ✣

The saga of the Jesse James gang is so well documented that we can add little new here. As in the Reno case, only one aspect of the Pinkerton-James imbroglio is germane to the Molly Maguire story. But this aspect is critically important.

The Pinkertons had been trailing Frank and Jesse James and their co-conspirators, the Younger brothers (Cole, James, John, and Robert), since 1867. It was an especially frustrating case, for the gang was extremely wily and, as in the Reno affair, Pinkerton had to cope with a countryside that (either through fear or admiration) was often on the side of the criminals. In July 1873 the gang, which had previously specialized in bank robberies—often with attendant killings—decided to try train robbery. They were successful, and the harried railroad, the Rock Island, naturally turned to Pinkerton, whose agency had concentrated heavily in railroad detective work. Pinkerton sent a number of agents into Missouri and Iowa with disastrous results. Within a few months three agents had been shot and killed by the gang (John Younger, in turn, was killed by Pinkertons in March 1874).

By mid-1874 Pinkerton was apoplectic with frenzy to pay back the gang. His agents were now refusing to take assignments in the case; even his son William hedged on going into the field. Pinkerton was by this time partially paralyzed, but the frustration of having his men shot down in cold blood almost got the best of him. He wrote Bangs that "if force was organized properly I would say there was no use for me going forward," but "I have no soldiers but all officers in my regiment—all are capital men to give orders, few will go forward except somebody goes ahead." Pinkerton declared, "I know that the James and the Youngers are desperate men, and that when we meet it must be the death of one or both of us." "My blood was spilt," he said, "and they must repay, there is no use talking, they must die . . . Mr. Warner and William refuse to go with the men to Mo., have both declared that they were not to be made a notch to be shot at . . . consequently, I make no talk but simply say I am going myself."[11]

But, as it turned out, Allan Pinkerton did not go in person. By the end of 1874 a force of armed Pinkertons had been put together. Soon a rumor came that the James brothers were to be visiting their mother at her farmhouse in Clay County, Missouri. This was in January 1875. A special train had been standing by, and when word came from a local informant to "attack Castle James," the Pinkerton "army" boarded the train, got off near the farm, and in the middle of the night surrounded the house. At a given signal, the attackers began firing into the house, and then threw a missile into a window that caused a terrible explosion. The Pinkertons vowed that the missile was merely a kerosene flare that had happened to strike the stove, causing an explosion. But it was widely believed by others that it was actually a bomb, deliberately thrown in to kill.

And kill it did. An eight-year-old half-brother of Frank and Jesse James was ripped apart and died almost immediately. The James's mother, Mrs. Samuel, had her arm blown off. But neither of the James brothers was hurt. They couldn't have been, for they were not there at all that night.[12]

The botched attempt created a furor, all of it directed against the Pinkertons. The *New York Times* devoted many columns to the story of the "Strange Acts of the Detectives" and castigated Pinkerton and the agency—"Every one condemns the barbarous method used by the detectives."[13] And, in a curious manifestation of public ambivalence, the James gang was looked upon with increasing sympathy during the following months, in spite of the fact that they had killed a number of men. At one point an amnesty bill to "pardon" the gang for all their past acts was proposed in the Missouri legislature. The attack on the Samuel house was only one factor here, for the thesis had also been built up that the gang was a victim of the circumstances of the Civil War (Jesse James had been one of William C. Quantrill's Confederate renegades right after the war) and that bygones should be forgotten for the sake of national unity. Jesse James even had the audacity to send letters to Southern newspapers advocating his case. One, in the Nashville *Republican Banner*, attempted to play on the Pinkerton incident for sympathy. James said "nine Chicago assassins and Sherman bummers" "crept up to my mother's house and hurled a misile of war (a 32 pound shell) in a room among a family of innocent women and children."[14]

But James could not give up crime, and a renewed series of atrocities soon turned the fickle public back to hating the gang. The case always remained a thorn in the side of Allan Pinkerton, though. Not only did he and the agency get a terrible black eye from the Samuel incident, but he was never able to revenge himself adequately against the gang. The Youngers were caught by local authorities in a Minnesota bank robbery; Jesse James was shot in the back and instantly killed by one of his own gang for the reward; and Frank James was captured and sent to prison. Pinkerton's plaintive vow to the widow of one of his murdered informants was never to be fulfilled: "Oh, how I've thought over Daniel Askew's murder and I hope the time will come when both you and I shall seek the same revenge. My own men have been slaughtered, as you know . . . those men the Youngers and James are red with my men's blood. I want to impress upon all the men in my company that they shall be avenged."[15]

❖   ❖   ❖   ❖   ❖

The Pinkerton–Jesse James case came to its climax at just the time when the McParlan reports on Molly activity began to take on an ominous note. Pinkerton agents were killed by Jesse James in 1874. The Samuel house bomb debacle occurred in January 1875; and a bitter wave of anti-Pinkerton public opinion rose in the weeks and months immediately following. Allan Pinkerton was embarrassed, frustrated, and boiling mad. Criminals still ranging the country unfettered were not only being looked upon sympathetically as the underdogs, but these very criminals were the killers of his own men. The worst of it was that nothing entirely satisfactory could be done about it. If the Jameses and Youngers were captured by the Pinkertons, the chance was great that past sins would be forgiven and that they would be free and clear under the blanket of amnesty. If the gang were killed by the Pinkertons, the agency stood a real chance of incurring further public censure and perhaps even lawsuits, or worse.

How, then, would the Molly Maguire atrocities have looked to Pinkerton at this moment? Here, too, were a group of criminals still running free; any efforts to bring them to justice had uniformly and miserably failed. False alibis, intimidation of witnesses, lack of documented legal evidence had combined to give the guilty parties a seemingly impregnable position.

There was one difference, though. Public opinion was bitterly against the Mollies. This had been true for over ten years—even more so now, because of the ill will engendered by the "Long Strike." The public did not often stop to make distinctions, careful or otherwise, between the union and the Mollies. Franklin B. Gowen himself saw to it that when people talked of the union they would talk of the Mollies in the same breath (and vice versa).

And this bitterness against the Mollies was no longer aimless and unorganized. The notion of forming vigilance groups had been openly advocated (even in the press) as far back as the late 1860's; with the advent of the volatile Tom Foster and his free-swinging paper, the *Shenandoah Herald*, this pressure for counteraction became stronger and stronger. It was true that all this had proved to be nothing but talk so far, and talk was very cheap in the rumor-ridden, idle environment of the coal fields in 1874 and 1875. Nevertheless, if an idea is discussed continually it often develops into action. And Foster kept the discussion going, even running a long feature on the San Francisco vigilante story. Foster and his supporters were playing with fire.

By the summer of 1875, Allan Pinkerton had received reports from McParlan that pointed to real crimes. On June 1 in Mahanoy City an AOH meeting had resulted in a plan to murder Bully Bill Thomas. And the plan turned out to be no idle barroom threat—Bully Bill had been assaulted and had barely come out of the affair alive. Then, in July and August, two dead men—Benjamin Yost, the Tamaqua policeman, and Gomer James, the Welsh bully—attested to the murderous aims of the Mollies. Even more disconcerting for Allan Pinkerton, McParlan had obtained confessions from all involved, but these confessions could not be well enough corroborated to be able to take the killers into court and obtain convictions. Again Pinkerton must have felt the situation threatening to thwart him. Criminals who had killed were going to go free—the most abhorrent of all things to the single-minded detective.

It is in this context that Allan Pinkerton took one of the most remarkable steps in the Molly Maguire case. It came in the form of a letter to George Bangs, his general superintendent, who was in Philadelphia at the time. The letter is dated August 29, 1875, eight weeks after the Yost murder, two weeks after the James murder, three days before the assassination of the mine boss Thomas Sanger (along with William Uren), and five days before the assassination of the mine boss John Jones. This letter is so important that we print it here in full:

Chicago, August 29/75

George H. Bangs, Esq.
Gen'l Supt., Philadelphia, Pa.
Dear Sir:

Your two letters of the 26th inst. relative to Mr. Cummins, and the M.M.'s were received yesterday. After reviewing the condition of affairs in the mining districts, and after mature deliberation, I indited the following dispatch to you:

> "Unless Cummins positively knows 'Mac' as connected with me, no danger letting him return until matters are disposed of; but if the slightest danger of his knowing 'Mac' as connected with me, withdraw him. If Linden can get up vigilence committee that can be relied upon, do so. When M.M.'s meet, then surround and deal summarily with them. Get off quietly. All should be securely masked. Don't speak to Charles Parish or anyone; endeavor to arrest those men when engaged in any illegal act, and on their own heads be the consequences. Yours amen."

I was aware of this grave deliberation, and when walking out I pondered over it. I thought of the matter on Saturday evening, and this morning, and I finally concluded to call on Mr. Warner and Willie, to lay the matter before them. They read your letters and my dispatches to you, after which I asked them to give an unbiased opinion with regard to the matter, simply to tell me what they thought, whether they believed in the action I was determined to take, or not. They assured me that it was perfectly right, and that they would act, disregarding all consequences.

With regard to Cummins. I don't think there is really anything wrong with him. I am afraid that beer has been the cause of all this. There is no doubt but that he will have to quit our employment as soon as convenient, but if there is no danger of his knowing "Mac" as being connected with me, I think it would be as well to let him remain, because he may be useful to us when matters culminate.

With regard to Mr. Parish, I think favorably of him but it is just as well to keep him out of the secret. We don't know how far we can trust him, although I think he is all right, and devoted to our interests, but there is no use taking in more men than we really require; therefore I say, leave him out entirely.

The M.M.'s are a species of Thugs. You have probably read of them in India. Their religion taught them to murder, to mark out their victims, and their plans by which they were to strike, and not to divulge anything even if they were brought to the stake. So it is with the M.M.'s. They are bound to stick by their oath, and to carry out their revenge. He, who they think does a wrong, is marked out, and he must die. It is impossible to believe that a jury in the mining districts would not give a verdict of guilty against the M.M.'s should they be brought to trial but I believe that some one on the jury would hang on, and get the guilty men to escape. The only way then to pursue that I can see is, to treat them in the same manner as the Reno's were treated in Seymour, Indiana. After they were done away with, the people improved wonderfully and now Seymour is quite a town. Let Linden get up a vigilence committee. It will not do to get many men, but let him get those who are prepared to take fearful revenge on the M.M.'s. I think it would open the eyes of all the people and then the M.M.'s would meet with their just deserts. It is awful to see men doomed to death, it is horrible. Now there is but one thing to be done, and that is, get up an organization if possible, and when ready for action pounce upon the M.M.'s when they meet and are in full blast, take the fearful responsibility and disperse.

This is the best advice I can give you. I would not keep this letter in Philadelphia, but if you want to preserve it, send it over to New York. Place all confidence in Mr. Linden, he is a good man, and he understands what to do.

If you think it advisable, bring the matter before Mr. Gowen, but none other than him.

In case of failure, bail may be required, Mr. Gowen will be able to furnish it by his understanding it.

Yours truly,
Allan Pinkerton[16]

There seems to be no doubt of the authenticity of this letter. It appears in serial in Pinkerton's letterbook; the transcriber was secretary "S," whose initials appear on most of Pinkerton's confidential contacts in the letterbook (including most of those going to members of the family); the signature is Pinkerton's. And in light of our knowledge of the circumstances of Pinkerton's affairs at this moment, the basic thesis of the letter seems consistent with his psychological predilections. The conclusion is clear: Pinkerton is advocating—actually planning for—vigilantism.

But admonitions, exhortations, boasts, threats, plans—all are merely *potentials* for action. Did action itself follow in this case?

✤　✤　✤　✤　✤

The public threats of vigilante action, voiced with increasing vehemence after the Sanger-Uren and Jones killings of 1875, did not go unnoticed by the Mollies. Some of the organization may have felt personal qualms, but the general reaction of the leaders was one of bluster, disbelief, and defiance. McParlan reported on September 2, "Excitement runs high. The Shenandoah *Herald* advises a Vigilance Committee organized. The Sleepers laugh at it, and say if any Irishman would suffer, let alone of themselves, by such a thing, they will sack the co. and burn it down. Not one out of 100 of them cares for themselves. They laugh at their fathers or mothers (of which most of them have got either one or the other) when they will remind them that there is a God in heaven."[17]

But McParlan himself was concerned lest the vigilantes turn on him, for there were many people who considered him the worst of the bunch. As he put it in his September 2 report, "you may depend it takes a man to keep pretty straight and more especially outsiders, who consider me a King of the Sleepers." Allan Pinkerton, in his book, quotes a letter that he says Linden sent to McParlan during this week:

A citizen by the name of Boyd remarked to me today that the only chance for an excitement in dull Tamaqua was when that man with the big head (alluding to the wig, I suppose) and blue coat came upon the street. Then people began to say to each other, "what a shame that such a fellow (this means you, McParlan) is allowed to live! He ought to be strung up!" You need to keep a sharp look out, wherever you are, for about everybody here is thinking that you are a suspicious fellow generally and a particularly bad Mollie![18]

Even if the exact words here were from Pinkerton's fertile imagination, the essence of the thought rings true. Though McParlan would not have been logically linked by outsiders to the Raven Run murders of Sanger and Uren—he had never even been in the area—he had been conspicuous in Tamaqua in the weeks before the Jones killing. He had frequented Carroll's saloon; he was often seen with Kerrigan; he was "sparking" the sister of Kerrigan's wife. He had been all over Tamaqua in his fruitless search for Kerrigan the day before Jones was shot. And of course he had been prominent in AOH affairs in Shenandoah—the heartland of Foster-pushed vigilante talk.

If the Mollies were not particularly upset by vigilante talk, they did not look with equal equanimity on the arrest of James Kerrigan, Edward Kelly, and Michael J. Doyle. All three were in the Mauch Chunk jail, with trial imminent. The AOH leaders in Schuylkill County were painfully aware that too many damning secrets were lodged in the brain of Kerrigan. The evidence against the three appeared to be largely circumstantial; even the murder gun, which had been found in the bushes on the mountain near where the three were arrested, could not be clearly identified as belonging to the threesome. Perhaps the combination of sharp lawyers, well-constructed alibis, and a bit of intimidation would pull them through. The Mollies immediately laid plans for the legal brains, the alibis, and the intimidation.

If the three were to be saved, the best lawyers would be needed, and because this required substantial funds, the various lodges began to amass a defense fund. They asked for subscriptions (McParlan contributed two dollars on September 29 and promptly put it on his expense account), and held balls and other special events to build up the "war chest." Two of the best lawyers of Schuylkill County, James B. Reilly and Len Bartholomew, agreed to take the case.

Along with the financial campaign, the building of alibis occupied much attention. McParlan went to the Wilkes-Barre area on October 4, explaining his move to the Mollies by promising to search for funds among the northern-district lodges (but probably also feeling it wise to be at least temporarily out of sight of any vigilantes). But the detective kept in close touch with the Schuylkill members by mail, and they reciprocated with the latest information on the alibis. Carroll wrote McParlan on October 12 that they had not yet succeeded in obtaining any witnesses to swear that they saw Kelly and Doyle get off the train from Pottsville at Tamaqua on the morning of the murder of John P. Jones, "but Alex Campbell thinks he will be able to find someone before the trial." The Mollies were soon successful, for McParlan reported two days later that a Mt. Laffee man would swear that he saw Kelly and Doyle going toward Pottsville the morning of the murder. Other witnesses were primed, too— "all have their parts learned and will swear to very much the same thing," McParlan commented.[19]

The trial opened on October 19 in Mauch Chunk, and McParlan hurried over from Wilkes-Barre to attend. Talking with the Mollies present, he soon garnered an imposing list of defense witnesses all set to perjure themselves on the stand. The defense began by demanding a change of venue, which was promptly denied. They then asked the court for a delay in the trial until the January 1876 term, and this was granted. No witnesses were called; thus the defense case was not yet public. Nevertheless, the Mollies were pleased, having apparently won the first round in the trial. The case seemed to be following the long-standing pattern: delay, forgetfulness by intimidated prosecution witnesses, alibis for the defendants, acquittal.

❖   ❖   ❖   ❖   ❖

Meanwhile, any hope that the arrest of the alleged assailants of Jones would bring a moratorium on violence was abruptly shattered on October 9. This was another pay-day Saturday night. Drink-befuddled senses made tempers flare—all the worse because of the increasing post-strike discrimination in the mines against the Irish. Scuffles were reported all over the region. But the worst occurred in Shenandoah. In one tavern an English miner was shot, in another, a Welshman—James Johns—had his throat cut and was robbed of his watch and $500. Both men were fearfully wounded, but both managed to survive. The assailant of the first man escaped; the man presumed to have attacked Johns was arrested, but turned out to have an ironclad alibi.

The Pottsville *Miners' Journal* in its next issue, October 15, 1875, flamingly recounted the night's horrors—" 'The dog is turned to his own vomit again' and the roughs in and around Shenandoah have had another night's fun." According to the paper the Shenandoah deputy sheriff had issued a public proclamation for a 9:30 p.m. curfew and promised that "an efficient posse" had been appointed to insure law and order. But the *Miners' Journal* was dubious of the posse's ability to carry through, for, as Ramsey pointed out, most of the law officers in Shenandoah were Irishmen, who were reluctant to arrest any fellow-countrymen. Ramsey gave voice to his personal frustration by printing an incendiary anonymous letter that spoke baldly for direct action. It had been "loudly proclaimed," the writer said, "that the next time shooting began a good many shots would be fired on the side of the people. What has become of the organization? And where were the peoples' marksmen on Saturday night last?"

Yes, where was "the organization" (and, incidentally, *what* was it) and where were the "peoples' marksmen"? Ramsey, without realizing it, might well have been addressing himself directly to Captain Robert J. Linden. The Pinkerton agent had gone to Philadelphia on September 15, according to his expense statement. He had returned to Pottsville that same evening. We have no other record of this meeting, but Pinkerton in his book mentions a secret meeting of Linden, Franklin, and McParlan in Pottsville at about this time. Pinkerton continues: "In a day or two McKenna was summoned to Philadelphia, thence traveled to New York, and had a meeting with General Superintendant George H. Bangs." Pinkerton then added, "The result of the journey the ensuing pages will explain."[20]

McParlan's expense statements do record that although he was in Tamaqua on September 15 (when Linden was in Philadelphia) he went to Philadelphia on September 19, to New York City on September 20, and thence back to Pottsville on September 22. The "ensuing pages" in Pinkerton's book explained this: "The work performed by McKenna while in New York and Philadelphia was very important and constituted a portion of the first really aggressive acts of the Agency against the formidable foe. It consisted in the preparation of classified and carefully arranged lists of all the Mollies, or members of the Ancient Order of Hibernians, in Luzerne, Northumberland, Columbia, Carbon, and Schuylkill Counties, their residence, occupation, standing in the society, and crimes they had been connected with. When completed, the schedule was given very extensive circulation throughout the United States, by publication in the principal newspapers."

A printed "List of the Members of the AOH." is extant. It contains 347 names, classified by town and noting for some names the post held in the AOH. It does not note the "crimes they had been connected with."[21]

Pinkerton's book continues, enigmatically, "It was but the prelude of the thunderbolt which was soon to cast consternation into the hearts of the leaders of the society. Our plans were formed for unrelenting and unending warfare upon them. They had for years carried everything unresistingly before them, but now a force, the secret emissaries of which for nearly three years had been ferreting out and marking their weak places, meanwhile sharpening and charging their own weapons for use, was to put its potent machinery suddenly in motion."

Did Pinkerton literally mean "sharpening and charging" weapons? What was the "potent machinery?" These questions soon became extremely relevant. For—sometime during this autumn of 1875—someone printed a startling document in the form of a one-page handbill, undated and headed "STRICTLY CONFIDENTIAL." This handbill is given verbatim as follows. It contains numerous errors; for example, "Boyle" in the second paragraph obviously should have been "Doyle," and "Charles McAllister" in connection with the Raven Run murders should have been "James McAllister."

STRICTLY CONFIDENTIAL

The following are FACTS for the consideration of the Vigilance Committee of the Anthracite Coal Region, and all other good citizens who desire to preserve law and order in their midst. viz:—

On June 28th, 1875, at about 5 A.M., an attempt was made to murder William Thomas, otherwise known as "Bully Bill," by John Gibbons and Thomas Hurley. Mr. Thomas was shot at and wounded by these men as he was quietly conversing with William Heilner, Stable Boss of Shoemakers Colliery, and was entirely unaware of his danger.—John Morris and Michael Boyle were accessories to the shooting, and present when it was done.

On July 5th, 1875, at 2 A.M., Police Officer Frank B. Yost, of Tamaqua, was shot and killed by Hugh McGehan as he, (Yost) was turning off the Gas of a Street Lamp a few rods from his residence.—James Boyle was present, and accessory to this murder, which was instigated by James Kerrigan.

On August 14th, 1875, at about 9 P.M. THOMAS Gwyther, a Justice of the Peace of Girardville, while standing at his office door in company with his daughter, was shot dead by William Love.

On the same date at about 11 P.M., Gomer James, a watchman, was shot and instantly killed at a Pic-nic at Glovers Hill; Shenandoah, by Thomas Hurley.

On September 1st, 1875, at about 7 A.M., Thomas Sanger, a Mining Boss, and William Uren, a Miner of Raven Run, were shot and fatally wounded by James O'Donnell, alias "Friday," and Thomas Munley, as the unsuspecting victims were on their way to their work.—Charles O'Donnell, Charles McAllister, and Mike Doyle were present, and accessories to this murder.

On September 3rd, 1875, at 7 o'clock, a.m., John P. Jones, a mining boss at Summit Hill, while on his way to work, was shot dead by Michael Boyle and Edward Kelly. This murder was instigated by James Kerrigan, who was accessory to the same.

RESIDENCES OF MURDERERS AND ACCESSORIES:—

John Gibbons, ... Member Molly Maguires', ... Shenandoah.			
Thomas Hurley, ... " " " , ... "			
John Morris, ... " " " , ... "			
Michael Doyle, ... " " " , ... "			
Hugh McGehan, ... " " " , ... Summit Hill.			
James Boyle, ... " " " , ... "			
William Love, ... " " " , ... Girardville.			
James O'Donnell, ... " " " , ... Weigans Patch			
Charles O'Donnell, ... " " " , ... "			
Charles McAlister, ... " " " , ... "			
Thomas Munley, ... " " " , ... Gilberton.			
Michael Doyle, ... Secretary , ... Mount Laffee.			
Edward Kelly, ... Member , ... "			
James Kerrigan, ... Ex-Body Master , ... Tamaqua.			

A specimen of this printed document (our source for the text just given) is in the files of the New York office of Pinkerton's National Detective Agency. The date of the handbill is unknown. The circumstances of its preparation, printing, and distribution are unclear. In the light of our knowledge from other sources, there seems to be no reason to doubt that it was produced in 1875 either by the Pinkertons or by someone else on information furnished by the Pinkertons. (For example, Wiggans Patch was also misspelled "Weigans Patch" on the printed Pinkerton list of the 347 AOH members). Through internal evidence one can feel reasonably sure that it was printed between September 3, 1875, the date of the Jones murder, and December 10, the date when a dreadful outrage was to take place at Wiggans Patch.

We pick up the thread of this handbill next in a Linden field report eleven days after Shenandoah's bloody night of October 9:

The operative has visited different places in the coal region with the view of giving necessary information to some of the leading citizens, advising them as to who the parties are who have committed the recent assassinations, and circumstances attending them, in order to place them fully on their guard against these outlaws, but as yet there seems to be so much apathy among the better class of citizens as well as the authorities, that no definite steps have been taken to make examples of the well known assassins.[22]

An additional piece of evidence is also available. In the manuscript collection of Archbishop James Frederic Wood is a copy, apparently in Wood's own handwriting, of a memorandum from Benjamin Franklin to Gowen, dated November 30, 1875. This contains a long list of murders committed between October 30, 1874, and October 9, 1875 (including all those on the "strictly confidential" list). And in the covering letter Franklin is quoted as stating, "the legal authorities of Schuylkill County have been notified but there seems to be an entire apathy on their part for various reasons to make an example of any of the parties charged with these offenses."[23]

We cannot feel very comfortable in our assumptions about the handbill, for there are a number of unanswered questions about the document and its possible use by Linden. Was there, in fact, a "Vigilance Committee of the Anthracite Coal Region"? There were certainly enough intimations around the region—the Shenandoah deputy sheriff's "efficient posse," the more and more frequent mention of a "detective corps" by Tom Foster in the *Shenandoah Herald*, even the Tamaqua citizens' committee that had privately hired the Pinkertons after the Yost killing. It might then be logical to assume that the handbill was primarily a "staff report" to an already existing organization, taken around by Linden to provide, as the first line of the handbill states, "FACTS." But Linden's report above makes us wary of this assumption, for it implies that because of "apathy" (or what might have been, in reality, fear), no one was willing to do more than talk. Again, though, caution would tell us that if in fact there was a secret organization dedicated to carrying through the final violent step, its members might well be reluctant to give any specific information about an intended action to a police officer or detective. Vigilantism was an illegal act, and a police officer or detective is charged with the prevention of such acts.

Just how "strictly confidential" the handbill was is not known. Though no copy appears to have fallen into the hands of the Mollies, they certainly knew that something was amiss. McParlan visited Shenandoah on October 29 and started on a round of the taverns with McAndrew. At Lawler's saloon, Muff Lawler said that he had been told that "the Molly Maguires were all known and that the next time a man was shot they would make it hot for the Mollies." All the men in the bar laughed at this, McParlan reported, but Lawler continued to maintain that "there was a screw loose somewhere."[24]

McParlan was also startled by the information that Tom Hurley had been arrested and was in jail, accused of two crimes. Bully Bill Thomas had evidently summoned up enough nerve to accuse Hurley legally of the assault on him in the stables on June 28. In addition, Hurley was also accused of the throat-slashing of the Welsh miner, James Johns, on October 9. Hurley's arrest disconcerted the Shenandoah Mollies for several reasons. The Thomas assault had been planned by a number of them, and although most of them probably had no notion that this made them accessories to the crime (the man who pulled the trigger was the only guilty party in their eyes), still Hurley knew a great deal. And the fact that Thomas had now come forward seemed to herald a stiffening attitude by the authorities. John Gibbons, Hurley's accomplice in the Thomas assault, was particularly nervous. Gibbons confided his fears to McParlan—he had just come from Lawler's, where Lawler "told him that there were traitors among the Mollies and advised him to clear out." Gibbons had pressed Lawler to tell him who the traitor was, but Lawler refused, saying that if he told, "it would put some men out of good jobs." Gibbons mentioned the conversation again to McAndrew that night and the bodymaster retorted that the spy was probably Lawler himself, a notion that McParlan must have been relieved to hear.[25]

In the first days of November, according to McParlan's November reports, the Mollies became increasingly perturbed about the possibility that an informer was in their midst. Something was wrong, for the coal and iron police were very active, even searching individual miners' homes for fugitives from various crimes. Their legal authority to do this was questionable—the limits of the jurisdiction of this private police arm were never very clear during this period. Evidently the county authorities had more confidence in Gowen's police than they did in the local authorities. And the misgivings about the local officers of the law were well-founded. McParlan's reports during November are filled with references to Mollies who were alerted to the threat of a potential arrest and spirited away; and often the alerters were the local police, the very men who had the responsibility of making the arrests.

McParlan himself aided an escape, although not realizing it at the time. The detective had proved a worthy bail-raiser in the past; now

Mrs. Hurley entreated him to raise the necessary amount (a high one because of the double crime) to free Hurley. McParlan was able to do so, and Hurley was let out of jail. A few weeks later Hurley disappeared, and there were rumors among the Mollies that he had jumped bail. John Kehoe indignantly accosted McParlan, demanding to know Hurley's whereabouts, as the county delegate had himself put up part of the money. There was an unverified story that Hurley had gone to England on the ship *Abyssinia*, but McParlan vowed to Kehoe that this was not true, that he knew Hurley was in hiding at Parson's Station with Mike Doyle (that is, Mike Doyle of Shenandoah, not Mike Doyle of Mt. Laffee). But the detective was to find that Hurley had jumped bail after all.

By mid-November the spy fears among the Mollies were rampant. Lawler was increasingly under suspicion, along with another Shenandoah Molly, Ed Monaghan, who had been seen talking with a prominent banker and with Tom Foster, the *Herald* editor, in the shadows of a Shenandoah side street at 2 o'clock one morning.

But if the Mollies' private affairs were filled with misgivings, fear, and mistrust, they continued to throw their weight around publicly. The hotly contested electioneering for county and state public offices had brought increasingly bitter innuendos that the Mollies had sold their votes *en masse* to representatives of the Republican candidate and incumbent governor, General John F. Hartranft, in exchange for the pardons of certain local Molly officials accused of embezzling funds. It would have been a curious switch, for the Irish had predominantly voted Democratic. The later Molly trials added further evidence on this accusation; but, before the 1875 elections, the Mollies hotly denied it. McParlan reported on November 2 that he went to the polls and voted "as his friends wanted him to." Hartranft was re-elected. Barney Dolan penned a particularly arrogant letter to the *Miners' Journal*, denying that he had engineered any payoffs, and Ramsey duly printed it, although piously editorializing that he did so only because he was dedicated to giving all sides representation. About the same time John Kehoe wrote the *Shenandoah Herald* a venomous letter, the essence of which was that the AOH had absolutely nothing to do with Molly Maguireism—the latter being exclusively the province of "drones of society . . . who hope by these means to receive an appointment . . . which would afford them an indolent living." In this case, though, Foster refused to print the letter, choosing to wait until the trials to make it public.[26]

As the weeks dragged on, the Mollies became increasingly suspicious of one another. A number of "trials" were held by the lodges, and numbers of members were expelled, mostly for "cowardice" for not taking active part in the defense plans for Kelly and Doyle at Mauch Chunk. Several other members were suspected as spies— even one of the bodymasters was accused of showing letters and other documents to "outsiders." There was a strong feeling in this case that the offending bodymaster "had ought to be put out of the way." Even one of the Molly lawyers had been heard "talking too much." On December 8, McParlan reported what to him must have appeared to be just another minor example of the tensions within the group: a band of Mollies from Gilberton and Wiggans Patch had beaten up another Irishman by the name of Quinn near St. Nicholas. One of the assailants, a Wiggans Patch man, was James "Friday" O'Donnell (who had been involved in the Raven Run killing, as duly noted in the "strictly confidential" handbill).[27] Two days later McParlan would have had every reason to reassess this incident, for Wiggans Patch was to become a name permanently imprinted in the Molly Maguire story.

✦   ✦   ✦   ✦   ✦

At 3 o'clock in the morning of Friday, December 10, 1875, Charles and Ellen McAllister were asleep in their bedroom downstairs, just off the kitchen. Their infant child lay between them. There would soon be another child, for Ellen was expecting. Upstairs, widow Margaret O'Donnell, Ellen's mother, was also asleep. It was a large house, a duplex with a center wall and a common cellar; the Cassidys lived in the other half. When Margaret O'Donnell's husband had died, she had been fortunate in being able to house, in addition to Ellen, Charles, and their baby, both her two unmarried sons. Their names: James "Friday" O'Donnell and Charles O'Donnell. They, too, were asleep upstairs this night, and so were four paying guests, Tom Murphy, John Purcell, James Blair, and James McAllister (brother of Charles).

In that first moment between deep sleep and startled awakening, various thoughts must have pushed forward to the consciousness of those ten people. "I thought it was old Murphy who had got up to light his pipe and had fallen downstairs," later reported Mrs. O'Donnell.[28] But the noise was the kitchen door being smashed in.

Charles McAllister jumped out of bed and ran to the cellar door, which opened into the bedroom. Turning in terror to his wife, he told her to stay in bed, after which he ran down the stairs and through the cellar toward Mrs. Cassidy's house. But Ellen McAllister did not stay in bed. Instead she rose, walked to the door leading into the kitchen and opened it. As her white-nightgowned form was outlined in the door a gun went off, a bullet pierced her right breast, and she cried "I'm shot." Charles McAllister later testified, "I heard my wife say that she was shot. The next time I saw her, she was dead. I went into the cellar. I went through the partition wall into Mrs. Cassidy's house. I remained there about fifteen minutes."[29]

Two men burst into Margaret O'Donnell's bedroom—"the one nearest to me put the pistol in my face." She backed off; the other man rudely brushed the pistol away. She tried to move to the door and one of the men gave her a glancing blow with his gun. "I calculate it was the butt end of the pistol that struck me."

Another pair went to Thomas Murphy's bed. "I raised up and asked what was the matter. He said put your hands above the clothes or else I will blow a hole through you." One of the men took a look at Murphy, said something to the other. "He told the man not to meddle with me, I was an old man."

John Purcell was next. "There were two more men masked over me, asked me my name. I said John Purcell. They tied me hand and feet to the bedpost."

James Blair, too. "I looked up and asked what the matter was. One man pulled bed clothes down. Do not know whether I got out alone or not. Took me down stair and one man tied me with rope [around neck]; tried to keep it off and rope was put on; took me out and asked my name and let me go; after rope was off did not take time to look at faces; went back into house."

James McAllister was brought down the stairs. In the yard he wrested himself free. He began running. Shots rang out; he was hit in the arm. He disappeared into the woods. James "Friday" O'Donnell also escaped.

Charles O'Donnell was grabbed in his bed by two men. (John Purcell heard him say, "Men, did I ever do anything to be afraid of you. I will go with you." Mrs. O'Donnell reported it as, "Boys, I never did anything I am afraid, I will go along with you.") He, too, broke away. Shots were fired at him. He fell. A ring of men surrounded him, pumping bullets into him. The men then disappeared.

Mrs. Sherry, a neighbor, was the first to reach him. "I found Charles O'Donnell lying with his face down and his clothes burning. I tore off of him what I could and then some men came up and carried him in." The *Shenandoah Herald* reporter added, "The head which had received no less than fifteen bullets and was in a shockingly crushed condition, was tied up in a white cloth. From the hips to the chin the body was crisped, there being no less than the marks of ten balls to be seen, and the firearms must have been held in such close proximity that the powder had actually roasted the flesh."[30]

The *Tamaqua Courier* had asked in September for action "sure, swift and terrible." The Wiggans Patch outrage was certainly swift. And if it was not quite "sure"—it would stretch the imagination to think of Ellen McAllister as one of the intended victims—nevertheless it was "terrible."

✤ ✤ ✤ ✤ ✤

"Who did it?" The question was on everyone's lips, for the Wiggans Patch massacre brought a public outcry of consternation, horror, and revulsion on a far greater scale than that of any of the previous killings. "If this state of affairs continues, no man will be safe hereafter," editorialized the *Tamaqua Courier*. Even Tom Foster of the *Shenandoah Herald* seemed appalled by the kind of action he had been so vociferously advocating for months. "One of the most atrocious outrages that has been perpetrated in this county," he bemoaned (after which he promptly eliminated any discussion of vigilantism from the pages of the *Herald*).[31]

Who *did* do the killings? We still do not really know, for the case has remained unsolved. A good many people participated in the attack and it is possible that some information was passed down to the descendants of one or more of them and could be known by someone living today. If so, he or she is not publicizing the information—perhaps it is just as well.

Early in the morning after the horrible night a crudely lettered note was found on the ground near the O'Donnell house. Its message was short but devastating: "You are the murderers of Uren and Sanger." In mid-morning the Mahanoy City coroner, a Dr. Hermany, arrived on the scene. After briefly examining the bodies of Charles O'Donnell and Ellen McAllister, and pronouncing that the cause of death was "so plain" that an autopsy would be unnecessary, he empaneled a coroner's jury and proceeded to cross-examine the witnesses, right in the O'Donnell front room. Tom Foster of the *Shenandoah Herald* was already on the scene, duly prepared to record the hearing in detail. While Hermany was cross-examining Mrs. O'Donnell as to whether she recognized any of the men in her room, a startling interruption came. John Kehoe, the Molly county delegate, strode into the room, and, on hearing the question to Mrs. O'Donnell, rushed up to her and said, "I order you not to answer that question." The startled Hermany inquired as to why Kehoe was even there. Kehoe replied that he was the brother-in-law of both Charles O'Donnell and Ellen McAllister, for his wife was another daughter of widow Margaret O'Donnell. "Dr. Hermany," Kehoe continued, "this business is going to be settled in another manner." The coroner promptly ordered Kehoe to remain quiet, the Molly leader grudgingly complied, and the hearing continued to its termination.

At this hearing Margaret O'Donnell was unable (or unwilling) to identify any of the men in the mob. But later in the day she changed her mind, for Kehoe himself made a formal charge against one Frank Wenrich, a well-known and highly respected butcher of Mahanoy City, charging him with the gun-butt assault on Mrs. O'Donnell. Wenrich was immediately arrested and a preliminary hearing held that afternoon. (All this was still the day of the murders —December 10.) By now Margaret O'Donnell was willing under oath to make a positive identification of Wenrich, and the butcher was committed to jail. An "immense and highly excited" crowd milled around the jail; so the following morning Wenrich was whisked away to safer keeping in Pottsville.

Two days later, on Monday the 13th, a habeas corpus plea by Wenrich was heard in Pottsville. Margaret O'Donnell was again asked to identify Wenrich and she obliged. District Attorney George Kaercher then flatly asked her if she had been told to do so by her son-in-law, Kehoe. She haltingly answered, "Yes." The judge promptly released Wenrich on $5,000 bail and Wenrich returned to Mahanoy City. The *Shenandoah Herald* said that about three hundred persons greeted him, followed him downtown, and "manifested much enthusiasm on his return," and that "he was busy receiving handshakes and congratulations until bed time." Kehoe's case had fallen through. But the Kehoe involvement added an enigmatic dimension to the already clouded question of who the assailants were. The papers were full of the crime, and many premises were advanced as to its origin. The *Miners' Journal* in Pottsville mentioned the earlier difficulties of the O'Donnell family with the Gilberton Irish, and the *Philadelphia Evening Telegram* called it a "clan fight." Just two days before, James O'Donnell had taken a large band to St. Nicholas and beaten up the Gilberton man, Quinn.[32]

But certain elements of the methods used at Wiggans Patch do not ring true as a faction-fighting case. The attackers were highly organized, a team being designated to capture each member of the house. They were all dressed alike; most of the witnesses commented on the long oilskin coats they wore. There was some difference of opinion as to whether they were masked; it seems that most were. Though all these devices had been used in Irish faction fighting— both Ireland's and America's versions—the high degree of apparent organization makes one wary of assuming it was a retaliation by the Gilberton group.

If not another clan, could it have been within the clan itself? There was a curious rumor to this effect, and it gained enough credence to have the Boston *Pilot*, hundreds of miles away, publish a perplexing comment a week after the killings. The Catholic paper said that "the shooting grew out of a previous shooting affair, the facts of which the O'Donnells were aware of, and it is thought the murderers found it necessary to silence them for fear of damaging evidence in their possession."[33] The *Tamaqua Courier* dropped the same hint in its issue of December 17: "No one hazards the opinion fully as to whether the outrage was committed by vigilantes as a retaliatory measure or whether the former friends of the deceased did the deed, on account of secrets exposed." Franklin Dewees, in his 1877 book on the Mollies, quotes John J. Slattery, an AOH member involved in a later trial, as stating that it was the work of John Kehoe. Dewees described Slattery's reasons:

> It appears that after the murder of Sanger and Uren, young Charles O'Donnell was much troubled in mind. It affected him to such a degree that his family became alarmed; John Kehoe, the brother-in-law, remonstrated with him, but O'Donnell still continued restless and disturbed. Kehoe became so indignant at his conduct that he went to Mrs. O'Donnell's house and thrashed him.
> O'Donnell's uneasiness remained, and it was feared by Kehoe that through him all the circumstances connected with the murder would be exposed. Slattery understood the state of affairs, and knew of Kehoe's feelings.
> On the morning of the 9th of December, Charles Mulhearn told Slattery he was going to Mahanoy Valley that day, and that a "job" was to be done at Wiggans Patch that night.
> On the 10th he heard of the murder. His suspicions were at once aroused. He did not see Mulhearn until about four days afterwards. When they did meet, Mulhearn made no reference to the matter. This increased Slattery's suspicions. He believes that had Mulhearn not known that the murder was not the work of the vigilance committee, he would have been much excited on the subject.[34]

This accusation was never tested in the courts. Even Dewees, as critical as he was of the Mollies, concluded, "It is difficult to believe that Jack Kehoe would deliberately compass the murder of the brothers of his wife." It is interesting, though, that Charles O'Donnell was the only man actually murdered (though both James O'Donnell and James McAllister had close calls). This whole story is made doubly intriguing by the strange conduct of Kehoe in the Wenrich case.

We must now add one further document to the pieces of evidence we have already noted. It is a handwritten copy of a letter supposed to have been written sometime during December 10, 1875, the same day of the early-morning killings at Wiggans Patch. We do not know to whom it is addressed; at the top are the words "Copy of

Report of J. McF [sic]." The handwriting appears to be one of the two sets of handwriting on the reports going to the railroad; perhaps the initial "L" at the end is that of Linden. (Linden had used the abbreviation "McF" for McParlan in at least one of his expense accounts.) The date the copy was made is indeterminate. This manuscript is now located in the files of the general offices of Pinkerton's National Detective Agency at New York, but no one today is really sure of its provenance. It reads as follows:

Pottsville, Schuylkill Co., Pa.
Friday, Dec. 10th, 1875

This morning at 8 A.M. I heard that a crowd of masked men had entered Mrs. O'Donnells house Wiggans Patch and had killed James O'Donnell alias Friday, Chas O'Donnell and James MacAllister also Mrs. MacAllister whom they took out of the house and shot (Chas Mac-Allisters wife). Now as for the O'Donnells I am satisfied they got their just deservings. I reported what those men were, I give all information about them so clear that the courts could have taken hold of their case at any time but the witnesses were too cowardly to do it. I have also in the interest of God and humanity notified you months before some of their outrages were committed, still the authorities took no hold of the matter. Now I wake up this morning to find that I am the murderer of Mrs. MacAllister. What had a woman to do in this case. Did the Sleepers in their worst time shoot down women. If I was not here the vigilant committee would not know who was guilty. And when I find them shooting women in their thirst for blood, I hereby tender my resignation to take effect as soon as this message is received. If there is any other job in the Agency that you may want me for I will accept it. If not I will go home to Chicago as I am sure I am sold anyhow by some of those men on the Committee and it is through them the Hon. James B. Reilly has got his information that there is something wrong. Now no doubt but there will be man for man taken and I do not see which side will have the Sympathizers. As for myself I will remain here until you dispatch for me to go down which I hope will be soon as this letter is received it is not cowardice that makes me resign but just let them have it now. I will no longer interfere as I see that one is the same as the other and I am not going to be accessory to the murder of women and children. Direct your dispatch to the Northwestern Hotel as it is not worthwhile to leave for a boarding house at present when I am going away anyhow. At 10:00 A.M. I got your letter and contents noted but as you see this alters state of affairs in genl hence there is no further use of comments, of course you may expect burning and murdering all over. Where we might have had a little quietness and now innocent men of both parties will suffer and I am sure the Sleepers will not spare the women so long as the vigilants has shown the example.

Respectfully submitted

J. McF

L.

Interpretation of this document is tricky. James Horan and Howard Swiggett, in their 1951 book *The Pinkerton Story*, conclude that "it disposes, we believe, of the charges that McParlan was ever an *agent-provocateur*." They quote a letter (now missing) that they state Benjamin Franklin sent to Allan Pinkerton: "This morning I received a report from 'Mac' of which I send you a copy, and in which he seems to be very much surprised at the shooting of these men; and he offers his resignation. I telegraphed 'Mac' to come here from Pottsville, as I am anxious to satisfy him that we have nothing to do with what has taken place in regard to these men. Of course I do not want 'Mac' to resign."[35]

McParlan does not state explicitly that he did not know of the vigilante plans beforehand. His indignation is not about the killing of Charles O'Donnell. (He was right about this murder, and that of Ellen McAllister, but did add two corpses that weren't!) He may or may not have known of Allan Pinkerton's letter to George Bangs. It does seem clear that he was not present at Wiggans Patch on the morning of December 10.

What of Franklin's letter to Pinkerton? Linden's expense statements show that on November 29 he traveled to Chicago, presumably for a conference with Allan Pinkerton. This was his first such trip since being assigned to the case. He returned to Philadelphia on December 7. His records in the Reading's files then show that he stayed in Philadelphia until December 12. It is true that an expense account can be faked and therefore does not prove actual physical presence; nevertheless, for want of further evidence we assume that Linden was nowhere near Wiggans Patch and, therefore, not personally participating. And there are no further records presently available to show where other Pinkerton men were on December 10. Here the matter stands. Clearly, Allan Pinkerton stood guilty of incitement to vigilantism. So, too, did many others. Thomas Foster, the *Herald* editor, had been indefatigable in his efforts. Colonel Ramsey of the *Miners' Journal* had followed in the footsteps of Bannan in subtly mentioning vigilante successes in other places. The "citizens' committee" in Tamaqua, the detective corps in the Coal and Iron Police in Shenandoah, and probably other similar groups had seeds of violence in them. Perhaps Allan Pinkerton was different from these in certain respects: he had had past experience with vigilantism (the precise nature of which we were not able to document definitively); he had abiding courage and personal drive; and he had an organization that knew violence firsthand. But we would be on weak ground in giving much weight to such circumstantial evidence in the Wiggans Patch situation.

Who killed Charles O'Donnell and Ellen McAllister? The answer is not known.

Part Four ✦ *The Great Molly Maguire Trials*

Chapter 11 ✦ McKenna Escapes

*T*HE WIGGANS PATCH killings profoundly shook the Mollies. How could such a complete and shatteringly accurate list of accused murderers have been put together for the "confidential" handbill? Who was behind its publication and its distribution? And who engineered the terrible night of blood at Wiggans Patch?

"The Mollies are now confident that there is a traitor in their midst," McParlan reported on December 11, 1875, the day after the killings. He said that "Pat Malone, Jerry Kane and several others from Mt. Laffee and also Patsey Collins . . . talk as if they would rather not have any one prosecuted in this case, even if they are found out, but want time to deliberate on the matter and then pay them off themselves." On the day Ellen McAllister and Charles O'Donnell were buried, the detective stayed in hiding, as it "would bring [me] in a public manner before the eyes of the public." But his report contained the intriguing fact that two Mollies of Port Carbon were drunkenly bragging that they were members of the vigilante mob, though Frank Keenan, bodymaster at Forestville, "was positive that neither man was there." A day later McParlan saw Kehoe, who said "he had not a doubt that Wenrich was one of the men but did not want him prosecuted as he knew very well it would not be a fair trial and he would rather let the affair blow over a little." Dennis Canning, another bodymaster, repeated the caution, saying that "all must keep quiet and they would soon find out who were the perpetrators." McParlan cautioned Superintendent Franklin that "the Mollies feel a terrible itching for vengeance," and that "there is no telling when or where they will act . . . but Foster of the *Herald* will be one of the condemned."[1]

Compounding Molly fears was the painful event of the capture in September of Edward Kelly, Michael J. Doyle, and Jimmy Kerrigan, immediately after the murder of the foreman, John P. Jones. These three possessed fearfully incriminating knowledge. The postponed trial in October had buoyed hopes; the long-standing pattern of delay, perjured defense, and acquittal seemed good for another round. But Wiggans Patch shattered any residual complacency. There was an implacable foe, a foe who knew too much already and apparently would stop at nothing to restore the balance of revenge. Early in January 1876, Hugh McGehan, who had been cited by McParlan as the actual trigger man in the Yost killing, reported that he was shot at while on the way home to his saloon. Miraculously, he escaped being slain, but several of the slugs were reported to have penetrated his clothes.[2] The "Vigilantes"—if in fact there was such a group—were apparently not satisfied by the Wiggans Patch debacle.

Scarcely had the Wiggans Patch shock subsided when new events intruded. The first came from one of the most feared sources—the Catholic Church.

The parish priests in the coal regions had remained badly split by the Molly Maguire issue. The Reverend Daniel McDermott's famous blast against the Mollies in 1874 in the *Freeman's Journal and Catholic Register,* followed by the "Declaration of the Seven Pastors," had already led to widespread denunciations of the Ancient Order of Hibernians, both collectively and individually. Other parish priests, particularly those farther up the fields in the Scranton diocese of Bishop O'Hara and those in the Pittsburgh area, had taken the opposite position. The age-old Church bugaboo of honest differences among priests setting parishioner against parishioner became a reality again. The *Freeman's Journal* pleaded:

The exceedingly ugly fact exists that while some Archbishops and Bishops declare, as of their personal and sure knowledge, that the A.O.H. is such a Society as falls under the condemnation of the Catholic Church, *other* Catholic Prelates treat the Society as composed for the most part of Catholics obedient to their duties.

These Most Rev. Prelates do not need us to tell them . . . that this open and opposite conduct—this practical *repudiation* by one Bishop of the official action of his brother Bishop . . . is, day by day, working loss of faith among the simple ones of the Catholic Church, and, among those of a less humble spirit is *bringing the authority of the Episcopate in this country into contempt!*[3]

James Frederic Wood had no doubts. Wood, who had become an Archbishop in February 1875, continued flatly opposed to the Molly Maguires. His famous pastoral in January 1864 had roundly condemned "the 'Molly Maguires,' the 'Buckshots' and others" (the "others" being the Fenians, the "National Brotherhood," the Masons, and the Odd Fellows). Not a formal excommunication, it was nevertheless a severe warning on the dangers of secret societies.

Wiggans Patch apparently moved Wood to renewed action. On December 15, 1875, he reissued the pastoral intact, significantly adding after "Molly Maguires" the additional words "otherwise the Ancient Order of Hibernians." The following Sunday it was read in most of the parish churches in Schuylkill County. This time there was no doubt about its being an excommunication.

The *New York Times* gave it full coverage, reporting Wood's message verbatim and then lengthily recounting the supporting remarks of one of the parish priests that Sunday—the Reverend Daniel O'Connor of Mahanoy Plane. O'Connor, who has already entered our story in a small way, will soon play a major role. Therefore, his words have added meaning: "A great portion of the trouble is caused by weak men and weaker priests." "Beware of the Molly Maguires. If you have a brother among them, pray for his repentance but have nothing further to do with him—and remember that he is cut off from the Church."[4] McParlan reported on December 26 that the O'Connor sermon had been reprinted in the *Shenandoah Herald* the previous day, and that there was general feeling among the Mollies that O'Connor had been paid off for it. The priest's words were harsh. Would he back them up under stress?

❖   ❖   ❖   ❖   ❖

If any authority carried more impact than the Church, it was the law. And here it was that the first real sense of doom began to creep over the Mollies. For it was the first Jones murder trial that opened the floodgates of the retribution which was soon to engulf so many people.

Separate trials had been demanded for each of the three accused murderers, and the case of Michael J. Doyle of Mt. Laffee had been chosen by the Commonwealth attorneys as the first. It was an astute move—Doyle was much less appealing in appearance and actions than Kelly, a young and innocent-appearing lad. The *Philadelphia Times* attributed to Doyle "a dogged and defiant expression . . .

more like a prize fighter or Fourth Ward rough." "The villain," echoed the *Miners' Journal*. Kerrigan might have made an equally good villain—"shrewd, cunning eyes, small stature and the uneasy, fidgety motion of his body," commented the *Miners' Journal*.[5] But the fact that he wasn't tried, that he sat as a spectator through the Doyle trial, knowing he was next, led to one of the greatest breaks for the Commonwealth.

The courtroom in Mauch Chunk was so jammed on January 18, 1876, that "danger was apprehended by some that all would go down into the shoemaker's shop under the court room, but luckily the beams held up." There was intense interest all over the southern fields; all local newspapers were fully represented with their fastest writers attempting to record every word of testimony. The *Philadelphia Times* reporter was apparently the only press outsider, and promptly antagonized the fiercely provincial locals by commenting on "the usual variety of shabby-looking rustics, dilapidated village loafers, and women with gaudy red shawls and crying babies." A *New York Evening Post* writer, from the safety of Manhattan Island, commented the next day on the "intrepidity" of the authorities in even bringing the accused men to trial "in the face of the possibility that a band of their comrades three or four thousand strong may, on any day, march into town, attack the Court House, release the criminals, and shoot down all opponents." The *Philadelphia Times* reporter promptly returned to Philadelphia, "scared home," according to Tom Foster of the *Shenandoah Herald*.[6]

Each side in the trial had amassed the best legal talent obtainable. District Attorney E. R. Siewers was aided by General Charles Albright for the Lehigh & Wilkes-Barre Coal Company (the murdered Jones had been their foreman), F. W. Hughes for Gowen's Reading Railroad, and Allen Craig for the Lehigh Valley Railroad. The defense was equally well represented; the local Mauch Chunk lawyers Daniel Kalbfus and Edward Mulhearn were aided by three popular and respected Pottsville attorneys, Len Bartholomew, Congressman J. B. Reilly, and John W. Ryon.

Three full days were taken up with the legal stratagems of both sides before the twelve jurors were selected. To the dismay of the defense, there were no Irish jurors; but a few "Pennsylvania Dutch" (Germans) who hardly understood English, gave a faint ray of hope. Even this was soon dimmed, however, for a parade of 122 prosecution witnesses soon built up solid evidence that Doyle had been in Lansford that day, had been observed walking rapidly toward the spot where Jones was shot, and, further, seen moments after the shooting running away with a pistol in his hand. Though no one testified he had actually seen Doyle shoot Jones, the circumstantial evidence was overwhelming.

The prosecution was on thin ice on only one point—a motive for the killing. McParlan's earlier reports to Gowen had clearly shown this motive:

> Kerrigan had been beaten up by policeman Yost;
> Hugh McGehan had been blacklisted by foreman Jones;
> Kerrigan, as Tamaqua bodymaster, agreed to "trade jobs" with James Roarity, Coaldale bodymaster;
> McGehan and James Boyle (with Roarity's and Kerrigan's help) murdered Yost;
> Doyle and Kelly (with Kerrigan's help) murdered Jones.

All this knowledge, though, stemmed directly from McParlan. McParlan was still "McKenna," was still in the fields, was still accepted as a loyal AOH confidant. How much Gowen actually told the prosecution about McParlan we do not know. But public disclosure of McParlan's role at this time would manifestly have been premature.

Nor was it needed. The prosecution introduced a bit of enigmatic evidence that Doyle's pockets had yielded not only an AOH button but also part of a letter from Jeremiah Kane, the AOH bodymaster at Mt. Laffee, to James Carroll of Tamaqua that seemed to imply certain instructions from Kane to Carroll about Doyle when the latter visited Carroll's vicinity. Nothing further was elicited in regard to this, but when the prosecution rested its case on January 31, few people had much doubt about the guilt of Doyle.

Many people, though, feared that even after such a strong case, the defense would wiggle the prisoner out from under by equally decisive, perjured testimony. Doyle's argument was anticipated with morbid fascination. The defense never materialized. The Doyle attorneys dumfounded the assemblage by announcing that they would call no witnesses. The case proceeded immediately to final summations. The prosecution repeated its multi-witness circumstantial web. Bartholomew opened the defense summation by agreeing that the murder itself was terrible, but pointing out that he was defending the man, not the crime. He agreed that Doyle was in Lansford that day, but only to hunt for work, and defended the AOH as "having for its object nothing that is bad except in the diseased eyes of the learned counsel for the Commonwealth." Kalbfus echoed the pleas.

But it was in vain. The jury returned on February 1, prepared with their decision. At this precise moment three dogs began fighting in the courtroom, adding a macabre touch to the verdict: "Guilty."[7]

A "brave verdict," said the *Miners' Journal*. The jurors had "nerve," for they were now "marked men." The ends of justice had finally prevailed. The first murder conviction in the history of either Carbon or Schuylkill County involving a Molly Maguire had been consummated. On February 23 he was sentenced to be hanged.

✣   ✣   ✣   ✣   ✣

But something else had happened during the trial—of even greater moment. And in February, just as the peak of the post-trial emotional excitement began to subside, this was made public. Jimmy Kerrigan had turned informer.

With each additional day's testimony in the Doyle trial, Kerrigan must have felt the hangman's noose tightening around his neck. During the trial Kerrigan and Kelly were left back at the jail in solitary confinement (they had been caught talking to each other through a drain pipe and had been moved to the solitary cells). The silence apparently broke Kerrigan's bold front. Sometime around January 28 he called to his cell a Coal & Iron policeman with the apt name Captain Peeler ("Peeler" was the old Irish tenants' derisive appellation for the constabulary) and poured out a confession to the astounded officer. Peeler immediately called in General Albright, F. W. Hughes, and a stenographer, and Kerrigan repeated the confession. He detailed the "trading" plans for the two killings, and fully implicated all the participants in both (being careful to shift his own role from an active to a passive one). Kerrigan's story was this:

Thomas Duffy, who had been beaten up with Kerrigan by Yost and Barney McCarron, was the one who instigated the trade.

James Roarity was contacted by Duffy (not by Kerrigan), had supplied one of the guns, and planned the policeman's death.

Hugh McGehan and James Boyle had been persuaded by Duffy (not Kerrigan) to do the job—and had done it.

Alexander Campbell, treasurer of the Storm Hill AOH, knew of the plans for both killings and had plotted the Jones killing with Kelly and Doyle the night before the murder.[8]

Of course, the authorities already knew some of the main facts through McParlan's reports—knew even that Kerrigan was now warping the account to put himself in a better light. But this was the break that was needed, a potential first-hand witness. As valuable as McParlan's reports had been, they had yet to produce usable legal evidence. In any case, Allan Pinkerton claimed that he had exacted a promise from Gowen right at the start that his detective would never have to be identified, would never be asked to testify in court. Now at least the Jones and Yost cases could be brought to trial with confidence.

And so apparently a bargain was struck. Kerrigan was promised immunity in exchange for a full and public confession followed by testimony in court. Kerrigan had taken the way that so many Irish back in Ireland had previously chosen. He had informed.

It was now imperative that Carroll, Duffy, Roarity, McGehan, Boyle, and Campbell be apprehended forthwith. Benjamin Franklin was notified in Philadelphia and came to Tamaqua on February 2 to meet Captain Robert Linden. Together with two other officers, Linden and Franklin rode over to Lansford to aid the authorities in setting up a posse (Linden's expense account notes "4 excursion tickets"). On February 4, the posse swooped down on the six suspects in their respective towns and they were quickly taken away to the Pottsville jail, leaving behind them an astounded populace.[9]

Rumors flew all over the region. The basis for the arrests was not yet known; the details concerning the confession were not made public until the habeas corpus proceedings for the arrested men on February 12. But the newspapers indulged in a bath of sensationalism. There was an informer . . . it might be Kelly, Doyle or Kerrigan . . . the authorities knew all . . . the Mollies were found out. Moreover, the papers implied that there were other sources for the authorities' moves. The *Miners' Journal* editor hit closer to the truth than he may have imagined: "Facts which were long ago in the hands of the authorities, and known to many others, although in such a shape that no use could be made of them, are now brought to life."[10] Just how many people were privy to McParlan's role is not clear. Probably the prosecutors in the Doyle case knew; the law enforcement officers may have, too. The newspapers probably did not. But the events were so startling and sensational that the press was hardly able to contain itself. McParlan was still "McKenna," but he must have been an increasingly uneasy Molly.

A few days later, before even the February 12 habeas corpus proceedings had identified Kerrigan as the informer, another series of arrests gave a new dimension to the situation. All during the Doyle trial there had been two types of rumors—almost diametrically opposite. First, it was whispered that the Mollies, arrogant and strong, were planning to storm the Mauch Chunk jail and rescue the prisoners. But, as the trial proceeded, other rumors were heard that the Mollies were for the first time afraid, were turning on their heels and escaping out of the county and the state (even the country). After the arrests of the five implicated by Kerrigan, these rumors mushroomed. The *Shenandoah Herald* of February 7 dignified them in print: "Even at this early date, rumors of a general exodus of the scum fill the air."

Gowen and company had already arrested all the participants in the Yost and Jones murders. But there were other murders. One killing had aroused particularly bitter feelings among the citizens of the Schuylkill fields—the shooting of the mine boss, Thomas Sanger, and his associate, William Uren, at Raven Run. McParlan had pinpointed the killers—he had met the five men and had heard their confessions shortly after they returned from the crime. We already know that these men were: James ("Friday") O'Donnell, Charles O'Donnell, Michael Doyle (of Shenandoah), Thomas Munley, and James McAllister. The first four names appeared on the "strictly confidential"document that had been surreptitiously circulated in the fall of 1875; Charles McAllister had been mistakenly named on the handbill as the fifth participant, instead of James. The handbill had directly accused the five it named as the killers of Sanger and Uren. We have seen that one of the five, Charles O'Donnell, was already dead, killed by an organized party at Wiggans Patch in December 1875, and that Charles McAllister's wife, Ellen, also died on that bloody night.

The authorities feared that the other four might slip through their fingers. Again a posse was formed, and on February 10 Thomas Munley was arrested in Gilberton and Charles McAllister (the

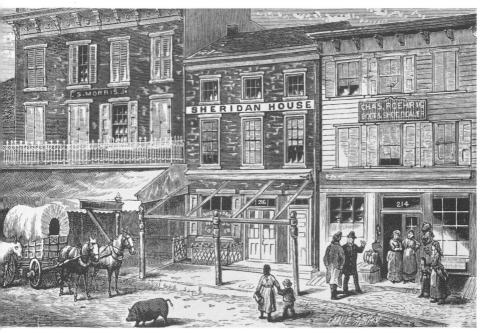

idan House, Pottsville, the tavern of Pat Dormer, a Molly Maguire leader.

st's conception of fight between "McKenna" (Pinkerton detective James McParlan)
a cheater at cards at the Sheridan House in 1873. McParlan is man with bare arms.
se and the following drawings are taken from Allan Pinkerton's book, *The Mollie
uires and the Detectives*, published in 1877.

McParlan (on knees) initiated as a Molly in "Muff" Lawler's bedroom, 1874.

Exterior of "Muff" Lawler's barroom and residence in the town of Shenandoah.

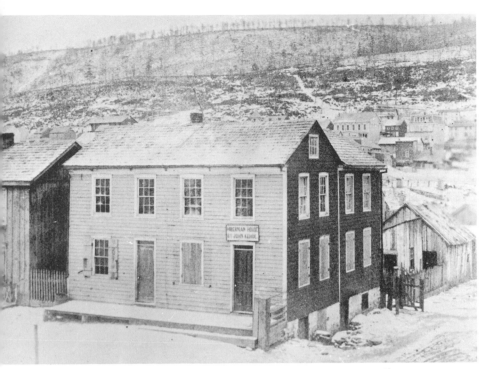

ernian House, Girardville, headquarters of John Kehoe, "King of the Mollies."

alt!" shouts Pinkerton detective Robert J. Linden, in charge of Coal & Iron Police,
ning back rioters at West Shenandoah Colliery, June 3, 1875. In center foreground
Parlan (waving stick) is pictured with his bulldog.

Attack on "Bully Bill" Thomas in stable at Shoemaker's Patch, June 28, 1875.

Murder of Gomer James at picnic in grove near Shenandoah, August 14, 1875.

rder of Thomas Sanger and William Uren at Raven Run, September 1, 1875.

rder of mine superintendent John P. Jones at Lansford, September 3, 1875.

James McParlan, now suspected by the Molly Maguires, is shown en route from She doah to Girardville in sleigh driven by Frank McAndrew in 1876. One of the men in rear sleigh is under orders to kill the detective at the first good opportunity.

Here the artist reconstructs the "Bully Bill" Thomas conspiracy trial at Pottsvill August 1876. John Kehoe and eight others were convicted of plotting and carrying 1875 attack on Thomas. Man in witness chair is presumably McParlan. RIGHT: 1879 Pinkerton list of "wanted" Mollies.

LIST OF FUGITIVE MOLLIE MAGUIRES,
1879.

WILLIAM LOVE.—Murderer of Thos. Gwyther, at Girardville, Pa., August 14th, 1875. Is a miner and boatman; 26 years old; 5 ft. 9 in. high; medium build; weighs about 150 lbs.; light complexion; grey eyes; yellow hair; light mustache; has a scar from burn on left side of neck under chin, and coal marks on hands; thin and sharp features; generally dresses well. Lived at Girardville, Schuylkill Co., Pa.

THOMAS HURLEY.—Murderer of Gomer Jamas, August 14th, 1875. Is a miner; 25 years old; 5 ft. 8 in. high; well built; weighs about 160 lbs.; sandy complexion and hair; small piercing eyes; smooth face; sharp features; large hands and feet; wears black hat and dark clothes; lived at Shenandoah, Schuylkill Co., Pa.

MICHAEL DOYLE.—Murderer of Thomas Sanger and Wm. Uren, September 1st, 1875. Is a miner; 25 years old; 5 ft. 5 in. high; medium built; dark complexion; black hair and eyes; full round face and head; smooth face and boyish looking generally; wears a cap. Lived at Shenandoah.

JAMES, ALIAS FRIDAY O'DONNELL.—Murderer of Sanger and Uren, is 26 years old; 5 ft. 10½ in. high; slim built; fair complexion; smooth face; dark eyes; brown hair; generally wears a cap; dresses well; is a miner and lived at Wiggan's Patch, Pa.

JAMES McALLISTER.—Murderer of Sanger and Uren, is 27 years old; 5 ft. 8 in. high; stout built; florid complexion; full broad face, somewhat freckled; light hair and moustache; wears a cap and dark clothes, lived at Wiggan's Patch, Pa.

JOHN, ALIAS HUMPTY FLYNN.—Murderer of Thomas Devine, October 11th, 1875, and Geo. K. Smith, at Audenreid, November 5th, 1863. Is 53 years old; 5 ft. 7 or 8 in high; heavy built; sandy hair and complexion; smooth face; large nose; round shouldered and almost humpbacked. Is a miner and lived at New Philadelphia, Schuylkill Co., Pa.

JERRY KANE.—Charged with conspiracy to murder. Is 38 years old; 5 ft. 7 in. high; dark complexion; short brown hair; sharp features; sunken eyes; roman nose; coal marks on face and hands; wears black slouch hat; has coarse gruff voice. Is a miner and lived at Mount Laffee, Pa.

FRANK KEENAN.—Charged with conspiracy to murder. Is 31 years old; 5 ft. 7 in. high; dark complexion; black hair, inclined to curl and parted in the middle; sharp features; slender but compactly built; wears a cap and dark clothes. Is a miner and lived at Forrestville, Pa.

WILLIAM GAVIN.—Charged with conspiracy to murder. Is 42 year old; 5 ft. 8 in. high; sandy hair and complexion; stout built; red chin whiskers; face badly pockmarked; has but one eye; large nose; formerly lived at Big Mine Run, Pa. Is a miner. Wears a cap and dark clothes.

JOHN REAGAN.—Murderer of Patrick Burns at Tuscarora, April 15th, 1870. About 5 ft. 10 or 11 in. high; 40 years old; small goatee; stoop shouldered; dark hair, cut short; coal marks on hands and face; has a swinging walk; wears shirt collar open at the neck.

THOMAS O'NEILL.—Murderer of Patrick Burns, at Tuscarora, April 15th, 1870. About 5 ft. 9 in. high; 35 years old; light hair; very florid complexion; red moustache and think red goatee; stoop shouldered; walks with a kind of a jerk; think has some shot marks on back of neck and wounded in right thigh.

PATRICK B. GALLAGHER, ALIAS PUG NOSE PAT.—Murderer of George K. Smith, at Audenreid, November 5th, 1863. About 5 ft. 8 in. high; medium built; dark complexion and hair; latter inclined to curl; turned up nose; thick lips; wears a frown on his countenance; large coal cut across the temple; from 32 to 35 years old; has been shot in the thigh.

Information may be sent to me at either of the above offices,

ALLAN PINKERTON.

FRANKLIN B. GOWEN
President of Reading Railroad

ALLAN PINKERTON
Head of the Pinkerton Agency

JAMES McPARLAN
Perhaps later than 1870's

JAMES KERRIGAN
One of the informers

wrong man for the Sanger-Uren killing) was arrested in Wiggans Patch. But "Friday" O'Donnell and Mike Doyle could not be found.

The newspapers chortled in headline glee—"More Mollies Scooped In," "More Mollies Gobbled."[11] But McParlan wasn't chortling. For Jimmy Kerrigan knew nothing of the Sanger-Uren killing. Kerrigan was the "informer" that the newspapers had been talking about; this now became known at the habeas corpus hearing on February 12 for the accused Jones-Yost murderers. But Kerrigan could not have informed for the Sanger-Uren killing. Would the Hibernians learn of the basis for the arrests at the habeas corpus proceedings for Munley and McAllister?

The newspapers had already been taken to task by the authorities for their irresponsible statements after the February 12 hearing. The judge had said that newspapermen could attend but that no written record or publication of findings could be made. Both the *Herald* and the *Miners' Journal* broke both rules. When the new habeas corpus case came up on February 23 in Pottsville, the judge abruptly called for a closed hearing, to the great disappointment of the immense crowd that had gathered. The *Miners' Journal* reported the next day that the judge "had reason to know that the ends of public justice had been defeated by the publication of the testimony at the previous hearing," and that "not even names should be published." The editor piously added that he had not received any "smuggled information." But the *Shenandoah Herald* editor clearly showed his pique for not being allowed to attend. The defense lawyers objected vociferously that not enough information was on the record to justify holding McAllister and Munley, but they were denied bail and remained behind bars in Pottsville.

The authorities' efforts in the habeas corpus proceedings to hide McParlan's role—efforts that apparently bordered on actually denying Munley and McAllister due process—were all in vain. Events now were convincing McParlan beyond doubt that if "McKenna" stayed in the coal fields very much longer, his life would be short.

One event involved Mary Ann Higgins. The detective's romance with the Irish girl had continued to burn brightly in spite of the encircling clouds of Molly activity. On February 16, McParlan had visited Mary Ann's home, thoughtfully bringing along a pint of whiskey for her father. Mary Ann's sister, Jimmy Kerrigan's wife, was also there. If the detective had meant to bring with him any condolences about Kerrigan's fate, he was quickly disabused of any such thoughts. For he found the Higgins family plotting an involved fabrication of alibis that had as its aim the pinning of the Jones and Yost killings on Kerrigan himself! Mary Ann's father, George Higgins, admitted to McParlan that he never had liked his son-in-law, had, in fact, never been in Kerrigan's home. When McParlan remarked that it would do no harm for Mrs. Kerrigan to visit the diminutive bodymaster in jail, both Mary Ann and Mrs. Kerrigan indignantly said they'd never go to see "the little rat." According to McParlan, Mrs. Kerrigan added, in a final bit of emphasis, that "she never wanted to see him either dead or alive." Irish hatred of "the informer" had even split a family.

Mrs. Kerrigan proposed to swear that her husband had come home on the night of the Yost murder, had admitted killing Yost, and had said that "if she ever spoke of it he would blow her brains out." Further, she was to say that Kerrigan had obtained the murder pistol from a man named Charles Mulhearn, not from Roarity, and Mulhearn would swear that he had sold it to Kerrigan many months before. "At this point," McParlan reported, "Miss Higgins observed that it would be very well to make things sure, and get a few cartridges belonging to Roarity's revolver, and bring them to court on the pretense that they were found in Kerrigan's drawer, and she was positive that they would correspond with the one found in Yost's body."

It was unsettling for McParlan to have to report to Franklin of the participation of Mary Ann in a plot which was designed not only to hang Jimmy but to enable some of his accomplices to go free. Duty came before love, though, and the details were sent on to Philadelphia.[12]

Even more disturbing, though, was a chance piece of information that the detective picked up during this romance-shattering evening. Mary Ann confided to him that after the arrest of the alleged Raven Run murderers, some people were saying that he—James McKenna —was the traitor that had informed. This was startling news. Both McParlan and the Mollies knew Kerrigan could not have informed about the Raven Run affair. And the detective was dismayed to find that the Mollies were putting other clues together.

The vindictiveness of Mrs. Kerrigan and Mary Ann Higgins paled in comparison to what McParlan soon learned was actually milling around in the Mollies' heads. The arrest of Munley and McAllister had led not only to general consternation but to a frenzied vengeance to pin the "black spot" on the unknown informer. And, McParlan learned, he really was the prime suspect.

❖   ❖   ❖   ❖   ❖

The events in these next crowded days of James McParlan's life rank in suspense with the best all-time detective exploits. McParlan's bravery—and sheer bravado—can hardly be denied, even though we can only incompletely document the evidence. In the absence of corroborative information, our clearest version comes from McParlan himself as he testified on August 10, 1876, in one of the trials. The detective may well have doctored certain facts for public consumption. Nevertheless, we have followed the detective through his two and a half years of adventures via his written reports, and it seems fair to let him tell in his own words what happened in these critical days in February 1876:[13]

"After the arrest of Thomas Munley and McAllister, there was a habeas corpus hearing here in this court. That was last February, I suppose; I am not positive as to the date exactly, without I refer to my reports. [Note: It was February 23.] I being in Pottsville for a couple or three days, probably nigh a week previous to that, I came up to the court-house upon the morning of the habeas corpus hearing. I met Frank McAndrew, and he informed me then that they were making bets . . . that I was a detective, and that I would go on the stand at the habeas corpus hearing. I told him it was not the fact; and I went and seen some parties that was there. I seen Danny Hughes and a few more; and Hughes said he knew it was not a fact, but that upon that morning that John Kehoe did not come himself, but he sent his wife down, and sent her into the saloon to tell Dan Hughes to tell everyone to beware of me; that I was a detective; that such was the report, and that he, John Kehoe, had it from responsible sources . . . the following day I went to Girardville and saw John Kehoe, and I asked him as to what about those reports? 'Well,' he said, 'I have heard it, and I heard it some time ago.' 'Well,' said I, 'what I want now is somebody to prove it. I am willing to let the society try me. I will stand a trial; and if I find out,' says I, 'a man that is lying about me, I will make him suffer, no doubt, to say that I am a detective.' Kehoe informed me that he had learned this from a conductor upon the Reading Railroad; that he was coming from Ashland . . . ; that this conductor had asked him into the baggage car to ask him if he had seen me or not; he made some reply, I forget what Kehoe said . . . Kehoe agreed that we should have a county convention to have me tried. I told Kehoe to name the time and the date and the place where this convention should be held, and he did. I guess it was somewhere about the 1st or 2d of March, that the convention was to be held in Shenandoah, in Ferguson's Hall. He then got me some paper and pen and ink, and he stated that he was too nervous to write himself, and he just wanted me to write, and sign his name, to each of the division masters in the county. He said he was a little nervous. I went upstairs in a room in the second floor, and I sat down and I wrote to every division master in the county. I knew all their addresses myself already where they lived. He came up, and I showed him the form of the letters, and handed them to him to read. He said they were all right, and I sealed them. The envelopes were stamped envelopes, and he took them with him to mail.

"I believe I stopped that night in Kehoe's, and the following day I came back to Pottsville. I reported all this. There was a number more told me. Patrick Butler, the body master of Lost Creek, he told me; he heard I was a detective, and that some men told him they must take action upon me. I said, 'I have the advantage of them; I will take action upon myself; I will have a meeting, and have a fair trial.' Upon I think the 26th day of February it was upon Saturday, John Kehoe came down to Pottsville, and he was in company with Manus O'Donnell, his brother-in-law . . . He said he was going to see Mr. Ryon, in order to have Mr. John W. Ryon retained for the defense of McAllister. In the afternoon I met him again, and I asked him what news. He told me it was going to cost him two hundred dollars, 'and,' said he, 'I got a good deal of news. The news is,' said he, 'that there is about two thousand five hundred men banded together in the county for the purpose of prosecuting the Ancient Order of Hibernians, and that there is positive proof that there is detectives amongst them, and that these detectives even gets money to go around and spend amongst them and find out all their secrets, and then turn around and either send them to the penitentiary or hang them.' Said I, 'There has been something in my mind for some time that there is something crooked going on, and that is the reason I am doubly cautious; but from whom have you received this information now?' 'From Mr. John W. Ryon,' said he; 'that is the man; he is after telling me in his office.'

"Upon the day previous to my trial, Kehoe was in Pottsville. I saw him in Dan Hughes's. I had a cigar with him. He asked me if I was going upon that evening to Shenandoah. I said 'Yes; I will be on hand for the trial to-morrow.' I engaged to meet him in the afternoon . . . I then met a man named Mullen, of somewhere near Tuscarora. Mullen told me what he had heard of me being a detective, and he considered that it would not be right to hold a meeting in Shenandoah. Some of them concluded I wanted to get all the officers and body masters assembled in Ferguson's Hall, and then have the whole crowd arrested by the Coal and Iron Police. I said to Mullen that was not possible; it was not legal, and it was not right to do such a thing as that, and, for fear there might be a suspicion, I told Mr. Linden he must not have a Coal and Iron Police there at all. I said, 'I believe I can fight them right through, and make them believe I am no detective.' The Captain was not very well satisfied, and believed I ran a very great risk, but I went. I got up to Shenandoah on the late train, and previous to getting to Shenandoah, I was in the smoking car. Manus O'Donnell came in, and informed me that Mrs. Kehoe was in the ladies' car, and wanted to see me . . . I asked her where was Mr. Kehoe; wasn't he along? She stated she thought he went up to Frackville on the afternoon train . . . She had been to see her mother, and I understood her to say she had been to Tamaqua. I suspicioned something was not right then, from Jack Kehoe telling me to be sure to be up that night, telling me he would be there and to be sure to be there.

"I was getting a little nervous. It was well known to McAndrew that I was bound to be up that night. I even wrote up to them, and always whenever I would be away there used to be five or six of them at the depot, and I would get all the news, and we would have a drink. That night when I got to Shenandoah none of them were there. I thought it was very strange. I had myself pretty well prepared: I was pretty well armed. I went along the street and met some citizens, but none of my old acquaintances that belonged to the organization. I came as far as James McHugh's saloon, and who belonged to the society, and spoke to him as I was passing by. He asked me in, and I went in. He says will you have anything to drink. I told him I did not mind having a bottle of porter. He got the bottle, and hardly could get the stopper out of it. I noticed that he was very pale. I asked him had he the ague, or was he out on a spree, or had he been sick. He said no, he was cold standing around. I asked him if he heard the report about me. He said he had, but he did not believe it, and he would be around the following day and see how things were going.

"Passing the Lehigh depot I met Mike McDermott; he was a member, and had been rather friendly with me always, but he hardly spoke. He passed by very quick; and just across the street from me I saw Edward Sweeney, another member, who was standing up against a lamp-post. I spoke to him; I hallooed across the street, and I said, 'Is that you, Sweeney?' He said, 'Yes,' and he came over. I said, 'Have you seen McAndrew?' He said, 'Yes.' I said, 'How long since?' He said, 'About an hour.' I said, 'Has he gone to bed?' He said that he thought not. We kept on down the street. I was very suspicious of Sweeney, and I got him to walk in front of me. I said my eyes were bad, and I could not see; that the pavements had holes in them, or something. I got him ahead of me, and I made up my mind to keep him there.

"When I got to McAndrew's there was a party posted inside and outside . . . I went in, and Sweeney came in and went out again. He said he was going to return home, but he returned after a little while with a little piece of snow, and throwed it over and struck McAndrew with it. McAndrew looked at me and said, 'My feet are sore; I guess I will take off my boots,' and Sweeney turned and walked out. From the rumors that were around, I was suspicious, of course, of everybody, and that seemed to be another clue that something was up, at least it appeared so to me.

"I then asked McAndrew about the meeting. He said he had a hall rented, and that it was all right. I bid him good night and when I got outside, instead of taking the usual road, I got in the swamp and crossed over and came out in front of my boarding-house. I went in, but I did not sleep much that night. The next morning I came over and seen McAndrew, and went up town and met Ned Monaghan, and a fellow named Carlin, the body master at St. Nicholas, and Florence Mahoney, the body master at Turkey Run, was there.

Nobody else seemed to come, but a little after 10 o'clock there came in a couple of drunken men from Mt. Laffee; one was a little drunk, and the other feigned a little drunk."

At this point a member of the prosecution asks McParlan "Who were they?" and the detective replies, "Dennis Dowling and James Doyle or Mike Doyle; I believe Mike Doyle was his first name." (If so, this must have been Mike Doyle No. 3, for one Michael Doyle was in jail and another was a fugitive.) McParlan continues, "I asked them if they had just arrived, and they said they had . . . "

PROSECUTION ATTORNEY: "Were they members of the Order?"

McPARLAN: "Yes; from Mt. Laffee. They said they had just come from the cars, and their appearance indicated they had not slept the night before. The fact was that there were no cars coming into Shenandoah at that time, and they had just come in, they said, right off the cars. Dowling turned and took me one side and asked me what was the matter. I said, 'Didn't you hear; don't you know what you are called here for?' He said no, and I told him, and he said they wouldn't believe that. I called for the drinks, and sent for Mc-Andrew, and took him in a rear room. Doyle kept getting drunker, and somebody took him away and put him to bed, or some place.

"I did not see Kehoe; he did not appear, and so I made up my mind that I would go and see him to see what was the matter and why there was no meeting. I went out with McAndrew and engaged a horse and cutter of Martin Delaney. Dowling and Ned Monaghan got another horse and cutter, McAndrew speaking for it, and they got in. I asked McAndrew how this thing was. He said, 'Look here; you had better look out, for that man who is riding in that sleigh behind you calculates to take your life.' He told me that Dennis Dowling was the man with Monaghan. He said, 'Have you got your pistols?' I said 'Yes.' He said 'So have I, and I will lose my life for you. I do not know whether you are a detective or not, but I do not know anything against you. I always knew you were doing right, and I will stand by you. Why don't they try you fair?' I made up my mind that I would keep my eye upon Dowling, and I did as well as I could. We stopped at Danny Munley's and took a drink, and after we came out McAndrew informed me positively that he had saved my life. He told me that John Kehoe had came to Shenandoah upon the afternoon previous, and that he . . . had spent a good deal of money amongst them, and that he told him, Mc-

Andrew, for God's sake to have me killed that night or I would hang half the people in Schuylkill County; and McAndrew said that he consented, and Kehoe and the men were satisfied, and they assembled just a little below the depot, twelve or fourteen of them . . .

Some of them had axes and some tomahawks, and some of them had the sledges which they used in the mines. They did not feel very much like shooting me. There was too many policemen around, and they did not want to make a noise, but I was to be inveigled down there and assassinated.

"He said, 'That is a fact; you will find out that you are in a queer company this minute.' I said, 'I do not give a cent; I am going down to Kehoe's,' and I did, and I reckon when I went there, there was no man more surprised than Kehoe. His plans had not worked worth a cent. I was still a live man, right in his presence, along with the man who was to have assassinated me. I asked him about the meeting, and he said that he had come to the conclusion that there was no use trying me, and I thought so too; that he had come to that conclusion from information he had received a little while previous, as there would be no use gathering a crowd there. I said, 'You had taken a great deal of trouble.' He said, 'You can go to Father O'Connor, and see him about it; you will find it all out.' He says, 'That is all I have to say.' I said, 'I will go to Father O'Connor, but I do not give a cent for any man in this county.' I took the opportunity of blowing a little. I went to Father O'Connor's, but I could see the movements while in Kehoe's; there was Philip Nash—"

A DEFENSE ATTORNEY: "Do you intend to state what you saw?"

McPARLAN: "I state what I saw in Kehoe's. Parties were there—"

PROSECUTION ATTORNEY: "Tell who were there?"

McPARLAN: "David Kelley was one, and Philip Nash was another; Thomas Donohue was there, and there was several more—a fellow by the name of Butler—and they were talking to McAndrew upon this subject. There was a good many there, and I stated that I would go to see Father O'Connor. A good many had left quite a while before we started, and then we started for Mahanoy Plane, and stopped at Collahan's, and when we got to Collahan's, Philip Nash and Tom Donohue were there. They had heard that I was going to see Father O'Connor, and they were ahead of me—but they probably might have had business about the Plane; Tom Donohue . . .

of Mahanoy Plane, he and Nash took McAndrew out and had a conversation, and after they came back they seemed quite uneasy. Nash went into Collahan's, and I went over to see Father O'Connor, but he was not home. I came back, and asked Collahan what was the matter, and he says, 'Those men there want to kill you right here; Dowling wants my revolver.' I said, 'Has he got one?' He said, 'Yes; but if I give him mine I will be unarmed myself.' However, Dowling was not a good hand at that kind of business, and he kept getting drunker, and he was so drunk that McAndrew told him he would not let him get in the sleigh, and he told Monaghan to get in the sleigh, and we drove away. I told McAndrew that if I saw Dowling make a motion toward me, I would shoot him—that I would sell my life pretty dear. But Dowling was drunk, so we left him at Collahan's, and we went to Shenandoah, and went straight to Mc-Andrew's house, and I said, 'I will go to my boarding-house.' He says: 'You will not go to your boarding-house.' I said, 'What is the matter?' And he said, 'It makes no difference; you will sleep with me.' And I did, and I was very glad of the chance, and the following morning I came down to Pottsville. Of course, I made out my report, and reported to Captain Linden. I went up, according to appointment, on that afternoon, in the noon train, to Mahanoy Plane, and I there met Dennis Dowling, and this Doyle, again in Collahan's. They were both sobered up a little then. I met McAndrew, and McAndrew told me he was going to see the thing through. He took me aside and said, 'It was a pretty lucky thing that you did not go home last night.' I said, 'Why—' "

DEFENSE ATTORNEY: "What is this for?"

PROSECUTION ATTORNEY: "We desire to have the whole narrative. First, because certain circumstances were drawn out by the cross-examination; and then we want to show it for the purpose of explaining an answer made to Mr. L'Velle's inquiry as to this society's attempts to prevent crime. [Martin L'Velle was another defense attorney.] I suppose the highest justice known to this organization is to hang a man by the neck in order to prevent him from divulging what he knows respecting the criminal deeds of one of its members."

PRESIDING JUDGE: "We will allow the evidence. The witness will proceed."

PROSECUTION ATTORNEY: "Go on and finish your narrative."

McPARLAN: "He stated that on the night previous—the night I slept with him—there came two or three men around by my boarding-house, and kept knocking about all night, but they did not manage to get the game, and they left an old carpet sack, so that they would be thought to be tramps. Of course, I had a different opinion as to their being tramps. I went to see Father O'Connor upon that occasion."

PROSECUTION ATTORNEY: "On that day?"

McPARLAN: "On that day, but, as usual, he was not at home: he had gone to Philadelphia. I returned back, and saw Dowling and the others. They were all very kind, and still talking with McAndrew. I bid them good-evening, and I took the train and came down to Pottsville that night. I did not feel like going back any more to Shenandoah. I saw Captain Linden upon that evening, and I told the Captain that I came to the conclusion that they had had a peep at my hand, and that the cards were all played. I said I would go up again, but I wanted him to keep a close shadow upon me. Captain Linden said he would, and he did so."

At this point we interrupt McParlan's testimony to report Linden's reaction to this conversation. He immediately wrote an emotional letter to the district attorney, George Kaercher, informing him of the new events. By now it seemed obvious that Father O'Connor was the source of information damaging to McParlan. Linden told Kaercher that "if the priest acknowledges himself wrong, all may yet be well. If on the contrary he proves his story correct the assassins are not only selected but have been kept at Shenandoah since last Wednesday to put him out of the way at once . . . I will be on hand to either prevent murder or arrest the parties and if I cannot save *my friend* I can easily die with him but it will cost the murderers more than one life . . . please don't blame me if someone is hurt in case shooting is begun for if *my friend* is killed Jack Kehoe can say his prayers in short mietre if I die for it."[14]

The day after the two detectives had their talk in Pottsville, McParlan finally saw Father O'Connor.

PROSECUTION ATTORNEY: "That was Saturday?"

McPARLAN: "On Saturday; but I did not see Dowling nor Doyle upon that day, I do not believe. I forget now, exactly, and I will have to refer to my reports to see whether I saw them on that day or not; I think not, but I seen Father O'Connor. I asked Collahan to go with me to Father O'Connor's, but Collahan said he did not wish to go there any more, because Father O'Connor and him had had some words in respect to a sermon which Father O'Connor had preached about the Mollie Maguires, or Ancient Order of Hibernians, and that he had abused Father O'Connor, and did not feel like going in. I told him I would go in alone.

"I went in and seen Father O'Connor. I was sitting in the hall waiting for Father O'Connor to come, and I heard footsteps and a man speaking while I was in the hall leading into another room. I heard this man speak and I knew his voice, and I heard him pull his chair alongside of the door; I supposed so from the motion. I heard Father O'Connor come in, and I told Father O'Connor I was James McKenna; that I was the man whom he had heard about, and that I was the man whom he had represented as a detective; that he had represented me as such and that it had ruined me, as I said, in the estimation of some of my fellow-citizens, and that they were greatly enraged against me, and from the fact that it was not true I would like him to deny it. He stated that he had not used my name, but that he had heard that I was a detective; and although he did not know me he thought that I was cognizant of crime long before the perpetration of it, and that I should have prevented it; that I acted as a stool pigeon—a common phrase among men—and that I knew all about crimes and took part in them instead of reporting them as a detective, and he did not think that it was right. He said that he had written a letter to Kehoe, and he had given it to a party to deliver, but the party had not delivered it but brought it back. He stated that he had told the men time and again that such would be their fate, but they would not hearken to his voice and would not leave the organization, and now they must suffer. He said I could go to Father Ryon of Mahanoy City, and Father Reilly, of Shenandoah, and they knew more about it than he did. He said that he had learned of it only a little while previous, and he said that he had went down himself to Philadelphia to find out something about me, and to find out how close I was connected with some other party who was in this region; but he did not name the party. He said, moreover, 'You were seen around Tamaqua about the time Kelly, Doyle, and Kerrigan were arrested, and you were seen in company with Kerrigan, keeping close company with him a little before Jones was shot.'

I told him I had business in Tamaqua; that I was sparking Kerrigan's sister-in-law, and, of course, I kept very close company with the brother-in-law. He laughed at that at the time, and he said he did not think there was any harm in that, that I had a right to go there. So I parted with Father O'Connor, and told him I would go and see Father Ryon and get things straightened out, and I would notify him of it, and he might inform the congregation that I was no detective. He stated that if I got things settled up in that way, he would be very happy to state so, as I had been injured in the estimation of my friends; but I had no notion of going to see Father Ryon or Father Reilly."

PROSECUTION ATTORNEY: "While you were there with Father O'Connor, did you defend or denounce the Ancient Order of Hibernians?"

McPARLAN: "I defended them in a loud tone. I stated that it was a good society; that I had belonged to it a good many years; I forget how many I said; that it was all right, and that the crimes which had been committed in the county were all attributed to the society, but that they were not guilty of these crimes, but tried to prevent crime, and all that sort of thing."

PROSECUTION ATTORNEY: "Why did you speak in this loud tone of voice?"

McPARLAN: "I was very well aware that Martin Dooley, a member of the Order, was sitting in the next room, and listening through the door, and I spoke loud enough so that he could hear."

PROSECUTION ATTORNEY: "How did you ascertain that Martin Dooley was sitting in the next room listening to your conversation?"

McPARLAN: "I heard footsteps coming along immediately after I got into Father O'Connor's, and I heard him speaking to the maid-servant, and I also heard him ask her for a chair. She gave him a chair, and I heard the chair move right over beside the door. I was standing in front of this door, but the door was closed."

PROSECUTION ATTORNEY: "You spoke in a loud tone of voice in defending this Order, so that he should have the benefit of your observations to Father O'Connor?"

McPARLAN: "Yes, sir, and that I should have the benefit of it also, to get out of there with my life."

PROSECUTION ATTORNEY: "What occurred then?"

McPARLAN: "I came out and went to Collahan's, and told Collahan that things were all right, and I said that I would go and see Father Reilly, and that I would go the following day; that I had to go to Pottsville that afternoon or evening. Tom Donohue was there, and Tom was well pleased, and said he was very glad to hear it. Then I left Collahan's and called into Dooley's. It was on my way—"

PROSECUTION ATTORNEY: "The same man?"

McPARLAN: "The same man. I saw Dooley, and he commenced to laugh. I told him how I got along, and Dooley said, 'I heard every word of it.' He said, 'I was in Father O'Connor's all the time, and it was a cute thing the way you gave your reasons for being in Tamaqua.' He said, 'You gave the society a pretty good lift.' I said, 'I know I did;' and he said, 'You were telling the truth.' Dooley seemed well satisfied that I came. I then went out of Dooley's and went to Frackville and took the train. Captain Linden shadowed me, and rode down in the same car. I left the county on the following morning."

PROSECUTION ATTORNEY: "You left the county?"

McPARLAN: "Yes, sir."

❧   ❧   ❧   ❧   ❧

Though "James McKenna" abruptly disappeared from the coal fields that day—March 7, 1876—the AOH'ers were still not sure that McKenna had been a detective. His continuing absence must have convinced many that they had found the bad seed in their ranks. Probably this is about as far as most carried their thinking. "He might have been a detective—if so, we can rest easier, he's gone for good now. Good riddance."

And James McParlan surely must have felt about the same. His tour of duty was over—he had performed the responsibilities he had been charged with; the reports were now resting in the hands of Franklin, Pinkerton and Gowen. Allan Pinkerton had apparently promised that he would never have to testify in court (a promise that Pinkerton stated he had first exacted from Gowen.) McParlan was finished with the Molly Maguire case.

But was he? Of course not.

❧   ❧   ❧   ❧   ❧

One of the intriguing elements of McParlan's story of his escape has to do with the role of the Roman Catholic Church, as demonstrated by Father O'Connor's actions. The Mahanoy Plane parish priest had been an open and bitter foe of the Mollies. One of the signers of the "Declaration of the Seven Pastors" in October 1874, he had subsequently followed Archbishop Wood in castigating the "Molly Maguires" and, finally, the AOH by name. His sermon in December 1875, commenting on Wood's excommunication pastoral, had been given wide publicity, even being reported in the *New York Times*.

But O'Connor had apparently been unaware of the other side of the equation. As much as he deprecated the AOH tactics, when he learned of the device being used by the opposition forces of Gowen he was outraged. The thought of a detective—an "informer" —operating in the fields and participating in the violence was anathema. He felt compelled, in spite of his hatred of the criminal element of the AOH, to notify Kehoe of the detective's presence. We might reasonably assume that O'Connor was unaware of just how deeply Kehoe himself was involved. Be that as it may, O'Connor's abiding concern for his wayward parishioners moved him to warn them of the desperate danger they were in.

Archbishop Wood now became involved in the story again. Wood may have known, before the general public or the AOH did, that Pinkerton detectives were operating in the coal fields under Gowen's hire. One cannot be certain when Wood first learned of Gowen's plans. Though his files contain a handwritten copy of the list of murders which Franklin sent to Gowen on November 30, 1875, this copy could have been made any time after that date.[15] But certain actions that Gowen now took will give us further clues.

The trial of Edward Kelly, the second man accused of the Jones murder, was held in late March and early April, 1876, in Mauch Chunk. Apparently the prosecution felt its case was so strong that it did not even need to use the testimony of Kerrigan. He was prepared to go on the stand as a prosecution witness, but the Commonwealth attorneys felt that his revelations would be wasted if allowed out merely for the Kelly trial. They were right. The defense efforts were desultory; Kelly was quickly convicted of murder in the first degree on the same testimony that had sealed Doyle's doom. On April 13 he was sentenced to be hanged. The populace had its second convicted Molly.[16]

But coming up now were trickier trials. One was the trial of Carroll, Boyle, McGehan, Duffy, and Roarity for the Yost killing. Another was the trial of McAllister and Munley for the Sanger-Uren murders (Campbell had asked for and received permission for a separate trial). Both were to be held in Pottsville. The Yost case was to be called first, probably some time in early May. Gowen was now spending a good part of his time directly on the trial preparations, as counsel to George Kaercher, district attorney for Schuylkill County. (Indeed, Gowen was about to take a substantial role in the trials themselves; how a busy rail president could afford such time is unclear!) And Gowen saw the prosecution facing two serious problems.

First, the latent anti-Catholic feelings in the coal regions could very well burst into the open if the O'Connor involvement in McParlan's discovery was given the wrong construction. If this happened, the case against the Mollies would degenerate into a diatribe of Catholic versus anti-Catholic, rather than a clean-cut issue of good versus evil. If the Catholic priests were thought to be sympathetic toward the Mollies, the large body of Catholic parishioners in the coal regions could easily turn against Gowen and the company. This would seriously weaken Gowen's case, even if there were convictions.

And the second problem was that there might not even be convictions, particularly in the Sanger-Uren case. Unlike the Jones murderers, the Sanger-Uren killers had not been clearly identified by the people of the vicinity. McParlan alone held the key. Otherwise the motive for the killings was unclear. Kerrigan could be of no help concerning this crime. Though McParlan had not been at Raven Run, though he had not been aware ahead of time that the killing was to be done, he had heard several first-hand confessions after the fact, and could clearly explain the motive. In sum, Gowen desperately needed McParlan's sworn testimony on the witness stand.

So Gowen put pressure on Pinkerton, and Pinkerton then put pressure on McParlan. Gowen apparently made his case in part on the basis that McParlan could clearly testify about his meeting with O'Connor and thereby put the priest and the Church in a better light. So far the public had only the rumors that O'Connor had been a vehicle for the discovery of the detective. Therefore, Gowen argued, the case would suffer, and so would the Church. McParlan was a Catholic; this appeal must have had real impact.

McParlan demurred at first. Why should he risk, at best, the bitter denunciations of his erstwhile Molly friends; at worst, assassination? As late as April 27 he still had not agreed. Charles Albright wrote George Kaercher, the district attorney, that "it looks very much as if we were not to get the testimony of the detective . . . It will be too bad if he fails us in this. I judge Mr. Linden controls this matter.[17]

Linden, supporting Gowen, finally prevailed. Gowen's arguments were too persuasive, particularly when Allan Pinkerton, McParlan's own boss, backed up the idea. McParlan reluctantly promised to appear on the witness stand.

On this basis, Gowen planned a further move—to put O'Connor himself on the stand in the Yost case, now scheduled for May 4. This would have been presumptuous without notification to Wood, and so Gowen penned a letter to the archbishop on May 14. In this letter is a further piece of evidence concerning Wood's knowledge of the case. Gowen said, "In my speech to the Jury, I will fully vindicate him [O'Connor] from any intention of association with the Molly Maguires. To do this effectively, however, and to put at rest all suspicions as to his position and that of the Church I would like to have your permission to state publicly that you have been for some time cognizant of the means I had taken to break up the association of Molly Maguires and that you earnestly desired to destroy or disperse their organization."[18]

Wood may have given his permission. At any rate, over and over during the following weeks Gowen repeated that the Church knew of the detective, knew of the plans, knew of the objectives. The rail president was a master of the art of public relations; if motivation research had been known in those days, Gowen would have been cited as an eminent practitioner of the "invisible sell."

By careful innuendo and implication Gowen subtly associated himself with Wood, so much so that for many years afterward the two were considered by many people to have acted in concert. Father O'Connor, on the occasion of a later squabble with Gowen over the Knights of Labor, wrote Gowen, "Archbishop Wood has been coupled with your name so often during the past two years that many believe ye are combined to run the P and R Co. and enslave the workingmen."[19] Gowen's plan to seat the Church at his right hand in his battle against the Mollies had succeeded famously.

But to many people in the coal regions O'Connor's actions in McParlan's discovery were unacceptable. Anti-Catholic bias lay just beneath the surface. To these people, Father O'Connor's actions repeated the age-old pattern in Ireland whereby the Catholic priest was thought to be explaining away atrocities against the English because of the deep vested interest held by the Church itself. Franklin Dewees, in his book on the Mollies published in 1877, spent several pages describing O'Connor's leak to Kehoe, using the old device of lengthily discussing the negative insinuations and then piously purporting to refute them by applying a "charitable" construction to the story.

That this fact should be urged by many as proof positive that the Roman Catholic priesthood, if not the Roman Catholic Church, are in sympathy with the "Molly Maguires" can readily be supposed. The prejudice existing against that Church in the minds of many is bitter and utterly unreasonable. There are those who through prejudice are prepared to believe any charge, however contrary to reason, against it, without any investigation, and to hold it responsible for intemperate language used by any man holding the priestly office, acting on his own responsibility, under strong provocation and influenced by the heat of passion.

This being the case, it can be a matter of no great surprise that the warning given to members of the "Molly" organization should receive the most uncharitable construction, especially as the act would seemingly bear it out. To shield criminals, to save them from punishment for brutal murder in the past, and to leave them to pursue unchecked a course of horrible crime in the future, is not in accordance with either the teachings of the Christian religion or the dictates of common humanity. Any steps tending to the relief of a terror-stricken people, who, feeling powerless, surrender unresistingly property and life itself to cold-blooded brutality, should, it would seem, receive the support of right-thinking men. That notice of the fact that James McKenna was a detective was given to members of the organization through Catholic priests has never been denied. The notice so given makes those pause and doubt who are most desirous not to believe, not even to imagine, the possibility of evil.

"Nevertheless," Dewees continued, "it is difficult to credit that any respectable portion of the Catholic priests sympathized with or countenanced in any way the Molly Maguires"—and "impossible" to believe that O'Connor would. Dewees then spent a full paragraph citing O'Connor's long history of public condemnation of the

Mollies, even complimenting him on his "handsome and commanding presence." But Dewees' summation left little doubt where he really stood:

Can it be possible that the inborn prejudice against an "informer," which seems to be part of the Irish nature, transmitted through generations, unconsciously influenced his mind contrary to his instincts, his nature, his education, and his religion? Can it be that when it was announced that a detective was in the midst of this lawless gang, contempt for the "informer" and pity for the unsuspicious criminal for the moment affected his judgment? . . . That his reasons were at the time satisfactory to his own mind is certain. His purity and honesty of purpose are unquestionable, but, in this matter, even in the exercise of the utmost charity his judgment must be regarded as at fault.[20]

The Church was not to be allowed to forget the Molly Maguire case.

❖   ❖   ❖   ❖   ❖

McParlan had been pressed to testify. Now his promise had to be kept.

What was later to be called "the first Yost case" was—in retrospect —the deciding case in the Molly Maguire trials. The case had been widely debated in the national press prior to its opening on May 4, 1876. On April 5 the *Bethlehem Times* published what purported to be Jimmy Kerrigan's actual verbatim confession. The metropolitan newspapers immediately picked up the item. On April 6 the *Philadelphia Inquirer* quoted Kerrigan as saying "the purpose of the Molly Maguires, or AOH, is to kill people and burn down buildings." The *New York Times* said on the same day that the operations of the Molly Maguires "are carried on under a charter granted by the Ancient Order of Hibernians." The next day the *Shenandoah Herald* denounced the "confession" as spurious—the *Herald* had already publicly leaked its version of Kerrigan's testimony in the February 12 habeas corpus proceeding, but had not been able to obtain the actual written version of the confession. No official testimony of Kerrigan had yet been made public, but the newspapers were now dangerously close to trying the case in the press.

Now the Hibernians as a group were drawn into the vortex. The Bethlehem Steel Company reportedly ordered all its employees who were AOH members to withdraw from the society under pain of dismissal if they refused, and one South Bethlehem priest denied the sacraments to all members of any family having an AOH member.[21] Patrick Ford's belligerent New York City paper, the *Irish World*, stoutly defended the order, even reporting that the Archbishop of San Francisco had sent its constitution to Rome, where it had been fully cleared "by the Propaganda."[22] But Gowen's plan to convict not only the individuals but the organization was already finding receptive ears.

On May 4, the day that the Yost trial opened, every space in the Pottsville courtroom was taken four hours before the court opened.[23] Crowds congregated around the front edges of the courtroom, at the back door, and outside all the way from the courthouse to the jail. The *Miners' Journal* the next day reflected the level of objectivity felt by the crowd, saying "all were anxious to see the alleged murderers and judge of their guilt by looking at their faces and figures." When the defendants, James Carroll, James Boyle, Hugh McGehan, Thomas Duffy, and James Roarity, came out of the jail the crowd pressed forward, and "wives, sisters, fathers, mothers, and brothers were permitted to grasp the flesh of their husbands, brothers, and sons and bid them be of good cheer." The prisoners were seated with their wives next to them. McGehan's young bride seemed hardly aware of what was transpiring, nor did Carroll's young son, who had climbed on his lap.

Neither side had left any details to chance. To plead the Commonwealth case before the panel of three judges, District Attorney George Kaercher called on Frank W. Hughes and General Charles Albright and added another attorney, Guy E. Farquhar. The second day of the trial President Franklin B. Gowen himself appeared for the prosecution and immediately pre-empted the spotlight. The defense was composed of Len Bartholomew, John W. Ryon, and Daniel Kalbfus, aided by another local attorney, Martin M. L'Velle.

The selection of the jury was bitterly fought over by both sides. In the Mauch Chunk trials of Doyle and Kelly, the defense had tried hard—with some success—to empanel several Pennsylvania Germans in the hope that their incomplete understanding of English would militate for an acquittal. But the general climate of the trials had clearly shifted because of the wide publicity given to the Mauch Chunk trials. Now it was the prosecution that sought German jurors.

In spite of defense efforts, Levi Stein was accepted though he admitted, "I don't understand much English." William Becker asked to be questioned "in Dutch as I am light on English . . . I would not understand the witnesses."[24] But after the prosecution asked if he was against hanging—and he answered that he was not—he, too, was accepted. Bartholomew was able to exclude one man who admitted that he was "a member of a society known as a vigilante committee." In spite of Bartholomew's efforts, though, the man would not name the organization, and the presiding judge finally ruled that it was not relevant.

The process of choosing the jury had intensely interested the immense crowd. But the following day—May 6—brought far the most stunning of all revelations to date about the Molly Maguires. George Kaercher began his opening statement with the news that James McParlan, a Pinkerton detective also known as "James McKenna," would be a prosecution witness.

The effect on the prisoners was profound. "Carroll was as if struck by lightning. He could scarcely get back the breath which seemed to be lost to him. Boyle shook like an aspen and the other prisoners became grave as judges. A thrill of excitement and astonishment went through the audience."[25] The fears that many of the Mollies had long harbored were now finally confirmed in one crushing flash of realization. Some must have thought, "This is the end."

As if this were not enough, just as Kaercher was finishing his address, a rumor flew through the courtroom that new Molly prisoners were outside, being led to jail in chains. It was true—"a wholesale band of Mollies of heavy caliber,"[26] eleven in all, had been searched out and jailed. They included Jack Kehoe, Schuylkill County delegate of the AOH; Dennis Canning, Northumberland County delegate; Chris Donnelly, Schuylkill County treasurer; Muff Lawler, McParlan's Shenandoah friend; Pat Butler, the Lost Creek bodymaster, and half a dozen other Mollies. The charges were not yet known. But the psychological impact of the arrests was overwhelming. The leaders of key lodges all through Schuylkill County and all the county officers were now behind bars. Few people that day would have been able—or willing—to distinguish between individual defendants and the AOH itself. The order, too, was on trial. "It now looks as if the very bottom itself had fallen out of 'Mollieism,' " said the *Shenandoah Herald*.

Late in the day on Saturday, May 6, 1876, James McParlan was called as a witness. The excitement was intense. McParlan had been hidden away until this moment; now he entered the side door of the courtroom, accompanied by Linden and two Pinkerton bodyguards. There was an immediate rush for the rail to see the "terror of the Mollies," dressed, according to the *Shenandoah Herald* reporter, "in the height of fashion."[27] Sworn in, McParlan seated himself easily in the witness chair for what was to be the most important four days in all of the Molly trials.

The detective handled himself well, answering the questions in a straightforward manner, without hesitation. Gowen was the chief questioner, and soon had the detective's main thread laid out for all to see. McParlan described his relation to the Yost case—that he was assigned to Tamaqua by Franklin after the killing, heard first-hand confessions from Carroll, Roarity, and Kerrigan, saw Roarity's pistol which had been borrowed by Kerrigan for use by McGehan and Boyle, had established that this was the same pistol used in the Jones killing and subsequently found in the bushes when the three Jones killers were apprehended. The detective pulled no punches in describing Kerrigan's role on the night of the killing—how Kerrigan planted the two killers and helped them escape—but did play down Kerrigan's motives, implying that it was Duffy who really wanted Yost killed. The evidence was terribly damaging to the five defendants, and it might well have been sufficient for the district attorney to obtain a conviction.

But it was not sufficient for Gowen. At the beginning of the second day of McParlan's testimony on the following Monday, the rail president's motives became obvious. District Attorney Kaercher submitted a written statement to the court that "the detective came to Schuylkill County to become familiar with the workings of a secret association known generally in this locality as 'Mollie Maguires' but the real name of which is the Ancient Order of Hibernians . . . that he became initiated as a member . . . that it was a practice for the members to aid and assist each other in the commission of crimes, and in defeating detection and punishment." In short, the prosecution wanted the AOH on trial, too.

The defense vehemently objected. But it was in vain, and merely gave Gowen a chance, when he questioned McParlan that day, to publicly denounce the AOH in Schuylkill County. Gowen magnanimously exonerated the AOH outside the coal regions, but accused the lodges in the county of being worse than the "Thugs" of India (an interesting reference which we already have heard from Allan Pinkerton in his letter concerning vigilantes in August 1875). The very courthouse was full of Mollies, Gowen continued—one of the county commissioners was not only a member, but had secreted murderers. Another member was actually jailer for the prisoners.

Gowen's accusations were a sensation. And the testimony was exciting. McParlan described how he joined the Shenandoah lodge, then launched into a description of the organization itself. The password and toast system, and the passing of the "goods" each quarter, were detailed. The limitations on membership (to Catholics), the local, county, state, and national organization were described, and the elusive international tie to the Board of Erin mentioned. But the clinching testimony came (after a last-ditch defense effort to keep it out) when McParlan described "the real purposes of the organization." The only object of the AOH in the county was to protect and avenge its members. Such a member brought his grievance to the attention of the bodymaster; if vengeance was deemed proper, the bodymaster either anonymously selected another member of the same lodge or asked another bodymaster for men. In the latter case, it was "trading jobs," on a reciprocal basis. After the job was done, there might be a reward for the successful assassin, provided the lodge (or at least its "inner circle") voted on it.

Thus the direst warnings of the alarmists that there was a giant "Molly Maguire" conspiracy were apparently confirmed by McParlan. A shudder of fear ran through the whole region, for it was not just two isolated killings but a whole master organization that they were seeing clearly for the first time. It was marvelously exciting lore for the newspapers, and the whole Molly story jumped to national prominence during these four days that McParlan was on the stand.

The defense attorneys readily perceived that if McParlan's testimony stood up, the whole fabric of defense, not only of this case but of all to follow, would be ripped apart. The detective had shown great facility on the stand, "considered by all . . . to be the sharpest witness that ever occupied the chair in this court."[28] While the revelations were startling, they were fully believable under the careful nurturing of the testimony by Gowen.

Bartholomew and Ryon probed and prodded McParlan for two days, trying to find a soft spot in his evidence. They scrutinized his past life, but could turn up nothing beyond the fact that he had held many different jobs. When asked about his various, often conflicting, stories of how "James McKenna" got his money, McParlan readily admitted, "Certainly they were all lies; I swear to that," but said these were justified in building his pose as a Molly. The detective denied having as part of his objective the searching out of labor union information. The defense efforts to imply that he personally was to profit from the investigations were defeated by McParlan's careful explanation that he was on straight salary and barred from receiving rewards of any kind.

We can add some verification for all these points on the basis of our earlier evidence through the detective's reports. McParlan was on straight salary—twelve dollars a week. His reports have very little on the union itself; obviously, he at least did not consider this his main charge. And the details of his various poses under the over-all disguise he adopted also mesh with information contained in the reports.

But all of these accusations were merely leading up to the central point of the defense—that James McParlan instigated and participated in the violence. Ryon elicited from McParlan on May 10 that he had been cognizant of three proposed shootings prior to their actual commitment.

One of these was the Jones killing. Ryon and Bartholomew went over and over the detective's movements on the days preceding the shooting. McParlan's reports have already told us that he went to Lansford with two Mollies, ostensibly to kill Jones, but that he was able to persuade them to return to Tamaqua after they got drunk. But, on finding after this that Kerrigan and two strangers had already left for Lansford for the killing, McParlan did not alert Franklin or Linden, pleading that he was shadowed by another Molly until too late to notify Jones. The defense closely questioned him on this, implying that there was enough time, after McParlan was alone, to notify Jones. But McParlan had a frank answer:

BARTHOLOMEW: Why did you not go over yourself, from Columbia House, five miles to save the life of a man you knew was going to be assassinated?

McPARLAN: My reason was that I was afraid of being assassinated myself.

BARTHOLOMEW: You would not take that risk to save the life of John P. Jones?

McPARLAN: I would not run the risk of losing my life for all the men in this Court House.

BARTHOLOMEW: You were playing the part of a detective and yet you would not take that much trouble to walk five miles?

McPARLAN: Walking the five miles was nothing; I would walk twenty, but it was the saving of my own life I was looking to.[29]

McParlan used the same frank reason to explain why he did not notify Sanger at Raven Run, though the detective did know of the threat a day before it was effected, and also why he had not notified "Bully Bill" Thomas the night before he was shot. It was an explanation that probably made personal sense to many of the spectators. Each could vicariously put himself in the place of the detective and ask himself, "Would I have been any braver than McParlan?"

Thus the defense was not able to pin any direct involvement on McParlan (though many writers in subsequent years have implied as much). McParlan frankly stated that he *did* know of upcoming violence in two cases of murder and one case of attempted murder. But whether he allowed the crimes to take place because he wanted to build a case for the Pinkerton agency, or whether he was only afraid of being found out, we will never fully know. On the basis of all the facts we now have, it seems unlikely that McParlan was an *agent provocateur*, though his pose as a leader in the Mollies pushed him perilously close at times.

The best of the efforts of the defense failed to shake McParlan's story, and when the detective stepped down from the stand on May 10, he had created, according to the *Miners' Journal* story the next day, "an ineffaceable impression on the jury."

✣   ✣   ✣   ✣   ✣

The Commonwealth might as well have rested their case right there had public opinion alone determined the trial result. But it was necessary to obtain as much legal corroboration as possible, lest McParlan's evidence be thrown out as hearsay. And here was where the other of the two key Commonwealth witnesses was to enter— Jimmy Kerrigan, the informer.

"The little sinner," as the *Miners' Journal* put it, was apparently terrified, but managed to get through his testimony on May 12 and 13 with only a few slips into profanity. He pinned the motive for the Yost killing on Thomas Duffy, and played down his own involvement. He was a victim of circumstances and threats, a pawn in the hands of James Carroll, the real power in the Tamaqua local. He had joined the organization thinking it was merely the AOH, but "found it out to be the Molly Maguires." He admitted his direct involvement in both the Yost and Jones killings, but averred that he was doing it under pressure in order to stay in the good graces of the rest of the organization. He corroborated McParlan's testimony on the events after the Yost murder, where McParlan obtained confessions from Kerrigan, Carroll, McGehan, and Roarity. Although obviously bending the facts of his own involvement, Kerrigan stuck to the prosecution story.

The defense again worked hard to shake the little Irishman's story. Ryon and Bartholomew raised some embarrassing personal questions, and at one point Kerrigan begged the judges, "Your honor, I think I ought to have some protection. They are my lawyers, and they ought not to ask me such questions."[30] (Before turning informer, Kerrigan had hired them as his lawyers.) He denied that he had ever told his wife he had killed Yost, or that he had ever threatened his wife if she were to tell. In fact, he said, she really said "It's damn good for him and I wish somebody would shoot Barney McCarron for the night he put my brother in jail." He denied that he had told Mary Ann Higgins that he had killed Yost because Yost "had pounded me on the head so often." It was true that he had helped the Yost murderers to escape—he had neglected to mention this at the habeas corpus proceedings—but it was on Carroll's direct order. Kerrigan denied that he had gotten dead drunk shortly after the Yost killing, and lain outside his house chanting over and over, "A man ought not to take away that which he could not give." He did plead being drunk on other occasions—for example, when McParlan approached him about men for the Jones killing. Kerrigan categorically denied being promised any favors for his turning state's evidence. He did admit that the district attorney and a reporter visited him, but when the defense asked, "Did not he say he would put you on Pinkerton's police force as a detective?" Kerrigan piously replied, "O No!"

Again the defense had been able to raise doubts, many in this case. Kerrigan was probably lying at several spots. Yet the key need of the defense, to shake McParlan's testimony, failed. A few more witnesses testified, one being Father O'Connor, who was allowed to testify briefly and corroborate that McParlan had visited him on Saturday, March 6. Then the prosecution closed its case.

Though the Commonwealth's spectacular evidence seemed to be so strong that nothing could overturn it, many people were still apprehensive about what the defense might be able to pull off. The *Shenandoah Herald* on May 15 called the case the "Greatest Issue Ever Tried in this or any other court in the Union" but said that it still expected "the roof of the court house sworn off this week." The pervasive fear of the perjured, false alibi—"drill swearing"—was hard to lose in the face of so many previous hung juries.

Daniel Kalbfus telegraphed the defense case in his opening address to the jury on May 13. There were really only two prosecution witnesses, he said, "a professed informer and a professional informer." McParlan "instigated these murders . . . offered rewards . . . was the prime conspirator of all . . . and his story is untrue." Kerrigan was the actual murderer of Yost; he had already confessed so to his wife. The AOH was a legitimate organization, in spite of so much bandying of the name "as to convict innocent men, without other evidence than that they were members of the organization." And the defendants were innocent.

The first defense witnesses began to build an alibi for James Boyle. One of the chief witnesses was John Mulhearn, who stated in his testimony on May 15 that he had seen Boyle in Summit Hill during the period on July 5 when both McParlan and Kerrigan had said he was in Tamaqua. Mulhearn was only partly through the testimony when the day's session was terminated.

When the trial opened again the next morning, the courtroom was thrown in an uproar when Gowen demanded that Mulhearn be arrested forthwith for perjury. Gowen's reasons stemmed from what he had learned from McParlan back in February when the detective visited Mrs. Kerrigan and Mary Ann Higgins. At that time, when Mrs. Kerrigan was planning the alibi for Boyle in order to pin the murder on her husband, she had mentioned that Charles Mulhearn would swear that he, not Boyle, had sold Kerrigan the pistol, and not a few days before but a full year before the killing. Gowen was either mistakenly—or deliberately—confusing Charles Mulhearn and

John Mulhearn. Gowen soon admitted to the court that he was mistaken in his identity, and John Mulhearn was allowed to take the stand again. But the point had been made unmistakably that a man could be tried for perjury for lying on the stand.

It seems incredible that any of the Mollies could have thought otherwise. But a great many did. Curious views of the law were held by many of the Irish in the coal fields. There was, first, the widely held view that in a murder planned and carried through by a group of people only the person who actually pulled the trigger was guilty. The concept of being an accomplice before the fact was only incompletely understood. Similarly, the notion that one could swear anything on the stand with impunity was clearly believed by a great many. Certainly there was little in the past history of ineffectual trials to disabuse them of the notion. "Drill swearing" appeared to be a highly dependable tactic.

Legally, of course, this is false. Yet one does need to prove that the perjurer did perjure. And this had always proved difficult, most often impossible, to do. The latent fear that the defendants would slip the noose by unprovable perjury so troubled Gowen that he privately made contact again with Archbishop Wood on the day the defense opened its case:

We know from our detectives who have been among the friends of the prisoners that arrangements have been made to procure quite a number of people, including many women, to swear to an *alibi* which is of course entirely false and which if sworn to in court will inevitably lead to the arrest and punishment of these poor misguided women for perjury.

It has struck me that possibly the presence in court of the parish priests known to these women as their pastors might have some restraining influence upon them . . . if you take the same view of this case that I do and see no objections to what I suggest I would be much obliged to you if you would telegraph the priest of the parish in which Lansford is situated as well as the priest of Tamaqua to go to Pottsville tomorrow and report to me there in the Court House.[31]

Wood complied, and both priests were in court the following day. But it was to no avail, for the apparent perjuring continued, and Gowen wrote Wood the next day, "I regret to say that their presence has not had the effect of restraining three or four witnesses from testifying to an alibi."

Several more minor defense witnesses testified, directly contradicting McParlan's and Kerrigan's stories. Once the defense objected to
Gowen's cross-examination, at which point the wily rail president
departed from the issue at hand and loosed a passionate diatribe that
"enough has been proved in this case, in the Court, in the last ten
days, to convict of murder in the first degree every member of that
organization in this county, for every murder that has been committed in it." He declared that "every member of that organization
is, not only in a court of conscience, but in the eyes of the law,
guilty of every murder as an accessory before the fact and liable to be
convicted and hanged by the neck until he is dead."[32] Gowen's
implications surely exceeded his legal backing; but there must have
been many an AOH member in the audience who for the first time
could see himself in his imagination dangling from the end of a
hangman's rope.

The star defense witness was to be Mrs. Kerrigan. Though the
defense was now aware that the prosecution had damning evidence
against her via McParlan's report of his February visit with her,
they gambled on putting her on the stand. She dutifully told her
story of Kerrigan owning the pistol, going out with it on the night
of the Yost killing and returning to tell her he had killed Yost, and
that he would kill her if she told. Although her story was true in some
of its details, it collapsed under Gowen's cross-examination. By in-
terspersing questions throughout the testimony he led her to imply
her motives for testifying against her husband. He first asked her if
it were true that she had said she would "see Jimmy hanged." She
denied it. But he was soon able to catch her by questioning her as to
why she did not go to see Kerrigan after he had confessed:

MRS. KERRIGAN: Because any man that done such a crime as that—
that done such a crime that he done, why should I turn around then,
and—
GOWEN: And what—go on.
MRS. KERRIGAN: That is all.[33]

Gowen skillfully elicited the fact that she had not felt this way until
after Kerrigan had confessed, and that the crime she was so against
was informing. She denied that she had called Kerrigan "the damned
dirty puppy," but was egged later into saying, "Why, because he
picked up innocent men for to suffer for his crime." She denied that

she had told McParlan anything on the day of the February visit of the detective. She finally admitted that the detective was there, but tried to pass the visit off as just another courting session with Mary Ann. Gowen asked her if she expected "he was going to be a brother-in-law of yours," but she was so demoralized at this stage of the questioning that she replied, "I do not know what I expected." Gowen needled her on why she hesitated so long in answering his questions. She pleaded heart trouble, but Gowen brought down the house with "Why is it, can you tell me, that you never get the heart disease when Mr. Ryon asks you a question?" Ryon immediately objected, and the presiding judge warned Gowen and asked the jury to "waive" the question. This type of subtle discrediting, however, took a heavy toll on the defense case. Gowen's questions, rather than Mrs. Kerrigan's answers, were looked upon as the facts. The wife's desperate efforts to hang her husband, the father of her children, collapsed under the brilliance of Gowen's courtroom technique.

At this point in the case, on Thursday, May 18, with Mrs. Kerrigan still on the stand, an unforeseen event added a last, macabre touch to the trial. Levi Stein, the Pennsylvania Dutch juror who had pleaded at the start that he didn't understand much English, became ill. The case was suspended for the day, pending Stein's recovery. The remaining jurors were held on hand, and the whole complicated legal machinery was held in abeyance for the sick juror. Over the next few days Stein's illness worsened. His mother was sworn in as a court nurse, and the area held its collective breath. All was unavailing. On May 25 Stein's illness, now diagnosed as pneumonia, reached a crisis and he died.

All of the work of the case was apparently in vain. The judges dismissed the jurors and the prisoners were remanded to the jail, to be held over until the next term of the court. The Commonwealth supporters were beside themselves with frustration; Stein's death was "to the delight of the Mollies and the sorrow of all good citizens." The *Miners' Journal* interviewed the jurors after their release and "all were agreed the defense hadn't a leg to stand on." Unless there was new testimony, all would have "not the slightest hesitation in bringing in a verdict of guilty against all five."[34]

The Commonwealth advocates viewed the abrupt end of the trial before a verdict as a terrible blow. All the testimony was out the window; all would have to be repeated again in a new trial. The prosecution's hand had been tipped; now the intervening weeks would allow all sorts of devious testimony to be manufactured by the defense. Just at the brink of the breaking of the Mollies forever, justice had been thwarted.

But if we look at what happened in this "trial that wasn't a trial," this apparently preliminary joust, we need only have the benefit of hindsight to find that all these fears were groundless. Gowen's masterful manipulation during the trial had planted all the seeds necessary for all the remaining cases. McParlan's and Kerrigan's testimony had truly convicted the defendants in the court of public opinion. Though no one knew it at this moment, the watershed in the Molly Maguire saga had been reached. The "first Yost case" was to be the definitive one. The case was a national sensation. Left now were only the legal details of trying the various defendants. There still remained most of the "Great Molly Maguire Trials." But their conclusion was already ordained.

Chapter 12 • The Day of the Rope

To recite the outrages of which President Gowen's company and its employees were the victims would be to print a volume of murder, plunder, and incendiarism, which, for fiendish violence, would read like a romance.

Threatening notices made fences, trees, and houses hideous with their brutal devices . . . Scarce a day passed without its blood-curdling tragedy.

Men who were tired of idleness, and would gladly have gone back to work, dared not. To labor was to provoke the wrath of the Mollie Maguires. Next came an order to leave the region, or a bullet, which cut short the offender's life. Breakers were fired, store houses robbed, workmen butchered, guards shot, and anarchy reigned supreme.

Philadelphia Inquirer, May 20, 1876

*I*T WAS now a newspaperman's field day. The Pottsville testimony was no longer legal evidence—for Levi Stein's abrupt death had cut the case back to a fresh starting point. But not in the eyes of millions of newspaper readers. The national press, exploiting the sensational story that emanated from the coal fields, quickly projected the case into wide notoriety—and to posterity.

Gowen's initial disappointment over the suspension of the Yost case must have rapidly faded as he saw the press react. Those papers following the *Philadelphia Inquirer's* bent must have particularly satisfied the rail president. Nothing in the trial had tied the Yost murder to labor-union activity. Nor had there been any implications that any other aspect of the AOH machinations were specifically linked to the W.B.A. or any other union effort. True, Hugh McGehan had nursed his grudge against Jones, the mine foreman, because of an alleged black-listing. And black-listing was a frequent antiunion device of the anthracite coal companies in this period. In this general sense the killing had overtones of labor-management tension. But the Yost case was a matter of personal grudge. The trial dealt only indirectly with the traumatic labor-capital struggle so much on the minds of those in the coal regions. Yet here was the *Inquirer* implying that strikes were continued by Molly pressure, and that even to work at all was to provoke "the wrath of the Mollie Maguires." Lost in the circular reasoning was the fact that McGehan had wanted to work, and had apparently killed because he was not able to.

And Gowen's tightrope performance in trying to pin the label of opprobrium on the locals of the AOH without turning the trial into an anti-Catholic attack had worked as well. The AOH itself was on trial, no doubt of it. And the Catholic Church was one of the tacit plaintiffs.

✤   ✤   ✤   ✤   ✤

The scene (and McParlan and Kerrigan) now shifted back to Mauch Chunk. Doyle and Kelly, the two trigger men in the killing of John P. Jones, were already convicted. Kerrigan was off the hook because he had informed. But one other Molly, Alexander Campbell, remained to be tried before the Jones case could be tidily closed.

Campbell stood accused of being an accessory before the fact, having allegedly helped to plan the shooting in his tavern the night before the deed. The trial opened on June 20, 1876, and the jury was empaneled forthwith, although it seemed almost impossible to find twelve people who had not heard of the case.[1] Several prospective jurors admitted that they had formed an opinion. But when asked by the Commonwealth if their opinions could be changed by testimony, they answered affirmatively—and were promptly accepted.

After the trial had been in session several days, one of the jurors became ill, and rumors flew through the town that the Stein case was going to repeat itself. But before the jurors could become uneasy for fear some mysterious power was diabolically at work, the man recovered and the trial proceeded. McParlan and Kerrigan gave their testimony with telling effect. The defense came close to accusing McParlan of actual murder ("if he saved a thousand lives it would not atone for the one he took").[2] But the prosecution promptly put Pinkerton superintendent Benjamin Franklin on the stand, who corroborated that Jones had not only been warned two weeks ahead of his death, but that a local protection committee had been formed to watch over Jones.

The eleven days of the trial produced little that appeared new, and on July 1 the jury took only a short time to bring in a verdict that Campbell was guilty of murder in the first degree. On August 28 he was sentenced to be hanged.

The jury's dispatch, however, belied the importance of the case. Whereas Kelly and Doyle were just *members* of the AOH, Alexander Campbell was an officer in his lodge and also, as the Franklin Dewees book put it, "a leader among leaders and a chief among chieftains."[3] Further, Campbell was found guilty, not of a minor crime, but of murder in the first degree, even though he was clearly not at the actual murder scene on the day of the killing. Campbell was "an accessory before the fact." And, said the Court, this was just as much a case of murder as if Campbell had pulled the trigger.

The defense immediately carried the case to the Supreme Court of the state. They alleged that many errors had been made—that the jury was incorrectly chosen on a loaded basis, that the collateral material on the AOH itself was irrelevant, that Kerrigan's testimony was inherently suspect. But their key point—the only one that might have truly overturned the Commonwealth in all the Molly trials— was that McParlan, too, was an accessory before the fact. "He counsels and encourages them to commit an act of murder, intending, *in his own mind,* to frustrate their designs. Without this encouragement . . . it is safe to assume they would not have attempted the murder . . . Why is not the detective an accessory before the fact?" When Pennsylvania's highest court finally heard the case, in late March of 1877, the justices discarded the plea, holding that "a detective who joins a criminal organization for the purpose of exposing it, and bringing criminals to punishment, and honestly carries out that design, is not an accessory before the fact, although he may have encouraged and counselled parties who were about to commit crime, if in doing so he intended that they should be discovered and punished, and his testimony, therefore, is not to be treated as that of an infamous person."[4]

Any hopes that the Mollies entertained of slipping the noose would have had to be based on breaking McParlan's story in the trial cross-examination or throwing out the testimony entirely by making McParlan an "infamous witness." The Yost "half-trial" and the Campbell full trial must have convinced them of the improbability of breaking the story. And, though they would not learn of it until most of the trials were over, the Supreme Court was to shut the door on the possibility of voiding the testimony. The wheels of justice were grinding.

So far, all three convictions (Kelly, Doyle, and Campbell) had been at Mauch Chunk, Carbon County. The Commonwealth had yet to obtain a conviction in Schuylkill County. And this loomed most important in Gowen's mind, for it was as district attorney of Schuylkill that he had failed in gaining a convictions record in the 1860's.

The Commonwealth could have immediately retried the Yost case. But it now appeared clear that the case was as good as won in spite of the abrupt ending before an actual conviction. There still remained many other crimes ready to be emblazoned in the press, and many other jailed defendants to be made public examples. One case, though, seemed to be uppermost in the minds of the populace, and to offer the most in terms of publicity. It was the Raven Run case—the killings of the mine boss, Thomas Sanger, and has associate, William Uren.

This would be a difficult case to win. The band of assassins had been incompletely observed by the various witnesses on that early morning, September 1, 1875. The motive for killing Sanger was cloudy; the shooting of Uren was apparently happenstance. And, worst for the prosecution, McParlan had not learned of the case until the day before the killing and knew nothing of the grudges leading to the motive for the crime. Kerrigan was out of the picture, having no connection whatsoever.

On the other hand, McParlan did know the crime was planned, and had even lent his coat to one of the killers. McParlan's position was that he was unable to notify Sanger because of close surveillance by other Mollies. But his report of September 1 shows that on the day of the killing he met the five men apparently involved and had a first-hand confession from all of them that they had just killed Sanger and Uren. Unfortunately, there was no further corroboration. Would McParlan's words alone stand up in court?

One of the five men, Charles O'Donnell, was already dead—shot at Wiggans Patch. Michael Doyle and James O'Donnell were fugitives. Two men were in jail, Thomas Munley and Charles McAllister (though, as it turned out, Charles's brother James should have been there in his place). Munley was now to be tried. The date was June 27; the place was Pottsville.[5]

Although dozens of Raven Run miners had witnessed the shootings (the entire shift was standing around, waiting to go down in
the mine) no one could be found who had clearly seen any of the
five faces. All had seen five men there, but the strangers' faces were
hidden under their coats (Michael Doyle's by McParlan's jacket).
The witnesses were bewildered; the action of the tragedy had been
too rapid. Only Robert Heaton, one of the managers of the mine,
who had rushed from his porch to exchange shots with the fugitives,
was willing to say that Munley was there. His testimony (on June
30) was weak, though. He was able to say only that he saw a man
sitting in a peculiar, constrained position, before the shooting, that
was similar to the way Munley was sitting in the courtroom.

Just as it looked as if Heaton's testimony would be insufficient,
the Commonwealth suddenly came by an additional witness via
one of those gratuitous jury-impressing breaks so welcomed by
trial lawyers. A Raven Run woman, Mrs. Jeanette Williams, im-
pelled by curiosity, visited the courtroom in Pottsville as the trial
was in session. As she sat down in the audience, she caught a side
view of Munley sitting in the prisoner's box. She apparently recognized him immediately. On the morning of the murder, when the
shots rang out, her young son rushed to the door and opened it. She
ran to hold him back, and at this moment a stranger with a pistol
in his hand passed the door. She had only an instant's side view of
the face. But, according to the prosecution (as they quickly got her
on the stand), that was enough for positive identification. Gowen
took full advantage of the drama of the moment: "The art of the
photographer has discovered a method whereby, in an instant of
time or less than an instant, in a pulsation of the heart, in the winking
of an eye, you can take the picture of a man while he is moving at
full speed before you. Why should not the eye of this woman be
able to do the same thing?"[6] With the additional backing of Mc-
Parlan's testimony on July 1 and 3 concerning the plans the day
before the murder and the confessions afterward, the prosecution
case appeared a good deal stronger.

But the defense took heart at the paucity of prosecution evidence
and pulled out all its stops. Munley's father, brother, and sister
testified that he had been at home that morning. Several of Munley's
friends corroborated them. It was a patently contradictory version
and the basis was laid for a perjury indictment of one or the other
side. McParlan's character was bitterly attacked by Ned Monaghan,

ex-constable of Shenandoah, AOH member and erstwhile friend of McParlan, who reported that "McKenna" had talked of killing Tom Fielders, a *Shenandoah Herald* reporter; had been arrested for stealing a peddler's watch; and had done most of the talking on the night of the AOH meeting to plan the killing of "Bully Bill" Thomas. Monaghan's testimony appeared damaging at the moment, but Gowen promptly turned the tables, first forcing Monaghan to admit that he had never notified anyone of the Fielders threat, then so confusing him in the testimony about the peddler that Monaghan admitted that it might have all been a joke. Finally, Gowen had Monaghan arrested for the "Bully Bill" story as being an accomplice present at the meeting.

Martin L'Velle, one of the defense attorneys, gave a vigorous summation of the defense case, bluntly raising questions of religious and racial prosecution and implying that the case was a thinly disguised attack on labor by capital. But this play to the jury's emotions was quickly blown away by the tornado of Gowen's concluding speech to the jury on July 12. It was one of the most remarkable single days in the entire Molly Maguire trial saga, perhaps rivaled only by that first day of McParlan's testimony that so shook the organization. The histrionic genius of the rail president was at its zenith as the crowded courtroom hung on every word of the speech. (Within days, it was reprinted in pamphlet form and thousands of copies sold.) It was clear that Gowen looked upon the Molly trials as a crusade and as personal vindication for his years of frustration in the role of district attorney and for his difficulties with labor as president of the Reading. This was his moment supreme.[7]

Patronizingly pointing out to the jury that, as a lawyer "who by experience, is somewhat skilled in the analyzation of testimony [and] perhaps better able than a jury to select those portions which bear on the real merits of the case," he began with a review of the evidence. Heaton's identification of Munley appeared suspect; Gowen slipped by it quickly: "Where can you get better identification than this? When a witness says, 'the man looked me full in the face, and I saw him; I was shooting at him and he was shooting at me, and I recognize this prisoner as the man,' of what avail is it that we did not ask the witness whether he recognized this prisoner by his face, or not, because the necessary and inevitable inference from what he said is that he did recognize him by his face."

The testimony of the surprise woman witness offered more possibilities, and Gowen made full use of them:

How much more to identification by a mother clinging to her offspring to keep him from danger . . . she said, "It seems to me that I could always see that face." In the dark visions of the night it was ever before her, and the face of the murderer was ever haunting the witness whom Providence had appointed for his identification. We did not know that she knew this. She was not subpoenaed as a witness . . . I can safely say that it looks to me as if the finger of God was here revealed, and as if it unerringly pointed out the evidence which the officers of the Commonwealth had not been able to secure.

Though the Commonwealth, Gowen continued, could readily win its case on the testimony of the witnesses alone, the jury had the privilege of knowing even more by the testimony of McParlan. The detective had come to the fields under a solemn pledge that he was never to be required to testify—"I would have been the last man in the world to have asked him to relieve me from the pledge" —but a "miraculous interposition of Providence had been vouchsafed to permit us to use the testimony." (This providential interposition was none other than McParlan's discovery by the Mollies!) "He was the blood-red wine marked 100," said Gowen, meticulously itemizing the detective's testimony. "What need I say further? An accomplice! McParlan an accomplice?" No, he *could not* let Sanger know—he would have forfeited his life. And he *did not* let two of the murderers, Michael Doyle and Thomas Hurley, escape; in fact, the Pinkertons would never rest until the two were apprehended. "Let them go to the Rocky Mountains, or to the shores of the Pacific; let them traverse the bleak deserts of Siberia; penetrate into the jungles of India, or wander over the wild steppes of Central Asia—they will be dogged and tracked and brought to justice."

Having figuratively carried his mesmerized listeners up to Heaven for divine sanction and around the world for the fugitives, Gowen now took them far below to Hades for a look at the antagonists they were dealing with:

This very organization that we are now, for the first time, exposing to the light of day, has hung like a pall over the people of this county. Before it fear and terror fled cowering to homes which afforded no sanctuary against the vengeance of their pursuers. Behind it stalked darkness and despair, brooding like grim shadows over the desolated hearth and the ruined home, and throughout the length and breadth of this fair land there was heard the voice of wailing and lamentation, of "Rachel weeping for her children and refusing to be comforted, because they were not."

In hidden places and by silent paths, in the dark ravines of the mountains, and in the secret ledges of the rocks, who shall say how many bodies of the victims of this order now await the final trump of God—and from these lonely sepulchers, there will go up to the God who gave them the spirits of these murdered victims, to take their place among the innumerable throng of witnesses at the last day . . . when their solemn accusation is read from the plain command of the Decalogue, "Thou shalt not kill."

Few in the crowded courtroom would have had time to stop and ask if things had actually been quite this bad, for Gowen hurried them on for a view of the Mollies back in Ireland. Here he called up the famous Trench story on the Shirley estate as his case example of the Ribbonmen "from which sprang the men known as Mollie Maguires." As to the defense allegations that the trial was anti-Irish, Gowen continued "I am myself the son of an Irishman, proud of my ancestry and proud of my race, and never ashamed of it except when I see Ireland has given birth to wretches such as these. These men call themselves Irishmen! These men parade on St. Patrick's Day and claim to be good Catholics! Where are the honest Irishmen of this county? Why do they not rise up and strike down these wretches that usurp the name of Irishmen?"

L'Velle's thinly veiled accusation that the trial was "Know Nothing" in character gave Gowen a ready-made opportunity to project Archbishop Wood back into the case: "I have the direct personal authority of Archbishop Wood himself to say that he denounces them all, and that he was fully cognizant of and approved of the means I took to bring them to justice." If this made the prelate a bit nervous, the next sentence almost appeared to put him in actual charge of the Pinkertons: "Archbishop Wood of Philadelphia, was the only confidant I had and fully knew of the mission of McParlan in this whole matter." Gowen noted that he himself was a Protestant, but concluded that "a good Catholic is better than a bad Protestant." This was too much for L'Velle, and he jumped to his feet with "I repel that remark."

Again and again Gowen harped on the theme of perjury. He cut to pieces the testimony of Munley's father and brother. Said Gowen: "This alibi was made up, but was not made up well. When two or three people get together to conspire to defeat the ends of justice, there always seems to be some loose ends . . . always seems to be some string hanging out that they forgot to take in." "There is no palliation for such testimony," Gowen continued, "but if there ever was a palliation . . . if there should be, at the last great day, before the final judge, any excuse for the enormity of this crime, it will be urged on behalf of a father who has striven to save his son from the gallows, and on behalf of one brother, who seeks to shield another from infamy and from shame."

But Gowen spared no vitriol for the other Munley witnesses, for "the time has gone by when the murderer, the incendiary, and the assassin can go home reeking from the commission of crimes, confident in the fact that he can appear before a jury and have an alibi proved for him." Gowen proclaimed "no more false alibis . . . no more confident reliance upon the perjury of relatives and friends . . . no more dust thrown in the eyes of juries."

L'Velle's innuendo that the whole case was a fabric of antiunion attacks hit too close to home for Gowen, and he carefully picked his way through his rejoinder, not once mentioning the word "union":

I became so much interested in the prosperity of this county, and in the development of its mineral wealth, that I saw it was a struggle between the good citizen and the bad citizen as to which should obtain the supremacy . . .

I took the pains to show that there was a secret association banded together for the purpose of committing outrages which have given a notorious character not only to the laboring people of the county, but to the whole county itself.

This was as far as Gowen wanted to go, for it was not yet a propitious time for a more direct link between the Mollies and the union.

If Schuykill County residents had ever felt that they had lost the loyalty of their illustrious son when he took the Reading presidency in Philadelphia, Gowen assured them that they were wrong, for "I said that I would come up into this county, where I first had learned to practice law, that I would take my place among the ranks of the counsel for the Commonwealth, and that I would stand side by side with him in the prosecution of these offenses until the last one was wiped off." In doing this, Gowen intimated, he was in real personal danger—"Is there a man in this audience . . . who longs to point a pistol at me? I tell him that he has as good a chance here as he will ever have again." But "let it take weeks, or let it take months, or let it take years, I have buckled on my harness and entered for the fight, and, God willing, I shall bear it out as bravely and as well as I can until justice is vindicated."

Gowen had taken three hours. The jury needed only one. On July 12, 1876, Thomas Munley was judged guilty of murder in the first degree. On August 28 he was sentenced to be hanged.

✠   ✠   ✠   ✠   ✠

The Commonwealth scorecard read well. The Jones murder was decisively vindicated—all the alleged participants were accounted for. Doyle, Kelly, and Campbell were convicted; and Kerrigan's body, if not also his soul, was firmly in the hands of the prosecution. Prospects in the Yost killing were very bright, despite the inconclusive first trial. And this would take care of Carroll, McGehan, Roarity, Boyle, and Duffy. One of the assailants at Raven Run in the killing of Sanger and Uren, Thomas Munley, was already convicted; another man, Charles McAllister, was in jail, apparently awaiting a like verdict. Just as securely behind bars were about a dozen other Mollies—a group that included most of the county officers, key bodymasters, and the county chairman, "King of the Mollies," Jack Kehoe. They were already variously indicted for several crimes, including the attempted murder of "Bully Bill" Thomas, the conspiracy to reward Tom Hurley for his murder of Gomer James, and the attempted assault on the two Major brothers.

But not all of the key figures were in such firm custody. Tom Hurley, for one, could not be found. Two of the Raven Run participants, Michael Doyle (of Shenandoah) and James "Friday" O'Donnell, were gone. William Love, who had allegedly killed Squire Gwyther on the same bloody night that Gomer James was killed, had fled and was still at large. And rumors of a wholesale exodus of other Mollies were now confirmed by missing faces. Even Frank McAndrew, McParlan's bodymaster confidant, was nowhere to be found.

McParlan had been mercilessly lambasted by L'Velle in the Munley trial for "collaborating to allow Doyle and Hurley to escape." From this, and from the detective's failure to notify Jones and Sanger, the defense had built up the image of McParlan as an accomplice. Gowen had promised that the Pinkertons would track these fugitives, even if they were in the "bleak deserts of Siberia," the "jungles of India," the "wild steppes of Central Asia."

McParlan was now lounging in the best hotels in the region, always in the company of other Pinkerton agents for fear of assassination, awaiting further calls for testimony. But Linden, still in the coal fields, and other Pinkerton agents elsewhere were continuing their investigations of other murders and searching for the fugitives. Both efforts were to pay dividends.

Linden was greatly aided by private, often anonymous, tips about various suspects. The improved climate of public opinion had made it easier for this—many people who would have feared Molly retaliation in the past now came forward. Often the accusations were loose and untrustworthy; sometimes they were even vindictive, and very often they were motivated by hopes for selfish gain, for the agency was not averse to paying "rewards" for information. The agents were deluged with offers of information, provided the giver would not have to testify publicly. Even close friends seemed willing to sell out the Mollies, provided there was cash involved. As one man put it, "I'm a poor man."[8]

Clearly, Hurley was the most wanted fugitive. His code designation in Linden's reports as "number 1" mirrored this. At first, McParlan, while still "McKenna," had kept in touch with him and had assured Linden that the situation was under control. But McParlan's exposure and flight left no doubt that the link was terminated, and Hurley temporarily became a phantom.

Linden was too occupied in Schuylkill County to chase him, and was forced to rely on other agents, mostly free-lancers, working on a tenuous day-by-day expense charge, and primarily interested in the reward money. The competition was intense. When Hurley's trail was picked up again in April 1876, one of these free-lancers wrote the Schuylkill district attorney, "If left to me, Captain Jack and Snyder not interfering, you will have Hurley for certain and the others possibly."[9]

But Hurley slipped the net again. In early June he was seen in Harrisburg, apparently on his way to Pittsburgh, and Linden wired his contact there to arrest. No fingerprint or wirephoto techniques being available then, Linden's physical description had to suffice: "5′ 8″ high, 160 lbs., hair and complexion sandy, sharp features, smooth face, small bright eyes, hands and feet large, wears slouch hat and work clothes, may have mustache and probably another name."[10] It was in vain, though, and Hurley dropped completely from sight.

Meanwhile new information on other murders was beginning to filter in, but not in definitive enough form to chance a formal indictment. In one case, Linden actually recommended that one of the suspects in an old killing be arrested "on general principles trusting to luck for a case against him."[11] But the district attorney decided against it, as the only evidence against the man had been furnished by Kerrigan and he "didn't want Kerrigan to carry any more."[12]

As the authorities began to fill in the gaps in the various cases, the reconciling of the fine line of distinction between those actually involved as accessories and those who were merely bystanders but did know critical pieces of evidence became increasingly troublesome. For example, one Hecksherville Irishman, Pat Brennan, touched the fringes of two of the cases. The night before the Raven Run shooting, Mike Doyle of Shenandoah, one of the triggermen and fugitives, had visited Brennan in the hope that he could borrow his false mustache. Brennan, instead of denying that he had one, said he would not part with it. Doyle told him to keep his mouth shut and left. The next day Sanger and Uren were dead. And two weeks earlier Brennan had also been in the wrong spot at the wrong time, for he had stood only three feet away from Gomer James at the picnic where Hurley gunned James down.

Brennan then felt he was on the spot, and, fearing Molly violence because he knew too much, left the area temporarily. Meanwhile, the mustache story became known to the authorities, and when Brennan returned, he was promptly arrested. Vehemently protesting that he had not left because of guilt but to save his own life, he demanded to be let out of jail, promising that he would not "run away." According to Linden, Brennan vowed that "if he kept his mouth shut, would get work, but if told on the parties, couldn't as would be killed." Unless they let him out, he would not tell anything—"they could keep him in jail as long as they liked—if couldn't get work, might as well be in jail." But Linden felt he might be a good witness "with delicate handling" and Brennan was not freed.[13]

Mike Doyle's whereabouts became increasingly interesting, for rumors were spread in the summer of 1876 about a strange incident supposed to have happened that spring, before Jack Kehoe's arrest. As Linden began to piece together the bits of information, the story that came out was startling. Kehoe apparently went to the national convention of the Ancient Order of Hibernians in New York City, held in March and April. (We cannot be certain even of this, for none of the extant records show his name.)[14] It was a sensitive time for the national organization, for the Catholic Church was putting increasing pressures on it. (The McParlan revelations of the AOH link to the Molly story were still not public information, as the "first" Yost trial was still a month off.) Resolutions were passed that "it is the most earnest desire of the AOH to think, judge and act in accordance with the government, teachings and practices of the Holy Catholic Church [and to] disown, denounce, protest against and ignore any connection with organizations, societies or bodies or individuals that hold, advance or do anything contrary to what their Church and Country demand of them."[15]

In the face of this, the story that came out on August 19 at one of the trials seemed a jarring note in the new piousness of the AOH, for Doyle was reported to have joined Kehoe at the convention, and the two together to have pleaded that Doyle was a fugitive—a potential millstone to the AOH—and therefore needed money to escape.[16] The convention (or perhaps the officers alone, or even chance members alone) then gave Doyle one hundred dollars, whereupon he took a boat for England. On August 13 Linden had been told that Doyle was in his home parish at Bellmullet, County Mayo. A report later in the month (August 26) said he had left for Australia to work on a railroad construction project.

The precise relationship of the national AOH to its embattled Schuylkill locals during this critical period remains an enigma. The records of the national convention and the national executive board, even if they survive, are unavailable—and probably would not tell us much anyway. So our main information is one-sided hearsay, duly reported in great detail by Linden. But this was enough to make quite a scare story for the authorities. On August 29, Linden reported that not only was money allegedly being sent from New York to Kehoe ($1100 being sent via Captain Gallagher, a state officer), but that the national grand secretary had assigned members to go to the coal fields and assassinate McParlan and Gowen. Nitroglycerin was to be "thrown among the lawyers . . . to blow the court house to hell even if one Mollie should be killed." An even wilder version was reported the next day: Twenty-five unmarried men were to be chosen; they were to split into two groups, one to sit in the front of the courtroom and the other in the back. The upper group, at the back, was to open fire on Gowen and McParlan; the front group was then to follow with a fusillade at the police. In the melee that presumably would result, they would all escape.[17]

In retrospect we can put very little credence in such hearsay. Nothing of this nature did transpire. Yet, at the time, it must have sounded ominous for the Pinkertons and Gowen. Assassination seemed to be a practiced art. Who could say it would not be tried again?

But if the perpetration of actual physical violence by the national organization seems less than credible, the persistent rumor of funds being collected by the AOH for a defense fund was harder to kill. In August, according to the *Shenandoah Herald*, the Philadelphia AOH lodge officers accused the national board of having ordered an assessment of five dollars from each of the six thousand lodges all over the country. The Philadelphia officers then voted the dissolution of the Philadelphia branch. The members were enraged by this and promptly held a rump session, repudiating the vote and suspending the officers for life. The membership was incited in this by a visiting priest from Ohio, who harangued Archbishop Wood for his denunciation of the AOH, for "no bishop had a right to brand by name any society" unless its constitution had been sent to Rome, together with documentation of its violence. The priest, as quoted by the *Herald*, saw the Molly issue as "a Know-nothing strike at every Irish organization," adding that "while the Schuylkill County assassins were murderers, their doings were instigated by the Workingmen's Benevolent Association."[18]

John McGuire, now the national head of the AOH, issued a statement that no money whatsoever had been sent to Pennsylvania, and that he regarded the Molly Maguires "as murderers, and as such would be entitled to no consideration from the order."[19] The *Pilot*, in Boston, one of the most influential of all Catholic papers, reported the whole story with shock, and promptly approached the Boston local of the AOH. The AOH officers there admitted that some "Black Sheep" were probably supporting Pennsylvania, but vowed they could not believe that the national board would actually have countenanced any such assessment.[20]

There the story died, for the veil of secrecy was again pulled around the organization. There may well have been such an assessment earlier in 1876, before the full import of the Molly debacle was clear. But by September it was manifestly clear that the

national had to repudiate the Pennsylvania group or be pulled
down with it.

❖   ❖   ❖   ❖   ❖

Doyle probably did go to Ireland. Others of the Mollies did, too.
Frank McAndrew went back (to Bangor, County Mayo), but
returned to the coal fields when he learned that his warning to
McParlan about the threat on his life was to gain him immunity
from trial.

Although there was a strong personal link between the Pennsylvania Mollies and their families and friends in "the old country,"
any organizational link between Pennsylvania and Ireland was slim
indeed. McParlan's testimony had planted the specter of a shadowy
"Board of Erin" back in Ireland diabolically pulling strings, the
ends of which were tied to the triggers of the blazing guns of the
Pennsylvania Mollies. There is no evidence that there was any truth
to this implication. There probably was a Board of Erin; it probably
did send passwords across to the American AOH in return for dues
money. But at this time—in the 1870's—the Board of Erin was far
out of the mainstream of Irish secret society and political activity.
Later it was to be a potent force, especially in Ulster, and to adopt
the name Ancient Order of Hibernians, popularized in the United
States.[21] By the turn of the century its political power was truly
feared, one analyst calling it "the Unknown Power Behind the Irish
Nationalist Party."[22] Though the Board may have dabbled in revolutionary activity during the Molly period, its impact was minuscule
in comparison to groups such as the Irish Republican Brotherhood—
the famous "Fenians." At any rate, the Board would not have
thought of Pennsylvania had it wished to loose a few bullets. The
English were too handy.

It is surprising, in fact, that the Molly Maguire story made so
little impact back in Ireland. The London *Times* carried a half-
column story early in June 1876 on the first Yost trial, but did not
mention the fact that Irishmen and Irish-based secret societies were
involved. The case was treated as a union aberration, and the
W.B.A. was taken to task as the power behind the Mollies. The
Times' chance to point a reproving finger at Ireland—a tactic the
paper was rather fond of—was apparently not perceived.[23]

And the article was not picked up at all in the Irish press. Not until six months later (when London's *Pall Mall Gazette* carried a long article on the progress of the trials) did the Irish newspapers feel that the trials were news. Several reprinted the *Gazette* piece intact without comment.[24] The article pinned the blame on the AOH, a society "deriving its authority from a foreign order existing in Great Britain," but only McParlan was mentioned as an Irishman. The *Cork Examiner* did see fit to make an editorial comment, but used most of its space to castigate, not Irish, but *British* secret societies: "The Prince of Wales is head of a secret society in England to which many of the nobility, gentry and trading classes are attached."[25] Again no one seemed to sense any Irish-British overtones in the American story.

This is curious, for the Irish in America were deeply involved in the struggle against England. The second abortive Fenian raid on Canada in 1871 was still a warm issue, the deportation of the Irish-based Fenians to the United States had filled the country with belligerent factions, warring among themselves, but all dedicated to a military attack on England. The Clan na Gael had been formed in America to keep a firm grip on Irish-American opinion, to organize anti-English opinion in America, and increasingly to combat the frequent proposals for an Anglo-American *rapprochement*.[26] Great quantities of money were collected and shipped across to Ireland, and various of the Fenian factions were committed to involving themselves actively in the hoped-for battle.

The many Irish benevolent lodges and societies in America stood in the wings on the actual "military" plans, vocally supporting and financing the Fenians. The Clan na Gael (known also as the "United Brotherhood") was perhaps the closest to the stage. The internecine warfare among all these groups made a very complicated fabric indeed. Some were more politically than militarily oriented; others were more interested in the potentials of the Irish vote for American politics.[27] Central to all efforts was the fact that all were "Irish" (though not necessarily born in Ireland).

The Catholic Church was the most potent single factor preventing the actual melding of the beneficent societies with the more revolutionary secret organizations. Its uncompromising attitude toward secret societies had already brought a negative ruling on the Fenians, and the pressure had already turned such groups as the AOH back toward the Church. Though the AOH continued to pour money into Irish causes—they were massive supporters of Parnell and the

Land League in the 1880's—they could not openly support the revolutionary groups.

As a result, the Clan na Gael began its own organization in the coal fields in early 1876. Dr. William Carroll, the chairman of the Clan Executive, wrote John Devoy, the Fenian leader, on January 12: "We are very glad to get a footing in the coal region, where hitherto all kinds of *so-called* Irish societies have held ground to the exclusion of the only *really Irish* Society of which I have any knowledge."[28] On February 8 he reported that "the cause goes bravely forward in the coal regions of Penna. . . . there are at least 200,000 of our men in these Penna. coal regions, who ought to wield a power in the [executive body] superior to that of New York." Relations with the AOH continued friendly, in spite of the fact that the Clan was proselyting AOH members.

But the Fenians and the Clan had no direct relationship with—and little concern for—what was happening in the Molly trials. Again, as in Ireland, the trials were not seen as having anything to do with Irish nationalism and the age-old battle between the tenant and the landlord. The Fenians and the Clan apparently had no desire to get embroiled in what they must have seen as a strictly American incident involving Irish-*Americans* in, as the London *Times* implied, an American labor-union squabble.

They were probably wrong here. The Molly incidents must have been a decisive influence in hardening the attitude of the Church toward secret societies. It turned many groups—such as the AOH—away from undercover support of Fenian revolutionary activity and toward the more legitimate parliamentary approaches such as Parnell's Land League. The Molly Maguire story must have influenced the Irish struggle for independence.

❖   ❖   ❖   ❖   ❖

The "second" Yost trial had only one really important difference from the "first." But it was a very large difference for the defendants, McGehan, Boyle, Carroll, and Roarity (Duffy had requested and been granted a separate trial). This time they were all found guilty of first-degree murder.[29]

The trial began on July 6, 1876, even before the Munley trial had finished. It ended on July 24. Gowen's spell-binding speech to the Munley jury on July 12 was nicely timed to straddle the two cases for maximum effect on the populace.

The "second" case moved along its foreordained path to its foregone conclusion. The evidence was the same, but with one important omission—Mrs. Kerrigan did not repeat her testimony that her husband had told her he had killed Yost. We do not know why she backed out. Franklin Dewees, in his 1877 book so heavily loaded toward the prosecution, had a ready answer: "It is stated that even before the conclusion of the first trial she had repented, and had determined to come upon the stand and tell the truth."[30] This could have been true. Or she could have backed out for fear of a perjury trial. Or she could have had a belated attack of conjugal loyalty (for she was reconciled with her husband after the trials). Now, almost ninety years later, we cannot be certain. The evidence presented appeared to implicate strongly all of the four defendants (and Kerrigan)—McGehan and Boyle for the actual shooting, Carroll and Roarity for prior knowledge and help in the plans. The McParlan reports appeared to corroborate the evidence. Pro-Molly writers over the years have bitterly attacked the Yost evidence, and have implied that it was Kerrigan alone who was the premeditating killer.[31] But at that time it was enough to convict the four.

Though Gowen's histrionic talents were not available for the prosecution's summations on July 22, General Charles Albright and F. W. Hughes filled in admirably and kept up the pressure on the AOH itself. (Their speeches, too, were soon widely available in paperback pamphlet form.[32]) Although the presiding judge pulled Albright up short when he tried to connect the AOH with the "Buckshot" draft riots of the Civil War, the General pursued one of the budding antagonisms now aroused by the trials, that of the threat to Schuylkill business interests. "It is almost inconceivable how this bad society has injured you and every property-owner in the coal regions," he said. Considering that capital is "naturally conservative," he continued, when the enterprises were "confronted by a body of men who seek to control the coal mines and capital invested in them . . . you can see how capital, how property, how life, how everything have been imperiled." In consequence, he concluded, "the business of this particular community was about being surrendered to lawless and desperate men." Albright made no direct mention of the union, and probably had intended no such implication. But Gowen did, later.

All the trials up to this point had been for murder. And all had resulted in first-degree murder convictions. All the defendants were headed for the gallows. Now a "lesser" case moved forward to the stage, to be tried in Pottsville beginning August 8, 1876.[33]

But it was lesser only for the crime—assault and battery with intent to kill William M. ("Bully Bill") Thomas—and for the potential punishment. In the importance and number of the defendants it was one of the greatest of all the Molly trials. For, charged with conspiracy in the case were nine men that included "King of the Mollies" Jack Kehoe; Christopher Donnelly, Schuylkill County treasurer; Dennis Canning, Northumberland County delegate; and three bodymasters, John "Yellow Jack" Donahue (Tuscarora), Michael O'Brien (Mahanoy City), and James Roarity (the Coaldale bodymaster already convicted in the Yost case). Frank McHugh, the Mahanoy City secretary, was the seventh man, and the prisoners' box was rounded out by two members, John Morris and John Gibbons, the only ones of the nine who were actually charged with the shooting of "Bully Bill" back on June 28, 1875. The crime had first been planned in the "convention" on June 1 of that year, and it was this conspiracy for which the nine were now being tried. McParlan had been at the convention. So, too, had William Gavin, the Schuylkill County secretary, but he had fled and was now one of Linden's fugitives. Michael Doyle and Tom Hurley had joined Gibbons and Morris in the actual assault, but now were missing, perhaps overseas. The nine on trial were the main body of the conspirators, though, and at the same time were the main body of the AOH leadership in the southern anthracite fields. Conviction here would be the peak plume in Gowen's already-feathered cap. The courtroom was jammed from the start of the trial to its finish. The metropolitan papers were there *en masse*, some even bringing staff artists to sketch the trial scenes.

The prosecution's key witness was McParlan, the only one at the trial beside the defendants who had attended the June 1 convention at Mahanoy City. Despite the defense efforts to confine the testimony to the specific charge, the prosecution introduced all the additional material on the criminal nature of the Hibernians that had made such an impression in previous trials. The Jones, Yost, and Sanger-Uren trials all showed that "jobs" had been traded between lodges, but the Thomas case went even further. It offered real opportunities for showing just how widespread the tentacles of the organization were: an actual conspiratorial convention attended by officers from even outside the county. Though the story was already old, McParlan's careful recounting showed it had plenty of punch left in it. With the help of "Bully Bill's" graphic description of being shot in the stable, the case seemed solid enough.

If it was not, though, a startling development made it solid beyond doubt. Frank McHugh, the youngest of the officers present at the convention, turned informer on August 10, in the middle of the trial. Piously proclaiming that "I think if they had all pled guilty it would have been better for their interests," he promptly corroborated McParlan's version of the convention. When attacked by the dumfounded defense as to why he had decided to change his plea, he said he had received no promise of immunity, though he admitted he did "expect a little less than I would receive had I sat listening to the evidence against me without defending myself— I expect less punishment than if I had not done it."

The defense was even further battered when the prosecution introduced a surprise witness, the warden of the county jail, George Byerle, who testified that Kehoe had told him, "If we don't get justice, I don't think the old man at Harrisburg will go back on us." The rumor that the Republican governor, John F. Hartranft, had become indebted to the AOH was already well known though unconfirmed. The Irish vote, normally Democratic, *had* gone Republican in the election the previous fall. Critics of Hartranft had already accused him of paying off by pardoning an embezzling Irish county commissioner. The defense castigated the warden's testimony as having nothing to do with the case, but the wily Gowen claimed that it was a tacit admission of Kehoe's guilt. Gowen's real motive was to make it politically inexpedient for the governor to intervene in any way. The story of the political horse trade was still cloudy, but it would become clearer during a later trial.

After McHugh's devastating testimony, the defense was forced to concentrate most of its efforts on trying to break McParlan's story, an effort in which they had been remarkably ineffective to date. The detective's involvement in the "Bully Bill" saga was not particularly savory. He had attended the convention; he had, according to some of the defendants, sided with Kehoe for the immediate disposal of Thomas. McParlan had even gone to Mahanoy City with Hurley, Gibbons, and his sometime roommate,

Doyle, to do the job. McParlan's testimony (and his reports) noted that he was then able to talk the three out of it. Later, the detective did know that those three, together with Morris, had left for another try, but he did not warn Thomas via Linden or Franklin. Again, McParlan's testimony and the reports gave the reason—he was guarded all night by another Molly. But the defense worked assiduously on the insinuation that McParlan's pose was really that of an *agent provocateur*. Defense attorney L'Velle went especially far in his summation: "He was their leader, their guide, and their general. He was the man who had the cash to supply the whiskey and fire the brain of these poor, susceptible, youthful enthusiasts. He was the man . . . From the time that he came into Schuylkill County until he left it, has not crime been increasing?" John Ryon, the other defense attorney, added what he thought the motive of McParlan to be: "It can be but for one purpose. To make himself a great detective, and give him a bureau under Mr. Franklin, he has to make some great and startling disclosures. It could not be done unless some lives were lost, some outrages committed."

These were strong words. But no stronger than Gowen's stinging address. The rail president, too, went further than he had gone even in the Munley case. He accused the AOH of deriving its authority from "a foreign land," and having as its purpose the same as that of the Irish secret societies, "to get the benefit of and use and enjoy the property of others without owning it, and without paying for it . . . to levy blackmail" so that the owners would "purchase peace and immunity" by employing members "in prominent positions." In effect, Gowen was accusing the Mollies of being labor racketeers, an allegation that had some slight substance in Pennsylvania but none in Ireland. Kehoe came in for particular attention as "the chief conspirator, murderer and villain," who in his position as saloon-owner made money "by his traffic in the souls of his fellow men." Referring obliquely to Wiggans Patch, Gowen averred that "we wanted no vigilance committee." He said, "No mother, through the long watches of the night bending over her sick infant, ever watched it with more tender solicitude than did I these men when I found their lives were threatened by lawless bands or vigilance committees."

Though Gowen soft-pedaled the tie with the union, he was probably surprised when Kaercher, the other prosecutor, frankly disassociated the two groups, using the actual words "the Labor

Union." Kaercher also reintroduced the Trench case from Ireland, succeeding only in demonstrating that he had read Steuart Trench's book, *Realities of Irish Life*.

The trial was one of the bitterest and most vindictive of all. The jury was out only twenty minutes—on August 12—bringing in a verdict of guilty for all defendants, with a recommendation of mercy for Frank McHugh. All except McHugh were given the maximum penalty: seven years in jail. And two days later, on August 14, all the defendants except Morris and Gibbons were brought right back in and tried for the conspiracy to murder the Major brothers, Jesse and William. The trial took only two days, and on August 15 seven more years were added to Kehoe's and Canning's sentences, shorter amounts to the others.[34]

And later in the day on August 15 another mass trial brought additional AOH officers before the bar, in this case accused of conspiring to reward Tom Hurley for his shooting of Gomer James.[35] McParlan had attended the county convention at Tamaqua on August 25, 1875, when Hurley had argued his case that he, not John McClain, had shot James and was therefore entitled to the reward. The detective had reported the participants then; they included not only Jack Kehoe, Chris Donnelly, Jack Donahue, and James Roarity, but also Patrick Dolan Sr. (Big Mine Run bodymaster), Francis O'Neil (head of the St. Clair lodge), and Patrick Butler (Lost Creek bodymaster), together with the missing Gavin and two other fugitive bodymasters, Frank Keenan of Forestville and Jeremiah Kane of Mt. Laffee. The last three were unavailable, but the rest, except Kehoe, were now brought to trial (the prosecution told the judge that it wished to save Kehoe's trial until later).

After the prosecution had finished its case (featuring McParlan again) the defense called Captain Robert Linden to the stand on August 18 and asked him a startling question—was he personally involved in the shooting at Jesse James' house back in Missouri? The detective successfully parried the question and it was dropped. The incident puzzled almost everyone. Even the *Shenandoah Herald*, which had been deeply immersed in the vigilante rumors, did not make the connection. But Linden and Allan Pinkerton must have swallowed twice on it.

In all the trials up to this point the defense attorneys had never put any of the defendants on the stand. Now, probably in desperation, they decided to try it. The Mollies were no match for the prosecution, though, and particularly so because they were all contradicting McParlan's version, now so well accepted. "Donnelly left the stand after receiving an awful raking," exulted the *Shenandoah Herald;* and Dolan was "pretty badly scratched."[36] But when Pat Butler was put on the stand, the house of cards tumbled down completely. Brought to the stand as a defense witness, he was properly vague, but when the cross-examiner began, he promptly turned full circle, and, before the shocked defense counsel, confessed on the stand. The trial was thrown into an uproar. The prisoners could not believe their ears—"Frank O'Neil actually rubbed his eyes to make sure he wasn't dreaming . . . Mike O'Brien suddenly became actually ghostly through terror and astonishment . . . Roarity actually gave his front teeth a rest and forgot to chew . . . 'Yellow Jack' gave up the attempt to take matters coolly, for it was too much, more than a man could be expected to bear calmly, to see a bodymaster like himself . . . go on the stand, apparently with the object of testifying in his old comrades' favor and turn around without a moment's warning and tell the truth." The jury took only fifteen minutes on August 22 to find all of the group guilty (with a recommendation of mercy for Butler).

Having a few days' respite before the next case, the newspapers bathed their columns in human interest stories on the Mollies. The *Herald* visited Mrs. Kerrigan, and found her in bitterly reduced straits. She and her children were down to "eating bread and water" and were to be evicted for failure to pay their rent. The poor woman mournfully reported that she was planning to sell her furniture, farm out the children, and "go out to service." When the reporter asked her if she would "live with Jimmy again," she said she would "if he promises to be kind to me, but if he is rough with me I won't stay with him a day." But, she added, "I'm not sorry I testified, and I told Jimmy in jail . . . that I would go on the stand against him again if the court wanted me to."[37]

Though the fruits of informing did not look promising, there was still more informing to come.

❖   ❖   ❖   ❖   ❖

The month of September 1876 brought more cases. But there were increasing signs that the Armageddon which Gowen and the authorities were so avidly seeking was beginning to trouble a few of the clearer-thinking people. Even some of the newspapers were raising doubts; a Hazleton paper warned that "the Mollie crusade is tending to fasten the idea that all Irishmen are Catholics, all Catholics members of the Ancient Order of Hibernians, and all Ancient Order men are Mollie Maguires . . . we protest the indecent haste of the trials."[38] The *Miners' Journal* retorted, "Write something sensible, Fincher, or shut up." But doubts kept coming back.

Especially was this so in the trial of Thomas Duffy, opening in Pottsville on September 6.[39] He, along with Kerrigan, had been beaten up by policeman Ben Yost. He had vowed revenge, had even been heard promising money for the officer's death. But, although his motive was bell-clear, his actual involvement in the plans leading to the shooting was not. McParlan had never known Duffy and could offer no direct testimony. Only Jimmy Kerrigan could testify that Duffy had offered Roarity ten dollars for Yost's death. The most damaging evidence against Duffy was that he had stayed at Carroll's the night of the shooting—July 5, 1875. The judge's charge to the jury in the case "leaned toward the side of mercy . . . hardly a soul in the courtroom but was satisfied Duffy's chances of acquittal were more than even."[40]

But on September 19 the jury confounded all by quickly bringing in a verdict of guilty of first-degree murder. "When the people recovered from the surprise," commented the *Shenandoah Herald*, "a feeling of perfect contentment stole over them." The reporter, as if trying hard to demonstrate this contentment, added, "they left the courtroom after assuring as many of the jurors as could be laid hold of that they were men of common sense."

The prosecution's haste appeared to be further confirmed on September 21 when Charles McAllister was brought into court after having been in the Pottsville jail since the previous February. He was accused of directly participating in the Raven Run killings, having been arrested on the word of McParlan. But the detective was now forced to admit publicly that he had made a mistake, that the culprit was really James McAllister, the look-alike brother of Charles. But McAllister had not a moment to breathe a sigh of relief, for he was immediately re-arrested for another shooting, that of James Riles on August 16, 1875. At least Riles had recovered, so it was not murder for which he was now being accused. Nevertheless, he was returned to jail.

The ranks of the informers were further swelled in September by the addition of Michael Lawler. As the *Herald* indelicately put it, "The 'Muff' Squeals." Lawler had ample reason to turn against his fellow Mollies, for after he had stepped down as bodymaster in Shenandoah, he had been widely suspected by the Mollies as a spy. Though he had been arrested shortly after the others, they would have nothing to do with him; no funds for legal help were available, and he was forced to use a court-appointed lawyer. Lawler, tried for being an accessory after the fact in the Sanger-Uren plans, corroborated the Commonwealth's evidence given previously. But, in spite of his admitted involvement, he pleaded innocent when the trial opened on September 21, 1876, and the confused jury could not reach a verdict a day later. He was retried on November 14 and 15 and convicted.[41]

Kerrigan's testimony in the case of the conspiracy to kill the Major brothers implicated four other men, two of whom conveniently turned state's evidence when brought to trial on September 22.[42] These two, J. J. Slattery and Charles Mulhearn, were political figures, and their evidence concerning Hibernian activity carried damaging weight. Though on September 23 the third man, Michael Doolan, was also found guilty with Slattery and Mulhearn, the fourth, John Stanton, was declared innocent, the first such verdict in the Molly cases.

With all the solicitous interest in the welfare of the Major brothers and "Bully Bill" Thomas—between the two cases over a dozen convictions had been effected—one might have expected that those three would rise to the occasion and move to the forefront of well-behaved, public-spirited citizens. But no, on September 26, right in the middle of the period of the trials concerning them, Jesse Major and Bully Bill got drunk in Pottsville, and, when Major "felt so exuberant that he slapped a woman," this "touched the chivalric feelings of Thomas, who said he never hit women."[43] An enormous brawl resulted, and both Major and Bully Bill were tossed in jail.

Fewer and fewer Irishmen were now willing to go on the stand to provide alibis, truthful or not. By now, "drill swearing" looked like a pretty dangerous avocation. But just to make certain on this point, the authorities brought in four of the witnesses in the Thomas Munley case and tried them for perjury during the week of September 25–30. Two were women, Mrs. Bridget Hyland and sixteen-year-old Kate Boyle. The other two were Barney Boyle, Kate's brother, and James Duffy. All were convicted easily, Barney Boyle drawing a three-year sentence and the others two and a half.

And the Thomas case continued to provide accessories; Ned Monaghan had mentioned in the Munley trial that he had attended the meeting concerning Bully Bill; therefore he was easy to convict. So was Thomas Donahue, having driven one of the culprits to the station after the crime.

❖   ❖   ❖   ❖   ❖

Except for the fugitives, the various cases in which McParlan had been involved were now rather well played out. The John P. Jones murder was fully accounted for. So was the Benjamin Yost killing. The Raven Run shooting of Sanger and Uren was not in quite such tidy shape. One participant in the shooting, Munley, was already convicted; the alleged instigator, Dennis "Bucky" Donnelly, was now indicted (and would subsequently be convicted of first-degree murder); another participant had been killed by the masked band at Wiggans Patch; but three of the gunmen, James "Friday" O'Donnell, James McAllister, and Michael Doyle, were still at large (and were never to be caught). Tom Hurley, the executioner of Gomer James, was likewise at large. The Thomas and Majors cases were well accounted for. Thus the McParlan-based Molly cases were mainly over.

But, as a result of Linden's continued field work and the rash of new confessions on the stand, a number of older crimes were resurrected. The murder of mine boss Morgan Powell back in 1871 was solved when Charles Mulhearn, confessing in the Major case, admitted that he had been along when Powell was shot. He implicated a number of men, and in a series of trials held in Mauch Chunk in late 1876, three were found guilty of first-degree murder and sentenced to be hanged: John "Yellow Jack" Donahue, Thomas Fisher, and Alexander Campbell (his second such conviction). Several others received major sentences.[44]

The biggest sensation of these trials had nothing to do with Morgan Powell, but rather Governor Hartranft. One of the informers, J. J. Slattery, testifying in the John Donahue trial on October 21, was asked about the alleged political "deal" in the

1875 elections. Slattery proceeded to spill the whole story before the court. As he told it, the story was this: He and John Kehoe were each given one thousand dollars by the state Republican party (through two prominent Schuylkill men) with the understanding that the AOH vote would be delivered, as far as possible, to the Republicans. Kehoe was to write to every AOH county delegate in the state. In turn, Slattery and Kehoe exacted an understanding "that when necessary we were to get pardons for our men." (McParlan had reported this to Franklin on November 25, 1875, although he had Slattery's payment being received instead by Bernard Doyle.)

Hartranft, the "old man at Harrisburg" (as Kehoe was reputed in the Thomas case to have called him), had already locked horns with Gowen over the imputation that Kehoe had any kind of influence over him. The governor wrote a stinging letter in late August denying Gowen's insinuations, and Gowen replied, "Hartranft is a liar if he charges me with having made any false statement whatsoever . . . give him my compliments."[45] But Gowen must have realized that he might endanger the whole Molly Maguire fabric if he let it become too stained with partisan politics. So he began ducking reporters' questions, retorting that "no matter how often Governor Hartranft may cross the scent, he cannot divert me from the chase" (i.e., the trials themselves).[46] Gowen now reissued an old 1860 resolution of the Reading Railroad that "it is the settled policy of this Company to keep aloof from political contests and to disapprove of any of its officers or employees taking any active part therein."[47] But the whole Slattery story was a fascinating one, albeit never fully authenticated in its details.

With the Morgan Powell case solved, other old cases were dug up on the basis of new evidence. By far the most important was the oldest case of all—a murder that took place over fourteen years before, in 1862. The murdered man was Frank Langdon. And one of the murderers was now alleged to be none other than the "King Molly" himself, Jack Kehoe.

Kehoe had already been tried and convicted twice. But both cases were only conspiracy cases, and the sentences were only seven years each. This was frustrating to the prosecution, because, in their view, Kehoe was the master planner and instigator behind most of the crime in Schuylkill County. Even if all the actual perpetrators—those present on the scene—could be tried, convicted, and hanged, it still might leave the "King of the Mollies" alive and only temporarily impotent.

But Kehoe *had* been involved in the Langdon case. Langdon had been an inspection boss in the mine employing many of the Kehoe family. It was his job to dock miners if the refuse content of their loads was too high. About three weeks before the murder, he had docked John Kehoe, whereupon Kehoe threatened to kill him. Then came the fatal night. A large group of people had assembled at the local hotel under request of Langdon to raise money for a Fourth of July celebration. A group of dissident miners in the crowd, including Kehoe, began annoying the assembled band by throwing pebbles at it. Langdon remonstrated with them, whereupon Kehoe spat on an American flag at the corner of the porch and was said to have told Langdon that if he would just step off the porch, they would kill him. Kehoe's father cautioned, "John, you ought not to do that," but Kehoe snapped back that he would do worse that evening.

Later, in the darkness, Langdon started home but was followed by one or more men, and beaten and stoned at least once, and perhaps twice or more. Several people saw these incidents but were unwilling or afraid to come to Langdon's aid. He was found semi-conscious by friends, but after resting overnight, he was able to walk to his own home the next day, a distance of a mile. A friend walked with him most of the way, and Langdon told him that he (Langdon) was going to die from the beating. And he was right, for two days later, after further attendance from a doctor (who may or may not have given him too strong a dose of heart stimulant) he succumbed.

There was not, however, enough viable evidence to bring any of the alleged participants, including Kehoe, to trial. That is, there was not enough evidence in 1862 to risk a trial. But now, in 1876, fourteen years later, there was. Though memories must have dimmed, the new-found willingness of people to testify gave the prosecution confidence. Kehoe and four others were indicted.

Two of the men, Neil Dougherty and John Campbell, were quickly convicted of second-degree murder when their trials were held in Pottsville on, respectively, November 24–30, 1876, and January 4–9, 1877. The other two, brothers named Columbus and Michael McGee, were later to be found innocent in May 1877. But these cases were all minor in comparison with the Kehoe case.[48]

And the prosecution took a bold gamble that it could prove a first-degree murder charge. A guilty verdict meant the rope.

The trial opened in Pottsville on January 9, 1877, before a packed house. The evidence presented by each side was contradictory. The night of the murder had been dark, the recognition by eyewitnesses incomplete. A father and his son, John Tyrell and John Tyrell, Jr., who had been together, who had found Langdon already beaten, and who had seen him beaten again, contradicted each other. Another witness swore he saw Kehoe back on the hotel porch at the very moment Langdon's cries were heard as he was being beaten. The threat that Kehoe was alleged to have made three weeks before and the further threat on the day of the killing weighed heavily against Kehoe as the prosecution strove to prove premeditation. With all the murky evidence in, the prosecution and defense made their final pleas to the jury. The Commonwealth put heavy emphasis on the grievances Kehoe was alleged to have nursed, and, relying on no less an authority than Chaucer, maintained that although it took fourteen years, "murder will out." The defense got into difficulties with their arguments, ending up contradicting themselves. Langdon's death probably resulted from the doctor's treatment, but if not, at least there was no premeditation. If either of the witnesses, the father or the son, was lying, then both would have to be considered so, as the jury could not be responsible for judging which one was incorrect. Finding themselves on weak ground here, the defense made much of the fact that the Coal & Iron police had conducted the investigation, rather than public authorities, and that the whole case was a fabric of capital depressing labor. While the jury was out, the courtroom hangers-on speculated on the verdict. Almost all felt he would be found guilty; most said it would be for second-degree murder. But one veteran maintained, "That jury is a first-degree one."[49] On January 16, 1877, John Kehoe was found guilty of first-degree murder. On April 16 he was sentenced to be hanged.

The dogged investigation of Linden, coupled with the multiplicity of informers, soon produced solutions for other old murders. The detective found a drunken Irishman, Daniel Kelly (alias Manus Cull, alias "Kelly the Bum"), languishing in the Pottsville jail and with promises of immunity soon had state's evidence on another famous killing, that of mine superintendent Alexander Rea, in 1868. Kelly implicated Patrick Hester, a well-known Hibernian from Columbia County, together with Peter McHugh, Patrick Tully, and several others. Hester, McHugh, and Tully were tried at Bloomsburg in early 1877 and all three found guilty of first-degree murder.[50]

And there would be other convictions before the books were closed on the Mollies.

✦ ✧ ✦ ✧ ✦

A RESCUE!

***

Startling News from Mauch Chunk

***

Doyle, Kelly, Fisher, Donohue, McKenna, and
Campbell Effect Their Escape

***

An Armed Force Outside and Traitors Inside the Walls

***

The Coal and Iron Police Drugged

***

A Pursuit Organized but no Results as Yet

***

T. B. Fielders, of the "Herald" Staff
Shot in the Ear

***

Captain Linden Bravely Attacks
the Retreating "Mollie Maguires"

***

Firing and Shouting His Indian War Cry
"ELAT SIHT EVEILEB TON OD"

Not all the readers of the *Shenandoah Herald's* issue of January 5, 1877, would have carefully reversed Linden's "Indian War Cry" in the last line above. As a result, some probably read through the entire lurid issue before they found out that it was a hoax, designed, said the editor, to prevent such a break from happening. But it was no hoax on January 8 when John Gibbons was actually caught tunneling out of the Mauch Chunk jail. Security was immediately increased in all the jails holding the Mollies and any such hope vanished.

With the key participants all sentenced, many to hang, the battles were now fought through the courts. Three cases, Carroll's (with Boyle, McGehan, and Roarity), Campbell's, and Duffy's, had gone to the Pennsylvania Supreme Court. When the rulings came on March 13 and 26 and May 21, respectively, they were all against the defendants. All were to hang.[51]

Now only the Pennsylvania Pardon Board stood between the men and eternity. A steady stream of letters now went forward to the board—from friends of the condemned asking for mercy, and from prosecution lawyers demanding that punishment be carried out. District Attorney Siewers of Mauch Chunk wrote the board that "vague rumors" had been heard of pardons for Kelly, Doyle, Campbell, and Donahue, the four men to be hanged in Carbon County. He objected vehemently, crying particularly bitterly against Campbell as being the "prime mover" and chief procurer of perjurers.[52]

Michael Doyle of Mt. Laffee, for one, however, had powerful forces speaking for him. The Rev. Daniel McDermott, the priest who figured so prominently in the Molly story, drafted a remarkable letter to the board petitioning for commutation of Doyle's sentence to life imprisonment, even though the priest was "certain beyond a doubt" that Doyle was guilty of the killing. Though Doyle had wanted to back out, McDermott continued, "anyone who knows the character of the Mollies well knows he could not have done so without losing his own life." The influence of the AOH "deprived him of the liberty of acting as his conscience dictated."[53] But all the various defenses were in vain.

The first ten of the condemned men were scheduled to be hanged on June 21, 1877, six at Pottsville (Carroll, Roarity, McGehan, Boyle, Munley, and Duffy) and four at Mauch Chunk (Kelly, Doyle, Campbell, and Donahue). As the day approached, rumors flew that a mass attempt at rescue would be made. At Mauch Chunk a request to Governor Hartranft had brought a squad of "Easton Greys with 26 muskets" to camp in the jail yard. Three of the four to be hanged at that place were connected with the John P. Jones shooting, and Mrs. Jones figured prominently in the news. She had made application to pull the lever which held the trap on the gallows, and her son had also applied. "Of course, both were refused," commented the *Mauch Chunk Democrat*.[54] She and two of her children showed up at the jail on the morning of the hangings. Edward Kelly asked to see her. "I have made your children fatherless, but I want you to forgive me," he was quoted as saying. "I hope God will forgive you," she replied. A moment later, in the hall, she inadvertently met Doyle's sister, who cried, "You have no business here; you ought not to be here." Shortly after, the four died together on a scaffold specially built for the occasion.

In Pottsville the sheriff had first thought of erecting a mammoth six-bed scaffold, but finally decided to hang the men two at a time. An immense crowd had gathered, blackening the hills around the jail yard. The scenes at dawn as the screaming women and sobbing children bid their husbands and fathers goodbye were sensationally reported in fulsome detail by the newspapers. Even a letter that James Roarity was said to have received from his father back in County Donegal, Ireland, was not sacred enough to miss the papers. Its pathos was too much for the editors to resist:

Meencorvick, June 6

Dear Loving Son:

I sit to write you the last letter that ever I'll write, again, and don't be afraid to meet your doom or your Judge. If you are going to suffer innocent I am sure God will spare your soul, and its far better to suffer in this world than in the world to come. No matter how long we suffer in this cursed world, its nothing beside eternity. Dear James, we are praying night and day for you; but it seems all in vain. But don't be afraid, God is merciful and good. And before you die, declare to your Judge and to the world whether you are guilty or innocent, and we are not sorry, for well I believe your letter saying you are innocent. But we are not sorry for your death, when you are going to die so.

And when your dear wife sees you, and the children; give them good encouragement, and keep yourself up. Certainly we are sorry; but what is the use? I did not tell your mother so far about it. And dear James, I don't know about Charles, where he is at all. All we heard he came down to Brooklyn.

So I hope, through the intercession of the Blessed Virgin, that you are going to meet with a happy death. I am sure you are; for since I heard of your sister and mother, we never stop praying night and day, in hopes still that God will spare you. And so He will and have that place prepared for you that will cause you joy and consolation during eternity, and it is not known until I be with you in the Kingdom of Heaven, so keep yourself stout in heart. I wish I was going to eternity along with you. I would be content; for, dear son, I don't know what to say or do, but really I'll be ever praying for you; and may the Lord of Heaven protect you in your last agony, and will. Don't be afraid. I am your loving father.

Columbus Roarty [sic]

Good bye for a while, for I'll shortly see you. We all join in prayer and with the help of God you will be all right.[55]

Boyle and McGehan came first, Boyle carrying a large, blood-red rose and McGehan with two roses in his lapel. The traps were sprung, and Boyle's rose fluttered to the ground. Carroll and Roarity were next, and both declared their innocence from the scaffold. The traps were sprung again and the Pottsville score rose to four. Munley and Duffy were last, Duffy having been held back on the chance that one of the others might exonerate him. None did, though, and the last two dropped through the trap. "Black Thursday," "Pennsylvania's Day With the Rope," had now climaxed the Molly Maguire story. Ten men hanged in one day— "Justice At Last," shouted the *Philadelphia Times*.[56]

And down to today that terrible day of retribution is bitterly remembered among the survivors of the hanged men. This is true both in the Pennsylvania coal fields and back in Ireland. For example, among the McGehan clan in County Donegal the story is still recounted of the family's gathering around the kitchen table on that day in 1877. Hugh McGehan had written them of his innocence and asked them to pray for him. And, so the story goes, at the moment of time when McGehan was on the gallows, the sky blackened as if by eclipse over the bogs of Glen Fin.

Already the blood-lust running rampant through the cases was beginning to pale. Many people were saying that if Duffy died, he would die an innocent man. Father McDermott, interceding again, was quoted as saying, "I know, beyond all reasonable doubt, that Duffy was not a party to the murder of Policeman Yost, and I think the same remark will apply with almost equal force to Carroll."[57] The priest would not go as far as to say both had had nothing to do with the planning of the crime. Yet there remained the uneasy feeling that there were degrees of guilt—that all of the ten were not equally guilty. Nevertheless, all ten were dead.

Chapter 13 * Closing the Record

*T*HE TEN who were hanged on that one June day in 1877 were just half of the total of twenty men who were finally executed for so-called "Molly Maguire" crimes. But eight of this second group, who had been involved in five murders, had no relationship to the conspiratorial inner circle based in Schuylkill County.* Their cases did not involve McParlan in any way, and only engaged the Pinkertons in the later investigations. Though all were solved by information stemming out of the earlier trials, liberally aided by further informing and confessing, they were considered to be Molly cases only because they involved Hibernian officers and members. Most stemmed from personal grudges (though one, that of the murder of Alexander Rae, was connected with a robbery). Some had elements of common tactics similar to those of the Schuylkill cases—such as trading of jobs and assignment of assassins' tasks by the bodymaster.

Two of the second ten, however, were Schuylkill County men whom McParlan knew and testified against. One was Dennis "Bucky" Donnelly. The other was John Kehoe.

Dennis Donnelly was belatedly brought to trial on November 17, 1877, after staying in the Pottsville jail for almost a year serving sentence for a minor crime.[1] Donnelly now stood accused of being the master mind behind the shooting of Sanger and Uren at Raven Run. He had been the Raven Run bodymaster at that time. McParlan had met him both before and after the shooting, but had never been in a meeting with him. The detective again described both the workings of the AOH and the details of his knowledge of the

* These eight were: Patrick Hester, Peter McHugh, and Patrick Tully, hanged on March 25, 1878, for the murder, in 1868, of Alexander Rea; Thomas Fisher, hanged on March 28, 1878, for the murder, in 1871, of Morgan Powell; James McDonnell and Charles Sharp, hanged on January 14, 1879, for the murder, in 1863, of George K. Smith; Martin Bergen, hanged on January 16, 1879, for the murder, in 1870, of Patrick Burns; and Peter McManus, hanged on October 9, 1879, for the murder, in 1874, of Frederick Hesser. They are discussed in Marvin Schlegel, *Ruler of the Reading: The Life of Franklin B. Gowen* (Harrisburg: Archives Publishing Co., 1947), pp. 146-152.

Raven Run shooting. But McParlan could only implicate Donnelly through certain bragging statements that the latter had made at the time of the habeas corpus proceedings on the Raven Run case on February 23, 1876, when Donnelly implied "he knew all about it." So it was necessary to fall back on testimony of two Mollies to convict Donnelly.

One was Dennis Canning, who was given an early pardon (from his convictions in the Thomas and Major brothers conspiracy cases) to come back on November 22, 1877, as Commonwealth witness to swear that Donnelly had boasted to him that he had arranged for the killing of Sanger.

But the most devastating evidence was by the other Molly. He was Patrick Butler, who had already provided one of the sensations of the trials by turning state's evidence while on the stand in the Gomer James case. Butler, under insistent prodding from the defense in his cross-examination on November 21, reluctantly admitted that he had not only gone scot-free from the earlier cases, but had subsequently been employed in Philadelphia as a detective for the Pinkertons. Butler enumerated earlier instances where Donnelly had tried to murder Thomas Sanger, supposedly because the mine boss was discharging Irishmen. The defense produced not only an alibi for Donnelly on the night before the killing, but also testimony that contradicted Butler and implied that Butler himself had ordered the killing.

The Commonwealth's evidence held sway, however. Dennis Donnelly was convicted of first-degree murder. He was hanged on June 11, 1878.

As for John Kehoe, after his surprising first-degree murder conviction in January 1877 for the killing of Frank Langdon the case was carried to the state Supreme Court. The justices rendered a lengthy opinion on October 1, 1877. They agreed that "the burden of raising the grade to murder of the first degree devolves on the Commonwealth" but, after reviewing the evidence, concluded that "all the ingredients necessary . . . were found to exist in this case" and affirmed the decision of the lower court.[2]

This left only the Pardon Board. Here Kehoe and his counsel made extraordinary efforts. When the plea for clemency was brought before the board on April 10, 1878, Kehoe presented sworn statements by John Campbell and Neil Dougherty admitting their own guilt but flatly vowing that Kehoe was not involved.[3] Kehoe petitioned under his own name, alleging that "the combination of great corporations reaching into the County of Schuylkill and having large numbers of paid police and agents . . . made use of the influence at their command to stimulate public sentiment against your petitioner and made it impossible for him to get a fair trial." He concluded that he would have been acquitted if he had not had "to encounter popular prejudice."[4] Kehoe went even further in a private letter in his own handwriting, undated but probably written sometime in March 1878:

Pottsvill Prison

Hon. W. R. Potts

My Esteemed friend. Thinking over the Cruelties that has Befallen me. By Bribery Perjury and Pregudise . . . I am under the sentence of Death. for a Crime I Never Committed which I will Prove to you. I am Convicted for the Beating or death of Frank Langdon that was Committed in Audenried nearly 16 years ago. I did not Get Justice in eighther Courts their is no evidence in my Case that should Convict me there was Good evidence that Proved my inocence But it was All Jug handled Justice. But iff I had sworn that Lie on Gov hartranft. I would Be Pardoned long ago they ofered one Both Money & Pardon if I would do it. Firgus Farquhar was appointed by Gowen to Pay the money. But I would not take it. they all know that I am inocent. Neil Dougherty & John Campbell was Convicted in the 2nd Degree on the same Charge on the 2nd of last april. Campbell Confessed in the Court that he seen Yellow Jack Donahoe Beating Langdon with a swingeltree he said their was no Person By at thy Beating onley him self & Donahoe. he said he would have told it before But he wanted to see they witnesses daming their souls on the stand By Pergury Donahoe was executed last June for the murder of Morgan Powel. the day Before he was hanged he Confessed to Capt Robbert J. Linden & Michael Donahoe of Mahanoy City that he was the man that Beat Langdon..he said he Beat him with a swingletree and that no Person saw him do it But John Campbell that John Kehoe was not there or Knowd nothing About it. Kerrigan Slattery & others said the same.. John W. Ryon Esq. will take my Case Before they Board of Pardons in april. so I must write to all my friends to try and do what they Can for Me. Now, Ramsey, what Ever their is in your Power I hope you will do it for me. I will Rite to John W. Morgan & Dr. McRibben you can see them. of Cours I Need not tell you who to see you Know them all yourself. I will write a long letter to John W. Rillinger him &

me used to Be Good old friends. Now my Dear Potts see all they Good men that you can to help you to Get me out of this Cursed Prison I am heart Broken. I hope that God will strenghten you and all my friends to obtain for me my humble and earnest Request. with Meutch Respets I Remain your humble servant . . . John Kehoe

P. S. dont for get what you told me when you seen me Last. Ramsey I never thought that men would Be so wicked they swore every way they wanted them . . . I would sooner die than swear a wilful lie on my fellow man Good By. J. Kehoe[5]

"Yellow Jack" Donahue was already hanged, as Kehoe said, and could not substantiate Kehoe's story. But Martin L'Velle, Donahue's attorney, told Kehoe's attorneys in a letter that in his very last interview with Donahue he had asked his client if Kehoe was guilty of the Langdon murder. "He answered emphasizing by slapping me on the knee," L'Velle continued, " 'He is as innocent, my son, as you are.' This reply gave me much anxiety, and I went at once and informed General Albright."[6] L'Velle volunteered to swear to this by affidavit.

Others apparently believed that Kehoe was guilty, but not of first-degree murder. A number of Girardville people, headed by Rev. Daniel O'Connor (the priest who had originally told Kehoe about McParlan), signed a plea for commutation to life imprisonment. They said Kehoe had "a wife and seven small helpless children who are destitute of wealth, rank or station," and further killing, after the more than a dozen hangings would "horrify and disgust the citizens . . . and awaken and arouse passions and animosities."[7] Even the vindictive *Shenandoah Herald* conceded that none of the cases of previous defendants "had half the bottom to stand on that Kehoe's case has."[8]

After the board failed to act in April, Governor Hartranft was quoted as saying, "All agree that he deserves the same punishment as that administered to his numerous guilty companions; however, he should not be hung for a crime that he was not clearly proven guilty of merely because he has been implicated in other dark deeds that, according to the law, would consign him to the gallows."[9] But, in spite of the governor's words, the board finally turned Kehoe down on September 4, 1878, by the effect of their tie vote of 2–2. Still Hartranft procrastinated about signing the death warrant. Some accused him of playing politics, for it was again an election autumn and there was always the Irish vote to worry about. In the Pottsville jail Kehoe was alleged to have said that Gowen had told Father Andrew Gallagher that, if the governor did not hang Kehoe, he would hang the governor.[10]

With the election past, Hartranft startled everyone by signing the warrant on November 21. Kehoe was stunned. "That's the end of it," he said when the warrant was read to him before a number of reporters.[11] In spite of an additional sworn statement, introduced at the last minute, that Kehoe was not present at the killing, the board turned a deaf ear. On December 18, 1878, Kehoe was sprung through the gallows trap. An error in the fastening of the rope made him fall slightly sideways and he swung to and fro for a full three minutes before strangling to death. In this gruesome manner occurred what the Miners' Journal called the "Death of Mollieism."[12]

✣   ✣   ✣   ✣   ✣

For the Irishmen of the southern coal fields, the Mollies were truly dead. Those parts of the AOH lodges that had been dubbed by McParlan "the inner circle" were no more. The key members had either swung from the gallows or were serving long prison terms.

In the process, the coal-region AOH lodges were themselves pulled under. In early 1877 Bishop William O'Hara of Scranton— in the northern anthracite field—dumfounded the organization by unexpectedly excommunicating the AOH and denying its members the sacraments.[13] The abrupt change of heart by the influential cleric produced a sensation throughout the ranks. When the 1877 national convention of the AOH opened in New York in early April, it was obvious that the Molly issue would have to be faced, and faced publicly.

This was a stormy session, attended by one hundred fifty-two delegates from twenty-six states. A Committee on Revision of the Constitution was formed and the Pennsylvania situation debated at length. At the end of the convention the usually secretive organization took the unprecedented action of issuing an "Address to the People of the United States." The position of the organization was given as follows: "For some time a stigma or cloud has rested over the Ancient Order of Hibernians on account of certain portions of Pennsylvania . . . the Order does not recognize any connection with . . . that terrible band of misguided men." After a searching investigation, it had been decided "to cut off from all connections with our organization the Schuylkill, Carbon, Northumberland and Columbia County lodges." The AOH said it realized that because of this action "a great number of good men would suffer for the misdeeds of a few . . . but the character of the organization was involved."[14]

Thus the national AOH completely disavowed its locals in the southern anthracite fields. These apparently became dormant; the official history of the Pottsville local states that the first lodge in the Schuylkill County was "Division No. 1 of Pottsville, chartered in March, 1887."[15]

The national convention also made sweeping changes in the constitution "to remove every cause of an objectionable nature so as to make our rules in harmony with the teachings of our Holy Church."[16] The same theme was stressed at the 1878 convention, and the organization was soon returned grudging recognition by the Church in most parts of the country. But it was to be many years before the AOH would fully live down the Molly Maguire incidents. Almost forty years later, in August 1916, at a large AOH convention in Pottsville, the leaders were able to persuade Archbishop Edmund F. Prendergast to say mass for them at its start. Promptly the Rev. Daniel McDermott, who had moved from New Philadelphia to Pottsville, where he was rector of St. Mary's Catholic Church, publicly denounced the AOH. He accused them not only of the Molly incidents but also of the murder of Dr. P. H. Cronin, a prominent Irishman connected with the Clan na Gael.[17] Not many people had as long and vivid a memory as Father McDermott. But the Hibernians were long troubled by the Molly Maguire image.

McDermott, though always violently opposing the AOH, could scarcely be accused of defending the employers. In 1877, shortly after the hanging of the first ten Mollies, the priest came out with a full-page letter to the *Freeman's Journal and Catholic Register* (New York), appropriately titled "Faults on Both Sides." The abuses of the Coal Exchange—the black list, the depressed wage, the antiunion attitudes—were bitterly criticized by the priest. McDermott then hit a sensitive spot: the killings at Wiggans Patch. Said he, "Who counseled, abetted and committed the Wiggans massacre has long been an open secret." And he asked, "Why have not the perpetrators . . . been brought to justice? Has a McParlan been sent among them?"[18]

The plight of the miners *was* still the same. The country remained imbedded in deep depression, and the conditions were reflected in the coal regions. The markets were demoralized through most of 1876, with wages by September one third below the $2.50 basis. Dissension in the coal combination over production quotas suddenly brought the complete demise of the combination, and Gowen and the other coal-rail magnates ruthlessly dumped coal on the markets. Prices tumbled, and wages followed. One of the biggest coal companies, the Lehigh & Wilkes-Barre, went into receivership in early 1877 and the market continued to sag through most of 1877. Each new corporate difficulty was quickly reflected in the miner's lot. There were strikes in the northern and central regions, and they were especially ugly. Both federal and state troops were finally sent to Scranton to quell the violence.

Compounding the tensions was a mushrooming dispute with the Brotherhood of Locomotive Engineers. Ever since Gowen had first sensed McParlan's effectiveness as a spy, he had employed other detectives on the railroad to keep him posted on any union activities. Thus he knew ahead of time the plans of his engineers in the early spring of 1877 to strike the Reading (engineers had carried off successful strikes earlier in the year on the Jersey Central and the Boston & Maine). Moving quickly, he gave the engineers on March 27 a choice of staying at work with increased benefits or being fired if they continued their membership in the union. The union struck, and Gowen countered by aggressively hiring new engineers and giving bonuses to the engineers and firemen who stayed. The union tried to frighten the public by insinuating that the Reading was running unsafe trains. But the quick, decisive moves by Gowen easily won the day and the strike failed miserably. Gowen sailed for Europe in early May to meet with the English stockholders, confident that union trouble had been put down again.[19]

Gowen came out far better than several other Eastern railroads did. For a series of events in July and August 1877 brought the country about as close to real revolution as it has ever been. Employees on the Baltimore & Ohio Railroad struck against a wage cut; the Pennsylvania Railroad employees followed. But this was no conventional strike. The strikers began seizing the trains. State militia were called up. In Baltimore the edgy troops fired into a mob, killing twelve people, and the mob retaliated by chasing the soldiers into the station and setting fire to it. Worse came in Pittsburgh; state militia from Philadelphia, attempting to disperse an ugly crowd, opened fire, whereupon the mob laid siege to the troops by holding them in the round house. By the time fresh troops arrived, more than two dozen men were dead.[20] These were but the worst of a widespread series of violent acts around the country, a great many touched off by the bitter labor-capital struggle that had been so accentuated by the deep depression.

When the anthracite miners of the northern fields attempted to bring the Schuylkill County employees out during the railroad strike, Gowen was able to forestall them through persuasion and through rapid action by Linden and the Coal & Iron police in dispersing a Mahanoy City mob on August 7.[21] Soon prices began to climb for the coal Gowen continued to send forward to the markets, and wages followed upward. Discontent died, and Gowen's ability to keep the southern fields working while the others were out now paid handsome dividends. In earlier years, the southern fields had gone out and had been undercut by the northern fields. Now the pattern was reversed.

Gowen's apparent success in the labor relations and marketing areas of the business were belied by a more deep-seated failure. Though the railroad continued to show fair earnings, it could not support the great debt created by the purchases of coal land. Dividend payments were stopped in July 1876, and the short-term debt climbed to over eight million dollars by early 1877. Gowen was again forced to borrow to pay the mounting interest charges; but a mortgage bond offering of ten million dollars fell miserably short, with only a bit over two million actually sold. The rail president spent the next three years urging bondholders to make various concessions and placating the dividendless stockholders. Finally, in 1880, the line went into receivership; and in 1881 Gowen lost his presidency. Relations between the new management and the English stockholders worsened, and in a complicated and exciting series of maneuvers Gowen won back the presidency and the English stockholders sold out at tremendous loss to new American stockholders, including William H. Vanderbilt, the head of the New York

Central. Gowen then launched a new series of expansions, but again they were ill-fated. He resigned in 1883 and the railroad fell into receivership again, finally to be bailed out by J. P. Morgan.

These fascinating years after the Molly Maguire incidents have been sketched here only in brief outline, for they are not central to our story, and are well covered in other books.[22] But the account of Gowen's involvement in the Molly Maguire story is not quite complete. After the Kehoe trial for the Langdon murder in early 1877, Gowen left the prosecution of the other cases to the various Commonwealth district attorneys—high time, felt many who were beginning to wonder if he intended to remain a railroad president. He had spent a great portion of the second half of 1876 in the courtroom despite the real difficulties at the railroad.

When he went to England in May 1877 to try to satisfy the English stockholders about the company's financial condition, he must have felt he needed a few red herrings to drag across his trail, for heavy emphasis was put on the Molly Maguire incidents. Thomas Wilde Powell said when he introduced Gowen:

As Englishmen, and as men of business, I think we have a good deal to thank Mr. Gowen for, besides his general character and reputation. He had the difficult task two or three years ago of attacking one of the most terrible and unscrupulous bodies of trades' union bullies and assassins that ever infected any region in the world. These men established themselves in the wild hilly country of Pennsylvania, among a rough population, many of whom were too willing to do their bidding. These men established a reign of violence and terror such as has had no parallel in any trades' union in contemporaneous history in this or in any other country. Mr. Gowen was exposed to threats of all kinds. He received threatening letters headed with drawings of death's heads and cross-bones, and other sketches of a similar character, but he was in no way daunted by these proceedings but fought the battle of his company fearlessly, brought some of these men to justice, and broke up their loathsome combination. The result is that he has now a contented set of men at work, who are satisfied with their employers, and that there now exists a reign of contentment and happiness where formerly there existed a reign of terror, bullying, burning and assassination.[23]

Gowen then replied with a theme that he was to reiterate many more times in the process of defending his management of the company:

We had to contend with a powerful and unscrupulous trades' union, which at one time controlled the entire coal fields, and which consisted of from 30,000 to 40,000 men, who by their officers established such a price for their labor as enabled a man of the meanest capacity to earn good wages, and then prevented any other man with more industry, or of greater skill, from doing more work than just sufficient to earn the same amount which the shiftless and inefficient required for his daily pay. There was no telling to what this system might have led, and we saw plainly that although we had acquired the ownership of the fee simple of the property, still we should not obtain the practical ownership of it unless we were permitted to do what we liked with our own.

After waiting and working for three or four years in constant strife, and after a suspension of business at one time for six entire months, we succeeded in breaking all this down, and for the first time since we acquired the title we found ourselves in the real ownership of the lands.

The railroad's annual report in January 1877 had made this even more specific:

A landed estate of two hundred and fifty square miles had to be taken from the control of an irresponsible trades-union, and its inhabitants rescued from the dominion of an oath-bound association of murderers which for years had held the life and property of every one engaged in any industrial pursuit subject to a secret tribunal, whose infamous decrees were carried into effect by the assassin and the incendiary. After more than four years of the most earnest and unremitting labor, the Company has been entirely successful in reclaiming its property. The labor unions have been practically dissolved; and it is truly believed that the great majority of the miners and laborers of the coal fields have been changed from enemies into friends and adherents of the Company. The secret association of Molly Maguires has been broken up, and every prominent leader of that infamous association who is not a fugitive from justice is today either under sentence and awaiting execution, in prison at penal servitude, or held in custody for future trial.[24]

Thus Gowen completed the verbal association—the union was beaten; the Mollies were beaten; the day was won for the company. If the W.B.A. or any other union were ever to attempt an organizing effort again it would find itself soaked in the brew of Molly Maguireism.

And this was exactly what happened to a famous successor, the Knights of Labor. The Knights had been in existence as a narrow trade union of tailors since late in the 1860's, but by the late 1870's the organization began picking up widely differing memberships, including many mining locals. When Terence Powderly, the Knights' most famous president, took over leadership from Uriah Stephens, the organization began earnest efforts to organize. The Knights of Labor was destined to achieve great notoriety and strength before its precipitous decline in the late 1880's. But before its growth could come, it had to live down the Molly Maguire name, though it had had nothing to do with the Mollies. At first the Knights of Labor was a secret organization, but was finally able to persuade the Church that its secrecy was designed only to protect it against its enemies and that Catholics were expressly authorized to reveal everything to ecclesiastical authorities.[25] But it was continually accused of being the Molly Maguires under another name.

One of Powderly's organizers put the twin problems of secrecy and Molly Maguireism succinctly:

Oh yes, Philadelphia is saying the name of the order shall not and be not divulged. I do not want to say anything. Go their yourself and you will hear every little child will tell the name of the order and the same out west. They say this we cannot rent a hall without showing our charter in the state of Illinois and then the people ask us our name and we dare not tell them. And the next thing the people say we have the Molly Maguires here—look out for murder, house burning and so on. I myself have quite a little of names. I am called member of a nameless Society. A Molly Maguire and in fact a Communist.[26]

Powderly himself cried out, "Our Order is not akin to the Molly Maguires . . . I am sick of that term being slung at us."[27] But, as Powderly aptly pointed out, "as long as workingmen had a willing ear to the slanders of capital just so long will capital be able to control us through our prejudices." Though "Communist" was also vying for position as a favorite epithet, the words "Molly Maguire" were still good for calling up stereotyped prejudices for most of the rest of the nineteenth century, particularly in the Pennsylvania hard-coal fields.

❖   ❖   ❖   ❖   ❖

The Molly Maguire saga was, then, a personal triumph for Franklin Gowen. And it was for Allan Pinkerton too.

The Molly Maguire investigation had come at a propitious time for the agency, for the deepening depression had brought it severe financial trauma. Even with the increased business of the Molly work, though, times remained hard for Pinkerton. And with the successful conclusion of the case, Pinkerton found himself faced with demands for salary increases from both Benjamin Franklin and Robert Linden (but apparently not from McParlan). Franklin had been receiving $2,000 a year, now wanted $3,000; Linden wanted an increase to $150 a month.

Pinkerton had been cooling toward Franklin for a number of months. "Philadelphia has been buoyed up a little in the way of business with the Molly Maguire cases," he wrote Bangs, "still take that away from them and where is Philadelphia?" It was not Franklin that built up the Philadelphia affair, but himself, Pinkerton continued. "It's the Agency they want, *not* Mr. Franklin." The Molly Maguires would soon be a thing of the past and, even there, "I beg him to remember that first the praise, honor and glory of breaking up the MM's belongs to MacParlan." There is no record of whether Franklin got his raise, but it is likely that he did not. He was soon accused by Pinkerton of showing signs of mental trouble and was replaced as Philadelphia superintendent by Linden.[28]

Just how much income did Pinkerton receive from the Molly Maguire cases? Gowen had estimated in 1876 that it had cost the railroad over four million dollars to take the five-month "long strike" of 1875, though the "determined stand" had resulted in "permanently rescuing" the company from the "arbitrary control of an irresponsible trades union."[29] Gowen's figures were somewhat arbitrary, but probably represented the lost revenues approximately. But Gowen's calculated effort to mix together the Molly Maguires and the W.B.A. has led some analysts of the Molly story to regard the four-million-dollar figure as the cost of searching out the Mollies during the 1870's.

Though the actual costs of that undertaking cannot be fully determined at this late date, we have some interesting new clues via the expense statements in the Reading Railroad files. McParlan's were always billed separately, and another statement covered all the remaining agents. There are many gaps in the list of statements still surviving, and we must tread carefully in generalizing. One of the most nearly complete years—as well as one of the busiest—was

1875. For the six and a half months of McParlan statements still extant, the total was $1,695.22, including salary. For the composite statement of Linden and nine others for approximately the same period it was $9,646.52. If we extrapolate, the total yearly cost in 1875 of the eleven agents was about $22,000. There were no provisions here for overhead and profit; apparently there was a separate billing on this. The total billing was probably under $50,000 for that year, and under $150,000 for the three major years of Molly investigation (1874, 1875, 1876)—quite a bit short of the imputed four million! Still, it was a substantial amount for a near-bankrupt railroad to be paying out.

But the monies made by Pinkerton in the actual Molly Maguire cases were only part of the total income accruing to the agency from the Reading. First, Pinkerton's detectives continued to be employed extensively by Gowen for other jobs on the Reading. We have already noted their use in the engineers' strike. And they were used even more for investigation of union activities in the coal fields—both a new version of the W.B.A. and the feared Knights of Labor. Many of the detective reports on these activities still survive, and they tell a fascinating story of pitched competition between the two unions, with old Protestant–Catholic and English–Irish tensions now compounded by the large influx of Eastern Europeans—the "Polanders" and the "Sclavs," to use the words of that day. It was a fertile field for detectives, and there was even a rough equivalent of a McParlan—operative N. Johnston—who was able to infiltrate a local of the Knights. The coal region was to be good business for Pinkerton for many years.[30]

The agency also profited handsomely from the Molly cases in its public reputation. Though there were occasional jibes at the methods used, Gowen's newsworthy explanations had clothed the agency efforts in an aura of success and righteousness that quickly brought in new business.

A fair proportion of this new business—apparently lucrative— entailed surveillance of labor unions. It was carried on without much public notoriety until 1892. Then occurred one of the most famous of all cases in which a detective agency opposed a labor union: the Homestead riot in the Pittsburgh area. The story is a complex one, and was finally made the subject of a full-scale investigation by the

United States Congress.[31] When strikers at the Carnegie steel plant at Homestead, Pennsylvania, saw two barges being towed up the Monongahela River, filled with three hundred Pinkerton detectives engaged by Henry Clay Frick as strikebreakers, they began shooting. The Pinkertons returned the fire but were driven back, and many were captured and manhandled by the strikers. Before the day ended, seven men were dead and over twenty injured. Though the Pinkertons were largely on the receiving end, the agency's reputation was tarnished by implications that it employed strong-arm tactics. The same accusations were made against detective agencies engaged in "labor spying" in the 1930's, when the "LaFollette report" in the United States Senate castigated the agencies, putting a heavy onus on the Pinkertons.[32] At this time public reaction was stronger, and the end result was that labor-union surveillance was dropped by all reputable detective agencies.

For Allan Pinkerton, the Molly Maguire case was the zenith of a long and famous career. He was able to publish his popular book, *The Mollie Maguires and the Detectives*, just after the first ten hangings. This, combined with Franklin Dewees' book, *The Molly Maguires*, put the agency's name on nearly everyone's lips. In all, Pinkerton published eighteen of these lucrative books, finally employing seven men just for this purpose.[33] All the books were ghost-written, Pinkerton dictating notes to the young writers. The *New York Times* chided Pinkerton on this: "Authorship is not his forte, and probably he could not write a reward handbill grammatically."[34] But we might want to dispute the learned paper after seeing Pinkerton's letterbook; his style in writing to his agents was colorful and pungent.

His role in the agency was less active after the Molly cases, not only because of his physical infirmities but because of a quarrel with his son Robert.[35] (Incidentally, Pinkerton's daughter married a man he did not like—Pinkerton's abiding interest in phrenology told him that "to look at _____'s head, phrenologically it predicts that he is not the man at all to produce happiness with Pussy.") By 1882, when he penned a long, rambling letter, filled with braggadocio, to William Gladstone, it was clear that he was out of the main stream of the agency's work. Another massive stroke killed him on July 1, 1884; he had lived just under sixty-five years.

No one could dispute the fact that he was the first in the country to give the name "detective" a respected and public image, in the process also making the word "Pinkerton" synonymous with it.

James McParlan, though, had a long career ahead of him and one more spectacular public role to play. The young detective (he was twenty-nine when he began the Pennsylvania saga) remained with Pinkerton's National Detective Agency for the rest of his life. He first took various private and governmental cases for the agency all over the country and South America, then settled in Denver, Colorado, to become head of the agency's office there. If his life was not exactly peaceful, at least he was no longer being given national publicity. Not, that is, until 1907, when a famous murder again put his name in newspaper headlines all over the country.

The murdered man was former Governor Frank Steunenberg of Idaho. Steunenberg had incurred the wrath of the militant Western Federation of Miners by using militia in labor disputes while he was in office. Now the finger was being pointed at key W.F.M. officials as plotters of his death.

The ex-Governor was blown up by a dynamite charge attached to his gate—and a miner hanger-on, Harry Orchard (alias Horsley or Hogan or Dempsey or Gaglan), was arrested for the crime. About ten days later McParland (who by now had added a "d" to his name) was called in on the case by Frank R. Gooding, then governor of Idaho. The detective went directly to Orchard's cell, where he quickly built a subtle set of psychological devices designed to make Orchard confess. As McParland later reported to Gooding, "I then cited cases in which the state witnesses went entirely free, and to put the matter more forcibly to him and to bring it home to the personal side of the present case, I cited and named personally the Mollie McGuires state witnesses who saved their own necks by telling the truth." McParland drew for Orchard a picture of Daniel Kelly, alias Manus Cull, alias "Kelly the Bum," being let off scot-free —"the good citizens of Columbia County, Pennsylvania, recognizing that Kelly had rendered a great service to the state, gave him about $1,000 in order that he might leave the country"—all this despite the fact that Kelly freely admitted he had personally put a ball through the head of Alexander Rae. McParland implied to Orchard that he was just a tool of the "inner circle," that Orchard's own attorney was really the attorney of this inner group and would advise him to remain silent until he was finally executed and they could breathe easy again. McParland reported he told Orchard he was "a man of intelligence and reasoning power as his forehead would indicate," and was not fool enough to take the punishment deserved by others. McParland piously told Gooding that he at no time promised Orchard immunity, and that he told Orchard that if he did want to confess, McParland must have "all the truth."[36]

McParland's arguments succeeded. In a startling 135-page confession, Orchard reconstructed a personal saga of crime that was almost beyond belief. He had murdered scores of men, said Orchard, most of these at the instigation of the W.F.M. "inner circle," consisting of president Charles Moyer, secretary-treasurer William "Big Bill" Haywood, and an influential member, George Pettibone. The three were promptly arrested and brought to Idaho.

The key trial was Haywood's; it opened in Boise, Idaho, on May 9, 1907.[37] The prosecution was headed by William E. Borah, who was about to begin his thirty-three years in the United States Senate. Though he was no Gowen, Borah made the most of the Orchard confession. But the defense this time was immensely stronger than in the Molly Maguire cases. Its leader was Clarence Darrow.

Darrow soon elicited the whole McParland involvement.[38] With his matchless technique of insinuation and sarcasm he sketched a picture of brutal capital depressing weak labor. Darrow reserved his bitterest blasts for the Pinkertons in his masterful eleven-hour summation on July 24 and 25. His treatment of McParland can be seen from the following sample:

Here is a piece of work, gentlemen of the jury, that will last as long as the ages last—McParland's conversion of Orchard! Don't you think this detective is wasting his time down in the Pinkerton office in the city of Denver? From the beginning of the world was ever any miracle like this performed before? Lo, and behold! A man who has spent his life as a Pinkerton—isn't a preacher—he has never been ordained except in the Pinkerton office. But here is a man who has challenged the world—Harry Orchard, who has lived his life up to this time, and he has gotten over what religion he ever had, and he meets this Pinkerton detective who never did anything in his life but lie and cheat and scheme (for the life of a detective is a living lie, that is his business; he lives one from the time he gets up in the morning to the time he goes to bed; he is deceiving people, and trapping people and lying to people and imposing on people;

that is his trade), and Harry Orchard is caught, and he meets this famous detective, who speaks to him familiarly about David and St. Paul and Kelly the Bum, and a few more of his acquaintances, and he speaks of them in the most familiar way. And then he holds out the hope of life and all that life could offer to Harry Orchard, and lo, and behold, he soon becomes a Christian. Now, gentlemen, Savonarola, who was a great preacher, and a mighty man in his day, is dead. He went up in flames long ago, and he cannot convert the world. John Wesley is dead. Cranmer is dead. Moody is dead. Pretty much all of them are gone. What is the matter with McParland changing the sign on his office, and going into the business of saving souls instead of snaring bodies? If he could convert a man like Orchard in the twinkling of an eye, I submit he is too valuable a man to waste his time in a Pinkerton detective office trying to catch men. He had better go out in the vineyard and go to work and bring in souls. A man who could wash Harry Orchard's soul as white as wool need not hesitate at tackling any sort of a job that came his way. He is a wonderful detective, but his fame as a detective would be eclipsed in a moment if he would go into the business of saving souls instead of catching men.

But I might suggest to this good man, who talks of St. Paul and David as if they had been shadows that he had used in his office, I might suggest to Mr. McParland, the wise and the good, who quotes the Bible in one moment and then tries to impose upon some victim in the next, who quotes Scripture in one sentence and then lies in the next, who utters blessings with one word and curses with the next, I might suggest to this good man that William Haywood has a soul, Moyer has a soul, Pettibone has a soul. Why not go to Moyer, Haywood and Pettibone and tell them some of your stories of St. Paul and David, and offer to wash their sins away?

Why not give some attention to the souls of the men whose bodies they are trying to consign to the tomb? Do you suppose McParland is interested in Haywood's soul? Do you suppose he is interested in Moyer's? Do you suppose he is interested in Harry Orchard's? Do you suppose he is interested in his own? Do you suppose he is interested in anything except weaving a web around these men so that he may be able to hang them by the neck until dead? And to do it, like the devil, he quotes Scripture. To do it, there isn't a scheme or a plan or a device of his wily, crooked brain that he won't bring into action, whether it is the Bible or detective yarns—there is none too good for McParland. And then he will have a lawyer to say: "Here, behold McParland's work. Here is Harry Orchard, with a pure soul and a clean heart, and he told you twelve men a story by which you can afford to take away the lives of three men." Well, all right, perhaps you will do it, but I don't think so.[39]

It was one of the most famous of all Darrow speeches. And it had the expected result. Haywood was found innocent, and Moyer and Pettibone subsequently also went free. Orchard was tried in May 1908 and was sentenced to be hanged; later his sentence was commuted to life imprisonment.

It was a bitter turn of events for the Pinkertons and for McParland. Their tactics were subjected to much abusive commentary, the very tactics that had been so well received in the Molly trials. But the Molly Maguires were tried in the 1870's, and Clarence Darrow was not there.

❖ ❖ ❖ ❖ ❖

McParland, like Allan Pinkerton, died peacefully—in 1919. But Franklin B. Gowen died violently. The rail president permanently lost his job with the Reading in 1883. He tried to get the presidency back in 1886 but failed. He returned to private law practice and was apparently doing well. But on Friday, December 13, 1889, he locked himself in a hotel room and shot himself in the head.

When the incredible news was made public, rumors immediately began to fly. It was not suicide, but murder—the Mollies had caught up with their Nemesis. Gowen had seemed in good health and spirits, and there seemed to be no earthly reason why he would take his own life.

Linden, now head of the Philadelphia office of the Pinkertons, immediately entered the case, and the papers were full of articles asking "Was Gowen Murdered?"[40] McParland was interviewed in Denver and was quoted as saying, "I don't see how he could have put an end to himself unless it was because he had over-taxed himself since leaving the Reading . . . he has been engaged in a desperate fight against Standard Oil." But after authorities sifted all evidence, they came to the reluctant conclusion that Gowen himself had pulled the trigger. Why he did it remains a complete enigma. Some anti-Gowen but pro-Molly Maguire writers have attributed the suicide to a guilt complex due to his handling of the Molly cases. Charles Smith, former president of the Reading, another Gowen enemy, commented sourly that "it was caused purely by mortification over his failure in the management of the road." At any rate, it put a grim ending to a major figure in the Molly Maguire saga.

Gowen's "murder" was not the only rumor of post-Molly retaliation and retribution. Some fascinating stories have grown up about the case. Some of these may well be true, though unprovable. Most are closer to the realm of anecdote, or even downright myth. There were legends that the "wrath of God" had taken vengeance on various participants in the Molly cases. John O'Dea, in his official history of the AOH, perpetuated these tales by making much of the fact that several of the prosecution did not die natural deaths.[41] And the story has persisted that on the night of the hanging of the first ten Mollies, two witnesses were murdered, and that within two weeks five of the prosecutors had met the same fate. This story has been reprinted as fact in otherwise sound books on criminology, despite the fact that there is no basis of truth in it whatsoever.[42] In an English book on the Mollies, published in the 1880's, seven specific murders and a number of incendiary fires were listed as being "Mollie retaliation."[43] No evidence can be found that any of these were linked to the Mollies.

But it was certainly true that enmities stemming from the Molly saga were deep and abiding. One need only visit the coal fields today, nearly a century later, to be convinced of the reservoir of ill feeling and suspicion about the case. Families were split when men informed. The violent emotions extended to wives and children. Patrick Hester's wife was reputed to have hired a gang to attack the wife of one of the men who testified against her husband; they planned to cut off her hair. Even some of the juveniles apparently formed secret organizations to carry on the animosities.[44]

Few of the fugitives were found. Hurley was reported to have come back to America, to have been arrested for a minor crime in 1886 in Gunnison, Colorado, and, when recognized as the Molly fugitive, to have committed suicide.[45] Harry Orchard asked McParland about this, and queried the detective as to why the Pinkertons did not bring Hurley back to Pennsylvania for trial. McParland reported that he replied, "It is easily explained. Hurley was simply the tool of Jack Kehoe . . . while I might have known where Hurley was located, as we had convicted all of the Inner Circle, including the leader of the gang, what did I want with convicting and hanging a poor unfortunate tool like Hurley."[46] But McParland had not really admitted he knew Hurley had been taken, only that he "might have known" where he was. It seems unlikely that fugitive "Number One" would really be forgiven by the Pinkertons.

Nothing further was ever heard of Michael Doyle of Shenandoah, William Gavin, James "Friday" O'Donnell, and James McAllister, nor of the other lesser lights. Jimmy Kerrigan, back with his wife and family, lived until 1903; Muff Lawler lived until 1900. Both were dogged the remainder of their days by the tag "squealer," and two famous folklore songs perpetuated their fame. The first stanza of each will give their flavor:

JIMMY KERRIGAN'S CONFESSION

You know I am that squealer they talk so much about,
And sure you know the reason, of which I have no doubt.
If not, I will tell you as nearly as I can,
So please in kindness listen to Jimmy Kerrigan.

MUFF LAWLER, THE SQUEALER

When Muff Lawler was in jail right bad did he feel,
He thought de-vil the rooster would he ever heel,
"Be-jabers," says Lawler, "I think I will squeal."
"Yes, do," says the Judge to Muff Law-ler.[47]

✤   ✤   ✤   ✤   ✤

So ended the Molly Maguire story. But the legend has grown over the years to become one of our classics in nineteenth-century labor relations. It was, plainly, more than a labor-management squabble, though, for behind the case were fundamental ethnic, religious, and personal tensions that mirrored the pressures of American life in the second half of that century.

The point of view of the property owners was well represented by the august *American Law Review*, which declared that "the debt which the coal counties owe to these men [the Pinkertons] cannot be overestimated, nor can the personal qualities of untiring resolution, daring and sagacity, in both principal and agent be too highly praised." It was, the *Review* concluded, "one of the greatest works for public good that has been achieved in this country and in this generation."[48] Indeed, the results of the investigations and trials must have gladdened property owners not only in the coal regions but all over the country. To them, in the post-Civil War period, revolution seemed to be in the air, with all the European tensions being transferred straight across to the United States. In the Molly case the property owners fought back with new tactics—and won.

The demonstrated success of these new tactics was one of the most important legacies of the Molly incidents. The use of the detective agency for internal surveillance of a union, though not a completely new idea, was adopted here on a scale not hitherto thought of, and with success and fame scarcely anticipated by the principals themselves. It is interesting to speculate on what might have happened in United States labor history had the Gowen efforts failed, had the LaFollette hearings been held in the mid-1870's rather than the mid-1930's, and had labor-union surveillance not been used as an employer device for these intervening sixty years. Though the Molly Maguire case did not alone bring about the widespread surveillance, it had a profound impact.

In addition, the heightened use of a private police force—here the Coal & Iron police—made a deep impression on employers. Shored up by their association with the Pinkertons, Gowen's own force became an efficient arm, deeply feared by the miners. Soon other railroads and industrial corporations were adopting and using the same device, sometimes with little regard for civil liberties.

The reasons for union organization still remained; and the desperate battle between labor and capital in the coal fields had many more bloody and bitter chapters to leave as heritage for the country. The Knights of Labor had real success for a brief period, but their fall, locally and nationally, was as precipitous as their rise, and by 1890 they were discredited and no longer a force. In the coal fields they were replaced by a new union that was destined to be the greatest—the United Mine Workers. Its president, John Mitchell, soon led it to both major triumphs and major failures. In 1902 he and George Baer, then president of the Reading, were called to the White House by Theodore Roosevelt, to settle a famous strike in the anthracite fields—the first such major intervention by a President. Baer earned himself a place in history at this time by being quoted as saying, "The rights and interests of the laboring man will be protected and cared for, not by the labor agitators, but by Christian men to whom God in His infinite wisdom has given the control of the property interests of this country."[49] Whether Baer really said this or not (he denied it), it earned him the undying name "Divine Right Baer."

The Molly incidents, then, did not settle the basic labor-relations dispute nor have any real effect on the conditions in the coal fields which led to so much tension. The atmosphere was still that of the company town, the dangers of coal mining still as frightful, the rewards still as low, and the life of the miner still as depressing and debilitating.

And, further, the case solved none of the ethnic and religious tensions. Despite the pious protestations of Gowen and other members of the prosecution, the case had strong "Know-Nothing" anti-Irish overtones. Though Gowen was not responsible for the fact that all the defendants were Irish, he was responsible for the heavy emphasis put into McParlan's testimony as to the Irish ties of the Mollies, the similarities to the Ribbonmen, and the clannishness, belligerence, and undisciplined nature of the Irish miner in Pennsylvania. It was a much more subtle brand of Know-Nothingism than that of a mob hanging an Irishman from a street-light pole, as was done in the 1840's.

The ethnic dimensions of the Molly Maguire story are probably far more important than has previously been considered. So very many of the Molly Maguire tactics in the coal fields stemmed directly from closely similar tactics in Ireland. The rationale behind the tactics was quite alike in both places. If one were a determinist in his brand of historical philosophy, he could easily conclude that the whole Pennsylvania development had about it a classic inevitability. Given the situation, so close to that of Ireland, the growth of a secret society might seem predestined. There had been other examples of Irish secret-society activity in the United States. For example, the clashes occurring among the Irish laborers building the Chesapeake & Ohio canal in 1834 were attributed in part to a shadowy New York–based secret society.[50] But there it was Irish versus Irish—really a faction fight. On the Illinois Central Railroad in the 1850's there were battles among Irish construction groups, apparently sometimes also involving Germans. Again, however, the emphasis was on faction fighting. In eastern Pennsylvania, though, it was Irish versus the English and Welsh. The parallels with Ireland were more direct.

The ethnic tensions in the coal fields were soon further compounded by the influx of a new group of miners, the East Europeans. The "Slav Invasion," as one writer called it,[51] came rapidly, starting in the late 1870's. By the turn of the century thousands upon thousands of people from these new countries had entered the anthracite fields to compete with the Irish for the jobs. Soon the second-generation Irish were considering themselves one step up on the economic and social ladder and now able to throw their weight about a bit with the new immigrants.

Religious differences were a powerful factor in America throughout these decades. The Roman Catholic Church was in a vulnerable position in nineteenth-century America, and this was nowhere better illustrated than in the Molly Maguire case. The heavily secular culture of the United States had as its central tenet the worship of individualism. Catholicism was finding the route to interpretation of the new industrial scene a rocky one. The Church's attitude toward the labor union exemplified its indecision. In addition, its attitudes toward an economically based secret society were also vacillating. Great numbers of the Church's constituency were the unskilled immigrants that constituted "labor" in most of these head-on clashes of nineteenth-century Darwinian individualism. On the other hand, the Church must have been reluctant to stand in opposition to so many industrial and political leaders who were the "capitalists" of the other side. Critics have pointed to the pragmatism and ambivalence of the Church in the Molly Maguire incidents, and not without reason. But the tight rope which had to be walked by the Church makes such judgments oversimplified and one-sided. The Molly Maguire incidents were serious for the Church, and the Church clearly recognized this as so.

❖   ❖   ❖   ❖   ❖

Why has the Molly Maguire story remained so popular? For many of the reasons we have just noted. It struck deeply at fundamental issues of nineteenth-century life and helped to shape the character of the nation in this critical period. But there is another basic reason, too. Given all the economic, ethnic, religious, and political dimensions, the Molly Maguire saga was, finally, a personal story. Personal success: Gowen's, McParlan's, Pinkerton's. Personal failures: Siney's, Kehoe's, and others. Personal virtues: courage, tenacity, boldness. Personal weaknesses: drinking, hating, informing, killing. The deepest of human passions were involved here; these passions finally determined the story. And it was quite a story.

Major Participants
in Pennsylvania Incidents

Notes ✱ *Index*

Major Participants in Pennsylvania Incidents

(Asterisks mark the twenty men hanged for so-called Molly Maguire crimes)

Albright, Charles—Lehigh & Wilkes-Barre Coal Company attorney representing prosecution in several Molly Maguire trials.

Allen, Major E. J.—pseudonym used by Allan Pinkerton as head of secret service of Union forces in Civil War.

Bangs, George H.—general manager of Pinkerton's National Detective Agency.

Bannan, Benjamin—editor, *Miners' Journal* (Pottsville).

Bartholomew, Len—Pottsville lawyer and AOH defense attorney.

Beard, Michael—Tamaqua citizen who hired Pinkerton's to investigate Yost killing.

Beard, Samuel—Tamaqua citizen instrumental in capturing participants in John P. Jones murder.

*Bergen, Martin—hanged in 1879 for murder of Patrick Burns in 1870.

Billingfelt, Esaias—Pennsylvania state senator opposing Gowen's efforts to incorporate coal company in 1871.

Boyle, Barney—convicted of perjury in Munley trial.

*Boyle, James—Summit Hill AOH member hanged in 1877 for murder of Benjamin Yost in 1875.

Boyle, Kate—convicted of perjury in Munley trial.

Brennan, Pat—Hecksherville man arrested for questioning in Raven Run and Gomer James murders.

Burns, Patrick—Silver Creek mine clerk murdered in 1870.

Butler, Patrick—AOH bodymaster at Lost Creek who turned state's evidence in conspiracy to reward Hurley for James killing.

*Campbell, Alexander—Storm Hill tavern owner, treasurer of Storm Hill AOH lodge, hanged in 1877 for murder of John P. Jones in 1875.

Campbell, John—miner convicted of second-degree murder in 1877 in the killing of F. W. Langdon in 1862.

Canning, Dennis—Locust Gap bodymaster, Northumberland County AOH delegate, convicted for Thomas and Majors conspiracies.

*Carroll, James—secretary of Tamaqua AOH, hanged in 1877 for murder of Benjamin Yost in 1875.

Carroll, Dr. William—Chairman of the Executive of the Clan na Gael.

Cosgrove, Edward—AOH member murdered in 1873; Gomer James tried and acquitted.

Crean, Lawrence—Girardville AOH bodymaster.

Cull, Manus—see Kelly, Daniel.

Cummings, P. M.—Pinkerton detective who infiltrated St. Clair local of W.B.A.

Curtin, Andrew—governor of Pennsylvania during Civil War draft riots.

Darcy, Michael—AOH member assigned to kill John P. Jones in company with James McParlan.

Dewees, Franklin—Pottsville attorney, author of 1877 book, *The Molly Maguires.*

Dolan, Barney—AOH county delegate for Schuylkill County preceding John Kehoe.

Dolan, Patrick, Sr.—Big Mine Run AOH bodymaster, convicted for Hurley conspiracy.

*Donahue, John ("Yellow Jack")—Tuscarora AOH bodymaster, hanged in 1877 for murder of Morgan Powell in 1871.

*Donnelly, Dennis ("Bucky")—Raven Run AOH bodymaster, hanged in 1878 for murders of Thomas Sanger and William Uren in 1875.

Donnelly, Christopher—Schuylkill County AOH treasurer, convicted in Thomas and Majors conspiracies and the conspiracy to reward Hurley for James killing.

Dooley, Martin—AOH member who eavesdropped when McParlan visited Father O'Connor.

Dormer, Patrick—AOH member, proprietor of Sheridan House, Pottsville tavern.

Dougherty, Daniel—Mahanoy City AOH member acquitted of murder of George Major.

Doyle, Michael—Shenandoah AOH member, McParlan's sometime roommate, alleged participant in Thomas shooting and Sanger-Uren murders; fugitive from justice.

*Doyle, Michael J.—Mt. Laffee AOH member hanged in 1877 for murder of John P. Jones in 1875.

Duffy, James—convicted of perjury in Munley trial.

*Duffy, Thomas—Tamaqua AOH member hanged in 1877 for murder of Benjamin Yost in 1875.

Dunne, Henry—Pottsville mine superintendent murdered in 1866.

Elwell, William—Columbia County judge who acted as arbitrator in 1871 anthracite wage dispute.

Farquhar, Guy—Pottsville attorney, member of prosecution in Molly Maguire trials.

*Fisher, Thomas—Carbon County AOH delegate, hanged in 1878 for murder of Morgan Powell in 1871.

Foster, Thomas J.—editor, *Shenandoah Herald*.
Franklin, Benjamin—superintendent of Philadelphia office, Pinkerton agency.

Gavin, William—Schuylkill County AOH secretary, allegedly implicated in Thomas conspiracy; fugitive from justice.
Gibbons, John—Shenandoah AOH member, participant in Thomas shooting, convicted of conspiracy.
Gowen, Franklin B.—president, Philadelphia & Reading Railroad and Philadelphia & Reading Coal & Iron Company.
Gwyther, Squire Thomas—Girardville justice of the peace murdered in 1875, allegedly by William Love.

Hartranft, John F.—governor of Pennsylvania during Molly Maguire trials.
Heaton, Robert—Raven Run mine owner, prosecution witness in Sanger-Uren murder trials.
Heisler, W. J.—captain in Reading's Coal & Iron police.
Hesser, Frederick—Northumberland County mine watchman murdered in 1874.
*Hester, Patrick—Northumberland County tavern owner and AOH bodymaster, hanged in 1878 for murder of Alexander Rea in 1868.
Higgins, Mary Ann—sister-in-law of James Kerrigan and sweetheart of James "McKenna."
Hughes, Frank W.—Reading Railroad attorney, member of prosecution in Molly Maguire trials.
Hurley, Thomas—Shenandoah AOH member alleged to have killed Gomer James, to have been involved in Sanger-Uren murders, and to have participated in the Thomas shooting; fugitive from justice.
Hyland, Bridget—convicted of perjury in Munley trial.

James, Gomer—Mahanoy City Welshman acquitted of murdering Edward Cosgrove in 1873, and himself murdered in 1875, allegedly by Thomas Hurley.
Jones, John P.—Lansford mine superintendent murdered in 1875.

Kaercher, George—Schuylkill County district attorney.
Kalbfus, Daniel—Mauch Chunk lawyer and AOH defense attorney.
Kane, Jeremiah—Mt. Laffee AOH bodymaster, alleged participant in conspiracy to reward Hurley for James killing; fugitive from justice.
Keenan, Frank—Forestville AOH bodymaster, alleged participant in conspiracy to reward Hurley for James killing; fugitive from justice.
*Kehoe, John—proprietor of Hibernian House, Girardville tavern, county AOH delegate for Schuylkill County, hanged in 1879 for murder of F. W. Langdon in 1862.

Kelly, Daniel ("Kelly the Bum," "Manus Cull")—confessed participant in murder of Alexander Rea in 1868; turned state's evidence.

*Kelly, Edward—Mt. Laffee AOH member hanged in 1877 for murder of John P. Jones in 1875.

Kerrigan, James—Tamaqua bodymaster implicated in John P. Jones and Benjamin Yost murders; turned state's evidence.

Langdon, Frank W.—Audenried mine foreman murdered in 1862.

Lawler, Ed—nephew of Michael Lawler.

Lawler, Michael ("Muff")—Shenandoah AOH bodymaster, implicated in Sanger-Uren murders; turned state's evidence.

Linden, Robert J.—Pinkerton assistant superintendent who operated as James McParlan's contact in coal fields and as a captain in Coal & Iron police.

Littlehales, William—Cass township mine foreman murdered in 1867.

Love, William—alleged murderer of Squire Gwyther in 1875; fugitive from justice.

L'Velle, Martin—Pottsville lawyer, defense counsel in Molly Maguire trials.

McAllister, Charles—arrested mistakenly for brother James in Sanger-Uren murders; convicted of shooting James Riles.

McAllister, Ellen—wife of Charles McAllister; murdered at Wiggans Patch in 1875.

McAllister, James—alleged participant in Sanger-Uren murders; fugitive from justice.

McAndrew, Frank—Shenandoah AOH bodymaster who aided James McParlan's escape in 1876.

McCann, John—alleged killer of George Major; fugitive from justice.

McCarron, Barney—Tamaqua policeman present when Benjamin Yost was murdered.

McClure, Alexander—colonel in Pennsylvania militia in charge of 1862 draft in state of Pennsylvania.

McDermott, Daniel—Roman Catholic priest in New Philadelphia (later in Pottsville), leader of anti-Molly faction, spokesman for the "Seven Pastors" in denunciation of AOH in 1874.

*McDonnell, James—hanged in 1879 for murder of George K. Smith in 1863.

McFadden, Charles—Roman Catholic priest in Mahanoy City.

McGee, Columbus and Michael—brothers acquitted of 1862 killing of F. W. Langdon.

*McGehan, Hugh—Summit Hill AOH member hanged in 1877 for murder of Benjamin Yost in 1875.

McHugh, Frank—Mahanoy City AOH secretary, turned state's evidence in Thomas case.

McHugh, James—Shenandoah AOH member who beat up Michael Lawler.

*McHugh, Peter—hanged in 1878 for murder of Alexander Rea in 1868.

McKenna, James—pseudonym used by Pinkerton detective James McParlan.

*McManus, Peter—Coal Run AOH bodymaster hanged in 1879 for murder of Frederick Hesser in 1874.

McParlan(d), James—Pinkerton detective who infiltrated Molly Maguires under pseudonym "James McKenna."

Major, George—chief burgess of Mahanoy City, killed in street fight in 1874.

Major, Jesse and William—Mahanoy City Welsh brothers, objects of AOH conspiracy to murder.

Monaghan, Ned—Shenandoah policeman and AOH member, convicted in Thomas conspiracy.

Morris, John—Shenandoah AOH member, participant in Thomas shooting, convicted of conspiracy.

Muir, David—Foster township mine superintendent murdered in 1865.

Mulhearn, Charles—Tamaqua AOH member convicted in Morgan Powell murder and Majors conspiracy.

Mulhearn, Edward—Mauch Chunk lawyer and AOH defense attorney.

Mulhearn, John—Tamaqua AOH member confused with Charles Mulhearn in first Yost trial.

*Munley, Thomas—Gilberton AOH member hanged in 1877 for murders of Thomas Sanger and William Uren in 1875.

O'Brien, Michael—Mahanoy City AOH bodymaster convicted in Thomas and Majors conspiracies and the conspiracy to reward Hurley for James killing.

O'Connor, Daniel—Roman Catholic priest in Mahanoy Plane who alerted John Kehoe on James McParlan's role as a detective.

O'Donnell, Charles—alleged participant in Sanger-Uren murders, killed at Wiggans Patch in 1875.

O'Donnell, James ("Friday")—alleged participant in Sanger-Uren murders; fugitive from justice.

O'Neil, Francis—St. Clair AOH bodymaster, convicted of conspiracy to reward Hurley for James killing.

O'Reilly, Henry F.—Roman Catholic priest in Shenandoah.

Pinkerton, Allan—Principal (president) of the Pinkerton's National Detective Agency.

Pinkerton, Robert—eldest son of Allan Pinkerton, assigned to New York City office of the agency.

Pinkerton, William—son of Allan Pinkerton, assigned to Chicago office of the agency.

Pleasants, General Henry—head of Reading's Coal & Iron police.
Powell, Morgan—Summit Hill mine superintendent murdered in 1871.

Ramsey, Robert—editor of Pottsville *Miners' Journal* after Benjamin Bannan.
Rea, Alexander—Columbia County mine paymaster murdered in 1868.
Reilly, James B.—Pottsville lawyer and AOH defense attorney.
*Roarity, James—Coaldale AOH bodymaster, hanged in 1877 for murder of John P. Jones in 1875.
Ryon, John W.—Pottsville lawyer and AOH defense attorney.

Sanger, Thomas—Raven Run mine foreman murdered in 1875.
*Sharp, Charles—hanged in 1879 for murder of George K. Smith in 1863.
Shepp, Daniel—Tamaqua citizen who hired Pinkerton's to investigate Yost killing.
Siewers, E. R.—Carbon County district attorney.
Siney, John—St. Clair labor leader, first president of W.B.A.
Slattery, J. J.—AOH member who turned state's evidence in Majors conspiracy case and implicated Kehoe in political payoffs.
Smith, Charles E.—president of Philadelphia & Reading Railroad before Gowen.
Smith, George K.—Audenried mine owner murdered in 1863.
Stein, Levi—German juror who died during "first" Yost trial.

Thomas, William M. ("Bully Bill")—Mahanoy City Welshman shot by group of AOH members.
*Tully, Patrick—hanged in 1878 for murder of Alexander Rea in 1868.

Uren, William—Raven Run miner murdered in 1875.

Welsh, John F.—John Siney's successor as president of the W.B.A.
Wood, Archbishop James Frederic—archbishop, Philadelphia diocese, Roman Catholic Church.

Yost, Benjamin—Tamaqua policeman murdered in 1875.

Notes

Chapter 1: Night Riders and Informers

1. The first miners in the anthracite fields were predominantly English and Welsh. It was not until the 1840's, and particularly during and after the famine that heavy Irish immigration came. See J. W. Coleman, *The Molly Maguire Riots* (Richmond, Va.: Garrett & Massie, 1936), pp. 20–21.

2. G. M. Trevelyan, *A Shortened History of England* (London: Longmans, Green & Co., 1942), p. 249.

3. T. W. Freeman, *Pre-Famine Ireland* (Manchester: Manchester University Press, 1957), p. 15; K. H. Connell, *The Population of Ireland, 1750–1845* (Oxford: Clarendon Press, 1950).

4. Connell, *Population of Ireland, passim.* For an analysis of the potato as a causal force, see also William L. Langer, "Europe's Initial Population Explosion," *American Historical Review*, October 1963, pp. 11–13.

5. Freeman, *Pre-Famine Ireland*, p. 3.

6. Edmund Curtis, *A History of Ireland*, 6th ed. (London: Methuen & Co., 1960), p. 93.

7. Curtis, *History of Ireland*, p. 117.

8. Especially important was the "Foster Act" of 1784, which granted liberal bounties for the export of wheat. See R. H. Murray and H. Law, *Ireland* (London: Hodder & Stoughton, 1924), p. 124, and John E. Pomfret, *The Struggle for Land in Ireland* (Princeton, N. J.: Princeton University Press, 1930), pp. 4–5.

9. 56 Geo. III, c. 88.

10. See Connell, *Population of Ireland*, chap i, for discussion of population estimates during this period. His "revised estimates," from which this figure is taken, are contained in his table 4, p. 25.

11. Freeman, *Pre-Famine Ireland*, p. 54.

12. J. E. Bicheno, *Ireland and Its Economy* (London: John Murray, 1830), p. 33.

13. *Digest of Evidence Taken before Her Majesty's Commissioners of Inquiry into the State of the Law and Practice in Respect to the Occupation of Land in Ireland* (Dublin: Alexander Thom, 2 vols., 1847 and 1848), I, 410, 411, 399. Commonly known as the "Devon Digest."

14. The observer is an anonymous writer in *State of the Nation 1822*, quoted in George O'Brien, *The Economic History of Ireland from the Union to the Famine* (London: Longmans, Green & Co., 1921), pp. 46–47.

15. Devon Digest (note 13, above), I, 428.

16. Devon Digest, I, 429.

17. Pomfret, *Struggle for Land*, p. 8.

18. O'Brien, *Economic History of Ireland*, p. 158.

19. Devon Digest, I, 156 ff.

20. John Stuart Mill, *Principles of Political Economy*, vol. I (Boston: Charles C. Little & James Brown, 1848), pp. 378–379.

21. Devon Digest, I, 8–9.

22. O'Brien, *Economic History of Ireland, passim*.

23. H. B. C. Pollard, in *The Secret Societies of Ireland* (London: Phillip Allan & Co., 1922), attempts to trace the "Defenders" back to 1565. His evidence is flimsy and circumstantial, however. W. E. H. Lecky, a more dependable historian, cites a number of these earlier forms in *History of Ireland in the Eighteenth Century* (London: Longmans, Green & Co., 1902), I, 357 ff.

24. 5 Geo. III, c. 8 (Ir.). See also *A Collection of Acts Relating to Tumultuous Risings of Persons, Etc.* (Dublin: George Grierson, 1795).

25. *Finn's Leinster Journal* (Kilkenny), Jan. 20, 1776.

26. See Lecky, *History*, II, 45–47.

27. See, especially, Francis Joseph Bigger, *The Ulster Land War of 1770* (*The Hearts of Steel*) (Dublin: Sealy, Bryers & Walker, 1910). Lecky also devotes space to the organization: II, 47–51.

28. Arthur Young, *A Tour in Ireland*, selected and edited by Constantia Maxwell (Cambridge, Eng.: Cambridge University Press, 1925), p. 45.

29. Lecky, *History*, II, 511.

30. *Report from the Select Committee Appointed to Inquire into the Nature, Character, Extent and Tendency of Orange Lodges, Associations or Societies in Ireland*, H. C., 1835 (377) XV, p. 6; 1835 (476) XVI, p. 213.

31. John Heron Lepper, *Famous Secret Societies* (London: Sampson Low, Marston & Co., 1932), p. 221.

32. These police reports are preserved almost intact from the year 1796 under the title *State of the Country Papers, 1796–1831* in the Public Records Office, Dublin. In the main they are reports from various local officials and citizens (especially the local magistrates and members of the constabulary) to the officials in Dublin Castle (especially the Lord Lieutenant). They represent a wide range of frankness and evasiveness, lethargy and purpose, courage and timidity. Very often they are suspect because the writer had a vested interest in reporting either activity or inactivity—sometimes it was to the advantage of the magistrate to show less activity than was actually occurring, other times the opposite. But as firsthand reports of the state of the country, the reports with all limitations are a highly valuable source of knowledge on disturbance.

33. James Cotter to the Lord Lieutenant, March 17, 1803, *State of the Country Papers*, I, 408/930/3.

34. James Cotter to the Lord Lieutenant, May 16, 1805; June 25, 1805, *ibid.*, 409/1031/86–8.

35. W. Gethin to Alex Marsden, June 3, 1803, *ibid.*, 408/902/41.

36. W. Gethin to Alex Marsden, May 30, 1803, *ibid.*, 408/902/40.

37. On "Black Conclusion" see A. Kerr to the Lord Lieutenant, Nov. 24, 1804, *ibid.*, 409/945/9. On "Standardmen" see James Cotter to the Lord Lieutenant, Dec. 29, 1806; Jan. 8, 1807, *ibid.*, 409/1091/42; 410/1120/41.

38. "Draft of a Report by Sergeant Moore—Threshers—Mayo, Sligo, Leitrim and Cavan," 1806, *ibid.*, 409/1092/5.

39. "Colonel Howard's Narrative and Observations concerning the Threshers," Nov. 28, 1806, *ibid.*, 409/1092/3.

40. This was 47 Geo. III, Sess. 2, c. 54 (1807). Earlier acts were 45 Geo.

III, c. 4 (1805); 47 Geo. III, Sess. i, c. 8 (1806–7). The laws are discussed in G. Locker-Lampson, *A Consideration of the State of Ireland in the Nineteenth Century* (London: Archibald Constable, 1907), p. 225.

41. "Draft of a Report by Sergeant Moore."

42. Nov. 28, 1806, *State of the Country Papers*, I, 409/1092/3.

43. See, for example, Oct. 17, 1806, *ibid.*, 409/1092/5; Dec. 7, 1808, 410/1192/9.

44. June 3, 1808 and June 9, 1808, *ibid.*, 410/1188/1-2; May 30, 1808, 410/1188/30–31.

45. April 20, 1804, *ibid.*, 409/980/47.

46. May 30, 1808, *ibid.*, 410/1188/30.

47. April 1, 1808, *ibid.*, 410/1192/1-2.

48. L. H. Jephson to Alex Marsden, March 16, 1805, *ibid.*, 409/1031/68–70.

49. For the case, *ibid.*, 408/980/62; 409/980/61-64; 409/980/95-97.

50. Feb. 28, 1811, *ibid.*, 412/1382/2-6.

51. Nov. 28, 1806, *ibid.*, 409/1092/3.

52. See, for example, *ibid.*, 411/1230/9.

53. *Ibid.*, 412/1386/14 and 412/1386/24.

54. Dec. 4, 1808, *ibid.*, 410/1188/62.

55. Jan. 6, 1811, *ibid.*, 411/1381/45.

56. March 18, 1811, *ibid.*, 412/1382/69.

57. Aug. 19, 1811, *ibid.*, 411/1381/18.

58. *Outrage Papers*, 1831, Province of Leinster, County of Carlow, document dated May 20, 1831. The *Outrage Papers* are preserved in the State Paper Office, Dublin.

59. Jan. 1, 1812, *State of the Country Papers*, I, 413/1401/7.

60. Jan. 25, 1804, *ibid*, 409/980/17. See also 409/1031/23 and 409/1031/43 for proclamation on houghing.

CHAPTER 2: WHO WAS MOLLY MAGUIRE?

1. Charles Whitworth to Viscount Sidmouth, June 5, 1816, printed in *The Annual Register for the Year 1816* (London: Baldwin, Cradock & Joy, 1817), pp. 402–417. See esp. pp. 403–404, 410.

2. "Précis of Report for Province of Ulster for August, 1829," *Outrage Papers* (State Paper Office, Dublin), 1829, R 18, p. 89.

3. June 21, 1843, *Outrage Papers*, County Monaghan, 23, 1843.

4. See, for example, Denis C. Rushe, *Historical Sketches of Monaghan from the Earliest Records to the Fenian Movement* (Dublin: J. Duffy, 1895), p. 94.

5. *Limerick Chronicle*, Oct. 17, 1821.

6. W. E. H. Lecky, *History of Ireland in the Eighteenth Century* (London: Longmans, Green & Co., 1902), I, 360.

7. April 10, 1822, *State of the Country Papers* (Public Records Office, Dublin), I, 433/2345/56.

8. Edmund Curtis, *A History of Ireland*, 6th ed. (London: Methuen & Co., 1960), p. 358.

9. G. Locker-Lampson, *A Consideration of the State of Ireland in the Nineteenth Century* (London: Archibald Constable, 1907), p. 107.

10. *Report of the Select Committee Appointed to Inquire into the State of Ireland*, H. C., 1825 (129) VIII, pp. 71–72.

11. Thomas Campbell Foster, *Letters on the Condition of the People of Ireland* (London: Chapman & Hall, 1847), pp. 20–21.

12. W. Steuart Trench, *Realities of Irish Life* (London: Longmans, Green & Co., 1868).

13. Dublin *Freeman's Journal*, Feb. 24, 1848.

14. *Freeman's Journal*, Dec. 19, 1847.

15. George Korson, *Minstrels of the Mine Patch* (Philadelphia: University of Pennsylvania Press, 1938), p. 240.

16. John O'Dea, *History of the Ancient Order of Hibernians and Ladies' Auxiliary* (Philadelphia: Keystone Printing Co., 1923), II, 771–772. O'Dea mentions several versions of the story but says the one quoted here is the "most likely" one.

17. *Ibid.* A similar version is found in Sean Milroy, "History of the A.O.H.," *The Hibernian* (Dublin), June 26, 1915, p. 5.

18. Denis C. Rushe, *History of Monaghan for Two Hundred Years 1660–1860* (Dundalk: William Tempest, 1921), p. 278.

19. Dublin *Evening Mail*, June 23 and July 9, 1845; *Freeman's Journal*, July 3, 1845.

20. Seamas MacManus, "The Capture of Molly Maguire," in *Irish Nights*, No. 6 (Dublin: 70 Strand St., circa 1903).

21. Michael Davitt, *The Fall of Feudalism in Ireland* (New York: Harper & Bros., 1904), p. 43.

22. O'Dea, *History*, II, 772.

23. Irish Folklore Commission, Dublin, Report by Sean Haughey on Parish of Inver, Barony of Banagh, County Donegal, Winter 1961, pp. 1–4.

24. *Ibid.*, pp. 8–10.

25. *Ibid.*, p. 12.

26. *Catholic Encyclopedia*, vol. XIV (London: Caxton Publishing Co., 1912), p. 72.

27. Lord Ashtown (Frederick Oliver Trench), *The Unknown Power Behind the Irish Nationalist Party* (London: Swan Sonnenschein & Co., 1907), p. 72.

28. *The Pastoral Address of the Rt. Rev. Dr. Doyle Against the Illegal Associations of Ribbonmen* (Dublin: J. J. Dolan, 1822).

29. *The Life of the Rt. Rev. James Doyle*, D.D., anon, by the author of "The Priesthood Vindicated" (New York: D. & J. Sadlier, n.d.), p. 59.

30. On St. Patrick's Fraternal Society, see next paragraph of text. The other five names appear in the report of the Roden Committee, i.e., *Report by the Lords' Select Committee Appointed to Inquire into the State of Ireland since the Year 1835 in Respect of Crime and Outrage*, H. L., 1839 (486 I–IV) XI, 194, 194, 384, 367, 540, respectively.

31. Roden Committee, XI, 386.

32. James J. Bergin, *History of the Ancient Order of Hibernians* (Dublin: Ancient Order of Hibernians, 1910), p. 29.

33. T. F. McGrath, *History of the Ancient Order of Hibernians from the Earliest Period to the Joint National Convention at Trenton, New Jersey, June 27, 1898* (Cleveland: T. F. McGrath, 1898), p. 52.

34. O'Dea, *History*, I, 425.

35. *Report from the Select Committee Appointed to Inquire into the Nature, Character, Extent and Tendency of Orange Lodges, Associations or Societies in Ireland*, H. C., 1835 (377) XV, p. 122.

36. O'Dea, *History*, II, 772.

37. Roden Committee, XII, 1125–1126.

38. Roden Committee, XII, 1126–1130.

39. Roden Committee, XII, 1133, 1125.

40. *Report of the Trial . . . of Richard Jones, Who Was Charged with Being a Member of an Illegal Society* (Dublin: Hodges & Smith, 1840), p. 23.

41. O'Dea, *History*, II, 884.

42. Bergin, *History*, pp. 32–33; O'Dea, History, II, 885–886.

43. Bergin, *History*, p. 35.

44. F. P. Dewees, *The Molly Maguires* (Philadelphia: J. B. Lippincott & Co., 1877), pp. 376–377.

CHAPTER 3: TENANT TROUBLES

1. Quotations in this paragraph are from G. Locker-Lampson, *A Consideration of the State of Ireland in the Nineteenth Century* (London: Archibald Constable, 1907), pp. 253–254.

2. *Burke's Landed Gentry* (London: Burke's Peerage, Ltd., 1952), p. 2305.

3. For family history see these writings of Shirley's son, Evelyn Philip Shirley: *Stemmate Shirleiana, or the Annals of the Shirley Family* (London: Nichols & Sons, 1873); *The History of the County of Monaghan* (London: Pickering & Co., 1879); *Some Account of the Territory or Dominion of Farney* (London: William Pickering, 1845).

4. Evelyn Philip Shirley, *An Account of Lough Fea House* (London: privately printed, 1859), pp. 4–5.

5. Newspaper clipping, Nov. 20, 1848, in vol. II of *Farney Bubble Book* (see next note). The clipping is labeled *Newry Examiner* in longhand but is more likely from *Newry Telegraph*.

6. His views appear in detail in the various documents preserved in the library of the family estate at Lough Fea, near Carrickmacross, County Monaghan, Ireland. Especially illuminating are vols. I and II of *Farney Bubble Book*, a collection of five scrapbooks containing original handbills, newspaper clippings, and some manuscript material. The *Bubble Book*, together with other Shirley MSS at Lough Fea, is catalogued in John F. Ainsworth and Edward MacLysaght, *Analecta Hibernica 20, Survey of Documents in Private Keeping*, 2nd series (Dublin: Stationery Office, 1958), pp. 257–278.

7. [Evelyn Philip Shirley], "Memoir of Evelyn John Shirley," in *A Funeral Sermon . . . in the Death of Evelyn John Shirley* (privately printed, 1858), pp. 15, 17.

8. The quotations are from the original handbills signed E. J. Shirley, dated respectively October 1833, Nov. 10, 1836, and Nov. 5, 1838, and preserved in *Farney Bubble Book*, vol. I.

9. Quotations on awards are from handbill dated Nov. 1, 1833, signed Alexander Mitchell, Agent, and preserved in *Farney Bubble Book*, vol. I.

10. Shirley's handbills of Nov. 14, 1839, and October 1833 in *Farney Bubble Book*, vol. I.

11. Same, October 1833 and Nov. 16, 1840.

12. Same, Nov. 5, 1838.

13. Same, September 1842.

14. Edward Porritt and Annie G. Porritt, *The Unreformed House of*

Commons, vol. II (Cambridge, England: Cambridge University Press, 1903), pp. 469–529.

15. The campaign is described in Shirley's diary, Shirley of Ettington MSS, CR 229, #174, Shire Hall, Warwick, County Warwickshire, England.

16. Shirley handbill of June 19, 1826, in *Farney Bubble Book,* vol. I.

17. Same, Nov. 4, 1837.

18. Unidentified newspaper dated Jan. 9, 1841, in *Farney Bubble Book,* vol. I.

19. Same newspaper.

20. Unidentified newspaper, *circa* April 1841, in *Farney Bubble Book,* vol. I.

21. *Outrage Papers,* County Monaghan, Carton 23, State Paper Office, Dublin. The quotation is from a police report dated Nov. 12, 1835.

22. Cf. Shirley handbills dated, respectively, Sept. 20, 1830; Nov. 4, 1837; Nov. 14, 1839, in *Farney Bubble Book,* vol. I.

23. Thomas Smollen to Earl of Dunraven, Feb. 15, 1869, *Farney Bubble Book,* vol. III.

24. Shirley handbill of April 1, 1843, in *Farney Bubble Book,* vol. I.

25. W. Steuart Trench, *Realities of Irish Life* (London: Longmans, Green & Co., 1868). The foregoing account is based on chap. v.

26. Denis C. Rushe, *History of Monaghan for Two Hundred Years, 1660–1860* (Dundalk: William Tempest, 1921), p. 279.

27. E. J. Shirley to Thomas Philip, Earl de Grey, April 3, 1843, *Outrage Papers,* County Monaghan, 1271.

28. Lord Rossmore to Thomas Philip, April 4, 1843, *ibid.*

29. E. J. Shirley to Thomas Philip, April 5, 1843, *ibid.*

30. Monaghan *Northern Standard,* April 8, 1843.

31. *Newry Examiner,* April 5, 1843.

32. London *Times,* April 11, 1843.

33. C. C. Gibson to E. J. Shirley, April 24, 1843. The letter is entitled "Observations on the Several Remedies Capable of Being Adopted for Recovery of the Rents Due by the Tenants of the Shirley Estate." Shirley MSS, Lough Fea Library, Carrickmacross, Ireland.

34. Monaghan *Northern Standard,* April 15, 1843.

35. *Returns of Counties, & in Which the Valuation Has Been Completed* . . . , 1840 (428) XLVIII, 385; *Comparison of the Amount of Value, as Given in the General Valuation of Ireland, with the Actual Rents* . . . , 1844 (513) VII, 674.

36. Richard Griffith to C. C. Gibson, May 5, 1843, Shirley MSS.

37. Diary, cited in note 15, above.

38. Dublin *Freeman's Journal,* April 27, 1843.

39. Unidentified newspaper, *circa* May 1843, *Farney Bubble Book,* vol. I.

40. May 13, 1843, in *Farney Bubble Book,* vol. I.

41. Trench, *Realities of Irish Life,* pp. 82, 85.

42. C. C. Gibson to Edward Lucas, May 30, 1843, *Outrage Papers,* County Monaghan, 1271.

43. See, especially, report of June 5, 1843, *Outrage Papers,* County Monaghan, 1271.

44. Same report.

45. *Outrage Papers,* report of June 8, 1843.

46. *Newry Examiner,* June 10, 1843.

47. Unidentified newspaper, *circa* July 1843, *Farney Bubble Book,* vol. I.

48. This paragraph based on Trench's letter to Shirley, Aug. 21, 1843, Shirley MSS.

49. "Mr. Thomas Elliot's Account of Emigration, 1844," in *Shirley Estate Emigrants, Spring 1844*, Shirley MSS.

50. Handbill, *circa* December 1846, signed Robert Rodgers, preserved in *Farney Bubble Book*, vol. II.

51. Handbill March 13, 1847, signed George Morant, *ibid.*

52. Handbill Sept. 15, 1846, signed Evelyn John Shirley, *ibid.*

53. *Punch*, Oct. 30, 1846, p. 178.

54. *Punch*, Nov. 7, 1846, p. 198.

55. Handbill December 1846, signed E. J. Shirley, *Farney Bubble Book*, vol. II.

56. See, especially, Dublin *Freeman's Journal* during February 1847, *passim.*

57. "Rough Draft of Arrears on the Shirley Estate," beginning Jan. 13, 1843, Shirley MSS, Lough Fea Library, Carrickmacross, Ireland.

58. Handbills May 4, 1847, and Jan. 1, 1848, signed George Morant, *Farney Bubble Book*, vol. II.

59. House of Commons, *Accounts and Papers*, 20 (1866), LVIII, 178.

60. *Dublin Evening Post*, Sept. 27, 1849.

61. *Dublin Evening Post*, Sept. 27, 1849.

62. Unidentified newspaper, *circa* September 1849, *Farney Bubble Book*, vol. II.

63. *Dundalk Democrat*, *circa* September 1849, *ibid.*

64. Dublin *Freeman's Journal*, Sept. 22, 1849.

65. *Annual Reporter*, 1852 (London: F. & J. Revington, 1853), pp. 2–3.

66. *Newry Telegraph*, Oct. 15, 1850.

67. *Dundalk Democrat*, Oct. 20, 1850.

68. *Dundalk Democrat*, Oct. 18 and 25, 1851.

69. Monaghan *Northern Standard*, Oct. 6, 1849.

70. *Dundalk Democrat*, Nov. 24, 1849.

CHAPTER 4: BLACK GOLD AND IRISH GREEN

1. T. W. Freeman, *Pre-Famine Ireland* (Manchester: Manchester University Press, 1957), p. 43.

2. Frederick Engels, *The Condition of the Working-class in England in 1844*, tr. Florence Kelley Wischnewtzky (London: S. Sonnenschein & Co., 1892), p. 61.

3. U.S. Bureau of the Census, *Historical Statistics of the United States, Colonial Times to 1957* (Washington: Government Printing Office, 1960), pp. 56–57.

4. Oscar Handlin, *The Uprooted* (Boston: Little, Brown & Co., 1951), chap. ii; Edwin C. Guillet, *The Great Migration: The Atlantic Crossing by Sailing Ship Since 1770* (New York: Thomas Nelson & Sons, 1937); George Potter, *To the Golden Door* (Boston: Little, Brown & Co., 1960), chap. xxiii; Edith Abbott, *Immigration: Select Documents and Case Records* (Chicago: University of Chicago Press, 1924), section I.

5. U.S. Immigration Commission, *Steerage Conditions*, Doc. no. 753, 61st Congress, 3rd Session (Washington: Government Printing Office, 1911).

6. *Niles' Weekly Register* (Baltimore), Sept. 27, 1834, pp. 55–56.

7. John Francis Maguire, *The Irish in America* (London: Longmans,

Green & Co., 1868), pp. 135–136. For a more comprehensive analysis of the typhus epidemic and its effects on the crossing see R. Dudley Edwards and T. Desmond Williams, eds., *The Great Famine* (Dublin: Browne & Nolan, 1956), chap. v and part 5 of chap. vi.

8. Maria Monk, *Awful Disclosures* (New York: Dewitt & Davenport, 1855). See Ray A. Billington, "Maria Monk and Her Influence," *Catholic Historical Review*, XXII (1936–1937), 283–296.

9. Maguire, *Irish in America*, p. 120.

10. As claimed by John O'Dea, *History of the Ancient Order of Hibernians and Ladies' Auxiliary* (Philadelphia: Keystone Printing Co., 1923), II, 830. Washington did attend a banquet of the organization in December 1781 and was presented with its ensign. Whether this made him a "member" has subsequently been the subject of some debate. Cf. Michael J. O'Brien, "Washington's Irish Friends," *Journal of the American Irish Historical Society*, XXV (1926), pp. 346–348; *Writings of George Washington*, vol. 23 (Washington, D.C.: U.S. Government Printing Office, 1937), p. 404.

11. Fergus MacDonald, *The Catholic Church and the Secret Societies in the United States* (New York: United States Catholic Historical Society, 1946), p. 4. See also Joseph Quigley, *Condemned Societies* (Washington: Catholic University of America, 1927), pp. 11–22.

12. James Edmund Roohan, "American Catholics and the Social Question, 1865–1900," unpub. thesis, Yale University, 1952, pp. 74–75.

13. *Ibid.*, p. 76.

14. Henry J. Browne, *The Knights of Labor and the Catholic Church* (Washington: Catholic University of America Press, 1949), p. 14.

15. *Acta et Decreta Coniclii Plenarii Baltimorensis II* (Baltimorae: Joannes Murphy, 1868), pp. 260–265.

16. Sister M. H. Yeager, C.S.C., *The Life of James Roosevelt Bayley, First Bishop of Newark and Eighth Bishop of Baltimore, 1814–1877,* (Washington: Catholic University of America Press, 1947), p. 309.

17. *Miners' National Record*, November 1874, p. 2.

18. Joseph L. J. Kirlin, *Catholicity in Philadelphia* (Philadelphia: J. J. McVey, 1909); J. T. Scharf and Thompson Wescott, *History of Philadelphia*, vol. II (Philadelphia: L. H. Everts & Co., 1884).

19. Richard J. Purcell in *Dictionary of American Biography*. (The middle name is there spelled "Frederick," but printed documents issued under Wood's name omit the "k.")

20. The observer's name was Joseph Neal. His words were recorded by Eli Bowen, *The Pictorial Sketch-Book of Pennsylvania and Its Scenery, Internal Improvements, Resources and Agriculture* (Philadelphia: Willis P. Hazard, 1852), p. 107, and are given here as quoted in C. K. Yearley, Jr.'s definitive work on the early business scene of Schuylkill County: *Enterprise and Anthracite: Economics and Democracy in Schuylkill County, 1820–1875* (Baltimore: Johns Hopkins Press, 1961), pp. 30–31.

21. Yearley, *Enterprise and Anthracite*, p. 31. His quotations are from Bowen, *Pictorial Sketch-Book*, p. 105.

22. *Pennsylvania Legislative Record*, 1876, p. 608.

23. *Miners' Journal* (Pottsville), March 19, 1853.

24. *Ibid.*, March 24, 1832.

25. *Ibid.*, March 20, 1841. The "noisy reveler" quotation March 19, 1842.

26. *Ibid.*, Oct. 3, 1857.

27. Wayland F. Dunaway, *A History of Pennsylvania* (New York: Prentice-Hall, 1935), chap. xxi; Alexander K. McClure, *Old Time Notes of Pennsylvania,* vol. I (Philadelphia: John C. Winston Co., 1905), chaps. xlvi, xlix.

28. Dunaway, *History of Pennsylvania,* pp. 502–3.

29. McClure, *Old Time Notes,* p. 545.

30. Joseph G. Rayback, *A History of American Labor* (New York: Macmillan Co., 1959), p. 109.

31. *Miners' Journal,* Aug. 9, 1862.

32. *Ibid.,* Oct. 25, 1862.

33. U.S. War Department, *War of the Rebellion: A Compilation of the Official Records of the Union and Confederate Armies,* series I, vol. XIX, part II (Washington: Government Printing Office, 1887), p. 479.

34. McClure, *Old Time Notes,* pp. 548–549.

35. *Ibid.,* p. 549.

36. *Miners' Journal,* Nov. 1, 1862; *War of the Rebellion,* p. 506.

37. *Cork Examiner,* Oct. 20, 1862.

38. *Kehoe v. Commonwealth,* Supreme Court of Pennsylvania, Eastern District, no. 29, July term, 1877, appendix, p. 11.

39. Irving Werstein, *July 1863* (New York: Julian Messner, 1959); David M. Barnes, *The Draft Riots in New York* (New York: Baker & Godwin, 1863); J. T. Headley, *The Great Riots of New York,* chaps. x–xx (New York: E. B. Treat, 1873).

40. *War of the Rebellion,* series III, vol. III (1899), p. 562.

41. Messages of Aug. 3 and 5, 1863, *ibid.,* pp. 620, 629.

42. Aug. 8, 1863, *ibid.,* p. 657.

43. *Miners' Journal,* Nov. 14, 1863.

44. Letters dated Nov. 7 and 9, 1863, *War of the Rebellion,* series III, vol. III (1899), pp. 1006, 1008.

45. *Miners' Journal,* Jan. 16, 1864.

46. Printed handbill in "miscellaneous" category of Molly Maguire Papers, Reading Railroad, Philadelphia.

47. *Miners' Journal,* Jan. 13, 1866.

48. *Ibid.,* March 30, 1867.

49. *Ibid.,* March 23, 1867.

50. *Ibid.,* April 13, 1867.

51. G. O. Virtue, "The Anthracite Mine Laborer," United States, *Bureau of Labor Bulletin,* November 1897, p. 731.

52. Conditions discussed in Marvin W. Schlegel, *Ruler of the Reading: The Life of Franklin B. Gowen* (Harrisburg: Archives Publishing Co. of Pennsylvania, 1947), p. 16; Jay O. Roads, "The Coal Region of Schuylkill County, Pennsylvania," unpub. MS., Pottsville, Free Public Library, pp. 101–103.

53. *Miners' Journal,* June 27, 1835.

54. *Ibid.,* July 9, 1842.

55. *Ibid.,* May 5, 1849.

56. *Ibid.,* May 19, 1849.

57. For biographical details I have relied heavily on Charles Edward Killeen, "John Siney, the Pioneer of American Industrial Unionism and Industrial Government," unpub. thesis, University of Wisconsin, 1942, p. 107.

58. State of Pennsylvania, *Report of the Committee on the Judiciary,*

General, of the Senate of Pennsylvania (Harrisburg: B. Singerly, 1871), p. 182.

59. Pennsylvania Bureau of Statistics of Labor and Agriculture, *First Annual Report, 1872–3*, part I, p. 232.

60. Killeen, "John Siney," p. 123.

61. *Miners' Journal*, Dec. 5, 1868.

62. The history of the coal-carrying railroads and their concomitant land operation is a complex story. The best single source covering all the companies is Jules I. Bogen, *The Anthracite Railroads* (New York: Ronald Press, 1927). Other general works of use are George Rogers Taylor and Irene D. Neu, *The American Railroad Network* (Cambridge, Mass.: Harvard University Press, 1956); George Rogers Taylor, *The Transportation Revolution* (New York: Rinehart & Co., 1951); Thomas C. Cochran, *Railroad Leaders, 1845–1890* (Cambridge, Mass.: Harvard University Press, 1933). Each of the six transportation companies has also been treated separately in one or more books; for a listing of these see Lorna M. Daniels, *Studies in Enterprise* (Boston: Graduate School of Business Administration, Harvard University, 1957), and Henrietta M. Larson, *Guide to Business History* (Cambridge, Mass.: Harvard University Press, 1950).

63. Killeen, "John Siney," p. 112.

64. *Miners' Journal*, March 27, 1869.

65. Pennsylvania Bureau of Statistics of Labor and Agriculture, *First Annual Report, 1872–3*, part II, p. 355.

66. *Miners' Journal*, May 8, 1869.

67. The complete employer proposal can be found in Killeen, "John Siney," p. 157.

68. *Wilkes-Barre Record*, quoted in *Miners' Journal*, July 17, 1869.

CHAPTER 5: GOWEN DECLARES WAR

1. *Hazard's Register of Pennsylvania*, vol. I (May 1828), p. 313.

2. Jules I. Bogen, *The Anthracite Railroads* (New York: Ronald Press, 1927), p. 35.

3. Philadelphia & Reading Railroad Co., *Report of the President and Managers*, Jan. 13, 1862.

4. Bogen, *Anthracite Railroads*, p. 44.

5. *Ibid.*, p. 43.

6. *Miners' Journal* (Pottsville), Sept. 28, 1867.

7. Marvin W. Schlegel, *Ruler of the Reading: The Life of Franklin B. Gowen* (Harrisburg: Archives Publishing Co. of Pennsylvania, 1947), p. 4.

8. *Ibid.*, p. 7.

9. *Miners' Journal*, Nov. 26, 1859, and July 6, 1861. Text of speech in issue of July 20, 1861.

10. *Ibid.*, Oct. 4, 1862.

11. *Ibid.*, Oct. 15, 1864.

12. *Pennsylvania Legislative Documents*, 1871, p. 1696. The events described in the text are mainly from Charles Edward Killeen, "John Siney, the Pioneer of American Industrial Unionism and Industrial Government" (unpub. thesis, University of Wisconsin, 1942), and the *Miners' Journal*.

13. Philadelphia & Reading Railroad Co., *Report of the President and Managers*, Jan. 10, 1870, p. 14.

14. State of Pennsylvania, *Report of the Committee on the Judiciary, General, of the Senate of Pennsylvania* (Harrisburg: B. Singerly, 1871), p. 58.

15. On this, cf. Killeen, "John Siney," pp. 214–219; Schlegel, *Ruler of the Reading*, p. 21; and Andrew Roy, *The Coal Mines* (Cleveland: Robinson, Savage & Co., 1876), pp. 82–83.

16. *Miners' Journal*, Aug. 27, 1870.

17. State of Pennsylvania, *Report of the Committee*, etc., p. 16.

18. This becomes particularly evident in the hearings before the Pennsylvania Senate investigating committee just two months later. Even at this period, though, Gowen's attitude had become more bellicose, as evidenced by the two letters he wrote Siney on December 30 and 31, 1870, later reproduced in these hearings. *Ibid.*, pp. 116–117.

19. *Miners' Journal*, Feb. 11, 1871.

20. State of Pennsylvania, *Report of the Committee*, etc., pp. 43, 53–59.

21. Schlegel, *Ruler of the Reading*, p. 25.

22. *Shenandoah Herald*, May 28 and June 4, 1870.

23. *Miners' Journal*, Aug. 6, 1870.

24. *Miners' Journal*, March 11, 1871, and *Shenandoah Herald*, March 5, 1871.

25. March 10, 1871, as quoted in Schlegel, *Ruler of the Reading*, p. 27.

26. State of Pennsylvania, *Report of the Committee*, etc., p. 12.

27. *Ibid.*, p. 19.

28. *Ibid.*, p. 33.

29. *Miners' Journal*, March 25, 1871.

30. Killeen, "John Siney" (note 12, above), p. 244.

31. Schlegel, *Ruler of the Reading*, p. 34.

32. State of Pennsylvania, *Report of the Committee*, etc., pp. 63–64.

33. *Pennsylvania Legislative Journal*, 1871, p. 835.

34. Schlegel, *Ruler of the Reading*, p. 35. See also Gowen to B. B. Thomas, Jan. 20, 1873, in *Pennsylvania Legislative Documents*, 1876, IV, 754.

35. *Miners' Journal*, May 27 and June 3, 1871.

36. Philadelphia & Reading Railroad, *Report of the President and Managers*, Jan. 9, 1871.

37. Bogen, *Anthracite Railroads*, p. 53.

38. Testimony of George deB. Keim in U.S. Congress, *House Reports*, 2nd Session, 50th Congress, Report no. 4147 (1887–1888), p. 201.

CHAPTER 6: ALIAS JAMES McKENNA

1. Allan Pinkerton, *The Mollie Maguires and the Detectives* (New York: G. W. Dillingham, 1877), p. 15.

2. John O'Dea, *History of the Ancient Order of Hibernians and Ladies' Auxiliary* (Philadelphia: Keystone Printing Co., 1923), III, 1032–1033. See also the version in James D. Horan and Howard Swiggett, *The Pinkerton Story* (New York: G. P. Putnam's Sons, 1951), pp. 130–131.

3. From biographical sketch of Pinkerton by Oliver W. Holmes (the historian) in the *Dictionary of American Biography*. This well-done short piece is the closest thing to a definitive biography of the detective. James Horan, who has written much about the Pinkerton Agency, covers Pinkerton himself in several books. See, especially, *Desperate Men* (New York: G. P. Putnam's Sons, 1949), "Introduction"; and *Pinkerton Story*, pp. 4–5.

4. Horan, *Desperate Men*, p. xiii.

5. For biographical details to the close of the Civil War, I lean heavily on the Holmes sketch cited above.

6. On the Baltimore plot see Norma Barrett Cuthbert, *Lincoln and the Baltimore Plot* (San Marino, Calif.: Huntington Library, 1945); Pinkerton's National Detective Agency, *History and Evidence of the Passage of Abraham Lincoln from Harrisburg, Pennsylvania to Washington, D.C.* . . . (New York: Rode & Brand, 1907).

7. Allan Pinkerton to Robert S. McLean, July 9, 1873, *Allan Pinkerton Letterbook, 1872–1875 in Pinkerton MSS, Library of Congress.*

8. The Pinkerton MSS in the Library of Congress consist of seven letterbooks as follows:

    1. Allan Pinkerton, 1872–1875.
    2. Allan Pinkerton, 1875–1883.
    3. George Bangs, 1869–1883.
    4. George Bangs, 1871–1872.
    5. George Bangs, 1872–1873.
    6. Letterbook, 1861, part I.
    7. Letterbook, 1861, part II.

In addition there is an office journal for the New York office covering the years 1865–1866.

9. Pinkerton's National Police Agency, *General Principles and Rules of Pinkerton's National Police Agency* (Chicago: George H. Fergus, 1867). Quotations *passim.*

10. Allan Pinkerton to George Bangs, Aug. 25, 1872, *Allan Pinkerton Letterbook, 1872–1875.*

11. Allan Pinkerton to George Bangs, Sept. 28, 1872, *ibid.*

12. Allan Pinkerton to Robert Pinkerton, Nov. 20, 1872, *ibid.*

13. Allan Pinkerton to Robert Pinkerton, Sept. 11, 1874, *ibid.*

14. Allan Pinkerton to William Pinkerton, Jan. 20, 1873, *ibid.*

15. Allan Pinkerton to William Pinkerton, Nov. 7, 1872, *ibid.*

16. Allan Pinkerton to Robert Pinkerton, Sept. 2, 1875, *ibid.*

17. Allan Pinkerton to George Bangs, Jan. 7, 1873, *ibid.*

18. Allan Pinkerton to George Bangs, May 18, 1874, *ibid.*

19. Allan Pinkerton to George Bangs, Aug. 25, 1872, *ibid.*

20. Allan Pinkerton to George Bangs, Oct. 2, 1872, *ibid.*

21. *General Principles and Rules* (note 9, above), pp. 10–11.

22. Allan Pinkerton to George Bangs, Sept. 24, 1873, *Allan Pinkerton Letterbook, 1872–1875.*

23. Allan Pinkerton to Miss Ella Hough, May 13, 1875, *ibid.*

24. Allan Pinkerton to George Bangs, Feb. 29, 1876, *Allan Pinkerton Letterbook, 1875–1883.*

25. Allan Pinkerton to Benjamin Franklin, Jan. 23, 1877, *ibid.*

26. Allan Pinkerton to William Pinkerton, Nov. 7, 1872, *Allan Pinkerton Letterbook, 1872–1875.*

27. Allan Pinkerton to George Bangs, Aug. 15, 1872, *ibid.*

28. Allan Pinkerton to Captain Fitzgerald, Aug. 15, 1872, *ibid.*

29. Allan Pinkerton to George Bangs, Oct. 17, 1872, *ibid.*

30. Allan Pinkerton to George Bangs, Nov. 16, 1872, *ibid.*

31. Allan Pinkerton to George Bangs, May 18, 1873, *ibid.*

32. George Smith to Franklin B. Gowen, Feb. 7, 1870, in Molly Maguire

Papers, Reading Railroad, Philadelphia.

33. Benjamin Franklin to Franklin B. Gowen, Oct. 9, 1873, *ibid.*

34. Benjamin Franklin to Franklin B. Gowen, Oct. 29, 1873, *ibid.*

35. Pinkerton, *Mollie Maguires*, p. 17.

36. Here I have drawn heavily upon McParlan's biography in Franklin P. Dewees, *The Molly Maguires* (Philadelphia: J. B. Lippincott & Co., 1877), pp. 79–83.

37. Robert A. Pinkerton, "Detective Surveillance of Anarchists," *North American Review*, November 1901, pp. 611–612.

38. O'Dea, *History*, III, 1033.

39. The original manuscript of McParlan's letter is in Reading Railroad's Molly Maguire Papers, "miscellaneous" category.

CHAPTER 7: IN SEARCH OF MURDER

1. Allan Pinkerton, *The Mollie Maguires and the Detectives* (New York: G. W. Dillingham, 1877), p. 27.

2. Arthur Conan Doyle, *The Valley of Fear* (New York: George H. Doran Co., 1914), near beginning of part II, chap. i.

3. Pinkerton, *Mollie Maguires*, p. 73.

4. *Ibid.*, p. 81.

5. *Ibid.*, pp. 83–84.

6. See, for example, Norman Abbott, "Murder was a Sleeper," *New York Mirror Magazine*, June 26, 1960, p. 15.

7. *The Pilot* (Boston), Nov. 29 and Dec. 24, 1873; Jan. 3, 1874.

8. Reading Railroad's Molly Maguire Papers, Philadelphia, Jan. 2, 1874.

9. Pinkerton, *Mollie Maguires*, pp. 99–100.

10. Reading Railroad's Molly Maguire Papers, Jan. 1–3, 1874.

11. *Ibid.*, Jan. 1–7, 1874.

12. *Ibid.*, Jan. 9, 1874.

13. *Ibid.*, Jan. 13. Pinkerton quotations from his *Mollie Maguires*, pp. 105–106.

14. Reading Railroad's Molly Maguire Papers, Jan. 15 and 23, 1874 (on Deenan); Jan. 17 and 20 (on Donnelly).

15. *Ibid.*, Jan. 24, 1874.

16. *Ibid.*, Jan. 21, 1874.

17. Pinkerton, *Mollie Maguires*, pp. 118–119.

18. Molly Maguire MSS, Historical Society of Pennsylvania, Philadelphia, McParlan reports dated Feb. 2 and 4, 1874.

19. *Ibid.*, esp. reports of Feb. 7, 12, 18, March 14, 22, 27, 30, 1874.

20. *Ibid.*, March 27, 1874.

21. *Ibid.*, March 20 and 22, 1874.

22. *Ibid.*, Feb. 8, 1874.

23. *Ibid.*, reports of Feb. 21, March 3, 7, 1874.

24. *Ibid.*, April 14. The versions given in Pinkerton's book (p. 144) exactly match those noted by McParlan in his report. See also, for purported full oath, F. P. Dewees, *The Molly Maguires* (Philadelphia: J. B. Lippincott & Co., 1877), p. 375.

25. Molly Maguire MSS, Historical Society of Pennsylvania, April 19, 1874.

26. *Ibid.*, April 30, 1874.

27. The three excellent older studies of Gowen and the Reading during this period, Jules Bogen, *The Anthracite Railroads* (New York: Ronald Press, 1927); Eliot Jones, *The Anthracite Coal Combination in the United States* (Cambridge, Mass.: Harvard University Press, 1914); and Marvin Schlegel, *Ruler of the Reading: The Life of Franklin B. Gowen* (Harrisburg: Archives Publishing Co. of Pennsylvania, 1947), have recently been supplemented by a first-rate new study, C. K. Yearley, Jr., *Enterprise and Anthracite: Economics and Democracy in Schuylkill County, 1820-1875* (Baltimore: Johns Hopkins Press, 1961). For a discussion of Gowen's contributions in the period 1871-1874 see, esp., Schlegel, chap. iii, and Yearley, chap. vi.

28. Quotations from *Miners' Journal* (Pottsville), Jan. 11 and Feb. 1, 1873. On the sale see the same publication, Feb. 22, 1873.

29. Schlegel, *Ruler of the Reading*, p. 37.

30. *Ibid.*, p. 39.

31. On the price-fixing and tonnage agreements see Jones, *Anthracite Combination*, pp. 40-41; U.S. Congress, *House Reports*, 2nd Session, 50th Congress, Report no. 4147 (1887-1888), pp. xlvi-xlvii.

32. *Miners' Journal*, Jan. 16 and 23, Feb. 13, 1874.

33. Records of Cummings' activity are found in two places: Reading Railroad's Molly Maguire Papers, entries dated from November 1874 to February 1875; and Molly Maguire MSS, Historical Society of Pennsylvania, Jan. 26 to May 3, 1874.

34. According to Pinkerton this meeting was held in Scranton on May 27, 1874, although no other reference to it can be found. Pinkerton, *Mollie Maguires*, pp. 188-189.

35. John O'Dea, *History of the Ancient Order of Hibernians and Ladies' Auxiliary* (Philadelphia: Keystone Printing Co., 1923), III, 1035, 1040. For a view that has generally been considered the left-wing version of the Molly Maguire story see Anthony Bimba, *The Molly Maguires* (New York: International Publishers, 1932).

36. Reading Railroad's Molly Maguire Papers, Oct. 2, 1874.

37. *Ibid.*, Sept. 11 and 13, 1874.

38. *Ibid.*, Sept. 8, 1874.

39. *Ibid.*, Sept. 16, 1874.

40. *Ibid.*, Sept. 15 and Oct. 2, 1874.

41. *Ibid.*, Oct. 21, 1874.

CHAPTER 8: THE LONG STRIKE

1. Reading Railroad's Molly Maguire Papers, Philadelphia, Nov. 27, 1874.

2. *Miners' Journal* (Pottsville), Nov. 6, 1874.

3. Reading Railroad's Molly Maguire Papers, Nov. 15 and 29, 1874.

4. *Ibid.*, Nov. 24, 1874.

5. *Miners' Journal*, Dec. 21, 1874.

6. Reading Railroad's Molly Maguire Papers, Nov. 25 and 30, 1874.

7. For further information on Welsh, see Charles Edward Killeen, "John Siney, the Pioneer of American Industrial Unionism and Industrial Government," unpub. thesis, University of Wisconsin, 1942, pp. 262-264; and *Shamokin Daily News*, Aug. 8, 1908, pp. 1-4.

8. Reports of P. M. Cummings for Nov. 2-Dec. 9, 1874, in Reading Railroad's Molly Maguire Papers.

9. McParlan's report of Dec. 5, 1874, *ibid.*

10. Killeen, "John Siney," pp. 204–272.

11. *Report of the Case of the Commonwealth vs. John Kehoe, et al.* . . . *for an Aggravated Assault and Battery with Intent to Kill Wm. M. Thomas,* stenographically reported by R. A. West (Pottsville: Miners' Journal Book and Job Rooms, 1876), pp. 87–88.

12. Allan Pinkerton, *The Mollie Maguires and the Detectives* (New York: G. W. Dillingham, 1877), p. 252.

13. These expense reports are separate, unnumbered manuscript pieces in the Reading Railroad's Molly Maguire Papers.

14. Document entitled "Memoranda" under name of James McParlan, Jan. 4, 1875, in the "miscellaneous" category of Reading Railroad's Molly Maguire Papers.

15. *Miners' Journal,* Jan. 15, 1875.

16. Reading Railroad's Molly Maguire Papers, Jan. 21, 1875.

17. *Ibid.,* March 17, 27, 28, 29, 1875.

18. On colliery fire, *ibid.,* Feb. 15 and 17, 1875. On the other two incidents, *ibid.,* March 6 and 26, 1875.

19. *Ibid.,* Feb. 25, March 24 and 30, 1875.

20. *Ibid.,* Feb. 18, 1875.

21. Pinkerton, *Mollie Maguires,* p. 257.

22. Reading Railroad's Molly Maguire Papers, March 17, 1875.

23. *Ibid.,* March 21, 1875.

24. Pinkerton, *Mollie Maguires,* p. 303.

25. Letter of James McParlan to Pinkerton's National Detective Agency, March 4, 1915, Pinkerton MSS, General Offices, Pinkerton's National Detective Agency, New York.

26. Reading Railroad's Molly Maguire Papers, April 14, 1875.

27. *Ibid.,* April 17 and 19, 1875.

28. Benjamin Franklin's memorandum, *ibid.,* date of April 28, 1875. See Pinkerton, *Mollie Maguires,* pp. 275–278, for a conflicting version of this meeting.

29. Pinkerton, *Mollie Maguires,* p. 280.

30. Linden now gives us an additional set of reports and expense accounts. Concerning this meeting on May 3, 1875, we have McParlan's report and Linden's expense account (Reading Railroad's Molly Maguire Papers).

31. *Miners' Journal,* April 2, 1875.

32. *Ibid.,* May 7, 1875.

33. Testimony Aug. 10, 1876, *Commonwealth vs. John Kehoe* (note 11, above), pp. 85–86.

34. *Ibid.,* pp. 198–199.

35. *Miners' Journal,* May 28 and June 11, 1875.

36. Original copies of these reports are found at the Reading Anthracite Company's general offices, Pottsville (formerly the Philadelphia & Reading Coal & Iron Company). Quotation is from letter of William Booth to Henry Pleasants, May 11, 1875.

37. Quoted in *Miners' Journal,* March 12, 1875.

38. Reading Railroad's Molly Maguire Papers, April 29 and May 6, 1875.

39. *Ibid.,* May 10, 1875.

40. *Ibid.,* May 11, 1875.

41. Pinkerton, *Mollie Maguires,* p. 291.

42. *Ibid.*, p. 294.

43. Reading Railroad's Molly Maguire Papers, Linden's reports of May 14 and 17, 1875.

44. John F. Welsh, letter "To the M and LBA of Schuylkill County," April 10, 1875, in the "miscellaneous" category of Reading Railroad's Molly Maguire Papers.

45. For this whole account see Robert Linden's reports of June 2 and 3, 1875, in Reading Railroad's Molly Maguire Papers.

46. Marvin W. Schlegel, *Ruler of the Reading: The Life of Franklin B. Gowen* (Harrisburg: Archives Publishing Co. of Pennsylvania, 1947), p. 72.

47. Pinkerton, *Mollie Maguires*, p. 332.

48. Linden's reports of June 4 and 5, 1875, in Reading Railroad's Molly Maguire Papers.

49. Joseph F. Patterson, "Old WBA Days," *Publications of the Historical Society of Schuylkill County* (Pottsville, 1909), IV, 380.

50. George Korson, *Minstrels of the Mine Patch* (Philadelphia: University of Pennsylvania Press, 1938), p. 225.

51. Schlegel, *Ruler of the Reading*, p. 75.

52. Detective reports from "A. T. L.," "C. M. P.," and "R. W. P.," May 7–July 12, 1875, in Reading Railroad's Molly Maguire Papers.

53. F. B. Gowen to John A. Ryan, May 7, 1875; F. B. Gowen to J. E. Wooten, May 6, 1875. Both letters are in the J. E. Wooten papers, Historical Society of Pennsylvania, Philadelphia.

CHAPTER 9: THE SUMMER OF 1875

1. *Report of the Case of the Commonwealth vs. John Kehoe, et al. . . . for an Aggravated Assault and Battery with Intent to Kill Wm. M. Thomas,* stenographically reported by R. A. West (Pottsville: Miners' Journal Book and Job Rooms, 1876).

2. *Ibid.*, p. 25.

3. *Ibid.*, p. 49.

4. Reading Railroad's Molly Maguire Papers, Philadelphia, May 9, 1875.

5. *Commonwealth vs. Kehoe*, p. 26.

6. *Ibid.*, pp. 122–125.

7. In the Reading Railroad's Molly Maguire Papers ("miscellaneous" category) is an undated document entitled "Memoranda," apparently in Franklin's hand and quoting from McParlan's reports (now missing) on this meeting. However, the fact that it is a separate piece, not in the regular series of detective reports, makes one wonder whether it might not have been written at a later date. Perhaps the more definitive account, within its own limitations, is the one McParlan gave at the Kehoe trial, and this is followed here. There is no major conflict between the two, however.

8. *Commonwealth vs. Kehoe*, pp. 27–28.

9. *Ibid.*, p. 28.

10. *Ibid.*, p. 28.

11. *Ibid.*, p. 58.

12. *Ibid.*, p. 82.

13. *Ibid.*, p. 59.

14. *Ibid.*, pp. 63, 64.

15. Allan Pinkerton, *The Mollie Maguires and the Detectives* (New York: G. W. Dillingham, 1877), pp. 320–321.

16. *Commonwealth vs. Kehoe*, p. 211.

17. *Ibid.*, p. 38.

18. The story of the killing of Yost is first found in James McParlan's reports of July 15–August 2, 1875, in Kaercher MSS, Mrs. George Keiser, Pottsville, Pa. Further details are found in *James Carroll, James Boyle, Hugh McGehan, and James Roarity vs. Commonwealth of Pennsylvania*, Supreme Court of Pennsylvania, Eastern District, no. 12, January term, 1877. Paper Book of Plaintiffs in Error, pp. 1–308 (see esp. pp. 54–55). The clearest picture of the planning and execution of this crime is contained in the testimony in the so-called "first" Yost trial, which was reported verbatim in the Pottsville *Miners' Journal* (Pottsville), May 5 to May 16, 1876.

19. *Tamaqua Courier*, July 8, 1875.

20. *Miners' Journal* (Pottsville), July 9, 1875.

21. Reading Railroad's Molly Maguire Papers, July 4, 1875.

22. Quotations from reports of July 3, 4, 3, and 6, respectively.

23. Pinkerton, *Mollie Maguires*, p. 359.

24. See especially McParlan's report of July 4, 1875.

25. Reading Railroad's Molly Maguire Papers, July 9, 1875.

26. *Denver Daily News*, Dec. 21, 1891.

27. The testimony is carefully analyzed in Marvin Schlegel, *Ruler of the Reading: The Life of Franklin B. Gowen* (Harrisburg: Archives Publishing Co. of Pennsylvania, 1947), chap. vi. Gowen took his case to the public, publishing his entire testimony in a widely distributed paperback book, *Argument of Franklin B. Gowen Before the Joint Committee of the Legislature of Pennsylvania . . . Atlantic City, New Jersey, July 29 and 30, 1875* (Philadelphia: Press of Helfenstein, Lewis & Green, 1875). The full text of the Committee's hearings is in *Pennsylvania Legislative Documents*, 1876, vol. IV.

28. Quotations from *Argument of Franklin B. Gowen*, pp. 76, 85.

29. "List of Outrages—1875" in Reading Railroad MSS, Reading Anthracite Co., Pottsville.

30. Benjamin Franklin to Michael Beard, Aug. 5, 1875, Kaercher MSS, Mrs. George Keiser, Pottsville, "Miscellaneous File."

31. Pinkerton, *Mollie Maguires*, p. 374.

32. Pinkerton, *Mollie Maguires*, p. 376. Expenditures are from expense accounts for the three dates, July 15, 16, 17, 1875, in Reading Railroad's Molly Maguire Papers.

33. Quotation is from Kerrigan's testimony in *James Carroll, et al.* (note 18, above), pp. 54–55.

34. Pinkerton, *Mollie Maguires*, p. 400.

35. *James Carroll, et al.*, p. 291.

36. Kaercher MSS, Mrs. George Keiser—McParlan's report of July 25, 1875.

37. *Ibid.*, July 27, 1875.

38. See McParlan's report of Aug. 27, 1875, in Kaercher MSS, and Robert Linden's report of Aug. 22, 1875, in Reading Railroad's Molly Maguire Papers.

39. Reading Railroad's Molly Maguire Papers, expense account of Aug. 14, 1875.

40. Last three paragraphs based on *Miners' Journal*, Aug. 20, 1875.

41. See McParlan's reports of Aug. 21-25, 1875, in Kaercher MSS, and Pinkerton, *Mollie Maguires*, pp. 422-423.

42. Reading Railroad's Molly Maguire Papers, Aug. 22, 1875.

43. Kaercher MSS, McParlan's report of Aug. 24, 1875.

44. *Ibid.*, Aug. 25, 1875.

45. *Ibid.*, Aug. 26, 1875.

46. Reading Railroad's Molly Maguire Papers, Linden's report of Aug. 28, 1875.

47. Kaercher MSS, McParlan's reports of Aug. 29 and 30, 1875.

48. The last five paragraphs from Kaercher MSS, Aug. 31, 1875.

49. *Ibid.*, Sept. 1, 1875.

50. Pinkerton quotation from his *Mollie Maguires*, p. 437. Otherwise the description of the murders is from James McParlan's reports of Sept. 1 and 2 (Kaercher MSS) and from the testimony in the trials of Thomas Munley and Dennis Donnelly (the latter was judged guilty of planning the murder). The Munley trial is reported verbatim in Pottsville *Miners' Journal*, June 29-July 14, 1876; the Donnelly testimony is printed in *The Evidence in the Case of Dennis Donnelly*, stenographically reported by E. D. York, official stenographer (Philadelphia: Allen, Lane & Scott's Printing House, 1878).

51. Kaercher MSS, Sept. 1, 1875.

52. The last two paragraphs from report of Sept. 2, *ibid.*

53. *Tamaqua Courier*, Sept. 4, 1875.

54. *The Evidence in the Case of Dennis Donnelly*, pp. 174-175.

55. Reading Railroad's Molly Maguire Papers, Sept. 2, 1875.

CHAPTER 10: WIGGANS PATCH

1. See, particularly, Hubert Howe Bancroft, *Popular Tribunals*, 2 vols. in *History of the Pacific States of North America* (San Francisco: The History Company, 1887). Covering the West in a more popular fashion is Wayne Gard, *Frontier Justice* (Norman: University of Oklahoma Press, 1949).

2. Richard Maxwell Brown, *The South Carolina Regulators* (Cambridge, Mass.: Harvard University Press, 1963), esp. pp. 135, 141-142. A recent over-all survey of vigilantism is John W. Caughey, *Their Majesties the Mob* (Chicago: University of Chicago Press, 1960).

3. James Elbert Cutler, in his *Lynch-Law* (London: Longmans, Green & Co., 1905) has the best analysis of the term "lynch." See also Thomas Walker Page, "The Real Judge Lynch," *Atlantic Monthly* (1901), pp. 731-743.

4. As reported by Cutler, *Lynch-Law*, p. 15, to be the wording in the council books of Galway. For the sake of our Irish background, the story is supposed to be this: The son had been sent to Spain to purchase a cargo of wine. He squandered the money but succeeded in obtaining credit from a Spanish friend. The friend accompanied him on the return boat, but the son pushed him overboard, thus hoping to destroy the only living evidence of the loan. A sailor saw the crime and told the father. The son was tried and convicted by the father to hang. But the public turned in sympathy to the son, formed a mob, and threatened to wrest the son from the father. The father, finding that he could not see the hanging effected in the legal way, conducted his son to the top floor of his home, gave his son a last

embrace and forthwith hanged him in plain sight of the mob below. But documentation for the story is slim—see Cutler for the available bibliographic sources. The story of the judge the Irish call the "Warden of Galway" is well-known in Irish lore.

5. James P. Horan and Howard Swiggett, *The Pinkerton Story* (New York: G. P. Putnam's Sons, 1951), pp. 11–59. Quotation on "brother" gangs from p. 14. The following account of the Reno gang and the vigilantes is based on the same book and a long article in the *New York Times*, Dec. 13, 1868.

6. *New York Times*, Dec. 19, 1868.

7. Allan Pinkerton to George Bangs, Nov. 1, 1874, *Allan Pinkerton Letterbook, 1872–1875, Pinkerton MSS, Library of Congress.*

8. Allan Pinkerton to A. P. Charles, Nov. 4, 1874, *ibid.*

9. Allan Pinkerton to Brig Gen. R. B. Marcy, May 8, 1873, *ibid.*

10. Allan Pinkerton to Benjamin Franklin, Oct. 9, 1872, *ibid.*

11. Allan Pinkerton to George Bangs, April 17, 1874, *ibid.*

12. This episode based largely on *New York Times*, Jan. 29 and 31, Feb. 1, 1875. For a view sympathetic to the Pinkertons, see James Horan, *Desperate Men* (New York: G. P. Putnam's Sons, 1949), chap. xi.

13. *New York Times*, Jan. 29 and Feb. 1, 1875.

14. *Republican Banner* (Nashville, Tenn.), July 7, 1875, as reprinted in full in *New York Times*, July 20, 1875.

15. Allan Pinkerton to Mrs. Daniel Askew, May 11, 1875, *Allan Pinkerton Letterbook, 1872–1875.*

16. Allan Pinkerton to George H. Bangs, Aug. 29, 1875, *Allan Pinkerton Letterbook, 1872–1875.*

17. Kaercher MSS, Mrs. George Keiser, Pottsville, Pa.

18. Allan Pinkerton, *The Mollie Maguires and the Detectives* (New York: G. W. Dillingham, 1877), p. 442.

19. Reading Railroad's Molly Maguire Papers, Oct. 12–15, 1875.

20. Pinkerton, *Mollie Maguires*, p. 451. Quotation in following paragraph from pp. 454–455.

21. A copy is in the "miscellaneous" category of Reading Railroad's Molly Maguire Papers.

22. Reading Railroad's Molly Maguire Papers, Oct. 20, 1875.

23. Archbishop James Frederic Wood MSS, American Catholic Historical Society, St. Charles Seminary, Overbrook, Pa.

24. Reading Railroad's Molly Maguire Papers, Oct. 29, 1875.

25. *Ibid.*, Oct. 29 and 31, 1875.

26. On the Mollies and the elections of 1875 see Dolan's letter in *Miners' Journal* (Pottsville), Oct. 15, 1875. On Kehoe's letter see *Shenandoah Herald*, June 8, 1876.

27. Reading Railroad's Molly Maguire Papers, Dec. 5 and 8, 1875.

28. *Shenandoah Herald*, Dec. 11, 1875, reporting the cross-examination of Mrs. O'Donnell in the arraignment of Frank Wenrich.

29. This and the following statements concerning that night are personal depositions given at habeas corpus proceedings before D. B. Green, Dec. 13, 1875. Kaercher MSS, Mrs. George Keiser, Pottsville.

30. *Shenandoah Herald*, Dec. 11, 1875.

31. *Tamaqua Courier*, Dec. 18, 1875; *Shenandoah Herald*, Dec. 11, 1875.

32. The *Miners' Journal,* Dec. 17, 1875, discusses the note left in the O'Donnell yard, and describes the habeas corpus hearing. The *Tamaqua Courier,* Dec. 18, 1875, describes Mrs. O'Donnell's change of mind. The *Shenandoah Herald,* Dec. 11, 1875, covers most comprehensively the coroner's jury. The *Philadelphia Evening Telegram* quotation is from the Dec. 11, 1875, issue.

33. *The Pilot* (Boston), Dec. 18, 1875.

34. F. P. Dewees, *The Molly Maguires* (Philadelphia: J. B. Lippincott & Co., 1877), pp. 239-240.

35. Horan and Swiggett, *Pinkerton Story,* pp. 353-354.

Chapter 11: McKenna Escapes

1. Reading Railroad's Molly Maguire Papers, Dec. 11-15, 1875, General Offices, Reading Railroad, Philadelphia, Pa.

2. As first reported publicly in the *Shenandoah Herald* of Feb. 5, 1876, after McGehan was arrested.

3. *Freeman's Journal and Catholic Register* (New York), April 8, 1876.

4. *New York Times,* Dec. 23, 1875.

5. *Philadelphia Times,* Jan. 19, 1876; *Miners' Journal* (Pottsville), Jan. 31, 1876.

6. Quotations are from, respectively, *Miners' Journal,* Jan. 21, 1876; *Philadelphia Times,* Jan. 19; *New York Evening Post* as quoted in *Miners' Journal,* Jan. 28; and *Shenandoah Herald,* Feb. 3.

7. Records of the various "Molly Maguire" trials in Carbon and Schuylkill Counties are extant in, respectively, the county courthouses in Mauch Chunk (now renamed Jim Thorpe) and Pottsville. These official records include the names of the prosecution and defense lawyers, the names of the jurors, the inclusive dates of the trial, and the disposition of the cases. In addition, official verbatim printed records of testimony remain for those cases going to the Pennsylvania Supreme Court, and unofficial verbatim printed records were also made for some of the other trials (see, for example, note 13 below). Fortunately, in addition to these records, the *Miners' Journal* and *Shenandoah Herald,* which had become dailies, began intensively covering the various trials. Here in the Doyle case, both papers closely paraphrased the testimony each day and printed it the following day. See, respectively, the *Miners' Journal* for Jan. 19–Feb. 1, 1876, and the *Shenandoah Herald,* Jan. 18–Feb. 1, 1876. Quotation of Bartholomew from issues of Jan. 31; quotation in next paragraph from *Miners' Journal* of Feb. 2. Beginning with the Yost trial in Pottsville in early May, both papers recorded and reported the testimony verbatim, and continued to do so for most of the trials of 1876 and early 1877. The combination of the two records aids the process of cross-checking and verification.

8. Our authority for the confession comes from several secondary sources. The *Shenandoah Herald,* in its issues of Feb. 14 and 19, 1876, and the *Miners' Journal* of Feb. 14, identify Kerrigan and quote their own version of his confession. F. P. Dewees, in his *The Molly Maguires* (Philadelphia: J. B. Lippincott & Co., 1877), pp. 248-249, also covers the story. Allan Pinkerton, in his *The Mollie Maguires and the Detectives* (New York: G. W. Dillingham, 1877), pp. 464-468, quotes what he states is the verbatim text. The

source for the dating of the confession in the text is the *Shenandoah Herald* story of Feb. 5, 1876, though the paper did not identify Kerrigan by name until Feb. 14. The precise nature of the bargain made was never fully documented, though later testimony in subsequent trials alluded to it.

9. The arrests are covered in the *Shenandoah Herald* and *Miners' Journal* of Feb. 5, 1876.

10. *Miners' Journal*, Feb. 5, 1876.

11. *Shenandoah Herald*, Feb. 10, 1876; *Miners' Journal*, Feb. 11.

12. Our source for this incident is a letter from Benjamin Franklin to George R. Kaercher, Feb. 19, 1876, Kaercher MSS, Mrs. George Keiser, Pottsville, Pa.

13. Our source for the pages that follow is *Report of the Case of the Commonwealth vs. John Kehoe et al. . . . for an Aggravated Assault and Battery with Intent to Kill Wm. M. Thomas*, stenographically reported by R. A. West (Pottsville: Miners' Journal Book and Job Rooms, 1876), pp. 92–98. The trial was held August 8–12, 1876.

14. Robert J. Linden to George R. Kaercher, March 4, 1876, Kaercher MSS, Mrs. George Keiser.

15. Handwritten copy of memorandum dated Nov. 30, 1875, from Benjamin Franklin to Franklin B. Gowen, in Archbishop James Frederic Wood MSS, American Catholic Historical Society, St. Charles Seminary, Overbrook, Pa.

16. Again the two newspapers supplement the official court records in Mauch Chunk by giving a close paraphrase of the line-by-line testimony. See *Miners' Journal*, Mar. 29–April 7, 1876, and *Shenandoah Herald* for same dates.

17. Charles Albright to George R. Kaercher, April 27, 1876, Kaercher MSS, Mrs. George Keiser.

18. Franklin B. Gowen to James Frederic Wood, May 14, 1876, Archbishop Wood MSS.

19. Daniel O'Connor to Franklin B. Gowen, March 14, 1880. Philadelphia & Reading Coal & Iron Company Letterbook No. 2, cited in Marvin W. Schlegel, *Ruler of the Reading: The Life of Franklin B. Gowen* (Harrisburg: Archives Publishing Co. of Pennsylvania, Inc., 1947), pp. 175–176.

20. F. P. Dewees, *The Molly Maguires* (Philadelphia: J. B. Lippincott and Co., 1877), pp. 253–256.

21. J. Walter Coleman, *The Molly Maguire Riots* (Richmond: Garrett & Massie, 1936), p. 115.

22. *Irish World*, April 8, 1876.

23. The court records in the county courthouse at Pottsville are supplemented by the verbatim testimony in both the *Miners' Journal* and the *Shenandoah Herald*. The inclusive dates are May 5 and May 18, 1876.

24. *Miners' Journal*, May 5, 1876.

25. *Ibid.*, May 8.

26. Quotations in this paragraph on arrests from *Shenandoah Herald*, May 6, 1876.

27. *Ibid.*, May 8.

28. *Ibid.*, May 9.

29. *Miners' Journal*, May 11, 1876.

30. *Ibid.*, May 13.

31. Gowen to Wood, May 14, 1876, Archbishop Wood MSS.

32. *Miners' Journal*, May 17, 1876.

33. *Ibid.*, May 18.

34. All quotations in this paragraph from *Miners' Journal* of May 26, 1876.

CHAPTER 12: THE DAY OF THE ROPE

1. This case went to the Pennsylvania Supreme Court, and therefore an official verbatim record of the testimony in the lower court was printed. See *Campbell versus The Commonwealth*, 84 Pa. 187. Again both the *Shenandoah Herald* and the *Miners' Journal* (Pottsville) published an unofficial verbatim testimony as each day of the trial progressed. Their quality is good when compared with the official record. But there were enough slips to make one careful; as the *Herald* reporter said on June 29, "Witness spoke in such a tone of voice that we could only catch a word here and there, and therefore gave the job up of taking down her testimony."

2. *Miners' Journal* (Pottsville), June 23, 1876.

3. Franklin P. Dewees, *The Molly Maguires* (Philadelphia: J. B. Lippincott and Co., 1877), p. 303.

4. *Campbell versus The Commonwealth*, 84 Pa. 187. Quotations from pp. 193, 187.

5. The extant official records in the Schuylkill County Court House at Pottsville contain the chronology of this case, its disposition, and the names of the prosecution, defense, judges, and jurors. Again, the *Shenandoah Herald* and the *Miners' Journal* provide unofficial verbatim records of the day-by-day testimony (see their issues of June 28–July 13). In addition, the final summation of the prosecution by Franklin B. Gowen was published in pamphlet form: *Argument of Franklin B. Gowen, Esq. . . . in the Case of the Commonwealth vs. Thomas Munley*, stenographically reported by R. A. West (Pottsville: Chronicle Book and Job Rooms, 1876).

6. *Argument of Franklin B. Gowen*, pp. 6–7.

7. The quotations in the following paragraphs are from *Argument of Franklin B. Gowen*, as follows: his initial statement to jury, p. 5; on Heaton identification, 6; on the woman witness, 7; quotations in the paragraph beginning "Though the Commonwealth," 30, 31, 19; quotation beginning "This very organization," 18; reference to Trench, 20; on Gowen's pride of Irish ancestry, 21; on Archbishop Wood, 22, 23; on alibis, 12, 13, 15; on L'Velle's innuendo about antiunionism, 16; and, finally, on Gowen's personal position in the case, 35, 24, 25. Both the *Herald* and the *Miners' Journal* printed Gowen's speech in its entirety.

8. Robert J. Linden's report of May 28, 1876, Kaercher MSS, Mrs. George Keiser, Pottsville, Pa.

9. H. C. Boyer to George Kaercher, April 8, 1876, *ibid.*

10. Linden's report of June 5, 1876, *ibid.*

11. Linden, May 25, 1876.

12. Linden, May 26, 1876.

13. Linden, May 27, 1876.

14. The convention was reported in greatest detail in *The Pilot* (Boston) of April 15, 1876. The *New York Times* of the same date also briefly covered it. The *Irish World* (New York) gave it excellent coverage (April 15,

1876), but spent most of its space on the role of the convention to form "military companies" to aid the "skirmishing fund" efforts of the Fenians. The actual minutes of the convention, if still extant, were unavailable.

15. *The Pilot* (Boston), April 15, 1876.

16. The allegation was made by Patrick Butler, one of the defendants in the trial of a number of the AOH for conspiring to reward Thomas Hurley for the murder of Gomer James. See the *Shenandoah Herald* and *Miners' Journal* of Aug. 20, 1876. The same accusation against Kehoe was made by J. J. Slattery on Oct. 21 in the John Donahue trial.

17. Robert J. Linden's reports of Aug. 29 and 30, 1876, in Molly Maguire MSS, Historical Society of Pennsylvania, Philadelphia.

18. *Shenandoah Herald*, Aug. 30, 1876. The newspaper did not name the priest.

19. *Shenandoah Herald*, Aug. 29, 1876, reprinting from an undated issue of the *New York Sun*.

20. *The Pilot*, Sept. 9, 1876.

21. See Eric Strauss, *Irish Nationalism and British Democracy* (New York: Columbia University Press, 1951), pp. 212–214; H. B. C. Pollard, *The Secret Societies of Ireland* (London: Philip Allan & Co., 1922), chap. ix; John O'Dea, *History of the Ancient Order of Hibernians* (Philadelphia: Keystone Printing Co., 1923), *passim*; James J. Bergin, *History of the Ancient Order of Hibernians* (Dublin: James Duffy & Co., 1910), *passim*.

22. Lord Ashtown (Frederick Oliver Trench), *The Unknown Power Behind the Irish Nationalist Party* (London: Swan Sonnenschein & Co., 1907).

23. *The Times* (London), June 7, 1876.

24. *Ballyshannon Herald*, Dec. 16, 1876; *Londonderry Standard*, Dec. 13, 1876; *Cork Examiner*, Dec. 13, 1876; *Newry Telegraph*, Dec. 12, 1876. The influential Dublin *Freeman's Journal* did not carry it, nor did Shirley's Nemesis, the *Dundalk Democrat*.

25. *Cork Examiner*, Dec. 14, 1876.

26. William O'Brien and Desmond Ryan, *Devoy's Post Bag*, vol. I (Dublin: C. J. Fallon, Ltd., 1948), p. xxxi.

27. The literature on this period of Irish-American organizations is voluminous. See, for example, O'Brien and Ryan, just cited; Charles Callan Tansill, *America and the Fight for Irish Freedom* (New York: Devon-Adair, 1957); Philip H. D. Bagenal, *The American Irish and Their Influence on Irish Politics* (Boston: Roberts Bros., 1882); Thomas Miller Beach, *Twenty-five Years in the Secret Service: The Recollection of a Spy by Major Henri Le Caron* (pseud.) (London: W. Heinemann, 1892); Arnold Schrier, *Ireland and the American Emigration* (Minneapolis: University of Minnesota Press, 1958).

28. O'Brien and Ryan, p. 127. Quotation in following sentence on p. 134.

29. Full records of this case are available, including official printed records of the testimony, for the case went to the Pennsylvania Supreme Court. See *Carroll, et al. versus The Commonwealth*, 84 Pa. 107. Both the *Shenandoah Herald* and the *Miners' Journal* provided their unofficial records of the verbatim testimony in their issues of July 6–July 25.

30. Dewees, *Molly Maguires*, p. 309.

31. See, especially, Anthony Bimba, *The Molly Maguires* (New York: International Publishers, 1932), pp. 82–100.

32. *The Great Molly Maguire Trials in Carbon and Schuylkill, Pa.: Brief Reference to Such Trials and Arguments of General Charles Albright and Hon. F. W. Hughes in the Case of Commonwealth vs. James Carroll, et al.* (Pottsville: Chronicle Book and Job Rooms, 1876). Albright's quotation in this paragraph is on p. 10.

33. The extant official records in the Schuylkill County Court House at Pottsville are similar to those noted for the Munley trial in footnote 5 above. The *Shenandoah Herald* and the *Miners' Journal* both published verbatim testimony in their issues of Aug. 9–14. In addition, an unofficial version of the verbatim testimony was published as a paperback book for sale: *Report of the Case of the Commonwealth vs. John Kehoe, et al . . . for an Aggravated Assault and Battery with Intent to kill Wm. M. Thomas,* stenographically reported by R. A. West (Pottsville: Miners' Journal Book and Job Rooms, 1876). This paperback additionally contained, as an appendix, the verbatim testimony of James Kerrigan in the trial for conspiracy to kill the Majors, which followed the Thomas case on Aug. 15, and also contained the verbatim testimony of Patrick Butler in the trial for conspiracy to reward Thomas Hurley for the murder of Gomer James, which was also held in Pottsville, beginning Aug. 17. The quotations in the following paragraphs come from this paperback, as follows: Frank McHugh's testimony, p. 117; warden George Byerle's testimony concerning Kehoe and Hartranft, p. 121; Martin L'Velle and John Ryon statements, pp. 195, 215; Franklin B. Gowen's statements, pp. 177, 184, 190; George R. Kaercher's reference to the "Labor Union" on p. 224.

34. Again the official records in Pottsville are supplemented by coverage of much of the testimony by the *Shenandoah Herald* and the *Miners' Journal* (Aug. 15–17). Though for the first time since the Doyle trial the newspapers did not report verbatim testimony, the reprinting of Kerrigan's testimony noted in footnote 33 above gives the key addition to the previous records.

35. There is verbatim testimony again in the *Shenandoah Herald* and the *Miners' Journal* (Aug. 19–23), supplemented by the printed record of Patrick Butler noted in footnote 33 above.

36. *Shenandoah Herald,* Aug. 21, 1876. The quotations of prisoner reactions to Butler's confession are also from this issue.

37. *Ibid.,* Aug. 22, 1876.

38. *Hazleton Mountain Democrat,* reprinted in *Miners' Journal,* Aug. 25, 1876.

39. Official verbatim records are available on the Duffy case, as it also went to the Pennsylvania Supreme Court. (See *Weekly Notes of Cases, Pennsylvania Supreme Court,* May 21, 1877.) The *Shenandoah Herald* and the *Miners' Journal* published full verbatim testimony (Sept. 7–20, 1876).

40. *Shenandoah Herald,* Sept. 20, 1876. Quotation in next paragraph also from this issue.

41. The court records in Pottsville are supplemented in both cases by verbatim testimony in the *Herald* and *Miners' Journal* (Sept. 22–23; Nov. 14–15, 1876).

42. Not all of this trial was covered by full verbatim testimony, though coverage is adequate. (See *Herald* and *Miners' Journal,* Sept. 23, 25, 1876.

43. *Shenandoah Herald,* Sept. 27, 1876.

44. The court records at Mauch Chunk again give chronology and par-

ticipants, and the *Herald* and *Miners' Journal* give verbatim testimony. For trial of John Donahue, see issues of Oct. 19–25, 1876; for trial of Thomas Fisher, Dec. 6–18; for trial of Alexander Campbell, Dec. 19–22.

45. *Shenandoah Herald*, Aug. 28, 1876.

46. *Tamaqua Courier*, Sept. 2, 1876.

47. Nov. 3, 1876, Reading Railroad, General Correspondence, 1876, Circular #12, Historical Society of Pennsylvania. (These records are separate from the Molly Maguire MSS in the same repository.)

48. The Neil Dougherty case and the John Campbell case are covered verbatim in the *Herald* and *Miners' Journal* of, respectively, Nov. 25–Dec. 1, 1876, and Jan. 5–10, 1877. The trial of Michael McGee was May 15–17, 1877; the two papers gave it modest coverage. Columbus McGee and John Chapman, another man involved in a minor way, were never tried. The Kehoe case has official, printed verbatim records, as the case went to the Pennsylvania Supreme Court (*Kehoe versus The Commonwealth*, 85 Pa. 127). The *Herald* and the *Miners' Journal* also reported unofficially the full trial verbatim in their issues of Jan. 10–17, 1877.

49. *Shenandoah Herald*, Jan. 17, 1877.

50. The testimony for this case is in the Pennsylvania Supreme Court files: *Hester et al. versus The Commonwealth*, 85 Pa. 139.

51. See footnotes 1, 29, and 39 above.

52. E. R. Siewers to Pennsylvania Pardon Board, May 21, 1877, and June 11, 1877, Alexander Campbell file, Pardon Board Records, Division of Public Records, Pennsylvania Historical and Museum Commission, Harrisburg, Pa.

53. Rev. Daniel McDermott to Pardon Board, June 13, 1877, Pardon Board Records, *ibid.*

54. *Mauch Chunk Democrat*, June 21, 1877.

55. *Shenandoah Herald*, June 22, 1877.

56. *Miners' Journal*, June 22, 1877; *Philadelphia Times*, June 22, 1877.

57. *Philadelphia Times*, June 22, 1877.

CHAPTER 13: CLOSING THE RECORD

1. Full official verbatim testimony is available for the Dennis Donnelly case, as it went to the Pennsylvania Supreme Court (see 6 W. N. Cases 104). Though the *Shenandoah Herald* and the *Miners' Journal* (Pottsville) did not now print verbatim testimony, both papers closely paraphrased the testimony, and the *Herald* did likewise for the summations to the jury. See issues of Nov. 17–26, 1877.

2. *Kehoe versus The Commonwealth*, 85 Pa. 127.

3. Both manuscript and printed copies of these two statements, dated March 23, 1878, are in John Kehoe file, Pardon Board Records, Division of Public Records, Pennsylvania Historical and Museum Commission, Harrisburg, Pa.

4. John Kehoe to Pardon Board, March 16, 1878, *ibid.*

5. John Kehoe to W. R. Potts, *circa* March 1878, Schuylkill County Historical Society MSS, Pottsville, Pa.

6. M. M. L'Velle to Messrs. Ryon, Garrett, and Campbell, April 1, 1878. John Kehoe file, Pardon Board Records.

7. Rev. Daniel O'Connor and others to Pardon Board, *circa* April 1878. John Kehoe file, Pardon Board Records.

8. *Shenandoah Herald*, April 11, 1878.

9. *Ibid.*, July 10, 1878.

10. Marvin W. Schlegel, *Ruler of the Reading: The Life of Franklin B. Gowen* (Harrisburg: Archives Publishing Co., 1947), p. 148.

11. *Miners' Journal*, Nov. 22, 1878.

12. *Ibid.*, Dec. 19, 1878.

13. *Pittsburgh Catholic*, Feb. 24, 1877; *New York Times*, Feb. 12, 1877.

14. Quoted in full in *Irish World* (New York), April 21, 1877.

15. *Pottsville Journal History*, newspaper clipping file, *circa* 1937, Pottsville Free Public Library, Pottsville, Pa.

16. *Irish World*, April 21, 1877.

17. *Philadelphia Ledger*, Aug. 19, 1916.

18. *Freeman's Journal and Catholic Register*, June 30, 1877.

19. Schlegel, *Ruler of the Reading*, pp. 157–161.

20. See Robert V. Bruce, *1877: Year of Violence* (Indianapolis: Bobbs, Merrill Co., 1959); James D. McCabe (Edward Winslow Martin, pseud.), *The History of the Great Riots . . . together with a Full History of the Molly Maguires* (Philadelphia: National Publishing Co., 1877).

21. Schlegel, *Ruler of the Reading*, pp. 164–165.

22. Schlegel, *Ruler of the Reading*, chaps. xiv–xviii; Jules I. Bogen, *The Anthracite Railroads* (New York: Ronald Press Co., 1927), pp. 54–65; Stuart Daggett, *Railroad Reorganization* (Cambridge, Mass.: Harvard University Press, 1908), chaps. iii–iv.

23. *Verbatim Report of General Meeting of Share and Bondholders of the Philadelphia & Reading Railroad, Held at the City Terminus Hotel, Cannon Street, London, June 6, 1877* (London: Charles Skipper & East, 1877). This was reprinted in the railroad's annual report: *Report of the President and Managers of the Philadelphia & Reading Railroad Company*, Jan. 14, 1878. Quotations are from pp. 120–121 and p. 129 of the latter.

24. *Report of the President and Managers of the Philadelphia & Reading Railroad Co.*, Jan. 8, 1877, pp. 27–28.

25. Henry J. Browne, *The Catholic Church and the Knights of Labor* (Washington: Catholic University of America Press, 1949); Fergus Mac-Donald, *The Catholic Church and the Secret Societies in the United States* (New York: United States Catholic Historical Society, 1946), pp. 146–149.

26. L. J. Bocker to Terence Powderly, June 16, 1877, Powderly MSS, File "Incoming 1871–1879," Catholic University of America, Washington, D.C.

27. Terence Powderly to William Hickey, May 17, 1882, cited in Browne, *Catholic Church and Knights of Labor*, p. 79.

28. For quotations, Allan Pinkerton to George Bangs, March 30, 1877, *Allan Pinkerton Letterbook, 1875–1883*, Library of Congress. Franklin's mental status discussed in letter of Oct. 30, 1877.

29. *Report of the President and Managers of the Philadelphia & Reading Railroad Co.*, Jan. 10, 1876, pp. 16–17.

30. These detective reports are part of the Reading Railroad's Molly Maguire Papers in Philadelphia.

31. "Labor Troubles at Homestead, Pa.: Employment of Pinkerton Detectives," U.S. House of Representatives Report no. 2447, 52nd Congress,

2nd Session (1893). See also James D. Horan and Howard Swiggett, *The Pinkerton Story* (New York: G. P. Putnam's Sons, 1951), pp. 223–238.

32. *Violations of Free Speech and Assembly and Interference with Rights of Labor, Hearings . . . on S. Res. 266*, 74th Congress, 2nd Session, Government Printing Office, Washington, D.C., 1936.

33. Allan Pinkerton to Robert Pinkerton, Feb. 29, 1876, *Allan Pinkerton Letterbook, 1875–1883*, p. 42. The eighteen Pinkerton volumes are listed in Richard W. Rowan, *The Pinkertons: A Detective Dynasty* (London: Hurst & Blackett, 1931), p. 244.

34. *New York Times*, Nov. 7, 1875.

35. Allan Pinkerton to Robert Pinkerton, May 22, 1879, *Allan Pinkerton Letterbook, 1875–1883*. The same letterbook contains the quotation on phrenology (in a letter to Robert Pinkerton, Nov. 22, 1876), and the letter to Gladstone, July 8, 1882.

36. James McParland to Frank R. Gooding, Jan. 22 and 25, 1906, "Pinkerton Reports" in James H. Hawley and William E. Borah MSS, Idaho Historical Society, Boise, Idaho.

37. The trial was covered in detail in most of the nation's press. See especially *New York Times* starting June 6, 1907. Perhaps the best book on the Steunenberg trials is Arthur Weinberg, ed., *Attorney for the Damned* (New York: Simon & Schuster, 1957), pp. 410–488. See also J. Walter Coleman, *The Molly Maguire Riots* (Richmond: Garrett & Massie, 1936), pp. 169–172; Clarence Darrow, *The Story of My Life* (New York: Charles Scribner's Sons, 1932), chap. xviii; Charles Yale Harrison, *Clarence Darrow* (New York: Jonathan Cape & Harrison Smith, 1931), pp. 120 ff; Irving Stone, *Clarence Darrow for the Defense* (Garden City: Doubleday, Doran & Co., 1941), pp. 185–247. The Pinkerton version of the trials is best expressed in Horan and Swiggett, *Pinkerton Story*, pp. 289–308.

38. *New York Times*, June 14, 1907.

39. Weinberg, ed., *Attorney for the Damned*, pp. 469–470.

40. For example, *New York Star*, Dec. 29, 1889; *New York Herald*, Dec. 24, 1889; *New York Sun*, Dec. 24, 1889. McParland quotation from *Denver Daily News*, Dec. 18, 1889. Smith quotation from Schlegel, *Ruler of the Reading*, p. 287.

41. John O'Dea, *History of the Ancient Order of Hibernians and Ladies' Auxiliary* (Philadelphia: Keystone Printing Co., 1923), III, 1045.

42. Originally quoted in *Prison Journal*, vol. 3, no. 4 (October 1923), p. 16; subsequently reprinted in Julia Johnsen, *Capital Punishment* (New York: H. W. Wilson, 1939), and in Harry Elmer Barnes and Negley K. Teeters, *New Horizons in Criminology*, 3rd ed. (Englewood Cliffs, N.J.: Prentice-Hall, 1959), p. 315.

43. Ernest W. Lucy, *The Mollie Maguires of Pennsylvania, or Ireland in America* (London: George Bell & Sons, 1882), pp. 64–65.

44. The story of Mrs. Hester is in *Pittsburgh Catholic*, March 17, 1877. The juvenile organization was mentioned in *The Pilot* (Boston), July 14, 1877.

45. The documentation that this man was actually Hurley is slim and inconclusive; see *New York World*, Aug. 19, 1886; *New York Times*, Aug. 20, 1876.

46. McParland to Frank R. Gooding, Jan. 25, 1906 (see note 36, above). See also *Denver Post*, May 19, 1919.

47. George Korson, *Minstrels of the Mine Patch* (Philadelphia: University of Pennsylvania Press, 1938), pp. 257–259, 267–268.

48. "The 'Molly Maguire' Trials," *American Law Review*, January 1877, pp. 234–235.

49. Foster Rhea Dulles, *Labor in America* (New York: Thomas Y. Crowell Co., 1949), p. 191.

50. See Richard B. Morris, "Andrew Jackson, Strikebreaker," *American Historical Review*, October 1949, p. 55; Walter S. Sanderlin, *The Great National Project: A History of the Chesapeake and Ohio Canal* (Baltimore: Johns Hopkins Press, 1946), pp. 115–122. The material on the Illinois Central incidents is covered in Paul W. Gates, *The Illinois Central Railroad and its Colonization Work* (Cambridge, Mass.: Harvard University Press, 1934), pp. 94–98.

51. Frank J. Warne, *The Slav Invasion and the Mine Workers: A Study in Immigration* (Philadelphia: J. B. Lippincott Co., 1904).

Index